A Guide to the NAI Arbitration Rules
Including a Commentary on Dutch Arbitration Law

KLUWER LAW INTERNATIONAL

A Guide to the NAI Arbitration Rules

Including a Commentary on Dutch Arbitration Law

Editors:

Bommel van der Bend

Marnix Leijten

Marc Ynzonides

Wolters Kluwer
Law & Business

AUSTIN   BOSTON   CHICAGO   NEW YORK   THE NETHERLANDS

Published by:
Kluwer Law International
PO Box 316
2400 AH Alphen aan den Rijn
The Netherlands
Website: www.kluwerlaw.com

Sold and distributed in North, Central and South America by:
Aspen Publishers, Inc.
7201 McKinney Circle
Frederick, MD 21704
United States of America
Email: customer.care@aspenpubl.com

Sold and distributed in all other countries by:
Turpin Distribution Services Ltd.
Stratton Business Park
Pegasus Drive, Biggleswade
Bedfordshire SG18 8TQ
United Kingdom
Email: kluwerlaw@turpin-distribution.com

Grateful acknowledgement is made to the NAI and ICCA for their kind permission to reproduce the materials in this book. Copyright is duly acknowledged.

In relation to the NAI Rules it is acknowledged that the NAI is the publisher and copyright holder. The text reproduced here is valid at the time of reproduction. As amendments may from time to time be made to the text, readers are referred to the website <www.nai-nl.org> for the latest version of the NAI Rules.

Printed on acid-free paper.

ISBN 978-90-411-2734-1

Printed in Great Britain.

Contributors:

Bommel van der Bend

Margriet de Boer

Leupien Giacometti-Vermeer

Mirjam van de Hel-Koedoot

Marnix Leijten

Eelco Meerdink

Rogier Schellaars

Marc Ynzonides

FOREWORD

We, members of the arbitration team of the Dutch law firm De Brauw Blackstone Westbroek N.V., herewith present our Guide to the NAI Arbitration Rules, including a commentary on Dutch arbitration law, with great pride and gratitude.

As Dutch lawyers specialized in acting as counsel for corporate clients and public entities in domestic and international arbitration proceedings, we were regularly confronted with the fact that no handbook exists on arbitration under the rules of the Netherlands Arbitration Institute that is accessible to those that do not master the Dutch language. In fact, hardly any comprehensive commentary on the NAI Rules seemed to exist except for the short explanatory notes that are part of the introduction to the NAI Rules. This while NAI Arbitration is the dispute resolution mechanism of choice of many Dutch corporations and public entities. NAI Arbitration is also surprisingly often agreed on by foreign parties selecting the Netherlands as a neutral venue for their potential disputes. The city of The Hague, for example, regards itself as 'The Legal Capital of the World', with noticeable success also in the sphere of commercial dispute resolution. Moreover, the NAI Arbitration Rules include a highly successful mechanism for parties to seek interim relief in summary arbitration proceedings. This mechanism has been inspired on the Dutch Code of Civil Procedure's provisions on summary proceedings before the President of the District Court, which provisions are almost exclusively known to Dutch lawyers. The broad sphere of application of such NAI summary arbitral proceedings is often an element of surprise to foreign parties that have opted for NAI Arbitration in their contracts. Writings on this mechanism in English are scarce. Having been confronted with this existing gap in literature on the NAI Arbitration Rules, our project was born. Against all odds, and despite extensive pressure from client work, we have managed to finalize this project, the result of which now lies in front of you.

This book has been written for those in-house counsel and practitioners that contemplate agreeing on NAI Arbitration in their contracts, as well as for in-house counsel, practitioners and arbitrators that get involved in NAI arbitration proceedings. Collectively, the writers of this book have been involved in numerous arbitrations over the last decade, including many NAI arbitrations. We have been involved as counsel to parties in such proceedings, as secretary to tribunals, as arbitrators and as counsel in court proceedings related to arbitration. In this context we have faced many questions on the NAI Arbitration Rules, advised on the interpretation and correct application of those Rules and defended such interpretation before tribunals and courts. We have attempted to lay down our experience in this book, and hope to trigger readers to comment on our views and supplement on our commentaries. We thus welcome any suggestions readers may have to make a future version of this guide more complete and better.

We have chosen to focus on the NAI Arbitration Rules, and to include references to and commentaries on rules of the Dutch arbitration act only where relevant. This guide thus does not provide a detailed and comprehensive overview of Dutch arbitration law. It consists of three parts. In Part I, we introduce the NAI, the Dutch arbitration act and the NAI Arbitration Rules. In Part II, a commentary is given on each provision of the NAI Arbitration Rules. In Part III, we address arbitration related court proceedings in the Netherlands under the Dutch arbitration act. Apart from our personal experience, we have drawn on case law from arbitral tribunals and state courts. Where relevant, we have also compared the NAI Arbitration Rules to the arbitration rules of other institutions, inter alia the ICC Rules of Arbitration and the UNCITRAL Arbitration Rules, and to the practice under such other Rules.

We owe a great deal of gratitude to many that have contributed to this book and that have supported our work on it. A special word of thanks is due to Wouter den Hollander, who as a student associate of our arbitration department has been an invaluable contributor to this book. We are also grateful to our firm, De Brauw Blackstone Westbroek N.V., not only for allowing us to devote the time and attention required to write this book, but also for motivating us to seek and fulfil many functions within the domestic and international arbitration scene. Although such functions are often not rewarded financially, they have contributed to our experience and thus to our practice and this book. We are also especially fortunate to have found Fredy von Hombracht-Brinkman, the current Administrator of the NAI, prepared to read a draft of this book. We have been able to make several improvements with her help. Finally, and most importantly, we thank our clients for trusting us to handle their arbitration disputes. We greatly enjoy the field of arbitration, and realize that it is only because of our clients that we get to work in this field every day.

The authors most appreciate receiving any comments and/or suggestions on guide.nairules@debrauw.com.

Bommel van der Bend
Marnix Leijten
Marc Ynzonides

Margriet de Boer
Leupien Giacometti–Vermeer
Mirjam van de Hel–Koedoot
Eelco Meerdink
Rogier Schellaars

CONTRIBUTORS

Bommel van der Bend joined the De Brauw Blackstone Westbroek in 1992 and has been a partner since 2000. He graduated at the University of Leiden and attended the *Europa-Institut* of the University of Saarbrücken (Germany). Bommel is particularly regarded for his expertise on international arbitrations, complex construction projects and European public procurement law. He has represented multinational corporations in large and complex arbitrations conducted under the NAI, ICC and UNCITRAL Rules. Bommel is the co-author of an authoritative handbook on European public procurement laws. He is the vice-president of the Governing Board of the NAI and a member of the Maasvlakte II Tender Board, an independent board of experts, advising on a major land reclamation project in the Rotterdam harbour area.

Margriet de Boer joined De Brauw Blackstone Westbroek in 2001, after obtaining her law degree from Amsterdam University. She also obtained a degree in French Language and Literature and in Translation studies. Since 2006, Margriet writes the annual chronicle on arbitration law for the Dutch Journal on Civil Litigation (*Tijdschrift voor Civiele Rechtspleging*). She has also published on Dutch procedural law.

Leupien Giacometti-Vermeer joined De Brauw Blackstone Westbroek in 2004, subsequent to obtaining her law degree from the University of Amsterdam. She has also studied at Columbia Law School. Leupien has lectured and published on Dutch procedural law.

Mirjam van de Hel-Koedoot joined De Brauw Blackstone Westbroek in 2001, subsequent to obtaining her law degree from Leiden University. She also studied at the Institut de Sciences Politiques in Paris and the University of British Columbia in Vancouver. In 2005, Mirjam joined the law firm of Hanotiau & van den Berg in Brussels, where she worked in the international arbitration practice of Professor Albert Jan van den Berg. In 2007, she returned to De Brauw's arbitration and litigation practice. Mirjam has written several publications on Dutch procedural law and arbitration.

Marnix Leijten has been a partner at De Brauw Blackstone Westbroek since 2004 and heads the arbitration department. Marnix joined De Brauw in 1996, subsequent to obtaining his law degree from Leiden University and a Magister Juris graduate degree from the University of Oxford. In 2003, he worked as a litigation associate at Cravath, Swaine & Moore LLP in New York. Marnix has been counsel to domestic and foreign clients in many national and international arbitrations and arbitration related court proceedings, predominantly cases conducted under the NAI, ICC, DIS and UNCITRAL Rules. Such cases include ones in the energy and natural resources, chemicals, technology, transport and construction sectors, as well as more generally cases concerning complex financial and corporate transactions and investor-state disputes. Marnix has been the Netherlands' member of the ICC Court of International Arbitration in Paris since January 2006, and frequently lectures and writes on arbitration and alternative dispute resolution.

Eelco Meerdink joined De Brauw Blackstone Westbroek in 2000. He graduated at the University of Utrecht and attended University College London Law School and Columbia Law School (LL.M.). Eelco publishes and lectures regularly in the field of arbitration. For several years, he held a position on the editorial board of *Tijdschrift voor Arbitrage*, the main publication on arbitration in the Netherlands.

Rogier Schellaars joined De Brauw Blackstone Westbroek in 2005 after having worked in Freshfields Bruckhaus Deringer LLP's arbitration group since 2002. He has obtained a bachelors degree in English law from the University of London and a civil law degree from Leiden University. Rogier has lectured English law for six years at Leiden University and also publishes regularly on Dutch procedural law and arbitration. He holds a position on the editorial board of *Tijdschrift voor Arbitrage*, the main publication on arbitration in the Netherlands, and the board of the NAI's under 40 group of arbitration practitioners, *NAI Jong Oranje*.

Marc Ynzonides has been a partner in De Brauw Blackstone Westbroek's litigation & arbitration practice since 2002. He joined the firm in 1996 after obtaining his PhD from Rotterdam University. Marc specializes in litigation and arbitration. He acts on behalf of national and international companies in all kinds of litigation and in all courts of the Netherlands, including the Supreme Court. He represents clients in both contractual and non-contractual claims. In arbitration he appears as counsel in both national and international arbitrations. He also acts as arbitrator. In international litigation and arbitration he regularly works with other international law firms. Marc is a member of the Dutch State Advisory Committee on Procedural Law. He also serves as a substitute judge in the Court of Appeal in Arnhem. Marc has written numerous publications and lectures frequently on various aspects of Dutch procedural law and arbitration.

CONTENTS

ABBREVIATIONS

BR	*Tijdschrift voor Bouwrecht* (Journal of Construction law)
DCC	Dutch Civil Code (*Burgerlijk Wetboek*)
DCCP	Dutch Code of Civil Procedure (*Wetboek van Burgerlijke Rechtsvordering*)
ECHR	European Convention on Human Rights
ECJ	European Court of Justice
HR	*Hoge Raad* (the Netherlands Supreme Court)
IBA	International Bar Association
ICC	International Chamber of Commerce
ICDR	International Centre for Dispute Resolution
ICSID	International Centre for Settlement of Investment Disputes
JBPR	*Jurisprudentie Burgerlijk Procesrecht* (Dutch Civil Procedure Case Law)
LCIA	London Court of International Arbitration
NAI	Netherlands Arbitration Institute
NJ	*Nederlandse Jurisprudentie* (Dutch Case Reports)
NJF	*Nederlandse Jurisprudentie Feitenrechtspraak* (Case Reports of Dutch Lower Courts)
RvdW	*Rechtspraak van de Week* (Dutch Case Law Weekly)
TK	Parliamentary Reports of the *Tweede Kamer* (Second Chamber of the Dutch Parliament)
TvA	*Tijdschrift voor Arbitrage* (Journal of Arbitration)
UNCITRAL	United Nations Commission on International Trade Law
WIPO	World Intellectual Property Organization

NOTE ON REFERENCES

A number of publications are referred to repeatedly throughout this book. For convenience, we have used the following abbreviations.

BOOKS

Bühler and Webster, 2008
   Bühler, M.W. & T.H. Webster, *Handbook of ICC Arbitration. Commentary, Precedents, Materials* (2nd edn, London, Sweet and Maxwell, 2008)
Burg. Rv, 2006
   Snijders, H.J., *Burgerlijke Rechtsvordering Boek IV Arbitrage*, supplement 305, August 2006 (Deventer, Kluwer, 2006)
Craig, Park and Paulsson, 2000
   Craig, W.L., W.W. Park & J. Paulsson, *International Chamber of Commerce Arbitration* (3rd edn, New York, Oceana Publishers, 2000)
Derains and Schwartz, 2005
   Derains, Y. & E.A. Schwartz, *A Guide to the ICC Rules of Arbitration* (2nd edn, The Hague, Kluwer Law International, 2005)
Fouchard, Gaillard and Goldman, 1999
   Gaillard, E. and J. Savage (eds), *Fouchard Gaillard and Goldman on International Commercial Arbitration* (The Hague, Kluwer Law International, 1999)
Fung Fen Chung, 2004
   Fung Fen Chung, C.S.K., *Bewijsmiddelen in het arbitraal geding* (Den Haag, SDU, 2004)
Meijer, 2008
   Meijer, G.J., *Overeenkomst tot arbitrage,* dissertation Erasmus University Rotterdam, 2008 (commercial edition forthcoming in 2009)
Parliamentary History Revision DCCP, 2002
   Van Mierlo, A.I.M. & F.M. Bart, *Parlementaire geschiedenis: herziening van het burgerlijk procesrecht* (Deventer, Kluwer, 2002)
T&C Rv
   Van Mierlo, A.I.M., C.J.J.C. van Nispen & M.V. Polak (eds), *Tekst en Commentaar Burgerlijke Rechtsvordering* (3rd edn, Deventer, Kluwer, 2008)

Vademecum Arbitrage, 2002
> Snijders, H.J. & G.J. Meijer (eds), *Vademecum Burgerlijk Procesrecht, Arbitrage* (Deventer, Gouda Quint, 2002)

OTHER DOCUMENTS

Draft Bill	Proposals to Amend the Fourth Book (Arbitration) Articles 1020–1076 DCCP as submitted to the Ministry of Justice (*Voorstellen tot Wijziging van het Vierde Boek (Arbitrage) Artikelen 1020–1076 Rv*)
Introduction to NAI Arbitration Rules	Enclosed in the official publication of the NAI Arbitration Rules
IBA Guidelines	IBA Guidelines on Conflicts of Interest in International Arbitration, approved by the Council of the International Bar Association on 22 May 2004
IBA Rules of Ethics	IBA Rules of Ethics for International Arbitrators
IBA Rules of Evidence	IBA Rules on the Taking of Evidence in International Commercial Arbitration, adopted by the Council of the International Bar Association on 1 June 1999
ICC Rules	ICC Rules of Arbitration, in force as of 1 January 1998
ICDR Rules	ICDR International Dispute Resolution Procedures (including Mediation and Arbitration Rules), as of 1 March 2008
ICSID Rules	ICSID Rules of Procedure for Arbitration Procedures
LCIA Rules	LCIA Arbitration Rules, in force as of 1 January 1998
NAI Rules	NAI Arbitration Rules, in force as of 13 November 2001, as published on the NAI website <www.nai-nl.org>
New York Convention	United Nations Convention on Recognition and Enforcement of Foreign Arbitral Awards, New York, 10 June 1958, United Nations, Treaty Series, Vol. 330, p. 38 No. 4739 (1959)
UNCITRAL Rules	The UNCITRAL Arbitration Rules, adopted on 15 December 1976
UNCITRAL Model Law	1985 UNCITRAL Model Law on International Commercial Arbitration, with amendments adopted in 2006
WIPO Arbitration Rules	WIPO Arbitration Rules, effective from 1 October 2002

PART I

GENERAL INTRODUCTION

CHAPTER 1

GENERAL INTRODUCTION TO THE NAI RULES

1.   The Netherlands Arbitration Institute

The Netherlands Arbitration Institute (NAI) is the most prestigious institute in the Netherlands for the arbitration of commercial disputes. During the 60 years of its existence, it has built up a solid reputation in dealing with national and international commercial arbitration. This reputation is attributable to the quality of arbitrators involved, the well-oiled organization of the NAI and the reputation of the people behind the NAI. The Governing Board of the Institute is currently chaired by Professor Albert Jan van den Berg, one of the world's leading commercial arbitrators. Honorary President of the Institute is Professor Emeritus Piet Sanders, author of the Dutch arbitration act.

The NAI was established on 22 June 1949 under the name 'Foundation for Dutch-American Commercial Arbitration'. The idea at that time was to create an institute for the administration of international arbitrations concerning disputes between companies in the Netherlands and in other countries, mainly in the United States of America.[1] However, shortly after its establishment, the NAI's objective was broadened and the Institute was given its current name on 23 December 1949.[2]

Unlike most other organizations in the Netherlands dealing with arbitration,[3] the NAI has no restrictions as to the subject matter of the arbitration (except for subjects that cannot be settled through arbitration).[4] The NAI is open to all kinds of commercial disputes, notwithstanding that disputes within industries having their own arbitration institutes are usually submitted to those institutes

---

[1]   P. Sanders, 'Het Nederlands Arbitrage Instituut', *Arbitrale Rechtspraak* 1959, 97-100.

[2]   Vademecum Arbitrage, 2002 (H.J. Snijders), 75-77. See for further information about the history of the NAI: the special issue of *Arbitrale Rechtspraak*, Sep. 1950, 259-286; P. Sanders, 'Het Nederlands Arbitrage Instituut', *Arbitrale Rechtspraak* 1959, 97-100; P. Sanders, 'Het NAI veertig jaar', TvA 1989, 143-144; P. Sanders, 'TvA/NAI 50 jaar', TvA 1999, 39-41; J.L.W. Sillevis Smitt, 'Het NAI 50 jaar. Enkele hedendaagse aspecten van een halve eeuw dienstverlening bij geschillenbeslechting', in *NAI 50 jaar. Arbitrage: In wiens handen?*, ed. NAI (Deventer, Kluwer, 2000), 13-21.

[3]   See Part I, Ch. 2, Section 3 for further information about those organizations.

[4]   See Part I, Ch. 2, Section 2 for further information about arbitrability.

(e.g., the construction industry[5]). Important areas in which disputes are often submitted to NAI arbitration include share purchase agreements, joint venture agreements, license agreements, franchise agreements, finance agreements, contractor agreements, distribution agreements and agreements for the sale of goods.[6]

The NAI is set up as an independent, non-profit organization in the form of a foundation (*stichting*) established under Dutch law. The NAI has no connection to the Dutch State, nor is it subsidized. The NAI has its registered office as well as its actual place of business in Rotterdam, the Netherlands. The objective of the NAI as described in its Articles of Association is to promote the use of arbitration, binding advice (*bindend advies*) and other legal methods to prevent, limit and resolve disputes.[7] This objective is pursued by providing trade and industry with rules for a well-organized arbitration procedure (the NAI Arbitration Rules), which may be used for arbitration and binding advice, as well as rules for a structured form of mediation in the form of a 'minitrial' (the NAI Minitrial Rules). Although the NAI strongly focuses on resolving commercial business disputes, individuals may also submit their disputes to NAI arbitration.

The NAI has an Executive Board and a Governing Board. The Executive Board is composed of the President, the Vice-President and the Secretary and Treasurer. The Governing Board consists of the three members of the Executive Board and the members of the General Committee (currently 21 members) and is charged with the management of the NAI. The Governing Board includes members with experience in arbitration from the legal profession, the business community and several universities as well as from the judiciary. Also, the Association of Chambers of Commerce in the Netherlands (*Vereniging Kamers van Koophandel in Nederland*), the Dutch division of the International Chamber of Commerce (ICC), the Association for Industry and Trade (*Maatschappij voor Nijverheid en Handel*) and the Institute of Chartered Accountants (*Nederlands Instituut van Registeraccountants*) are usually represented.

The NAI is managed by the Administrator, who is also the Director of the NAI as provided for in the NAI Articles of Association. The Administrator has a central role in NAI arbitration (see also the comments on Article 1). The Administrator is assisted by the NAI Secretariat.[8]

---

[5] There is, however, a recent tendency in the construction industry that parties opt for NAI arbitration because of dissatisfaction with arbitration under the Arbitration Rules of the Arbitration Council for the Construction Industry in the Netherlands (*Raad van Arbitrage voor de Bouw*).

[6] NAI annual report 2006, published in TvA 2008, 43-44.

[7] See Art. 2 of the NAI Articles of Association.

[8] See for the current members of the Executive Board, the Governing Board, the General Committee and the Secretariat <www.nai-nl.org> and Appendix 1 to the NAI Rules.

The NAI itself does not act as arbitral tribunal. The role of the NAI in arbitrations is limited to administering arbitrations, from the submission of the request for arbitration to the deposit of the arbitral award with the Registry of the District Court.

The *Tijdschrift voor Arbitrage* (Journal of Arbitration; TvA) is published by Kluwer under the auspices of the NAI. This journal contains articles and court judgments related to arbitration (primarily in Dutch), as well as arbitral awards (in their original language). TvA is the most important, if not the only, Dutch journal containing (excerpts of) arbitral awards rendered under the NAI Rules.

2. The NAI Arbitration Rules

The NAI has its own Arbitration Rules. These Rules contain the basic rules for an arbitration administered by the NAI. Apart from more general provisions, these Rules concern the appointment of arbitrators, the arbitral procedure, the possibility of summary arbitral proceedings, the arbitral award including the possibility of rectifying and supplementing this award, and the costs of arbitration.

The present version of the NAI Rules, which will be commented on in this book, is the version that entered into force on 13 November 2001. It applies to arbitrations that have commenced after this date.

The NAI Rules have been carefully harmonized with the Dutch arbitration act set forth in the Dutch Code of Civil Procedure (DCCP). Occasionally, the NAI Rules repeat what has already been provided for in the DCCP. However, on certain points the NAI Rules depart from the non-mandatory rules of the DCCP. At times other arbitration rules provided inspiration for such departures. For example, the so-called list procedure for the selection and appointment of arbitrators (described in the comments on Article 14) has been derived from the arbitration rules of the American Arbitration Association (AAA).[9] In addition, the NAI Rules occasionally also govern subjects on which the DCCP is silent, for example the language to be used in the arbitral proceedings and the possibility of introducing counterclaims. Part II will indicate how each article of the NAI Rules compares to the equivalent rule in the DCCP (if any).

The NAI Rules do not comprise a comprehensive arrangement for conducting arbitrations. First of all, the NAI Rules leave the actual organization of the proceedings to the arbitral tribunal, which allows the arbitrators to adapt the proceedings to the specifics of the individual case. Second, the parties may deviate from the NAI Rules, except where the NAI Rules are based on mandatory rules in the DCCP and the arbitration is seated in the Netherlands. These two aspects are discussed in more detail in the comments on Article 23.

The NAI Rules distinguish between domestic and international arbitration. An international arbitration is defined as an arbitration in which one of the parties

---

[9] P. Sanders, 'Het NAI veertig jaar', TvA 1989, 143-144.

is domiciled outside the Netherlands at the time of commencement of the arbitration (see Article 1(g) and the comments on that provision). The qualification 'international arbitration' primarily entails that certain time limits provided for in the NAI Rules will be doubled (Article 5(2)).

The NAI Rules do not distinguish between arbitrations with a place of arbitration in the Netherlands and arbitrations with a place of arbitration outside the Netherlands.[10] The underlying idea is that the NAI Rules are equally fit to apply if the place of arbitration is outside the Netherlands. However, as will be explained in further detail in the comments on Article 22, parties should carefully consider whether to opt for NAI arbitration if the place of arbitration is outside the Netherlands, as the NAI Rules have been specifically harmonized with the DCCP and the DCCP does not apply if the place of arbitration is situated outside the Netherlands. This is particularly true where arbitrators may be inclined to interpret the NAI Rules that have been derived from the DCCP in accordance with Dutch procedural law and the associated case law.

3. The NAI Rules and Other Means of Dispute Resolution

Contrary to what the name 'Arbitration Rules' suggests, the NAI Rules do not merely apply to dispute resolution by means of arbitration; they also cover dispute resolution by means of binding advice (*bindend advies*). Binding advice is explained in the comments on Article 3. As set out in the comments on Article 3, we are of the opinion that binding advice based on the NAI Rules is not to be preferred. If the parties nevertheless opt for binding advice, they should realize that due to the nature of the Dutch concept of binding advice, under Dutch law (i) neither the parties nor the binding advisor can rely on the state court's assistance, (ii) a binding advice is not subject to recognition and enforcement in the same way as an arbitral award and (iii) the grounds and procedures applying to the setting aside of a binding advice are entirely different from those applying to the setting aside of an arbitral award. Against this background, in order to avoid possible discussions as to whether the parties have agreed on binding advice or on arbitration under the NAI Rules, we note that an arbitration clause should clearly stipulate whether disputes will be settled by arbitration or by binding advice in accordance with the NAI Rules (see also Article 1, note 3 (NAI recommended arbitration clause)).

The NAI Rules contain no provision on mediation. However, since the NAI not only aims to promote arbitration and binding advice, but also other legal means to prevent, limit and resolve disputes, the NAI adopted its Minitrial Rules in 1995 and has recently adopted Mediation Rules. Minitrial is a particular structured form of alternative dispute resolution, in which a mediator and a representative of each of the parties to the dispute form a committee that – after a thorough preparatory process headed by the mediator – try to facilitate

---

[10] However, there are examples of provisions that distinguish between arbitration seated in and outside the Netherlands, for example summary arbitral proceedings (see Arts 42a(3) and 50(1)(b)).

the settlement of the dispute. The success of Minitrial proceedings ultimately depends on the parties' willingness to reach a compromise. If they are unable to do so, the dispute will have to be settled by arbitration or by the courts. According to the NAI's annual reports, Minitrial is rarely used in practice.[11] Now that the new Mediation Rules have been adopted, this will probably be even less in future. For that reason we will not elaborate on the Minitrial Rules in this guide. The Mediation Rules also fall outside the scope of this publication. More information on the Minitrial Rules and the Mediation Rules can be obtained from the NAI.[12]

Since alternative dispute resolution techniques, such as mediation and Minitrial, are never a guarantee that the dispute will be resolved, we recommend that parties choosing such forms of alternative dispute resolution also make arrangements for the event that the alternative dispute resolution does not succeed. This leads to multi-tier dispute resolution mechanisms, in which various forms of alternative dispute resolution may be followed by, for example, arbitration in accordance with the NAI Rules. In that case it is recommended that the arbitrators have not been involved in any way in the resolution process preceding the arbitration, in order to prevent a challenge of the arbitrator or the setting aside of the arbitral award based on a lack of impartiality of the arbitrator (see Part II, Section 3 and Article 33, note 2, as well as Part III on the setting aside of awards). Should there nevertheless be a particular reason to appoint a person as arbitrator who has acted as mediator before the arbitration, it is recommended that all parties involved clearly consent to this in advance and explicitly waive their right to challenge the arbitrator or the award on the basis of that prior involvement.

4. Interpretation of the Arbitration Agreement and the NAI Rules

4.1. Interpretation of the Arbitration Agreement

The NAI Rules apply if the parties unequivocally declare the NAI Rules applicable in their arbitration agreement. This normally does not pose problems if the parties use the wording of the model arbitration clause recommended by the NAI in their arbitration agreement (which is discussed in more detail in the comments on Article 1(e)). If the parties draft their own arbitration clause, they should make sure that it is clear that they have agreed on arbitration in accordance with the NAI Rules.[13]

It is a matter of interpretation whether the parties have actually agreed on NAI arbitration. The arbitration agreement should be interpreted in accordance with

---

[11] See for example the information from the annual report 2006 of the NAI, as published in TvA 2008, 43-44.

[12] See <www.nai-nl.org>.

[13] Practice shows that if parties have drafted their own arbitration clause, this sometimes results in pathological arbitration clauses. See H.J. Snijders, 'Pathologische geschillenbeslechtingsclausules', TvA 2005, 1-3.

the law that applies to the arbitration clause.[14] Pursuant to Article 1053 DCCP, the arbitration agreement must be considered and assessed as a separate agreement (the separability or 'séparabilité' of the arbitration agreement). Parties only rarely make a separate choice of law for their arbitration clause. Usually, the parties consider it sufficient to choose the law applicable to the agreement in which the arbitration clause has been included. This choice of law does not necessarily pertain to the arbitration clause (whether it does so is a matter of interpretation), due to the separability of the arbitration agreement. If it does not, the law applicable to the arbitration clause must be determined based on the applicable rules of private international law. This involves the rules of private international law that apply in the country of the court which ultimately will have to rule on the interpretation of the arbitration clause (the 'lex fori'). In the Netherlands, the general rule is that the applicable law is the law of the country with which the arbitration agreement is most closely connected. This implies that either the law of the country where the place of arbitration is situated or the law (declared) applicable to the agreement incorporating the arbitration clause will be used as the starting point.[15] If the parties wish to avoid uncertainty with regard to the law applicable to the arbitration agreement, it is recommended to make a choice of law in the arbitration agreement. The law declared applicable to the arbitration agreement may thus be a different legal system than the law declared applicable to the agreement itself. The parties may, for example, make an explicit choice of law with regard to the arbitration agreement if they wish to have all aspects of the arbitration governed by the law of the place of arbitration and this law is not applicable to the agreement itself. The application of different legal systems to different parts of the agreement is referred to as 'dépeçage'.[16]

Under Dutch law, the interpretation of the arbitration agreement is based on the so-called 'Haviltex' formula, referring to the Supreme Court case which established the rules for contract interpretation.[17] A contract is not interpreted solely based on the wording of the agreement. Contract interpretation also requires an examination of the meaning that each of the parties was reasonably entitled to ascribe to the statements and conduct of the other party and to what each of the parties was reasonably entitled to expect from the other party in this regard.[18] More weight is attributed to the linguistic meaning of the wording of the agreement when professional parties are involved who conducted extensive negotiations regarding their agreement.[19] The same goes if the relevant

---

[14] The same applies for questions regarding the legal validity of the arbitration clause.

[15] See G.J. Meijer 2008 (T&C Rv), Art. 1020 DCCP, note 2.

[16] See also Fouchard, Gaillard and Goldman, 1999, para. 1436 and 1555.

[17] HR 13 Mar. 1981, NJ 1981, 635.

[18] HR 13 Mar. 1981, NJ 1981, 635, para. 2.

[19] HR 19 Jan. 2007, RvdW 2007, 108; HR 29 Jun. 2007, NJ 2007, 576.

agreement has been negotiated by third parties with the aim to apply to a broader group of individuals who have not been involved in the negotiations.[20] It can be argued that the same applies where the parties have simply incorporated the standard arbitration clause recommended by the NAI.

In exceptional cases the parties declare the NAI Rules applicable to their arbitration but they decide not to have the NAI administer their arbitration, usually with a view to save on administration costs. Such arbitrations are also referred to as 'wild arbitrations' and are not recommended. Apart from the fact that a wild arbitration is an irregular free ride, it is bound to suffer numerous defects, in particular since the role of the Administrator is critical to many of the NAI Rules.

4.2. Interpretation of the NAI Rules

Under Dutch law, arbitration rules referred to in the arbitration agreement are deemed to form an integral part of the arbitration agreement. Therefore, a reference to the NAI Rules in an arbitration clause entails that the NAI Rules become part of the arbitration agreement. Accordingly, the NAI Rules need to be interpreted in accordance with the rules of law that apply to the arbitration agreement.

If Dutch law applies, it is relevant that the Supreme Court ruled that arbitration rules should be interpreted in accordance with the linguistic meaning of the wording. In addition, international arbitration practice should be taken into account, if the relevant arbitration rules are applied in the international arena.[21] Practice shows that arbitral tribunals and state courts are inclined to take the provisions of the DCCP and the associated case law of the state courts into account when interpreting the NAI Rules, because a substantive number of provisions in the NAI Rules are derived from the DCCP. However, it is arguable whether Dutch procedural law should always be decisive when interpreting the NAI Rules, in particular in so far as international arbitrations are concerned.

The interpretation of the NAI Rules is particularly relevant in connection with the possibility of setting aside arbitral awards based on a breach of the tribunal's mandate. When assessing whether the arbitral tribunal exceeded the boundaries

---

[20] The Supreme Court has accepted this rule for example in regard of Collective Labour Agreements that are negotiated by labour unions on behalf of their members, Collective Labour Agreements that have been declared compulsory applicable in accordance with the relevant Dutch statutory provisions, and the standard terms of insurance policies that have not been subject to separate negotiations by the parties to the agreement; HR 17 Sep. 1993, NJ 1994, 173; HR 31 May 2002, NJ 2003, 110, respectively HR 16 May 2008, NJ 2008, 284.

[21] The Supreme Court accepted this rule in regard of the ICC Rules (HR 17 Jan. 2003, NJ 2004, 384). There is no reason why the same rule should not apply to the NAI Rules in case of international arbitrations.

of its mandate, it is relevant whether the tribunal conducted the proceedings in accordance with the applicable procedural rules.[22]

5. Main Characteristics of NAI Arbitration

Although all aspects of NAI arbitration will be discussed at length in Part II, this general chapter gives an overview of the most important characteristics of NAI arbitration. The purpose is to offer the reader the opportunity to get a general picture of several features of NAI arbitration at a glance.

First, the central role of the Administrator ensures a well-oiled administration of the arbitration, also thanks to years of experience and adequate support from the Secretariat. The Administrator is involved in the arbitration from start to finish, although the intensity of the involvement varies during different stages of the arbitration. The Administrator has a crucial role in relation to the appointment of the arbitrators, as discussed below (Articles 12-15). The NAI Rules furthermore allocate clearly defined tasks to the Administrator, for example the receipt and forwarding of documents when the arbitral tribunal has not yet been appointed (Articles 6 and 7), sending the arbitration file to the arbitral tribunal after its appointment (Article 20), adding a secretary to the arbitral tribunal upon request (Article 39), determining the fees of the arbitral tribunal (Article 58), and sending the arbitral award to the parties and depositing the arbitral award with the Registry of the District Court (Article 50) as required by Article 1058 DCCP. The Administrator also has an important role apart from the tasks explicitly allocated to the Administrator in the NAI Rules. After the arbitrators have been appointed, the Administrator monitors the course of the arbitration in order to assist the arbitral tribunal where necessary, for example in arranging hearings and providing names of possible experts. Moreover, the Administrator sees to it that the arbitration proceeds expeditiously and that no unnecessary delays occur in rendering an arbitral award. The Administrator also informally reviews a draft of the arbitral award before it is officially rendered by the arbitral tribunal. Part II contains more information on these formal and informal tasks of the Administrator.

Second, NAI arbitration is characterized by the use of the list procedure in cases in which the parties themselves did not provide for the appointment of arbitrators (Articles 14 and 15). The NAI has a confidential file containing the names of approximately 250 people who are registered as arbitrators with the NAI. These persons, including both generalists and specialists in various fields, have been carefully selected and typically all have experience with arbitrations. The NAI provides training to these persons to expand their knowledge of arbitration law. The NAI's file with names of possible arbitrators is undoubtedly the most important asset of the NAI, as it enables the NAI to quickly and readily

---

[22] HR 17 Jan. 2003, NJ 2004, 384 and HR 28 Sep. 1990, NJ 1991, 230.

appoint arbitrators whose qualities are geared to the nature and subject of the arbitration in question as much as possible in every arbitration in which the parties did not provide for the (method of) appointment of arbitrators. The list procedure is a procedure in which the Administrator first presents a list of potential arbitrators to the parties. The parties may delete from this list the names of persons against whom they have overriding objections and list the remaining names in the order of their preference. After the lists have been returned, the Administrator appoints the arbitrators on the basis of the parties' preferences. If the lists returned do not contain a sufficient number of names of persons who are acceptable as arbitrator to each of the parties, the Administrator himself may invite one or more other persons to act as arbitrator. However, if deemed appropriate the Administrator may also decide to send the parties a second list of potential arbitrators for selecting the (remaining) arbitrators. The Administrator tends to appoint as many arbitrators as possible on the basis of the first list. The appointment of arbitrators is completed if the persons invited accept their appointment.

Third, it should be pointed out that the standard NAI arbitral procedure starts with one round of submissions followed by an oral hearing after which an arbitral award is rendered. The parties may make different arrangements and the arbitral tribunal may organize the procedure based on the needs of the subject dispute. For example, the arbitral tribunal may order a second round of written submissions, which is in fact commonly done. NAI arbitrations do not use a system of Terms of Reference, as provided for in the ICC Rules,[23] but further detailed agreements on the arbitral procedure, resembling such Terms of Reference, may be agreed upon by the tribunal and the parties if they wish to do so (see also the comments on Article 23).

Fourth, unless the parties have agreed otherwise, the arbitral tribunal has considerable freedom in determining and applying rules of evidence. The arbitral tribunal is not bound by detailed rules for the examination of witnesses and experts and the submission of documents. The arbitral tribunal may in principle determine how to deal with these issues. In respect of the conduct of witness examinations in the form of Anglo-American cross-examination, it is noted that this is not part of the Dutch legal system and culture – although the Dutch legal system is not hostile to the use thereof in arbitration. This means that if parties have agreed on the possibility of witnesses being cross-examined, or if the arbitral tribunal has determined that cross-examination will take place, this type of witness examination will be conducted. However, even if cross-examination will take place, the parties should take into account that the examination of witnesses is likely to be conducted with a lesser degree of adherence to specific formalities for cross-examination than might be expected by parties rooted in a system of law

---

[23]   Article 18(1) ICC Rules. See Derains and Schwartz, 2005, 250 et seq.

where cross-examination is traditionally used. The arbitral tribunal, in particular, is likely to take a more active role than may be expected by such parties.

Fifth, pursuant to Dutch arbitration law and the NAI Rules, the (partial) final arbitral award in an arbitration seated in the Netherlands must be deposited with the Registry of the District Court in whose district the place of arbitration is located (see Articles 50(1)(b) and 1058(b) DCCP). This deposit triggers the commencement of time limits within which the parties may request rectification, correction, supplementation or the setting aside of the award.

Sixth, the NAI Rules do not provide for the possibility of arbitral appeal. Nevertheless, the parties may agree upon such appeal, also when the NAI Rules apply. However, in that event the parties should bear in mind that they will also have to provide for the entire appeal procedure including time limits for lodging an appeal and associated formalities. To our knowledge, appeal is virtually never agreed upon in NAI arbitration practice.

Seventh, the NAI Rules include the right of a party to request interim or provisional measures both in separate summary arbitral proceedings and during a pending arbitration on the merits. The possibility of separate summary arbitral proceedings aimed at urgently obtaining interim measures is a fairly unique and successful feature of NAI arbitration. This possibility is derived from the Dutch rules of summary proceedings before the President (*voorzieningenrechter*) of the District Court. Foreign parties in particular should take note of the possibilities offered by summary arbitral proceedings so that they can make appropriate use of these possibilities or know what to expect if the other party commences summary arbitral proceedings (see also the comments in Part II, Section 4).

Finally, NAI arbitrations are characterized by confidentiality. The principle of public access to the proceedings applying to public administration of justice does not apply in arbitrations. In arbitration, the parties can claim confidentiality.[24] There is, however, no provision in the NAI Rules or the DCCP specifically imposing on the parties the obligation to keep all information exchanged in the context of the arbitration – including submissions – confidential. As with most other arbitration laws and rules, confidentiality as point of departure is apparently considered to be so obvious that it has not been embedded as such in any specific provision (see, however, the comments on Article 55 concerning the publication of the arbitral award).[25] If the parties have an interest in securing absolute confidentiality beyond the usual practice, it is advisable to enter into a specific confidentiality arrangement between the

---

[24] See for the relation between Art. 6 ECHR and arbitration European Commission on Human Rights 27 Nov. 1986, NJ 1997, 505.

[25] The Draft Bill (see Part I, Ch. 2, Section 7) contains a new Art. 1069A on the principle of confidentiality. This article stipulates that an arbitration is confidential and that all persons that are directly or indirectly involved in the arbitration have to observe confidentiality, unless and insofar as disclosure (or publication) arises out of the law or an agreement between the parties. Art. 55 of the NAI Rules on the publication of the award may qualify as such an agreement between the parties.

arbitral tribunal and the parties or to request the tribunal to issue a confidentiality order. In the case of an agreement, careful attention should be given to the complex issues that may follow from confidentiality arrangements in the context of arbitrations and related proceedings before state courts (see Part I, Chapter 2, Section 5).

6.   Contractual Relationships under the NAI Rules

In ad hoc arbitrations (which are discussed in more detail in Part I, Chapter 2, Section 3) the contractual relationships are clear. If the arbitration is governed by Dutch law, an agreement of instruction (*overeenkomst van opdracht*) as referred to in Article 7:400 DCC is established between the parties and the arbitral tribunal. The parties instruct the arbitral tribunal to resolve their dispute by means of an arbitral award, for which service the parties will have to pay a fee to the arbitral tribunal.

In institutional arbitrations, the contractual relationships are more complex due to the involvement of the arbitration institute. With regard to NAI arbitrations, the following applies, assuming that the arbitration is governed by Dutch law.[26] An agreement of instruction is established and forms the basis of the relationship between the parties and the arbitral tribunal, not only if the parties themselves have appointed arbitrators but also if the arbitrators have been appointed according to the list procedure of the NAI Rules. In the former case, the parties are deemed to have jointly instructed the individual arbitrators, regardless of who requested an arbitrator to act as such. The appointment of the arbitral tribunal by the parties must be confirmed by the Administrator (Article 15(1)), to ensure and safeguard the quality of the arbitrators appointed (see also Article 13(3)). In the latter case, in which the arbitral tribunal is appointed according to the list procedure, the Administrator appoints the arbitrators on behalf of the parties. In both cases the Administrator confirms the appointment, on behalf of the parties, in a letter of appointment addressed to the individual arbitrators.

In addition to the agreement of instruction between the parties and the arbitral tribunal, an agreement of instruction is also established between the parties and the NAI. This agreement entails that the parties instruct the NAI to administer the arbitration from start to finish; the NAI is deemed to perform all tasks as set forth in the NAI Rules. Naturally, the most important task in this context is to arrange the formation of an arbitral tribunal. The parties have to pay administrative expenses for the services rendered by the NAI.

Finally, a contractual relationship is established between the NAI and the arbitral tribunal. In our opinion, this agreement has a sui generis nature. In the relationship between the arbitral tribunal and the NAI, the arbitral tribunal is required to

---

[26]   See for further information F.D. von Hombracht-Brinkman, 'Taken en verantwoordelijkheden van arbitrage-instituten bezien in het licht van de driehoeksverhouding partijen – instituut – arbiters', TvA 1994, 1-21.

properly perform the instruction received from the parties to resolve their dispute. The NAI, on the other hand, is required to properly administer the arbitration and perform various other tasks: for instance, asking for the payment of a deposit by the parties and paying arbitrators from such deposits during and upon conclusion of the arbitral proceedings. Where necessary, the NAI provides assistance to the arbitral tribunal and ensures a smooth financial settlement of the arbitration.

Contrary to the agreement of instruction between the parties and the arbitral tribunal, which is set forth in the letter of appointment mentioned before, the agreement between the parties and the NAI and the agreement between the NAI and the arbitral tribunal is not generally recorded in writing. Those agreements are deemed to be encompassed in the manner in which the parties, the NAI and the arbitral tribunal deal with one another and the correspondence that initiates each arbitration. The foregoing assumes that all parties have accepted the applicability of the NAI Rules. However, especially in situations where the respondent claims that the arbitral tribunal has no jurisdiction based on the fact that there is no valid arbitration agreement, it is recommended to ensure that all parties involved in the arbitration, including the respondent, explicitly acknowledge that arbitration under the applicability of the NAI Rules is involved, for example, by requiring that appearance in the arbitral proceedings (either in writing or during a hearing) constitutes acceptance of the NAI Rules.

The above is relevant in connection with the exclusion of liability as set forth in Article 66, since such exoneration requires that there is a contractual relationship between the parties involved (see also the comments on Article 66).

What has been set out above relates to the most important actors involved in NAI arbitrations. Attention should also be given to possible other parties that may be involved in arbitration, such as tribunal-appointed experts, the secretary to the tribunal, interpreters and court reporters. It is outside the scope of this publication to address the various relationships in detail and to assess the legal qualification thereof under specific laws that may apply. However, abstracting from the applicable laws, the following may be observed on the basis of the applicable provisions of the NAI Rules.

Article 31(1) indicates that tribunal-appointed experts are appointed by the arbitral tribunal. Accordingly, tribunal-appointed experts normally carry out their activities on the basis of a contractual relationship with the arbitral tribunal only. There is usually no separate relationship between the experts and the parties or the NAI. The tribunal-appointed expert's activities are usually paid for by the Administrator from the deposit as provided for in Article 59. Occasionally, arbitral tribunals prefer to arrange for experts to be paid directly by the parties. Such arrangement in itself will not bring about a contractual relationship between the parties and the tribunal-appointed experts. However, the specific wording of the arrangement may indicate otherwise. The same goes for specific arrangements providing for the exclusion or a limitation of liability in favour of the tribunal-appointed experts.

Pursuant to Article 39, a secretary to the arbitral tribunal may be provided for by the Administrator, upon request of the arbitral tribunal. This provision seems to indicate that the secretary is acting on the basis of a contractual relationship with the NAI only, in the absence of separate contractual relationships with the arbitral tribunal and/or the parties. The inapplicability of the exclusion of liability in Article 66 is pointing to the same.

In international arbitrations under the NAI Rules the practice seems to be that the parties arrange for their own interpreters and court reporters. Accordingly, the interpreters and court reporters work at the instruction of the parties and there are no separate contractual relationships with the arbitral tribunal or the NAI. The arbitral tribunal can, however, also decide to instruct the necessary interpreters and court reporters itself, or to have them instructed by the NAI Secretariat. If this is the case, they will carry out their activities on the basis of a contractual relationship with the arbitral tribunal or the NAI respectively and their services will be paid from the deposit referred to in Article 59.

The mere absence of a contractual relationship between the parties on the one hand and tribunal-appointed experts, interpreters and court reporters on the other hand, does not preclude that the latter may be held liable for their activities by the parties. Under certain circumstances, the conduct of such parties may be tortuous. In that event, the parties may wish to seek compensation on the basis of tort (*onrechtmatige daad*). If tribunal-appointed experts, interpreters or court reporters wish to limit their liability, it is recommended that they request the parties to explicitly accept an exclusion or limitation of liability.

CHAPTER 2

ARBITRATION IN THE NETHERLANDS

1.   The Dutch Law of Arbitration

The DCCP, also referred to as the 'Dutch arbitration act', contains the – mainly mandatory – statutory provisions of Dutch arbitration law. Book IV of the DCCP is devoted entirely to arbitration law. The greater part of the provisions (Title 1 of Book IV) involves arbitration in the Netherlands. Only a few provisions (Title 2 of Book IV) deal with arbitration outside the Netherlands.[27] These provisions will not be discussed in this chapter (see the comments on Articles 1075 and 1076 DCCP in Part III, Chapter 3, on the recognition and enforcement of foreign arbitral awards).

A proper understanding of the NAI Rules, based as they are on the Dutch arbitration act, requires a general knowledge of Dutch arbitration law. Where relevant for the understanding of the NAI Rules, we refer to the relevant provisions of the Dutch arbitration act. In addition, this guide outlines the main features of Dutch arbitration law, including topics not provided for in the NAI Rules, but applicable to arbitrations seated in the Netherlands (see specifically this Chapter 2 and Part III on post-arbitration court proceedings). We also refer to the various handbooks for an extensive explanation of Dutch arbitration law.[28]

Title 1 of Book IV regarding Arbitration in the Netherlands applies if the place of arbitration is situated in the Netherlands (Article 1073 DCCP). This is a mandatory rule and the parties may thus not deviate from that provision by agreement. Whether national or international arbitration is involved is irrelevant. An international arbitration only involving foreign parties is also subject to Dutch arbitration law when the place of arbitration is in the Netherlands. If the place of arbitration is outside the Netherlands, Dutch arbitration law does not apply. In that case, the law of the country in which the place of arbitration is located will typically be held to apply. The definitive answer to this question will, however

---

[27]   Those provisions only regard the jurisdiction of the Dutch court if the parties agreed upon arbitration outside the Netherlands and the recognition and enforcement of foreign arbitral awards.

[28]   Burg. Rv, 2006 (H.J. Snijders), comments on Book IV of the DCCP; P. Sanders, *Het Nederlandse arbitragerecht. Nationaal en internationaal* (Deventer, Kluwer, 2001) and Vademecum Arbitrage (H.J. Snijders et al.), 2002.

and in principle, have to be provided by the law of the country in which the place of arbitration is located, including the issue of whether the parties may deviate from such laws.

The applicable arbitration law must be distinguished from the substantive law to be applied by the arbitral tribunal. The applicability of Dutch arbitration law based on the place of arbitration by no means implies the applicability of Dutch substantive law. Instead, the arbitral tribunal determines which substantive law applies based on the agreement and/or the rules of private international law. When in doubt, discussion may arise regarding the question of whether provisions are part of the domain of arbitration law or the domain of the applicable substantive law. From a Dutch law point of view this could involve rules regarding evidence, as these are usually deemed to be part of arbitration law. However, under Dutch law most of the rules regarding the division of the burden of proof between the parties are part of substantive law. In many situations, the DCC stipulates which of the parties has the burden of proving particular facts. From an international perspective, how a certain rule of law compares to Dutch arbitration law and whether Dutch arbitration law offers room for the applicability of that rule based on the fact that the rule is part of the domain of the applicable substantive law will have to be assessed on a case-by-case basis.

The Netherlands is a party to the New York Convention. The spirit of this Convention is usually adhered to in the Netherlands. The grounds for refusing the recognition and enforcement of foreign arbitral awards in the Netherlands are interpreted narrowly and applied with restraint (for more information on the recognition and enforcement of arbitral awards, see Part III, Chapter 3).

2. Arbitrability of the Subject Matter

The NAI is a general arbitration institute that is open to all commercial disputes, regardless of the subject matter and regardless of whether a dispute has a contractual basis. Hence, disputes for which it is possible to opt for arbitration via an industry-related arbitration institute can also be submitted to NAI arbitration. The only restriction is that arbitration cannot be used to ascertain legal consequences that may not be freely determined by the parties (Article 1020(3) DCCP). This involves the legal consequences in respect of which the legislature or the courts through case law have determined that these can only be ascertained by state courts.

This exclusive jurisdiction of the state courts comprises subjects in which dispute resolution results in a ruling that has legal effect in relation to everyone ('*erga omnes*'), and not just to the parties to the dispute. By their nature, such rulings cannot be rendered by arbitrators because an arbitral award can only have binding effect on parties that agreed to arbitration. This specifically relates to subjects that are traditionally not submitted to arbitration, such as numerous family law disputes (e.g., divorce, adoption and family supervision), bankruptcy petitions and moratorium of payments requests. Rulings regarding the legal validity of decisions and resolutions of legal entities are also, by their nature, deemed to apply '*erga omnes*'; this means that the state court's jurisdiction to rule on this validity is exclusive.[29] The same is assumed for rulings regarding the legal validity of patents and trademarks.

Moreover, there are also subjects that require some form of state involvement through bailiffs (*deurwaarders*) or the police. These matters are, in principle, also subject to the exclusive jurisdiction of the state courts. Examples of this include the (effectuation of) requests for protective measures (such as a prejudgment attachment), requests to hear reluctant witnesses and claims for committal due to failure to comply with a judicial order.

Furthermore, non-arbitrability applies to subjects that are deemed to be so important that dispute resolution is exclusively reserved for the state courts. This usually regards subjects directly or indirectly involving third-party interests. Examples include dispute settlement schemes in mass tort cases, inquiries into company affairs (*enquête*) and possible class actions. Although in the past, there has been debate whether disputes regarding leases can be submitted to arbitration, there is now a growing consensus that this is possible.[30]

The common denominator in all the examples set out above is that the subject of the dispute and the relief requested is a matter of public policy. If such is not the case, arbitration is generally possible. However, the mere fact that rules of public policy are involved does not bar a dispute from being submitted to arbitration. For example, the arbitral tribunal which is to rule on claims regarding an agreement may also rule on the question of whether all or part of this agreement is in breach of Article 81 EC Treaty. This is not altered by the fact that this latter provision is deemed to be a rule of public policy, albeit that the award can be scrutinized in setting aside proceedings as to whether it complies with such a rule (see further Article 1065 DCCP, note 6 in Part III, Chapter 1).

3. 'Ad hoc' versus Institutional Arbitration

Arbitrations that are not administered by an arbitration institute or a similar organization are referred to as 'ad hoc' arbitrations. One disadvantage of ad hoc proceedings is that the parties themselves, if necessary with the assistance of the President (*voorzieningenrechter*) of the District Court, must provide for the appointment of arbitrators (Article 1027 DCCP). Another disadvantage is that the parties themselves, or if they fail to do so, the arbitral tribunal, must agree upon the applicable procedural rules. However, the other side of the coin is that the parties do not have to incur any costs for the administration by the arbitration institute.

---

[29] HR 10 Nov. 2006, NJ 2007, 561. See also P. van Schilfgaarde, 'De Hoge Raad en de arbitrabiliteit van een vordering tot vaststelling van de nietigheid of vernietiging van een besluit', TvA 2008, 7-14.

[30] Burg. Rv, 2006 (H.J. Snijders), Art. 1020 DCCP, note 5(e).

The parties can eliminate the drawbacks mentioned above by declaring the UNCITRAL Rules applicable to their arbitration clause. This would mean that widely recognized arbitration rules apply to the arbitration, even though the arbitration is not administered by an arbitration institute. However, this does not negate the fact that the parties will still miss out on the many advantages such an institute can offer. If the parties refer to the UNCITRAL Rules, it is recommended that they also include the appointing authority in their arbitration clause. The NAI is prepared to act as the appointing authority (see Article 14(7) NAI Rules). If the parties have failed to designate an appointing authority or in the unlikely event that this authority fails to appoint arbitrators or fails to do so timely, the parties can turn to the Secretary General of the Permanent Court of Arbitration in The Hague, who ultimately arranges for the appointment of arbitrators under the UNCITRAL Rules.[31]

Arbitrations that are administered by an arbitration institute or a similar organization are referred to as institutional arbitrations. One advantage of such arbitrations is that to a greater or lesser extent, the arbitration institute arranges for the appointment of arbitrators. Another advantage is that a general framework for the rules of procedure is set forth in rules so that the parties and the arbitrators largely know in advance how the arbitration will proceed. On the other hand, the parties will incur additional costs for the administration by the arbitration institute. Save for exceptions (reference is made in particular to cases involving a minor financial interest), these costs, however, by no means outweigh the advantages which the parties will experience from an arbitration being administered by the arbitration institute.

The NAI is the most well-known and also the only general arbitration institute in the Netherlands. The other arbitration institutes in the Netherlands are more or less industry related. The most important industry-related institute is the *Raad van Arbitrage voor de Bouw* (Arbitration Council for the Construction Industry).[32] This is one of the few arbitration institutes whose Rules provide for the possibility of an arbitral appeal. As an example, the following industry-related arbitration institutes are noted: the *Stichting Geschillenoplossing Organisatie en Automatisering* (Foundation for the Settlement of Automation Disputes);[33] NOFOTA (the Netherlands Oils, Fats and Oilseeds Trade Association);[34]

---

[31]   See <www.uncitral.org/uncitral/en/uncitral_texts/arbitration/1976Arbitration_rules.html>. See for more information on the UNCITRAL Rules: P. Sanders, 'Commentary on UNCITRAL Arbitration Rules', in *Yearbook Commercial Arbitration*, ed. P. Sanders, Vol. II (Deventer, Kluwer, 1977), 172-219; D.D. Caron, L.M. Caplan & M. Pellonpaa, *The UNCITRAL Arbitration Rules. A Commentary* (Oxford, Oxford University Press, 2006).

[32]   See <www.raadvanarbitrage.nl>. More information can be found in Vademecum Arbitrage, 2002 (D.E. van Werven), 439-483.

[33]   See <www.sgoa.org>. More information can be found in Vademecum Arbitrage, 2002 (D.T.L. Oosterbaan), 589-601.

[34]   See <www.nofota.com>. More information can be found in Vademecum Arbitrage, 2002 (P.W. van Baal), 231-260.

the *Scheidsgerecht Gezondheidszorg* (Arbitral Tribunal for the Healthcare Industry);[35] the *Raad van Arbitrage voor Metaalnijverheid en Handel* (Arbitration Council for the Metal Trade and Industry), the *Koninklijk Instituut van Ingenieurs (KIVI)* (Arbitration Institute for Engineers).

In an international context, at least from a Dutch perspective, the ICC International Court of Arbitration is the most important general arbitration institute.[36] One of the special features of ICC arbitration in deviation of NAI arbitration is the use of 'Terms of Reference', in which the parties and the tribunal agree at the outset of the proceedings on the positions and claims of the parties and on those issues in dispute that the arbitral tribunal has to decide. Furthermore, NAI arbitration does only provide for an internal and informal system of review of draft awards by the Administrator, which does not compare with the thorough scrutiny by the ICC Court. As a consequence, the costs involved with NAI arbitration (both the administrative costs and the arbitrators' fees) are usually considerably lower than the costs of ICC arbitration.

Other important international arbitration institutes are the World Intellectual Property Organization (WIPO) Arbitration and Mediation Center,[37] the International Centre for Settlement of Investment Disputes (ICSID),[38] the AAA International Centre for Dispute Resolution (ICDR),[39] the London Court of International Arbitration (LCIA),[40] the Stockholm Chamber of Commerce,[41] and the Swiss Chambers of Commerce (Swiss Rules of International Arbitration).[42] We suffice to note that parties may wish to consider these alternatives to NAI arbitration, whether it be because of their particular expertise (WIPO and ICSID), or because of regional preferences. A comprehensive comparison with the arbitration rules of these institutes falls outside the ambit of this book.[43]

---

[35] See <www.scheidsgerechtgezondheidszorg.nl>. More information can be found in Vademecum Arbitrage, 2002 (A.T.B. de Vries), 513-538.

[36] See <www.iccwbo.org>. More information on ICC arbitration can be found in Bühler and Webster, 2008; Derains and Schwartz, 2005; Craig, Park and Paulsson, 2000.

[37] See <www.wipo.int>.

[38] See <icsid.worldbank.org>.

[39] See <www.adr.org>.

[40] See <www.lcia-arbitration.com>.

[41] See <www.sccinstitute.com>.

[42] See <www.sccam.org>.

[43] See the following handbooks on the rules of these institutes. On the ICSID: L. Reed, J. Paulsson & N. Blackaby, *A Guide to ICSID Arbitration* (The Hague, Kluwer Law International, 2004); C.H. Schreuer, *The ICSID Convention. A Commentary* (Cambridge, Cambridge University Press, 2001). On the LCIA: P. Turner & R. Mohtashami, *A Guide to the LCIA Arbitration Rules* (Oxford, Oxford University Press, forthcoming 2009). On the Stockholm Chamber of Commerce: F. Madsen, *Commercial Arbitration in Sweden* (Oxford, Oxford University Press, 2006). On the Swiss Chambers of Commerce: G. Kaufmann-Kohler & B. Stucki (eds), *International Arbitration in Switzerland. A Handbook for Practitioners* (The Hague, Kluwer Law International, 2004).

The arbitration rules of the above-mentioned institutes will only be referred to if that enhances a better understanding of the NAI Rules. In most cases, reference is made to both the ICC Rules and the UNCITRAL Rules, as these are the most common arbitration rules from a Netherlands perspective, that serve as an alternative to the NAI Rules.

4.　Mandatory versus Supplementary Rules of Law

The NAI Rules have been carefully harmonized with the arbitration law set forth in the DCCP. Dutch arbitration law distinguishes between rules of mandatory law and rules of supplementary law. As mandatory law rules cannot be deviated from, the NAI Rules either do not contain rules on issues covered by mandatory law, or contain rules which are in perfect harmony with mandatory law. Deviations are possible where Dutch arbitration law involves rules of supplementary law. The NAI Rules actually use this possibility in various instances.

A provision of supplementary nature is typically identified by an explicit reference to the fact that the parties may agree differently, or otherwise mentions the possibility of the parties making their own arrangements. An important example of this is the arrangement regarding the appointment of arbitrators (Article 1027 DCCP). If such reference is absent, rules are generally of a mandatory nature. However, there are also statutory provisions that do not include the reference mentioned above and which nevertheless are of a supplementary nature. In view of this, whether or not a rule is mandatory law must be determined on a case-by-case basis. For example, the rule that the arbitral tribunal must be composed of an odd number of arbitrators (Article 1026(1) DCCP) must be designated as mandatory law, since the legislature deliberately excluded the possibility of an even number of arbitrators. On the other hand, the rule that an arbitrator must accept his mandate in writing (Article 1029(1) DCCP) is generally not regarded as mandatory in nature, even though there is no reference to the possibility that the parties can agree otherwise.

5.　Role of the Dutch State Courts

In Dutch arbitration law, state courts play a considerable role. This is true both during the arbitral proceedings and thereafter.

During the arbitration, the state courts act as a safety net if issues arise that the parties and/or the arbitrators are unable to resolve. For example, the courts can be called on for numerous aspects surrounding the appointment and replacement of arbitrators (Articles 1026-1030 DCCP), challenge of arbitrators (Article 1035 DCCP), hearing of reluctant witnesses (Article 1041 DCCP), for the purpose of gathering information regarding foreign law (Article 1044 DCCP), and in consolidating related arbitrations (Article 1046 DCCP). In all these cases, parties have ready access to the courts, which means that arbitrations can be facilitated in numerous situations in which arbitrations threaten to come to a standstill. Where necessary, this role of the courts during arbitrations is discussed in more detail in Part II.

Once the arbitral proceedings have ended (i.e., when the final award has been rendered), the courts fulfil a monitoring function. On the one hand, the courts fulfil this function within the scope of a possible proceeding to set aside (Articles 1064-1065 DCCP) or revoke (Articles 1064(1) and 1068 DCCP) the award; on the other hand, the courts fulfil this function within the scope of a proceeding to grant leave to enforce an arbitral award (Articles 1062-1063 DCCP). In all these proceedings, which are addressed in more detail in Part III, the courts tend to act with restraint when exercising this monitoring function in order to prevent such proceedings from being used (or abused) as some form of disguised appeal against arbitral awards. Nevertheless, this monitoring function has a preventive effect, thus increasing the quality of arbitration, as arbitrators want to prevent their arbitral award from being set aside or failing to qualify for recognition or enforcement.

However, the courts' role within the scope of arbitrations also has a downside. As soon as a court is called on, confidentiality is no longer guaranteed, since the public has access to the public administration of justice (Articles 27 and 28 DCCP) and these days, court decisions are widely published, sometimes in legal journals and frequently on the internet. There are only very limited possibilities for a hearing behind closed doors (Articles 27 and 28 DCCP) and for having decisions made anonymous before they are published. Since confidentiality agreements are still an uncommon feature in arbitration agreements and arbitration rules to date, it is uncertain to what extent the courts are likely to cooperate in adopting an extraordinary arrangement for maintaining confidentiality. There are rare examples where the courts turned out to be willing to agree to some kind of special arrangement, while deviating from normal practice, but keeping within the boundaries of the DCCP.

6. Arbitration Law as a Necessary Supplement to the NAI Rules

As is common to all arbitration rules, the NAI Rules do not contain fully self-sufficient rules. The rules of arbitration law as set forth in the DCCP have to be applied to various matters because these are not (and indeed often cannot be) covered by the NAI Rules. Where necessary, those subjects are addressed in Parts II and III of this guide. Here only a brief account is given of the most important subjects that have not been provided for in the NAI Rules.[44]

Pursuant to Article 1021 DCCP, an arbitration agreement is evidenced by a 'document' (*geschrift*). A document that only refers to general terms and conditions that contain an arbitration clause meets this requirement. Electronically recorded data can also be designated as a document. Article 1021 DCCP merely

---

[44] The arbitrability rules as set forth in Art. 1020 DCCP have been discussed above in Part I, Ch. 2, Section 2.

contains a requirement of proof and not a requirement of existence. Proof by means of a document is, in principle, only required when the existence of the arbitration agreement is challenged by the defendant. However, this fine distinction virtually never plays a role in practice. As a rule, arbitration agreements are set forth in writing. In NAI arbitrations, a copy of the arbitration agreement must be submitted when the request for arbitration is filed (Article 6(3)(e) NAI Rules).[45]

The NAI Rules provide for the situation in which the arbitral tribunal is confronted with a claim for lack of jurisdiction (Article 9). Article 1022 DCCP involves the reverse situation, namely the situation in which a court is confronted with a claim for lack of jurisdiction because of the alleged existence of an arbitration agreement. Such a claim must be made before, or at the latest together with, the first substantive defence, failing which a court will assume jurisdiction.

Article 1022(3) DCCP provides for the possibility of a party to an arbitration agreement to request a state court to order a witness or expert examination, a site visit or a inspection before the appointment of the arbitral tribunal. Some District Courts have interpreted the time limits in Article 1022(3) DCCP as to relate to the moment on which the state court renders a decision on the request and not to the moment on which the request was filed and, accordingly, dismissed a request in the case that the arbitral tribunal was constituted after the request had been filed with the court, but before a decision had been taken thereon.[46] The idea behind this is that once the arbitral tribunal is able (i.e., when all[47] arbitrators are appointed) to proceed with witness and expert examinations, site visits and inspections, state courts should not do so anymore. After all, witness and expert examinations, site visits and inspections should preferably be done in the presence of the arbitral tribunal that will determine the case, as its presence is crucial for its ability to interpret and evaluate the evidence that is gathered in this way. In this respect, the gathering of evidence before the state court as envisaged by Article 1022(3) DCCP is not preferable. Such gathering of evidence could, however, prove to be useful for example if there is reasonable fear of embezzlement of the evidence before the arbitral tribunal is constituted, or if the evidence is necessary for assessing the chances of success in arbitral proceedings.

---

[45]   As noted by G.J. Meijer in his dissertation *Overeenkomst tot Arbitrage* (Meijer, 2008), the evidentiary requirement of an instrument in writing operates in practice as an additional constitutive requirement for the formation of the arbitration agreement. This is also the reason why in the Draft Bill, which will be discussed below in Part I, Ch. 2, Section 7, Art. 1021 DCCP is to be amended to the effect that the requirement of a written instrument becomes a constitutive requirement for the formation of an arbitration agreement.

[46]   See, for example, the Haarlem District Court 18 Jun. 2002, JBPR 2003, 18; Amsterdam District Court 1 Oct. 2002, JBPR 2003, 19 and G.J. Meijer 2008 (T&C Rv), Art. 1022 DCCP, note 3(c).

[47]   See Amsterdam District Court 1 Oct. 2002, JBPR 2003, 19 and G.J. Meijer 2008 (T&C Rv), Art. 1022 DCCP, note 3(c).

Article 1028 DCCP includes rules providing for the event that one of the parties takes a preferred position in the arrangement for the appointment of arbitrators. In that case, the other party can request that the arbitrators be appointed by the President (*voorzieningenrechter*) of the District Court instead of in accordance with the arrangement agreed upon.

The mandate for the arbitral tribunal can be terminated pursuant to Article 1031 DCCP. The parties can do this jointly, for example when they have reached an amicable settlement or if they are collectively dissatisfied about the way in which the arbitral tribunal is carrying out its mandate. Either of the parties can also individually request the President (*voorzieningenrechter*) of the District Court to terminate the arbitral tribunal's mandate on the ground that, taking into account all circumstances, the speed with which the arbitral tribunal is carrying out its mandate is unacceptably low. Remarkably, the NAI Rules do not contain any provisions regarding the termination of the arbitral tribunal's mandate, other than provisions for costs if the mandate is prematurely terminated (Article 62(2)).

Article 1032 DCCP includes rules that apply if one of the parties dies. These rules are limited to natural persons, of course, and rarely play a role in NAI arbitrations. See the comments on Article 6(3)(a) and (b) for a discussion of the issue of legal succession in legal entities.

Article 1044 DCCP provides for the possibility for arbitrators to obtain information regarding foreign law through the President (*voorzieningenrechter*) of the The Hague District Court. In practice, arbitrators do not use this option, not only because the parties themselves usually provide information on foreign law based on opinions, but also because doing so will result in considerable delays in the progress of the arbitration.

By virtue of Article 1046 DCCP, arbitrations with related subjects can be consolidated in the Netherlands, unless the parties agree otherwise. Since consolidation as a rule considerably complicates arbitrations, excluding this possibility of consolidation in the arbitration agreement is usually recommended. This results primarily from the process that is to lead to consolidation of arbitrations. Once consolidation has been decided on in principle, arbitrators still have to be appointed and agreements have to be made with regard to the rules which will apply to the consolidated proceedings. All of this is especially complex if the consolidated arbitrations were subject to different rules or regulations. Once consolidation has been ordered, proceedings involving three or more parties frequently[48] ensue. Such proceedings may naturally become highly complex as a result thereof. In addition, the fact that a request for consolidation must be submitted to the state courts may compromise confidentiality of the (existence of) arbitral proceedings. Against this background, the possibility of consolidation should only be considered in the event of legal relationships that are very closely

---

[48]   This only differs in the case of consolidation if arbitrations are involved which were pending between the same parties.

related, because in such cases it might be strongly preferable to have different disputes resolved at the same time and by the same arbitrators to avoid conflicting decisions. Unless the parties have excluded the possibility of consolidation, consolidation must be realized by means of proceedings before the President (*voorzieningenrechter*) of the Amsterdam District Court. The President may also order partial consolidation.

Article 1050 DCCP includes rules governing arbitral appeals. As already set out, the possibility of arbitral appeal is virtually never used in NAI arbitrations. For the event of an arbitral appeal, Article 1055 DCCP empowers the arbitral tribunal to declare its decisions provisionally enforceable in those cases where the state courts would also be authorized to do so. The point of departure is that all condemnatory decisions can be declared provisionally enforceable. If an award is declared provisionally enforceable, the arbitral award can be enforced despite an appeal having been lodged against the award. If the arbitral award has not been declared provisionally enforceable, an appeal has suspending effect, so that no further enforcement is possible as from the time the appeal was lodged. The provision of Article 1050 DCCP differs in this respect from the rules governing setting aside proceedings. In principle, setting aside proceedings do not have suspending effect. If claimant in the setting aside proceedings has an interest in freezing possible enforcement measures, it should request for suspension in separate (summary) proceedings (see the comments on Article 1066 DCCP in Part III). Under Dutch law, if the arbitral award is overturned on appeal and the claim is wholly or partially dismissed, the previous enforcement must be designated as a wrongful act, which entails an obligation to pay damages. The same applies in cases where an arbitral award is set aside.

Article 1056 DCCP[49] empowers the arbitral tribunal to impose penalties in those cases where the state courts would have the same power. Penalties can be imposed in regard of all orders to act or refrain from acting in a particular way, with the exception of orders to pay a monetary sum (Article 611a DCCP). In NAI arbitrations, where the possibility of an arbitral appeal is usually not available, the arbitral tribunal is advised to use its power to impose penalties with restraint, as such penalties are in principle definitive. Any penalty imposed can only be reversed in the event that it is fully or partially impossible to comply with the arbitral tribunal's order. In that case, the President (*voorzieningenrechter*) of the District Court can be requested to cancel, suspend or reduce the penalty (Article 1056 DCCP). In this regard it should be noted that penalties are regarded as disciplinary measures aimed at stimulating a party to comply with the order. The penalties are definitively due for the mere reason that the relevant party failed to comply with the order, even if the order itself is subsequently reversed.

In addition, the DCCP includes rules regarding the enforcement of arbitral awards (Articles 1062 and 1063), setting aside and revoking arbitral awards

---

[49] Article 1056 DCCP provides that the provisions of Arts 611a to 611i DCCP inclusive, regarding the penalty to be imposed, shall apply accordingly.

(Articles 1064-1068). More information on these rules is given in Part III of this guide.

In all cases where the President (*voorzieningenrechter*) of the District Court is requested to interfere in aid of arbitration, his decision is final and cannot be appealed against (Article 1070 DCCP). This exclusion of appeal can only be circumvented in extremely exceptional circumstances, for example if the President breached a party's right to be heard. In some cases, a practising lawyer (*advocaat*) must represent the requesting party and submit the case documents to the President; in other cases, this obligation does not apply (Article 1071 DCCP). Article 1072 DCCP stipulates those cases in which the parties themselves can make agreements in respect of the President of the District Court who will have jurisdiction to deal with a specific request.

7. Plans for Reform

The most recent fundamental review of the Dutch arbitration act as included in the DCCP dates from 1986. On the occasion of that legislative amendment, which was initiated by Professor Piet Sanders, the arbitration act was expanded and drastically modernized. Fairly soon afterwards, it was argued that the arbitration act should be brought more in line with the wishes of the international arbitration practice.[50] This did not lead to any legislative activity though. In 2002, significant changes were incorporated into the DCCP, but those changes flowed primarily from the reform of state court proceedings in first instance. Apart from a few marginal amendments, the arbitration act was left largely as it was, although it was announced that a review of the arbitration act would follow at a later stage.[51] This challenge was accepted by Professor Albert Jan van den Berg. At the end of 2006, he presented '*Voorstellen tot wijziging van het Vierde Boek (Arbitrage) Artikelen 1020–1076 Rv*' (Proposals to Amend the Fourth Book (Arbitration) Articles 1020-1076 DCCP) to the Ministry of Justice.[52] The Proposals represent a complete Draft Bill with explanatory notes. The Draft Bill was prepared in close consultation with a working group comprised of various arbitration specialists.

According to the explanatory notes to the Draft Bill (pages 7-9), the most important proposed changes are the following:

(a) In order to implement the Directive on unfair terms in consumer contracts[53] it is proposed to include the arbitration clause on what is referred to as the black list of Article 6:236 DCC; as a result, an arbitration clause in general conditions is deemed to be unreasonably onerous in relation to

---

[50] See A.J. van den Berg, *Hoe gastvrij is Nederland voor de internationale arbitrage?* Oration at Erasmus University Rotterdam (Deventer, Kluwer, 1990).

[51] Parliamentary History TK 1999-2000, 26.855, No. 5, 3.

[52] This can be found at <www.arbitragewet.nl>. An earlier version of the Draft Bill was published in TvA 2005 Special, also including a few articles by arbitration specialists responding to parts of the Draft Bill.

[53] Council Directive 93/13/EEC of 5 Apr. 1993 on unfair terms in consumer contracts, OJ L95/29.

consumers and thus voidable, unless the clause allows the consumer to opt for settlement of the dispute by a state court.

(b) Further arrangements will be introduced for the provisional gathering of evidence before a state court before the appointment of an arbitral tribunal.

(c) Distinct and extended time limits for non-Dutch parties are deleted. This will, however, not result in a reduction of the applicable time limits, because at the same time, all time limits are set at three months, which is the current time limit for non-Dutch parties.

(d) The President (*voorzieningenrechter*) of the District Court may appoint the third arbitrator in the event that the parties have already appointed two arbitrators and it is only the appointment of the third arbitrator that poses a problem.

(e) Institutional rules for the challenge of arbitrators may replace the possibility to challenge arbitrators before the President (*voorzieningenrechter*) of the District Court. This is an improvement – also for the NAI – since the statutory rules and the institutional rules for challenging have never been properly harmonized and can easily lead to confusing situations where parties are forced to initiate parallel proceedings at the same time, both aimed at the same goal, not knowing which procedure is going to evolve quickest and what effect one procedure will have on the other (see also the comments on Article 19).

(f) The provisions regarding the arbitration clause are arranged more logically and the text of a number of provisions has been clarified. Moreover, a number of provisions have been added to address gaps in the text of the arbitration act perceived in the national and international arbitration practice.

(g) Arbitrators are empowered to order provisional measures other than in summary arbitral proceedings.

(h) The provisions governing arbitral appeal are moved to a different section and expanded.

(i) The automatic revival of the state courts' jurisdiction in the event that the jurisdiction of the arbitral tribunal is denied will be abolished. This is an improvement, as the current system is too rigid. There are certainly situations in which it is not necessary to relegate jurisdiction fully to a state court.[54]

(j) Arbitral tribunals will no longer have to deposit the arbitral award with the office of the clerk of the relevant District Court. The Netherlands is the only country requiring such deposit. Against this background, it makes sense to amend the rules pertaining to the deposit.

---

[54] For instance, arbitrators in an NAI arbitration may declare that they have no jurisdiction, because the clause refers to arbitration in accordance with the rules of a different arbitration institute. In this case, a State Court should not regain jurisdiction.

(k) The time limit for initiating a claim to set aside an arbitral award will be simplified, by linking this time limit exclusively to the date of receipt of the arbitral award. This change is related to abolition of the requirement to deposit arbitral awards, to which the current time limit is linked. Taking the date on which the arbitral award is received as the starting date for the time limit poses some difficulties if the date of receipt is not clear or if there are several dates of receipt.

(l) Claims to set aside an arbitral award will be assessed by the Court of Appeal as court of first instance, after which it is only possible to appeal to the Supreme Court on limited grounds. Currently, setting aside proceedings start before the District Court; the Draft Bill thus takes out one instance. This is an improvement as primacy should lie with the arbitration and therefore provisions for setting aside the arbitral award should be as limited as possible.

(m) Remission after the setting aside of an award will be introduced. This will allow the arbitral tribunal to be reinstated and redress the grounds for setting aside itself. This is also an improvement. Pursuant to the current system, insofar as the award is set aside the relevant issue in dispute has to be litigated from scratch before the state courts.

(n) A system is introduced in which – unless the parties agree otherwise – a state court becomes competent only if the arbitral award is set aside based on the absence of a valid arbitration agreement. Again, given the primacy of arbitration as means of dispute resolution chosen by the parties, this is an improvement.

(o) A statutory basis will be provided for the principle of confidentiality of arbitral proceedings. Explicitly embedding this principle in the arbitration act promotes clarity and certainty. Currently, there is no formal rule governing confidentiality of arbitral proceedings.

(p) Rules regarding the exclusion of liability of arbitrators and arbitration institutes will be introduced. The NAI has already provided for such an exclusion in the NAI Rules. Liability of arbitrators and arbitration institutes should be as exceptional as liability of a court judge.

(q) It becomes possible to request the Dutch state courts for assistance in the gathering of evidence in the event of an arbitration that is seated outside the Netherlands. This seems to be a useful addition, but it remains to be seen whether this possibility will be used frequently.

Where appropriate and instructive, further attention will be given in Parts II and III to various recommendations of the Draft Bill, especially where the Draft Bill or the explanatory notes thereto contain useful recommendations. The most recent information from the Ministry of Justice is that (parliamentary) review of the Draft Bill and the current arbitration act has been relegated to the bottom of the list of legislative priorities. If this message is added both to the fact that the

Ministry must spend a lot of time and resources to issues relating to European legislation that effects the DCCP and also to the fact that the need for a review as proposed in the Draft Bill has been questioned,[55] it seems reasonable to conclude that it will take quite some years before the Draft Bill may ultimately result in legislation.

---

[55] For example, see P. Sanders, 'Fundamentele herbezinning. De herziening van onze Arbitragewet en UNCITRAL's Modelwet', *Tijdschrift voor Civiele Rechtspleging* 2005, 95-96 and H.J. Snijders, 'Algemene beschouwingen bij het Voorontwerp tot herziening van de Nederlandse arbitragewetgeving', TvA 2005 Special, 1-9.

PART II

A COMMENTARY TO THE NAI RULES

GENERAL PROVISIONS (Articles 1-5)

ARTICLE 1 – DEFINITIONS

In these Rules, the words and phrases listed below have the following meaning:

(a) 'NAI': Netherlands Arbitration Institute, Foundation (Stichting), with its seat in Rotterdam;

(b) 'Governing Board': the Governing Board of the NAI;

(c) 'Executive Board': the executive section of the NAI Governing Board as provided for in the NAI Articles of Association;

(d) 'Administrator': the Director of the NAI as provided for in the NAI Articles of Association and in case a director is lacking the member of the Executive Board appointed as such by the Governing Board, or their deputy nominated by the Executive Board;

(e) 'arbitration agreement': the agreement by which parties bind themselves to submit to arbitration an existing dispute between them (compromis; submission agreement) or disputes which may arise between them in the future (arbitration clause) out of a defined legal relationship, whether contractual or not; this agreement shall be proven by an instrument in writing; for this purpose an instrument in writing which provides for arbitration or which refers to standard conditions providing for arbitration is sufficient, provided that this instrument is expressly or impliedly accepted by or on behalf of the parties;

(f) 'arbitral tribunal': an arbitral tribunal of one or more arbitrators, composed in accordance with Section Three or Section Four A (summary arbitral proceedings) of these Rules;

(g) 'international arbitration': an arbitration in which at the moment of commencement of arbitration as referred to in Articles 6 and 42b of these Arbitration Rules, at least one of the parties is domiciled or has its seat, or, in the absence thereof, has his actual residence outside the Netherlands.

1. Definitions

Article 1 is intended to clarify certain terms used in the NAI Rules by providing definitions of these terms. These definitions will be discussed below. The NAI Rules also use other terms than those defined by Article 1. Most of these terms originate directly from the DCCP and will be discussed in the comments on the relevant article of the NAI Rules.

2. NAI, Governing Board, Executive Board, Administrator (Article 1(a)-(d))

Article 1(a)-(d) defines the NAI, its Governing Board, its Executive Board and the Administrator, based on the relevant Articles of Association of the NAI. The background and structure of the NAI have been discussed in the General Introduction to the NAI Rules (see Part I, Chapter 1). Additionally, and more specifically in respect of application of the NAI Rules, the following can be noted on the role of the Governing Board, the Executive Board and the Administrator in the arbitral procedure.

In actual arbitral proceedings administered by the NAI, the Administrator, who is assisted by the NAI Secretariat, has a much more important role than the Governing Board and the Executive Board, whose roles are limited in the actual proceedings. The Executive Board has a role in the recommending, evaluation and approval of candidates for the General Panel of Arbitrators (which is discussed in more detail in the comments on Article 14) and in the challenge of an arbitrator pursuant to Article 19(7): if a challenged arbitrator does not withdraw his motion on his own volition, the Executive Board will decide on the merits of the challenge. The role of the Governing Board is limited to exercising a veto against candidates for the General Panel of Arbitrators if necessary.

Article 1(d) defines the Administrator as 'the Director of the NAI as provided for in the NAI Articles of Association and in case a director is lacking the member of the Executive Board appointed as such by the Governing Board, or their deputy nominated by the Executive Board'.[56] A deputy director will take the Director's place if the Director is not free to act in a specific case, for example because he has a direct or indirect personal or professional relationship with (one of) the parties or counsel involved.[57] Thus, even the appearance of a biased administration is avoided.

The tasks of the Administrator in arbitral proceedings follow from many provisions in the NAI Rules (see also Part I, Chapter 1, Section 5). The general responsibility of the Administrator is to safeguard the quality of NAI arbitration, not only by the selection of the arbitrators whose names will appear on the list of arbitrators (see the comments on Article 14), but also by reviewing the draft

---

[56] See for the present Director <www.nai-nl.org> or Appendix 1 to the NAI Rules.
[57] NAI 19 Jan. 1989, TvA 1991, 62.

arbitral award (although this review usually does not relate to points of substance as this may be the case in the scrutinizing of the award by the International Court of Arbitration in ICC arbitrations;[58] see also the comments on Article 49). More in particular, the Administrator has an important role in the process of appointing arbitrators (see Articles 12 et seq. and 42f). The Administrator, for example, determines the number of arbitrators, absent an agreement of the parties. Also, the Administrator compiles the list with names of arbitrators if the arbitrators are to be appointed in accordance with the list procedure of Article 14. Furthermore, the Administrator closely monitors the entire arbitral process from the moment the request for arbitration is filed until the deposit of the final award. Sometimes, the Administrator even provides assistance thereafter, for example in the event of a request for rectification of the award (Article 52), a request for an additional award (Article 53), or an objection to publication of the award (Article 55). The role of the Administrator during the various stages of the arbitration will be discussed in more detail in the comments on the relevant articles.

In order to enable the Administrator to perform his or her duties, a copy of all written submissions and communications from the parties to the arbitral tribunal or vice versa must be sent simultaneously to the Administrator (Article 20).

3. Arbitration Agreement (Article 1(e))

3.1. Definition

Article 1(e) provides a definition of the most important prerequisite for arbitration: the arbitration agreement. The submission of a dispute to arbitration requires an agreement to arbitrate, which is generally referred to as arbitration agreement. An arbitration agreement may take the form of an arbitration clause in a contract, for example, referring possible future disputes arising out of that contract to arbitration, but it can also take the form of a submission agreement (referred to under Dutch law as *compromis*), in which the parties agree to submit an existing dispute between them to arbitration. Hence, depending on whether the arbitration agreement is entered into for an existing dispute or for possible future disputes arising from a specific relationship, it may, according to Article 1(e), either take the form of a submission agreement or of an arbitration clause.

> The definition of arbitration agreement in Article 1(e) is derived from Articles 1020(1) and 1020(2) DCCP, which also define the arbitration agreement as the agreement by which parties bind themselves to submit to arbitration either an existing dispute between them or disputes which may arise between them in the future (see Article 1020(2) DCCP) out of a defined legal relationship, whether contractual or not (see Article 1020(1) DCCP).

---

[58]   See Art. 27 ICC Rules.

Apart from the possibility of Articles 1020(1) and 1020(2) DCCP to submit existing or future *disputes* to arbitration, Article 1020(4) DCCP provides for the possibility to submit to arbitration:

(a) only the determination of the quality or condition of goods;
(b) only the determination of the amount of damages or of a monetary debt; and
(c) the supplementation or amendment of a legal relationship arising from agreement or otherwise ('filling of gaps').

The submission to arbitration of only such determinations or the supplementation or amendment requires an explicit agreement. A 'regular' arbitration agreement providing for the submission of disputes to arbitration as such does not provide an arbitral tribunal with the required jurisdiction to only make (i.e. outside the context of a dispute) determinations, supplements or amendments as meant by Article 1020(4) DCCP.

It should be noted, however, that the determination of the quality or condition of goods, or the determination of an amount of damages or a monetary debt *in the context of* a dispute, falls within the definition of Article 1020(1) DCCP and does not require a separate arbitration agreement on the basis of Article 1020(4) DCCP. Hence, a general arbitration agreement (providing that all disputes arising from a certain legal relationship will be submitted to arbitration) allows the arbitral tribunal to determine the quality or condition of goods or the amount of damages in the context of a dispute submitted to it. In the context of a dispute, the arbitral tribunal may also be allowed to supplement or amend a legal relationship without an explicit agreement pursuant to Article 1020(4)(c) DCCP, if the applicable substantive law allows such supplement or amendment. If, for example, Dutch law applies, Article 6:248(1) DCC allows an arbitrator to supplement or amend a contractual relationship between parties if the principles of reasonableness and fairness so require. Also Article 6:258 DCC allows an arbitrator to amend a legal relationship at the request of a party in the event of unforeseen circumstances of such nature that it would unacceptable according to the principle of reasonableness and fairness to expect the agreement to remain unchanged.

3.2. *Validity and Proof*

In line with the DCCP, the NAI Rules do not pose any formal requirements for a valid agreement to arbitrate. Therefore, an arbitration agreement can be concluded orally or even be implied in an established trade usage. However, if one of the parties (timely) contests the validity of the arbitration agreement, the existence of the arbitration agreement must be proven by a written document (referred to in Article 1(e) as 'an instrument in writing') that has been accepted, either explicitly or implicitly, by the other party. The requirement of written proof, contained in Article 1(e), results directly from Article 1021 DCCP.[59] In this respect, a written document referring to standard conditions that provide for arbitration is also

---

[59] For an elaborate discussion on the requirements of a valid arbitration agreement under Dutch law, in particular Art. 1021 DCCP, see the dissertation of G.J. Meijer (Meijer, 2008).

sufficient, provided that this document is expressly or impliedly accepted by or on behalf of the parties. If the place of arbitration is located in the Netherlands, the existence of an arbitration agreement may also be proven by electronic means pursuant to the applicable provisions in the DCCP (see below).

Although the NAI Rules do not pose any formal requirements for a valid agreement to arbitrate, parties should bear in mind that the effectiveness of an arbitration clause first of all depends on proof of its existence. This proof is not only crucial in the arbitral proceedings itself, but also in possible subsequent recognition and enforcement proceedings. Therefore, it is strongly recommended in practice that an arbitration agreement be laid down in writing, or at least can be proven by a written document that has been accepted, preferably explicitly, by the other party.

Article 1(e) is based on Article 1021 DCCP, which contains a similar provision regarding proof of an arbitration agreement.[60] Additionally, Article 1021 DCCP explicitly states that an arbitration agreement may also be proven by electronic means, pursuant to the implementation of the Directive on electronic commerce in the Internal Market.[61]

Furthermore, Article 1020(5) DCCP provides that an arbitration agreement may also take the form of an arbitration clause included in articles of association or regulations that are binding upon the parties. Such a clause can be included, for example, in the articles of association of a private company with limited liability or a public limited company (providing for arbitration in case of a dispute between the company and the shareholders, or between the shareholders) or in the articles of association or regulations of an association[62] (providing for arbitration in case of a dispute between the association and its members or between the members).

3.3. NAI Recommended Arbitration Clause

The NAI recommends that parties wishing to have recourse to NAI arbitration include the following standard arbitration clause in their contracts:

'All disputes arising in connection with the present contract, or further contracts resulting therefrom, shall be finally settled in accordance with the Arbitration Rules of the Netherlands Arbitration Institute (*Nederlands Arbitrage Instituut*).'

This standard arbitration clause recommended by the NAI is available in Dutch, English, French and German and may be used without prior permission and free of charge.[63]

---

[60] The Draft Bill proposes to change the requirement of a written arbitration agreement as proof of the existence of the arbitration agreement into a condition for the existence of an arbitration agreement.

[61] Directive 2000/31/EC of the European Parliament and of the Council of 8 Jun. 2000 on certain legal aspects of information society services, in particular electronic commerce.

[62] NAI 11 Jul. 2001, TvA 2003, 12-14.

[63] See <www.nai-nl.org>.

The use of the standard NAI clause is not mandatory and parties are free to use different wording for their arbitration clause. Should the circumstances require a tailor-made arbitration clause, the NAI is also willing to advise on the drafting of a specific arbitration clause.[64] However, whatever arbitration clause is used, the parties should always ensure that it is carefully drafted. Simple, clearly drafted arbitration clauses will avoid uncertainty and disputes as to their meaning and effect, whereas ambiguous or badly phrased arbitration clauses cause delay and may impede the arbitration process. A clearly drafted arbitration clause will minimize the risk of time and financial resources being expended on disputes regarding, for example, the jurisdiction of the arbitral tribunal or the process of appointing arbitrators.

As to the recommended NAI arbitration clause, although it does refer to settlement of disputes in accordance with the *Arbitration* Rules of the NAI, it does not refer explicitly to the settlement of disputes *by arbitration*. As the NAI Arbitration Rules also provide for settlement of disputes by means of binding advice (*bindend advies*; see the comments on Article 3), it is recommended – to avoid any misunderstanding – that parties add the words 'by arbitration' between 'shall be finally settled' and 'in accordance with (. . .)' in the NAI recommended arbitration clause.

As to the standard NAI arbitration clause, disputes 'in connection with' the contract are generally deemed to encompass claims arising from tort (*onrecht-matige daad*) insofar as these claims are related to the contract or the contractual relationship between the parties.[65] Hence, if parties wish to exclude recourse to arbitration for contract-related tort claims, they should rephrase the standard NAI arbitration clause or explicitly exclude claims arising from tort. The same applies should the parties wish to exclude the possibility of binding advice under the NAI Rules (see also the comments on Article 3).

As a general rule, the parties should be explicit in their arbitration clause and clearly indicate their wishes and preferences in relation to the way in which possible arbitral proceedings should be conducted. Article 1020(6) DCCP specifically provides that if an arbitration agreement refers to arbitration rules, these arbitration rules are deemed to form an integral part of the arbitration agreement. Hence, a reference to the NAI Rules in an arbitration clause entails that the NAI Rules become part of the arbitration agreement between the parties. However, since the NAI Rules leave the parties a choice in respect of certain

---

[64] See <www.nai-nl.org>.

[65] In relation to the scope and wording of arbitration clauses, see for example: A. Redfern, M. Hunter, N. Blackaby & C. Partasides, *Law and Practice of International Commercial Arbitration* (London, Sweet and Maxwell, 2004), 152-155; D. St. John Sutton & J. Gill, *Russell on Arbitration* (London, Sweet and Maxwell, 2003), 60, No. 2-075; P.D. Friedland, *Arbitration Clauses for International Contracts* (New York, Iuris Publishing, 2004), 46-48.

matters, it may be desirable for the parties to agree on those matters beforehand and also to stipulate in the arbitration clause itself:

- *The number of arbitrators*
  Absent an agreement on the number of arbitrators by the parties, the number of arbitrators will be determined by the Administrator to be either one or three (see Article 12). Further particulars as to the choice of the number of arbitrators will be set out below, in the comments on Articles 1(f) and 12.
- *The qualifications of the arbitrators*
  The NAI Rules do not give any guidance as to the qualifications of the arbitrators, except for the provision in Article 16(2) that in international arbitrations either party may require that the chairman of the arbitral tribunal – or the sole arbitrator as the case may be – shall not have the nationality of one of the parties. It is not uncommon to agree in the arbitration agreement on the qualifications of the arbitrators. Parties regularly agree for example that the chairman of the arbitral tribunal shall be a legal professional with extensive experience in resolving disputes through arbitration. Parties also stipulate on a regular basis that the co-arbitrators or at least one of them shall have specific expertise in cases where the contract relates to such expertise and such expertise is deemed to be a prerequisite for adequately understanding the mutual obligations flowing from the contract. It is often hard to predict whether such qualifications will actually turn out to be advantageous once the dispute has arisen. After the dispute has arisen the parties' needs may be quite different from what they expected when the contract was concluded. It is obviously much easier to determine one's needs once the nature of the dispute has become clear. However, at that time it may be difficult to reach common ground at all, taking into account that the parties often have conflicting interests at the outset of a dispute. Stipulating the arbitrators' qualifications in advance is therefore normally the best option, requiring careful weighing of all possible scenarios and the type of disputes that are likely to arise under the contract. In doing so, the parties should take into account that the appointment of only one single expert arbitrator may turn out to be disadvantageous, because the relevant issues are likely to be decided by that very arbitrator without substantial involvement of the other arbitrators, whereas in addition such decision may very well be taken on the basis of considerations that have not been explicitly discussed in front of the parties. This risk may in particular be assessed negatively, if the expert arbitrator has actual no particular expertise and experience in regard of the specific issue that is at stake. Some disputes relate to expertise that is so specific and rare that it is hardly possible to find an expert that really has the relevant expertise and on top of that has no conflicting interests. In such cases the better option may be to rely on arbitrators that do not consider themselves as experts and are

therefore clearly in a position that they need to be informed by the parties and their experts, and possibly a tribunal appointed expert, in order to be able to decide the matter.

– *The method of appointment of the arbitrators*

Absent an agreement on the method of appointment of the arbitrators, the appointment will take place in accordance with the list procedure of Article 14. See the comments on Articles 13 and 14 for further particulars concerning the method of appointment of the arbitrators.

– *The place of arbitration*

If the place of arbitration has not been agreed upon by the parties, the place will be determined by the arbitral tribunal (see Article 22(1)), or, for summary arbitral proceedings as referred to in Section 4A, the place of arbitration will be Rotterdam, the Netherlands (see Article 42a(4)). Given that the place of arbitration is a legal concept that determines, inter alia, the applicable arbitration law, it is strongly recommended that the parties agree on the place of arbitration, either in their arbitration clause or subsequently, at the outset of the arbitration. The choice of the place of arbitration will be discussed in more detail below in the comments on Article 22. It is noted here, however, that the place of arbitration is a legal concept and does not determine the physical place where hearings are to be held. The arbitral tribunal may hold hearings at any place that it deems appropriate, even outside the country where the arbitration is seated (see Article 22(3)).

– *The language of the arbitration*

To avoid uncertainty at the commencement of the arbitration, the parties are advised to agree on the language or languages in which the arbitral proceedings will be conducted. In the absence of an agreement of the parties, the language of the arbitration will be determined by the arbitral tribunal (see also the comments on Article 40(1)). Parties should be aware that the language of the agreement and the nationality of the arbitrators do not necessarily determine the language of the arbitral proceedings. It may be a good argument that the language of the agreement and the parties' correspondence in the execution of the agreement should also be used in the arbitration. The same goes for the argument that the arbitration should be conducted in a language in which all arbitrators are fluent. However, the arbitral tribunal is in no way obliged to follow such arguments. Therefore, it is inevitable to stipulate the language of the arbitration, if the parties wish to obtain certainty in this respect. By the same token the language of the arbitration does not determine the nationality of the arbitrators. If for instance an arbitration clause stipulates that the arbitration has to be conducted in two languages, to allow both parties to arbitrate in their mother tongue, such provision does not induce the Administrator to appoint arbitrators of the respective nationalities. It does not even induce the Administrator to appoint arbitrators that are equally fluent in both languages. Of course it may be advisable for the Administrator to do so, in order to meet the parties' obvious expectations. However, if the parties wish such expectations to be adhered to under al circumstances they should stipulate the relevant qualifications of the arbitrators in the arbitration agreement.

– *The decision standard*

It is recommended that the parties indicate the decision standard that they require the arbitral tribunal to apply. Article 45(1) provides that in a domestic arbitration, the arbitral tribunal will decide as amiable compositeur, unless the parties agreed to authorize the tribunal to make its award in accordance with the rules of law. The opposite applies in an international arbitration, where, according to Article 45(2), the arbitral tribunal will make its award in accordance with the rules of law, unless the parties agreed to authorize it to decide as amiable compositeur. In practice the two decision standards will normally not lead to a different approach by the arbitral tribunal, whereas it is normally hard to imagine that the outcome of the arbitration would have been different if the other decision standard was used (in particular this applies in case Dutch law is the substantive law of the contract). The two decision standards are most of all food for scholarly debate with only little relevance in Dutch practice. For a more elaborate explanation of the difference between the two decision standards, see the comments on Article 45.

– *The law governing the contract*

Pursuant to Article 46, if the arbitral tribunal has to decide in accordance with the rules of law and a choice of law has been made by the parties, the arbitral tribunal will make its award in accordance with the rules of law chosen by the parties (see the comments on Article 46). If the contract containing the arbitration clause contains also a provision on the law applicable to the contract, there is no need to repeat this choice of law in the arbitration clause. However, in the case of a submission agreement, where the parties submit an existing dispute between them to arbitration, the parties may wish to explicitly include a choice of law in their arbitration agreement, either because no choice of law has been made before (e.g. in the contract to which the dispute relates) or because the parties wish to change a previous choice of law.

– *The law governing the arbitration agreement*

Although the question of which law applies to the arbitration agreement itself is a very complicated one and a choice of law in this respect is hardly ever made in practice, it may be advisable in certain circumstances to stipulate in the arbitration agreement the law governing the arbitration agreement itself.[66] This may be the case in international arbitrations

---

[66] See for an elaboration on the law applicable to the arbitration agreement and an explicit or implicit choice of law for the arbitration agreement: Meijer, 2008, 337-364 (Ch. 7.4).

involving parties of multiple nationalities or state parties, where questions may arise regarding the validity of the arbitration agreement (see also above under 'Validity and proof' and Part I, Chapter 1, Section 4.1).

– *Exclusion of consolidation of arbitrations*

Although the NAI Rules do not contain provisions regarding the consolidation of arbitral proceedings, Article 1046 DCCP does provide for the possibility of consolidating arbitral proceedings pending before different arbitral tribunals in the Netherlands if the subject matters of these proceedings are connected. A request for consolidation must be made with the President (*voorzieningenrechter*) of the Amsterdam District Court. The parties may exclude the possibility of consolidation, but if they wish to do so, they are advised to state this explicitly in the arbitration agreement. Usually, there will not be a need for the possibility of consolidation. This might, however, be different if there are several interrelated contracts providing for arbitration in the Netherlands. See also the comments on Article 41.

– *Arbitration agreement operative also after setting aside of arbitral award*

Article 1067 DCCP provides that the jurisdiction of the courts will revive as soon as a decision setting aside the award has become final, unless the parties have agreed otherwise. Although it is rarely seen in practice, it may be advisable to include in the arbitration agreement an arrangement that the arbitration agreement remains operative also after the award has been set aside. See also the comments on Article 1067 DCCP in Part III, Chapter 1.

– *Summary arbitral proceedings*

Parties may exclude the possibility of summary arbitral proceedings on the basis of the NAI Rules, but they need to explicitly agree on such exclusion (see Article 42a). However, if the place of arbitration is in the Netherlands, summary proceedings may be initiated before the President (*voorzieningenrechter*) of the District Court even if the parties have excluded the possibility of summary arbitral proceedings, as this possibility of summary proceedings before the President of the District Court cannot be excluded (Article 1022(2) DCCP).

– *Other (procedural) matters*

A wide range of other (procedural) matters may be agreed upon beforehand within the limits of the applicable arbitration law and the NAI Rules. The parties may, for example, also agree on: multi-tier dispute resolution (e.g. only arbitration after mediation), final offer or 'baseball' arbitration,[67] confidentiality of the arbitration (see Part I, Chapter 1, Section 5 and Chapter 2,

---

[67] Final offer, last offer or 'baseball' arbitration is a specific form of arbitration that is frequently adopted in the United States and is slowly beginning to also be recognized in civil law countries as a useful tool

Section 5 and Article 55), applicable rules of evidence (see Article 27), possibility of discovery, final cut-off date for delivery of evidence, prorogation of jurisdiction to the Court of Appeal for setting aside proceedings (see the Article 1064 DCCP in Part III, Chapter 1, note 3) etc. However, be advised that by making detailed arrangements or by agreeing beforehand to deviations from the NAI Rules, the parties might agree to a way of conducting the proceedings which turns out not to be the best way once the arbitration is underway. Although the parties may always change any arrangements made, this may not be so easy in practice once an arbitration has been initiated. Finally, when varying the standard NAI arbitration clause or adding language to it, it is essential to ensure that the added language does not conflict with the arbitration rules selected. The NAI practically only refuses to administer an arbitration if the subject matter of the dispute is not arbitrable[68] or if one or more of the arbitrators that were appointed by the parties do not, in the opinion of the Administrator, offer sufficient safeguards for a sound arbitration.[69] Nevertheless, parties run the risk that the NAI will refuse to administer their arbitration, if the arbitration clause seeks to alter the NAI Rules or includes provisions that may be considered by the Administrator to be incompatible with the NAI Rules.

4. Arbitral Tribunal (Article 1(f))

According to Article 1(f), the arbitral tribunal consists of one or more arbitrators appointed in accordance with Section 3 (or in case of summary arbitral proceedings, Section 4A). The arbitral tribunal in NAI arbitrations is normally composed of either one or three arbitrators. Although the NAI Rules do not preclude the parties from agreeing on a number of arbitrators other than one or three, it is extremely rare in practice that parties do so. For a more detailed discussion on the number of arbitrators, see the comments on Article 12. For the (contractual) relationship between the arbitrator(s) and the parties, and the NAI and the parties, see Part I, Chapter 1, Section 6.

---

in the speedy resolution of disputes. In baseball arbitration, the powers of the arbitrator concerning the award are narrowed down to a choice between two final offers submitted by the parties. Without being able to adjust either offer, or to opt for a solution somewhere between the two, the arbitrator is bound to choose between the two. Thus, baseball arbitration makes it impossible for the arbitrator to compromise. One of the parties wins entirely, while the other inevitably loses entirely. This way, the parties are each impelled to provide a realistic offer that will appeal to their opponents. This will bring the parties' positions much closer together, since extreme positions and 'bargaining material' are filtered out. See C. Borris, 'Final Offer Arbitration from a Civil Law Perspective', *Journal of International Arbitration* 24, No. 3 (2007), 307-317.

[68] For a general explanation of the concept of arbitrability under Dutch law, see Part I, Ch. 2, Section 2.

[69] See Article 13(3) and the comments thereon.

5. International Arbitration (Article 1(g))

In Article 1(g), an international arbitration is defined as an arbitration in which at the moment of commencement of the arbitration (as referred to in Articles 6 and 42b), at least one of the parties is domiciled or has its seat or, in the absence thereof, its actual residence outside the Netherlands. The moment that determines whether an arbitration qualifies as domestic or international is fixed at the moment of commencement of the arbitration. This is to prevent that a change of domicile or actual residence during the arbitration raises difficulties in the application of the NAI Rules that particularly apply to international arbitration (such as Article 45 concerning the decision standard to be applied by the arbitral tribunal).

Although the Introduction to the NAI Arbitration Rules[70] states that the NAI Rules, like the Dutch arbitration act, do not distinguish between domestic and international arbitration, the NAI Rules do contain a number of provisions that are either explicitly or implicitly tailored to international arbitration:

- Article 5(2) concerning longer periods of time;
- Article 16 concerning the nationality of arbitrators;
- Article 40 concerning the language in which the arbitration is conducted;
- Article 45(2) concerning the decision standard to be applied by the tribunal in international arbitration, absenting a choice by the parties;
- Article 46 concerning the applicable law;
- Article 48(4) providing for the possibility of a dissenting opinion in an international arbitration.

The NAI Rules also contain provisions that may be particularly relevant in international arbitration, but are not especially tailored for it. Examples are:

- Article 19(10) concerning the period of time for a challenged arbitrator to withdraw, which is doubled if the challenged arbitrator is domiciled or has his actual residence outside the Netherlands; and
- Article 22(2), allowing the arbitral tribunal to hold hearings, deliberate, and examine witnesses and experts at a place other than the place of arbitration, either within or outside the Netherlands.

With the exception of Article 5(2) on extended periods of time and Article 16 on the nationality of arbitrators, the above-mentioned provisions also apply to summary arbitral proceedings as provided for in Section 4A.

ARTICLE 2 – FIELD OF APPLICATION (ARBITRATION)

These Rules shall apply if parties have agreed to arbitration by the NAI or to arbitration in accordance with the NAI Rules.

---

[70] See the Introduction to NAI Arbitration Rules, para. 3.1.

1.   General Comments

Article 2 stipulates that for the NAI Rules to apply to an arbitration between parties, the parties must have agreed – in the arbitration agreement – to arbitration by the NAI or to arbitration in accordance with the NAI Rules. Essentially, these are two ways to express the same thing, i.e. the parties' wish that the arbitral proceedings be governed by the NAI Rules. The effect of the wording of Article 2 is that it is placed beyond doubt that a mere reference to 'arbitration by the NAI' will be deemed to include an agreement to arbitrate in accordance with the NAI Rules. It must be assumed that the requirements for the arbitration agreement in general (see Article 1(e)) also apply to the agreement referred to in Article 2. This means that there are no formal requirements for the validity of the agreement, but that if its existence is contested, the agreement on NAI arbitration must be proven by a written document. Article 2 also covers the situation where the parties that have concluded an arbitration agreement that initially did not refer to NAI arbitration (but for example ad hoc arbitration), later on specifically agree on NAI arbitration.

2.   Effect

The NAI Rules set the procedural framework for NAI arbitral proceedings. Apart from the NAI Rules, the arbitral proceedings are necessarily also governed by the *mandatory* provisions of arbitration law of the country where the arbitration is seated. If there is a conflict between the mandatory provisions of arbitration law and the NAI Rules, the mandatory provisions prevail. If the arbitration is seated in the Netherlands, however, such conflict is not likely to occur, given that the NAI Rules are for the most part based on the Dutch arbitration act.[71] In addition, the arbitral proceedings are governed by the *supplementary* provisions of arbitration law of the country where the arbitration is seated, insofar as these provisions concern rules or subjects that are not covered by the NAI Rules (such as, under Dutch arbitration law, the provision concerning consolidation of arbitrations in Article 1046 DCCP).

ARTICLE 3 – FIELD OF APPLICATION (BINDING ADVICE)

1. These Rules shall apply accordingly if parties have agreed in writing to binding advice by the NAI or to binding advice in accordance with the NAI Rules.
2. If parties have agreed to arbitration, but the arbitral tribunal finds that a dispute is wholly or partially incapable of settlement by arbitration, the arbitral tribunal is authorized to render its decision wholly or partially in the form of a binding advice.

---

[71] For a general discussion of the Dutch arbitration act, see Part I, Ch. 2, Section 1.

3. In case of binding advice, no deposit of the decision with the Registry of the District Court takes place. The period of time for correction (Article 52) and for rendering an additional decision (Article 53) shall expire 30 days after the day the decision is received.

1. Binding Advice (*Bindend Advies*)

The NAI Rules not only provide the procedural framework for arbitral proceedings, but also intend to provide procedural rules for an alternative way of resolving disputes between parties, by means of so-called binding advice (*bindend advies*).

In the Netherlands, binding advice[72] was first developed in practice as a type of informal private dispute resolution. It is only since 1 September 1993 that the DCC provides for binding advice as a species of settlement agreement (*vaststellingsovereenkomst*; see Articles 7:900-7:906 DCC). Binding advice is based on a contract between parties. By contract, parties agree in advance to be bound by the decision (binding advice) given by one or more third parties who have been appointed by the parties as binding advisors. Once rendered, the binding advice is deemed part of the parties' agreement (Article 7:900(1) and (2) DCC). As a consequence, the party who fails to comply with a binding advice is in breach of contract. Except for the requirements of due process that also apply to binding advice proceedings (which, however, follows only implicitly from Article 7:904(1) DCC), neither the DCCP nor the DCC contains any procedural rules regarding binding advice.

Under Dutch law, binding advice can be agreed upon for a disputed or a non-disputed matter. In the case of binding advice for a non-disputed matter, the parties have the binding advisor fill in certain 'gaps' in their contractual relationship, rather than resolve a dispute between them. The parties may, for example, request the binding advisor to determine a purchase price or to establish the value of goods or real estate.[73] In the case of binding advice for a disputed matter, the binding advisor is requested to decide upon a dispute between the parties. This type of binding advice closely resembles arbitration, although there are relevant differences.

---

[72] See for binding advice and settlement agreement under Dutch law in general: Burg. Rv, 2006 (H.J. Snijders), General notes to Book IV, note 7; A.C. van Schaik, *Bijzondere overeenkomsten*, Asser-Van Schaick 5-IV (Deventer, Kluwer, 2004), 211-244; G.J. Meijer, 'Bindend advies en de vaststellingsovereenkomst', in *Tot persistit! Opstellen aangeboden aan H.J. Snijders* (Arnhem, Gouda Quint, 1992), 51-67; A.A. van Rossum, *Vaststellingsovereenkomst*, Monografieën Nieuw BW B-80 (Deventer, Kluwer, 2001).

[73] For the avoidance of doubt it should be noted that the same power of '*filling the gaps*' may be granted to arbitrators pursuant to Art. 1020(4) DCCP. See Art. 1, note 3, under 'Definition'.

An important difference between arbitration and binding advice is that arbitration results in an award by a tribunal that is enforceable at law. Decisions made by binding advisors are not enforceable at law as such, but are only contractually binding on the parties. That means that if a party does not comply with the binding advice, the only available remedy for the other party is claim active performance of the agreement by the party in breach in legal proceedings before a court.

Another difference is the possibility of reviewing the substance of a decision by state courts. As set out in Part III, Chapter 1, an arbitral award may be set aside if the arbitral tribunal has not complied with its mandate by failing to decide on a claim or to take into account an essential defence (Article 1065(1)(c) DCCP), if the award does not contain grounds (Article 1065(1)(d) DCCP) or if its contents violate public policy (Article 1065(1)(e) DCCP). Apart from these limited grounds for setting aside, the court is not allowed to rule on the contents of the motivation of the arbitral tribunal. The approach is somewhat different for binding advice. Pursuant to Article 7:904(1) DCC, a decision of a binding advisor is open for setting aside by a court if it were unacceptable according to the principles of reasonableness and fairness that a party is bound by the decision of the binding advisor, given the contents of the decision or the way in which the decision was made.[74]

As is the case for arbitration (see Article 1020(3) DCCP), binding advice may not be agreed upon with regard to rights and obligations of which parties cannot freely dispose. Pursuant to Article 7:902 DCC, a binding advice is invalid if it, as to content or purport, violates good morals or public policy.

Parties who have agreed to refer a matter to binding advice cannot submit a claim before state courts or in arbitral proceedings.[75] A binding advice agreement does, however, not preclude the possibility of requesting injunctive relief from the President (*voorzieningenrechter*) of the District Court in summary proceedings.[76]

2.   Binding Advice Agreement (Article 3(1))

Article 3(1) provides that the NAI Rules govern binding advice proceedings if the parties have agreed to binding advice by the NAI or to binding advice in accordance with the NAI Rules (which basically means the same). Article 3(1)

---

[74] Case law shows that there is no general answer to the question to what extent a binding advice must contain the grounds for the decision. For an example where the binding advice was set aside by lack of the reasons for the decision, see Arnhem Court of Appeal, 13 Nov. 2001, NJ 2002, 248 and also HR 20 May 2005, NJ 2007, 114 (Gemeente Amsterdam/Honnebier). In a case comparable to the latter, however, the decision of the binding advisors was considered sufficiently motivated and was not set aside (HR 24 Mar. 2006, NJ 2007, 115 (Meurs c.s./B.V. Nederlandsche Woningfinanciering Maatschappij)). On these decisions, see also M.H. de Boer, 'Kroniek arbitragerecht', *Tijdschrift voor Civiele Rechtspleging* 2006, 55-56.

[75] See Burg. Rv, 2006 (H.J. Snijders), General notes to Book IV, note 7.

[76] See President of the Amsterdam District Court 7 Oct. 1982, KG 1982, 183.

requires that the parties have agreed on binding advice by the NAI in writing. As is evident from the comments on Articles 1(e) and 2 above, the requirement of an agreement in writing does not apply to arbitration. In practice, however, this distinction is not particularly relevant, since also an arbitration agreement will usually be in writing, as the existence of it must be proven by a written document.

When drafting a binding advice agreement, it is essential to ensure that the clause is clear and does not give rise to any misunderstanding. It happens in practice, for example, that parties use terms that clearly indicate that they wish to agree to binding advice, but at the same time use terms that seem to indicate that they wish to submit their dispute to arbitration. Although the NAI does not recommend a standard binding advice clause, the arbitration clause can be amended to apply to binding advice proceedings as follows:

> 'All disputes arising in connection with the present contract, or further contracts resulting therefrom, shall be settled by means of binding advice in accordance with the Arbitration Rules of the Netherlands Arbitration Institute (Nederlands Arbitrage Instituut).'

3. NAI Rules and Binding Advice Proceedings

Article 3(1) provides that the NAI Rules shall apply accordingly to binding advice proceedings. In that respect, Article 3(3) incorrectly suggests that there is only one exception to this rule, being that in case of binding advice, no deposit of the decision with the office of the clerk of the District Court is required, as is the case for arbitral awards.

It needs to be emphasized that the NAI Rules have been written first and foremost to apply to arbitral proceedings. As arbitration and the statutory rules applicable to arbitration differ from binding advice in many respects, it is not realistic to think that the NAI Rules can simply be applied accordingly to binding advice proceedings. The NAI Rules contain several provisions that by law or by their very nature only apply to arbitration and do not (and cannot) apply accordingly to binding advice. Examples are Article 22 relating to the place of arbitration (this concept does not have any relevance in relation to binding advice) and the competence of the President (*voorzieningenrechter*) of the District Court in case of a challenge of an arbitrator, which is provided by the law (Article 19(8)).

Given the specific characteristics of binding advice and the fact that the NAI Rules are completely tailored to arbitration, we would not recommend the use of the NAI Rules for binding advice proceedings.

4. Disputes Incapable of Being Settled by Arbitration (Article 3(2))

Article 3(2) provides that if parties have agreed to arbitration and the arbitral tribunal finds that a dispute is wholly or partially incapable of being settled by arbitration, the arbitral tribunal is authorized to render its decision wholly or partially in the form of a binding advice.

First and foremost, contrary to what the wording of Article 3(2) may suggest, this Article does not apply to matters that are precluded from settlement by arbitration because they are not arbitrable pursuant to Article 1020(3) DCCP. As set out above, these matters are also precluded from settlement by binding advice, on the basis of Article 7:902 DCC. Article 1020(3) DCCP provides that an arbitration agreement may not lead to the determination of legal consequences of which the parties cannot freely dispose. Inarbitrable matters are assumed to include certain disputes relating to family law, the granting of bankruptcy orders, intellectual property, the status of private companies with limited liability, the status of public limited companies and the formal validity of corporate resolutions.[77] Hence, disputes regarding matters of which the parties cannot freely dispose cannot be submitted to arbitration nor to binding advice.

That being said, the practical relevance today of Article 3(2) is limited. The reason is that Article 3(2) was enacted under the former Dutch arbitration act, under which only *disputes* could be submitted to arbitration. The former arbitration act did not provide for the possibility now contained in Article 1020(4) DCCP to have solely the quality or condition of goods or only the amount of damages or of a monetary debt determined in arbitration. Also, it did not provide for the possibility of filling in gaps or modifying a contract by arbitrators. Therefore, doubt existed as to the arbitrability of these matters. In such cases, Article 3(2) brought relief, as it provided the arbitral tribunal with the authority to render such decisions wholly or partially in the form of a binding advice.

The present arbitration act, however, explicitly provides for the possibility to submit the aforementioned determinations to arbitration, provided the parties have explicitly agreed thereupon (see Article 1020(4)(a) and (b) DCCP). Moreover, the present arbitration act provides for the possibility to authorize an arbitral tribunal to supplement (filling in of gaps) or to amend a legal relationship arising from agreement or otherwise, again provided the parties have agreed thereupon (see Article 1020(4)(c) DCCP). Given that these matters are currently considered arbitrable, Article 3(2) no longer plays an important role. Article 3(2), however, remains relevant in those cases where the parties did not make use of the possibility provided for in Article 1020(4) DCCP, but want the arbitral tribunal to render a decision as meant in Article 1020(4) DCCP after all. If this is the case, the most logical way to proceed is for the parties to grant the arbitral tribunal the relevant power after all. Then again, Article 3(2) may come into play if the defending party refuses to cooperate.

Finally, we note that we do not know of any cases in which Article 3(2) has been applied. Parties in NAI arbitration will rarely realize that the arbitral tribunal is authorized to render its decision (partially) in the form of a binding

---

[77] For a general explanation of the concept of arbitrability under Dutch law, see Part I, Ch. 2, Section 2.

advice if the dispute is incapable of being settled by arbitration, because the parties did not explicitly agree thereon. It is therefore recommended to exclude the applicability of Article 3, or to give the arbitral tribunal a full mandate in respect of the settlement of the dispute by arbitration, also regarding the filling in of gaps and the like, if necessary.

5.   No Deposit of the Decision (Article 3(3))

As already mentioned above, Article 3(3) notes only one of the differences between binding advice proceedings and arbitral proceedings, being that in the case of binding advice, no deposit of the decision with the office of the clerk of the District Court if required, as is the case for arbitral awards. The reason for this is that for binding advice, there is no legal basis for such deposit as there is for arbitration (see the comments on Article 50). As a binding advice is not deposited, the periods of time for rectification and correction of the decision (Article 52) and for rendering an additional decision (Article 53) are not linked to the date of deposit, but to the date of receipt of the decision. Article 3(3) provides that the periods of time for correction and for rendering an additional decision will expire 30 days after the day the decision is received.

ARTICLE 4 – NOTICES

---

1. Notices shall be given or confirmed in writing, such as by letter or rapid written communication.
2. If there is more than one claimant or respondent, the number of copies of notices and other written submissions to be submitted shall be increased accordingly.

---

1.   Notices (Article 4(1))

According to Article 4(1), notices in the arbitral proceedings shall be given or confirmed in writing, such as by letter or rapid written communication. The term 'notices' refers to all communications between the parties, the arbitral tribunal and the Administrator, except for written submissions such as the request for arbitration, the short answer and other memorials (which submissions are referred to separately by Article 4(2) and, for example, also by Article 20(2))).

Article 4(1) stipulates that a notice or the subsequent confirmation of a notice in writing may be given by letter or rapid written communication (such as telex, telefax and currently usually also e-mail).[78] As Article 4 does not set any requirements as to the manner in which letters are to be sent, any manner seems to fulfil the requirement of a written notice. However, in order to avoid disputes on the

---

[78]   See Art. 1021 DCCP and Art. 6:227a DCC regarding written agreements in electronic form.

receipt or even the dispatch of written communications, it is recommended to use a type of written communication that provides proof of receipt by the addressee, such as telefax or registered mail with return of receipt. Important documents or notices will usually be sent by courier. The exact manner in which communications have to be sent will usually be determined by the arbitral tribunal, for example in a procedural order at the outset of the arbitration (see Article 23(2)) or may be agreed upon between the parties during a (procedural) meeting with the arbitral tribunal (see Article 23(4)). The arbitral tribunal might, for example, determine that communications must be sent by e-mail or telefax, and that subsequently, the original must be sent by courier or by registered mail. In general, it is increasingly becoming common practice that communications are sent by e-mail also in arbitral proceedings.

It follows from the wording of Article 4(1) ('given or confirmed in writing') that notices may also be given orally, provided that they are subsequently confirmed in writing. The rationale behind this rule is of course the possibility to provide proof of the oral notice. Oral notices will usually be given during hearings or in meetings or (video) conference calls with the arbitral tribunal. Obviously, Article 4(1) does not require the confirmation in writing of each and every oral communication given during such hearing, meeting or conference call. A confirmation in writing can be limited to the arrangements made or, for example, any important objections raised or remarks made by a party during such hearing or conference call.

In respect of oral notices, a complication may arise regarding unilateral contacts between the arbitral tribunal and one of the parties. Article 10(2) stipulates that in the course of the proceedings, an arbitrator may not have any contacts with only one of the parties concerning matters regarding the proceedings, unless he has obtained the prior consent of the other parties and of the co-arbitrators (if the tribunal consists of more than one arbitrator). Therefore, oral notices can only be given either in the presence of all participants in the arbitration (all arbitrators and all parties) or, if not all parties or arbitrators are present, with the consent of the parties and the possible co-arbitrators. If the parties and possible co-arbitrators have agreed to a unilateral contact between the arbitrator and one of the parties, it seems to follow from Article 4(1) that also notices given during such unilateral contact need to be confirmed in writing, with a copy to *all* other parties, possible co-arbitrators and the NAI Secretariat.

2. Number of Copies (Article 4(2))

Article 4(2) provides that if there is more than one claimant or respondent, the number of copies and other written submissions to be submitted shall be increased accordingly. The meaning of this provision is not immediately evident. However, it follows from the Dutch text, which is clearer, that apart from the copies meant for the arbitrators, the secretary to the arbitral tribunal and the

Administrator, the number of copies to be submitted depends on the number of parties on the other side. For example, if there are four respondents and claimant submits its statement of claim, it should do so in four copies for the respondents, i.e. one plus three extra copies for each additional respondent. The background of this rule is a practical one: the requirement that submissions have to be filed in a sufficient number of copies ensures that the NAI or the arbitrators do not have to make copies.

Article 20(2) provides that after the Administrator has transmitted the arbitration file to the arbitral tribunal, the parties have to send their notices and other written submissions directly to the arbitral tribunal, with a copy to the Administrator. Although not required by Article 4(2), it seems logical to provide extra copies if the arbitral tribunal is composed of more than one arbitrator or if the arbitral tribunal is assisted by a secretary.[79] As the arbitral tribunal determines the manner in which the procedure is conducted (see Article 23(2)), the arbitral tribunal may also establish rules as to the number of copies that is to be supplied. Furthermore, it is up to the parties to agree on the manner in which and to whom copies of notices and other written communications will be sent in a (procedural) meeting with the arbitral tribunal (see Article 23(4)). In practice, parties agree to send each respondent multiple copies, depending on the number of individuals involved from the respondents' organizations in order to avoid extensive copying after receipt of the communications. Moreover, it may be considered common practice to provide electronic versions of written submissions in a searchable format.

Both Articles 20 and 4 do not address the way in which copies of notices and written submissions are to be sent to the other party. In practice, however, the arbitral tribunal will either determine at the outset of the arbitration that copies of notices or written submissions must be sent simultaneously to the arbitral tribunal, the Administrator and the other party or parties, or the arbitral tribunal will itself forward notices and submissions received from a party to the other party or parties. Article 4(2) seems relevant only in the latter case.

Although Articles 6(4) and 7(4), dealing with the number of copies to be submitted of the request for arbitration and the short answer (see the comments on those articles), seem fairly clear about the number of copies that have to be provided (i.e. five copies), Article 4(2) also applies to Article 6(4) and 7(4).[80] Thus, if there is more than one party on the other side, the number of copies should be increased accordingly for the request for arbitration and the short answer as well. That not only saves the NAI Secretariat or the Administrator, that will communicate a copy of the request and the short answer to the other party or parties, the trouble of making additional copies, but also avoids possible mistakes made in copying. In addition, providing the increased number of copies

---

[79] This also seems to follow from Arts 6(4) and 7(4), which provide that both the request for arbitration and the short answer must be filed in five copies, of which three will be intended for the (future) arbitrator(s), one for the Administrator and one for the other party.

[80] Differently: Vademecum Arbitrage, 2002 (H.J. Snijders), 96.

right away prevents delay, given that the Administrator may ask for additional copies and even suspend action if the request for arbitration has not been filed in sufficient copies.

ARTICLE 5 – PERIODS OF TIME

1. For the purposes of these Rules, a period of time shall start to run on the day a notice is received unless these Rules or the arbitral tribunal explicitly provide otherwise.
2. In an international arbitration, the periods of time referred to in Articles 7(4), 12(3), 13(2), 14(3), 14(9), 19(3), 19(7), 57(5) and 59(6) shall be doubled.
3. The Administrator is, at the request of a party or on his own motion, authorized to extend or to shorten in exceptional cases the periods of time referred to in Articles 7(4), 12(3), 14(3), 14(9), 57(5) and 59(6).
4. For summary arbitral proceedings as regulated in Section Four A, the periods of time which are determined in those provisions or in accordance with those provisions, apply.

1.   General Comments

This Article contains some general provisions regarding periods of time that should be observed during the arbitration.

2.   Commencement of Periods of Time (Article 5(1))

According to Article 5(1), a period of time provided for in the NAI Rules starts to run on the day of receipt of a notice, unless explicitly provided otherwise in the NAI Rules or by the arbitral tribunal.[81] This rather flexible moment of commencement of periods of time could conceivably cause some problems, for example if the parties do not receive a notice on the same day or if a party knowingly frustrates or delays the receipt of a notice (e.g. by refusing to accept or to collect registered mail or by blocking its mailbox). However, in practice, this provision generally does not cause any difficulties. Due to means of communication like e-mail and telefax, parties will usually receive notices on the same day. If, in an exceptional case, a party knowingly frustrates or delays the receipt of a notice, the notice might be deemed to be received on the day the notice would normally have been received by the addressee.[82]

---

[81] This provision differs from Art. 2(2) UNCITRAL Rules, Art. 3(4) ICC Rules, Art. 4.6 LCIA Rules and Art. 4(e) WIPO Arbitration Rules, which all provide that a period of time shall begin to run on the day *following* the day when a notice or other communication is received.

[82] See Art. 46 DCCP regarding the consequences of a refusal to accept a writ served by a bailiff.

A period of time runs until 12 p.m. on the last day of the applicable period. In order to avoid problems with physical delivery, it is, however, recommended to contact the NAI Secretariat or the arbitral tribunal as the case may be in advance when planning to deliver documents (for example by courier) to the NAI after business hours.

Article 5 remains tacit on what happens if the last day of a period is an official holiday or a non-business day. In practice, if a period of time ends on a day that is not a business day, the NAI extends that period of time until the first business day that follows. This is in line with international practice as appears from other arbitration rules[83] and with the Dutch General Extension of Time Limits Act (*Algemene Termijnenwet*).[84] In our view, a similar provision should be added to the NAI Rules, should the NAI Rules be amended in the future. For the time being, it is recommended to ask the Administrator for a written confirmation of the end of a period of time, should this period end on a day that is an official holiday or a non-business day.

Article 5(2) applies to time periods in regard of submissions to the Administrator and activities to be executed by the Administrator. It is assumed that the other provision, including that in regard of the commencement of time periods, apply equally to terms set by the arbitral tribunal in the absence of a different ruling by the arbitral tribunal. In practice most arbitral tribunals set similar rules in a procedural order or an additional arbitration agreement entered into by the parties and the arbitral tribunal. NAI tribunals are advised to do the same in order to avoid misunderstandings.

3.   Doubled Periods of Time in International Arbitration (Article 5(2))

As discussed above in the context of Article 1(g), the NAI Rules contain certain provisions in order to meet the special needs of international arbitration. One of these provisions is Article 5(2), which doubles specific periods of time provided in the NAI Rules in the event of an international arbitration as defined in Article 1(g). According to Article 5(2), the periods of time referred to in the following articles are doubled in an international arbitration:

- Article 7(4) regarding the period for filing the short answer;
- Article 12(3) regarding the period within which agreement must be reached on the appointment of the chairman of the arbitral tribunal if the parties agreed on an even number of arbitrators;
- Article 13(2) regarding the period within which the parties must have complied with the method of appointment of arbitrators agreed upon by the parties;

---

[83]   See also Art. 2(2) UNCITRAL Rules, Art. 3(4) ICC Rules, Art. 4.6 LCIA Rules, Art. 4(e) WIPO Arbitration Rules.

[84]   See Art. 1 General Extension of Time Limits Act (*Algemene Termijnenwet*).

– Article 14(3) regarding the period within which the list with names of possible arbitrators has to be returned to the Administrator;
– Article 14(9) regarding the period for appointment of the arbitrators in accordance with the list procedure;
– Article 19(3) regarding the period within which a challenge and the grounds therefore must be notified;
– Article 19(7) regarding the period within which a challenged arbitrator must withdraw;
– Article 57(5) regarding the period for payment of the administration costs due after a second reminder in writing by the Administrator;
– Article 59(6) regarding the period for payment of the deposit for costs after a second reminder in writing by the Administrator.

These provisions may be considered outdated and seem to stem from a period in time when communications with foreign countries were considered considerably more burdensome than communications within the Netherlands. With the modern means of communication this difference does not seem to apply anymore. In light thereof we could imagine the NAI changing the relevant rules in accordance with the proposed reform of the DCCP by abolishing the difference between terms in national and international arbitrations.

4.   Adjustment of Periods of Time (Article 5(3))

Article 5(3) authorizes the Administrator to extend or to shorten the periods of time referred to in specific articles of the NAI Rules. These articles concern the stages of the arbitration in which the arbitral tribunal has not yet been composed or in which the final award has been deposited and consequently, the assignment of the arbitral tribunal has terminated. It concerns the following articles (the subject of which has been briefly stated above in the comments on Article 5(2)): Articles 7(4), 12(3), 14(3), 14(9), 57(5) and 59(6).

The Administrator may use its authority to extend or to shorten the specified periods of time at the request of a party or on his own volition, but only in exceptional cases. It is left to the discretion of the Administrator whether a case is sufficiently exceptional to adjust a period of time. In this respect, it rarely happens that a period of time is shortened by the Administrator.

Once the arbitral tribunal has been constituted, the arbitral tribunal is authorized, according to Article 23(3), to extend in exceptional cases a period of time fixed by it or agreed to by the parties (see also the comments on Article 23(3)).

5.   Periods of Time in Summary Arbitral Proceedings (Article 5(4))

Article 5(4) stipulates that for summary arbitral proceedings as regulated by Section 4A, the periods of time which are determined in those provisions or in accordance with those provisions, apply. These provisions will be discussed below, in the comments on the articles regarding the summary arbitral proceedings.

SECTION 2

COMMENCEMENT OF ARBITRATION
(Articles 6-9)

ARTICLE 6 – REQUEST FOR ARBITRATION

1. An arbitration commences by the filing of a request for arbitration with the NAI Secretariat.
2. Both in case of an arbitration clause and in case of a submission agreement, the arbitration shall be deemed to have commenced on the day the request for arbitration is received by the NAI Secretariat.
3. The request for arbitration shall contain the following particulars:
   (a) the name and address of the claimant, his place of domicile, seat or actual residence, as well as his telephone, telefax and telex numbers;
   (b) the name and address of the respondent, his place of domicile, seat or actual residence, as well as his telephone, telefax and telex numbers;
   (c) a brief description of the dispute;
   (d) a clear description of what is claimed;
   (e) a reference to the arbitration agreement; a copy of the latter shall be submitted simultaneously;
   (f) the name(s) and address(es) of the arbitrator(s), their place of domicile or actual residence, as well as their telephone, telefax and telex numbers, insofar as parties themselves have appointed the arbitrator(s);
   (g) the method of appointing the arbitrator(s), if parties have agreed to a method of appointment different from the list-procedure provided in Article 14;
   (h) the number of the arbitrators, if agreed by the parties;
   (i) the place of arbitration, if agreed by the parties;

      (j) the preference, if any, of the claimant for the number of the arbitrators and/or for the place of arbitration, if not agreed by the parties;

      (k) to the extent applicable, further particulars as to the arbitral procedure, e.g., the nationality of arbitrators as referred to in Article 16(4).

4. The request for arbitration shall be filed in five copies. If the request for arbitration is not filed in a sufficient number of copies, or does not comply with all requirements listed in the preceding paragraph, the Administrator shall contact the claimant in order to obtain additional copies or completion as necessary. The Administrator is authorized to suspend action on the request for arbitration until the requirements mentioned above have been complied with. The suspension does not prejudice the provisions of paragraph (2).

5. As regards the requirements of paragraph (3)(e), in case a request for arbitration is contained in rapid written communication, it is sufficient for the claimant to quote literally the text of the arbitration agreement provided that, as soon as possible after the commencement of the arbitration, the claimant communicates a copy of the arbitration agreement to the Administrator.

6. The Administrator shall communicate to the claimant a written acknowledgement of receipt of the request for arbitration, making mention of the date of receipt.

1. General Comments

A NAI arbitration is commenced by filing a request for arbitration with the NAI Secretariat. No specific form (other than that it follows from this article that such request has to be in writing) is prescribed for the request for arbitration. A simple letter will suffice. Also, a standard form for the request for arbitration is available with the Secretariat free of charge. This form can also be downloaded from the NAI website. Although no specific form is prescribed, the request must contain the information specified in Article 6(3)(a)-(k), such as the name and address of both the claimant and the respondent, a brief description of the dispute, a clear description of the claim and a reference to the arbitration agreement. The information contained in the request (as well as in the short answer) is meant primarily to inform the Administrator of the nature and circumstances of the dispute so as to facilitate the selection of the arbitrators and to determine the amount of administration costs due (see Article 57). Therefore, the request may be brief and to the point. The claimant will have a full opportunity to present its case in the statement of claim. An extensive request for arbitration is basically useless and unnecessarily costly to the claimant.

2. Filing of the Request

Article 6(1) establishes the principle that the request for arbitration is submitted by the claimant to the Secretariat rather than to the respondent directly. It is the responsibility of the Administrator to communicate a copy of the request for arbitration to the respondent (see Article 7(1)). However, counsel for claimant may be subject to rules of conduct stipulating that he has to send a copy of the request directly and simultaneously to (counsel for) the respondent.[85]

Although a request for arbitration will usually be sent to the Secretariat by mail or courier, Article 6(5) explicitly provides for the possibility that the request is contained in 'rapid written communication' (see also Article 4(1) on notices). Hence, the request may be filed by telefax and also by e-mail. This may be necessary under pressure of time or in case of imminent expiry of statutory or contractual time limits for bringing a claim. If the request is filed by means of rapid communication, such as by telefax or e-mail, it is sufficient for the claimant to quote the text of the arbitration agreement in the request. The required copy of the arbitration agreement must be filed with the Secretariat as soon as possible thereafter.

Article 6(4) provides that the request shall be filed in five copies. According to Article 4(2), if there is more than one respondent, this number shall be increased accordingly. When a request is filed by telefax or by e-mail, the claimant shall as soon as possible thereafter provide the original hard copies of the request in the number required by the NAI Rules, as well as a copy of the arbitration agreement.

When a request for arbitration is received by the Secretariat, the Administrator will acknowledge its receipt in writing by sending a letter to the claimant confirming the (date of) receipt of the request (Article 6(6)). Ordinarily, this will be done as soon as possible, mostly within one or two days, after receipt of the request. If the request has not been filed in a sufficient number of copies or does not contain all the information required by Article 6(3)(a)-(k), the Administrator will contact the claimant in order to obtain additional copies or completion as necessary (Article 6(4)). The Administrator is authorized to suspend action until sufficient copies and/or the required information have been supplied (Article 6(4)). However, non-compliance with the obligations of Article 6(3) and 6(4) does not affect the date of commencement of the arbitration as provided in Article 6(2) (see note 3).

---

[85] See for counsel who are subject to the Dutch Rules of Conduct, Art. 15 of these Rules.

3. Date of Commencement of the Arbitration

Article 6(2) fixes the date of commencement of the arbitration, both when there is an arbitration clause and when there is a submission agreement (*compromis*). The arbitration shall be deemed to have commenced on the day of receipt of the request for arbitration by the NAI Secretariat (as mentioned in the letter to the claimant on the basis of Article 6(6)).

> This rule differs from the statutory provisions of Articles 1024 DCCP (for a submission agreement) and 1025 DCCP (for an arbitration clause). In the case of a submission agreement, Article 1024(2) DCCP provides that the arbitration commences by the conclusion of the submission agreement, unless otherwise agreed by the parties.
>
> In the case of an arbitration clause, Article 1025(1) DCCP provides that the arbitration commences on the day of receipt of a written communication, in which the future claimant informs the other party that it initiates arbitration, unless otherwise agreed by the parties. Both articles, thus, allow the parties to agree otherwise, which is often done by including in the arbitration clause a reference to arbitration rules that derogate from the statutory rules, such as the NAI Rules.

By linking the commencement of the arbitration to the date of receipt by the Secretariat of the request, the NAI Rules ensure that the parties will have no difficulty in establishing the date of its commencement.[86] The date of commencement of the arbitration is of obvious importance with regard to relevant statutes of limitation or if the arbitration is required to be commenced by a particular date for other reasons. For example, the date of commencement of the arbitration is decisive in cases in which a pre-judgment attachment has been made by the claimant and the arbitration constitutes the claim in the principal action. In that event, the arbitration must be commenced within the timeframe set in the leave for pre-judgment attachment by the President (*voorzieningenrechter*) of the District Court (Article 700 DCCP). Also, the date of commencement of the arbitration is relevant for the commencement of the time limit for the appointment of arbitrators (see Article 14(9)), as well as, for example, for a request to the competent court pursuant to Article 1046 DCCP (if applicability of this provision has not been excluded by the parties) to consolidate an arbitration with another arbitration if the subject matters of the two arbitrations are connected.

It follows from Article 6(4) that failure to provide a sufficient number of copies of the request or non-observance of the requirements as to the information to be provided in the request is without prejudice to the date of commencement of the arbitration. That means that the date on which a request for arbitration is received by the Secretariat is decisive, even if the provisions of Article 6 have not been

---

[86] The ICC Rules contain a similar provision in Art. 4(2) and the LCIA Rules in Art. 1.2. However, in arbitral proceedings not administered by an arbitration institute, such as arbitrations under the UNCITRAL Rules, the proceedings are deemed to commence on the date of receipt of the request by the respondent.

properly complied with. A different approach seems appropriate when the contents of the request are so defective that it does no longer allow the Administrator to adequately fulfil its obligation to appoint the arbitrator and the respondent to draft the short answer. This criterion will only be met in exceptional cases.

For the respondent, a possibly negative consequence of Article 6(2) and 6(4) is that arbitral proceedings may be deemed to have commenced before the respondent is aware of this, unless the applicable rules of conduct require claimant's counsel to send the request for arbitration (and other submissions) also directly to the respondent (and claimant's counsel has indeed done so). In any event, the Secretariat will normally see to it that the respondent is notified of the filing of a request for arbitration as soon as possible. Whether the request is notified to the respondent if the request does not satisfy the provisions of Article 6(3)(a)-(k) or has not been filed in a sufficient number of copies, is up to the Administrator to decide. As mentioned before, Article 6(4) allows the Administrator to suspend action until the claimant properly complies with the requirements. Since the suspension does not affect the date of commencement of the arbitration (see above), the Administrator should, however, exercise this authority with restraint, at least insofar as it would entail that the respondent is not notified of the request until the request meets all requirements. In this respect, the Administrator may notify the respondent of the filing of the request for arbitration without inviting the respondent to submit a short answer thereto until all the requirements have been properly complied with by the claimant.

4.   Information to be Contained in or Provided with the Request

As already noted, the request for arbitration serves as an introduction to the arbitral procedure and is meant primarily to inform the Administrator of the nature and circumstances of the dispute so as to facilitate the designation of the arbitrators and determine the amount of administration costs due. The same applies for the short answer (see Article 7). The NAI Rules explicitly provide that the filing of the request and the short answer do not prejudice the right of the parties to submit a statement of claim and a statement of defence, respectively (see Articles 8 and 24(1)). Hence, the request and the short answer may be brief. Once the arbitrators have been appointed, the parties will have the opportunity to fully present their case.

4.1. Identification of the Parties (Article 6(3)(a) and 6(3)(b))

Article 6(3)(a) and 6(3)(b) provide for the identification in the request of both the claimant and the respondent. The identification of the parties in the request is not only important for the Administrator, but also dictates who will be the parties in the arbitration. In this respect, the claimant may be required, especially in cases involving multiple parties or complicated corporate structures, to carefully consider the relevant arbitration agreement in determining who should be the claimant(s) and respondent(s), in order to avoid jurisdictional issues or issues relating to the enforcement of the award at a later stage. In particular, the claimant(s) should ensure that the party or parties identified as the respondent(s) in the request are also a party to the relevant arbitration agreement. If not, this may give rise to a plea as to lack of jurisdiction of the arbitral tribunal by the respondent(s), which will considerably slow down the arbitral proceedings and may even lead to the tribunal declaring that it lacks jurisdiction. Therefore, it is advisable to verify whether the parties still exist and/or whether they still have the same name. Also, it is advisable to verify whether, under the applicable law, third parties have become a party to the arbitration agreement. It is, however, up to the claimant to make sure that the request is based on the correct information and it is up to the respondent to determine its position in this respect and, if necessary, to submit a plea for lack of jurisdiction. The Administrator should refrain from interfering and should in particular refrain from conducting its own investigations. If not, the Administrator's conduct could come into conflict with the principles of due process which, in turn, could give rise to a challenge of the award.[87]

> In principle, only the parties to the arbitration agreement are bound by the arbitration agreement. However, under Dutch law, some specific third parties may – under specific circumstances – become a party to the arbitration agreement. For example, in the case of the assignment of a claim, with respect to which the original parties have agreed to arbitration, the assignor is bound to this arbitration agreement Articles 6:145 and 6:142 DCC). The same applies to subrogation (Article 6:150 DCC in conjunction with Articles 6:145 and 6:142 DCC), as well as to the transfer of a contract as a whole (*contractsoverneming*; Article 6:159(2) DCC) or a debt (*schuldoverneming*; Article 6:157(1) DCC). Furthermore, the third party that accepts a third-party condition (*derdenbeding*) will be a party to the agreement, including the arbitration agreement, on the basis of Article 6:254 DCC.[88] In other cases, it is a question of contract interpretation whether a third party will be a party to the agreement, for example if a guarantor has signed the contract.

Once the claimant has decided who to designate as parties in the arbitration, their description, pursuant to Article 6(3)(a) and (b), will normally not be problematic. Given, however, that the request will be notified to the respondent by the Secretariat on the basis of the information provided in the request without verifying the correctness of that information, the claimant must ensure that the address details are accurate. If not, this might delay the actual commencement of the arbitral proceedings because the request will not reach the respondent.

Finally, it may be helpful to provide (in the request for arbitration or in a covering letter) at least some detail about the ownership and control of the parties in the request, as well as the names and contact details (including e-mail address)

---

[87] Fortunately, the Administrator seems to adhere to a restrictive policy in this respect and challenges on the ground of the Administrator's conduct are unprecedented to date.

[88] See also Arts 6:11 DCC, 7:850 DCC in conjunction with Art. 6:11 DCC, Art. 7:868 DCC, Art. 8:441 DCC and Art. 8:415 DCC. See for a more elaborate discussion on this subject Burg. Rv, 2006 (H.J. Snijders), Art. 1020 DCCP, note 7; G.J. Meijer 2008 (T&C Rv), Art. 1020 DCCP, note 3(f)-(g).

of the parties' counsel, although the NAI Rules do not require the claimant or the respondent to do so. This information may be important for the Administrator to have in order to assess the *prima facie* independence and/or impartiality of the arbitrators whose names will appear on the list (see Articles 10 and 14). Also, this information gives potential arbitrators a better opportunity to assess whether there are any conflicts of interest.

4.2. Description of the Dispute and Description of What is Claimed (Article 6(3)(c) and 6(3)(d))

Although the request for arbitration determines the commencement of the arbitration, there is no requirement to elaborate the claim in detail in the request. Article 6(3)(c) merely requires 'a brief description of the dispute' and Article 6(3)(d) 'a clear description of what is claimed'. The NAI Rules allow the claimant the freedom to provide more detail with respect to the facts as well as the legal basis of its claims. As a minimum, however, a brief description of the factual and legal basis of the claim, as well as a clear description of the relief sought suffice. To the extent possible, the description of the relief sought should include an indication of any amounts claimed, not only for the information of the respondent, but especially for the benefit of the Administrator in order to fix the advance on costs for the arbitration. The administration costs due by the claimant are determined on the basis of the amount of the claim (see Article 57(2)). Also, the arbitrator's fees are determined, inter alia, on the basis of the amount in dispute (see Article 58(1)).

Requests for arbitration are commonly not submitted with any supporting documentation or documentary evidence, except for a copy of the arbitration agreement, as required by Article 6(3)(e) (see below).

The filing of the request for arbitration does not prejudice the right of the claimant to submit a statement of claim, once the arbitrators have been appointed. All details regarding the nature of the dispute and the claim will generally be given in the statement of claim. In order to leave the possibility open of putting forward additional grounds and arguments for its claims, depending on the possible defences raised by the respondent in its short answer, it is wise for the claimant not to go into more detail in the request than required by the NAI Rules.

As stated above, Article 6(3) merely requires the request to hold a 'clear description of the claim'. The actual claim is presented in the statement of claim following the appointment of the arbitral tribunal. Accordingly, any changes to the claim in the statement of claim, compared to the description in the request for arbitration cannot be regarded as an amendment of the claim within the meaning of Article 34.

4.3. Arbitration Agreement (Article 6(3)(e))

The submission of a dispute to arbitration requires an agreement to arbitrate, generally referred to as arbitration agreement. This arbitration agreement may take the form of an arbitration clause in a contract, referring future disputes to arbitration, but it can also take the form of a submission agreement, in which the parties agree to submit an existing dispute to arbitration (see the comments on Article 1(e)).

Article 6(3)(e) requires the claimant to refer to the relevant arbitration agreement in the request and to submit a copy of that agreement with the request. As indicated above, it is sufficient for the claimant to quote literally the text of the arbitration agreement in the request if the request is filed by means of rapid written communication (such as by telefax or by e-mail), provided that a copy of the arbitration agreement is submitted to the Administrator as soon as possible thereafter (see Article 6(5)). It is not required that the contract in which the arbitration agreement has been incorporated will be filed in its entirety, especially not if it is a voluminous contract. It will usually suffice to file the page(s) that contain the arbitration agreement, as well as other relevant pages of the contract, such as the pages that contain the identification of the parties to the contract and the signature pages.

The requirement to submit a copy of the arbitration agreement may pose a problem if there is no written arbitration agreement. It follows from Article 1(e) that an agreement to arbitrate need not fulfil any formal requirements and may be concluded orally.[89] However, if one of the parties (timely) contests the validity of the agreement, the existence of the agreement must be proven by means of a written document that has been accepted, either explicitly or implicitly, by the other party (see Article 1(e) and the comments on this article). In practice, however, arbitration agreements will commonly be laid down in written form.

> Article 1021 DCCP contains a similar provision on the proof of an arbitration agreement.

4.4. Arbitrator(s) to be Appointed, Method of Appointment (Article 6(3)(f)-(h) and 6(3)(j))

Since the request for arbitration serves as an introduction to the arbitral procedure and is also meant to facilitate the designation of the arbitrators, Articles 6(3)(f)-(h) and 6(3)(j) require the claimant to provide in the request relevant particulars concerning the arbitrators to be appointed, including, if applicable, their number and the parties' choice of arbitrators. However, this does not apply if the parties have already appointed the arbitrator(s) (see below).

> Article 1027 DCCP provides that the arbitrator or arbitrators shall be appointed in the manner agreed by the parties. The parties may also assign the appointment of one or more arbitrators to a third party.

As discussed below, the NAI Rules provide for a specific method of appointment of arbitrators on the basis of a list of names of possible arbitrators, composed by

---

[89] This is also possible under Dutch arbitration law. If the place of arbitration is outside the Netherlands, it depends on the (mandatory) provisions on arbitration agreements in that country whether an arbitration agreement may be concluded orally.

the Administrator (see Article 14). If the parties did not make an arrangement to the contrary by agreeing on a method of appointment different from the list-procedure or on appointment of specific arbitrators in the arbitration agreement, the appointment will occur in accordance with the list-procedure. As a practical matter, this means that there is no need for the claimant to nominate or appoint one or more arbitrators in the request. If, however, the parties have agreed to deviate from the list-procedure of Article 14 and to appoint arbitrators themselves, the request should contain a description of the method of appointment of the arbitrator(s) (Article 6(3)(g)), the number of arbitrators (Article 6(3)(h)), as well as – if already possible, depending on the chosen method of appointment – the name and address details of the arbitrator(s) nominated by the claimant (Article 6(3)(f)).

Where the arbitration agreement does not specify the number of arbitrators, the claimant should indicate the number of arbitrators that it wishes (Article 6(3)(j)). In the absence of an agreement on the number of arbitrators, the Administrator will determine the number of arbitrators (either one or three), taking into account, among other factors, the preferences of the parties (see Article 12(2)).

As a practical matter, it may be useful for the claimant to indicate the preferred qualifications of the arbitrators who are about to be appointed. If the respondent does not object in the short answer, the Administrator will generally (try to) take such suggestions into account when composing a list with the names of arbitrators. In practice the Administrator may ask the respondent whether indeed it has no views on the requested qualifications of the arbitrators. Expressing such qualifications always requires, however, a judgment call to be made. If the respondent opposes the claimant's wishes, it is uncertain what the Administrator will do. The Administrator may try to avoid taking any measures at the beginning of the arbitration that one of the parties has explicitly rejected. Taking into account that the selection of the arbitrators always involves considerable room for appreciation, the Administrator may just try to compose a list of arbitrators that leaves the parties' debate on the qualifications of the arbitrators irrelevant by selecting arbitrators who meet other qualifications that make them fit for resolving the dispute. If one has to deal with a counterparty that tends to reject any proposal simply because it was made by the claimant, it may therefore be more fruitful to remain tacit on the qualifications of the arbitrators and leave it to the Administrator to come up with a list of qualified candidates. If parties do not express any views on the qualifications for arbitrators, the Administrator will nevertheless try to select potential arbitrators that have relevant qualifications in view of the description of the dispute.

4.5. Place of Arbitration (Article 6(3)(i))

The request for arbitration should mention the place of arbitration, if it has been agreed by the parties in the arbitration agreement. If the place of arbitration has not been agreed by the parties, Article 22(1) provides that the place of arbitration will be determined by the arbitral tribunal, once constituted. The arbitral tribunal must notify the parties and the Administrator in writing of the place so determined. As a practical matter, if the place of arbitration has not been agreed by the parties, the parties may wish to suggest a place for arbitration that suits them.

The place of arbitration is a legal concept. Article 22(2) provides that hearings and deliberations of the tribunal may be held and witnesses and experts may be examined at any other place that the arbitral tribunal deems appropriate, either in or outside the Netherlands.

See for a more elaborate discussion the comments on Article 22.

> As will be discussed below (see the comments on Article 22), the place of arbitration is relevant for the applicability of Book IV of the DCCP. Pursuant to Article 1073(1) DCCP, Title 1 of Book IV only applies if the place of arbitration is in the Netherlands. Also, the place of arbitration determines with which District Court the arbitral award has to be deposited, where a request for execution of the award has to be filed and where possible setting aside proceedings have to be initiated. In addition, the place of arbitration will in most instances determine which law governs the procedural aspects of the arbitration.

4.6. Further Particulars as to the Arbitral Procedure (Article 6(3)(k)); Language of Arbitration

To the extent applicable, Article 6(3)(k) requires and allows the claimant to furnish further particulars as to the arbitral procedure, other than those mentioned in Article 6(3)(a)-(j). These particulars may include, for example, comments as to the nationality of the arbitrators and/or the arbitrator who will act as chairman of the tribunal as referred to in Article 16(4). As mentioned above, the claimant may also wish to indicate its wishes in regard of the potential arbitrators' qualifications. The claimant may also include prior agreements between the parties on witness statements, the possibility of a statement of reply and rejoinder, or – failing such agreements – the claimant may indicate its preferences in this respect.

Article 40(1) stipulates that the arbitral proceedings must be conducted in the language or languages as agreed by the parties[90] or, in the absence of such agreement, in the language or languages determined by the tribunal. Although the language(s) of the arbitration can be deemed relevant information for the Administrator for composing the list of possible arbitrators (particularly when the arbitration is to be conducted in a language other than Dutch or English), Article 6(3), strangely enough, does not explicitly require the claimant to provide information as to the language in which the arbitration is to be conducted. This information, apparently, is covered by the general description 'further particulars as to the arbitral procedure' of Article 6(3)(k).

If the parties have agreed in the arbitration agreement on the language of the arbitration, the request for arbitration should ordinarily be submitted in that language (although Article 6 does not actually say so). If the claimant

---

[90] See also the comments on Art. 1(e).

chooses to draft the request in a different language, the respondent may ask for a translation (Article 40(3)). If the request is in another then the agreed language, the NAI Rules do not prevent the Administrator from notifying the request to the respondent. However, the Administrator will generally make sure that the respondent understands that language. If deemed necessary, the Administrator may require the claimant to provide a suitable translation before taking any further action. Again this will only result in a delay of the arbitral proceedings, but does not affect the date of commencement of the arbitration.

If the parties have not agreed on the language of the arbitration, the submission of the request for arbitration in either claimant's own language or the language of the relevant contract can be regarded as good practice. However, the Administrator may ask for a translation.

ARTICLE 7 – SHORT ANSWER

1. The Administrator shall communicate a copy of the request for arbitration to the respondent, along with mention of the date of receipt, and shall invite him in writing to submit a short answer thereto.

2. The short answer shall also contain the preference, if any, of the respondent for the number of the arbitrators and/or for the place of arbitration, if not agreed by the parties, as well as, to the extent applicable, any further particulars as to the arbitral procedure.

3. In the short answer the respondent may introduce a counterclaim against the claimant in accordance with the provisions of Article 25(2). The requirements mentioned in Article 6(3)(c), (d) and (e) apply accordingly to the counterclaim.

4. The respondent shall file the short answer with the Administrator in five copies within 14 days[*] after receipt of the invitation mentioned above.

5. The Administrator shall communicate a copy of the short answer to the claimant.

[*] This period of time is doubled in an international arbitration (Art. 5(2)).

1.   General Comments

Contrary to certain other arbitration rules (such as the UNCITRAL Rules and the ICSID Rules), the NAI Rules provide for the filing of a short response to the request for arbitration by the respondent prior to constituting the arbitral tribunal. Article 7 provides for the submission by the respondent of a short answer in response to the request for arbitration. In the short answer, the respondent *may* also introduce counterclaims or include a plea as to the lack of jurisdiction of the arbitral tribunal. The word may indicates that this is, however, not compulsory. The respondent is also free to introduce its counterclaim only in the statement of defence, or to introduce a revised counterclaim in the statement of defence. In addition a plea as to lack of jurisdiction may also be presented in the statement of defence for the first time. Any such information in the short answer will only serve to provide the Administrator and the future arbitrators with more detailed information as to the nature of the dispute. The legal relevance of such information in the short answer is, however, negligible. Here again, one might argue that an extensive short answer is useless and overly costly to the defendant.

2.   Filing of the Short Answer

The short answer has to be filed with the Administrator in five copies (Article 7(4), see also Article 4(2)). The Administrator will forward one copy of the short answer to the claimant(s) (Article 7(5), see also Article 4(2)), which will usually be done upon receipt of the short answer by the Administrator. The other four copies filed by the respondent will be retained by the Administrator for the Secretariat and the arbitral tribunal. The fact that the Administrator forwards a copy of the short answer to the claimant does not prevent the respondent from sending an additional copy to the claimant directly, if it wishes to do so or if any applicable rules of conduct so require.[91]

Just as for the request for arbitration, the NAI Rules do not lay down any requirements concerning the manner in which the short answer is to be transmitted to the Administrator. However, just as for the request for arbitration, it follows from the NAI Rules that the short answer will have to be in writing. As a practical matter, the short answer will usually be sent to the Administrator by mail or courier. The NAI Rules, however, do not exclude filing by telefax or by e-mail, if necessary under the pressure of time. In that event, the respondent should ensure that the original five copies of the short answer are received by the Administrator as soon as possible thereafter.

3.   Time Limit

The Administrator will forward a copy of the request for arbitration to the respondent. In this communication, the Administrator must mention the date of receipt of the request for arbitration by the Secretariat (which date marks the date of commencement of the arbitration; see Article 6(2)) and invite the respondent to file a short answer to the request (see Article 7(1)).

Subject to obtaining an extension of time pursuant to Article 5(3), the respondent is required to file the short answer with the Administrator within

---

[91]   See for counsel who are subject to the Dutch Rules of Conduct, Art. 15 of these Rules.

14 days after receipt of the Administrator's invitation (see the comments on Article 5(1) on the commencement of time periods). Pursuant to Article 5(2), this time limit is doubled in an international arbitration, thus allowing the respondent in an international arbitration 28 days to file the short answer.[92] The NAI Rules limit the period for filing the short answer to no more than 14 days. Compared to other arbitration rules this period can be considered extremely short, even in international arbitrations, where the period is doubled. Where the claimant may have taken months in the preparation of the arbitration and the request, the respondent only has 14 (or, as the case may be, 28) days to locate, retain and brief counsel and prepare the short answer. Although the short answer can be very brief and the respondent may postpone the introduction of a counterclaim and a plea as to lack of jurisdiction until the submission of a full statement of defence after the appointment of the arbitral tribunal and the submission of the statement of claim by the claimant, this time period can easily be too short for retaining outside counsel and taking the first steps in adopting a defence strategy. The possibility of an extension does only partly provide a suitable solution in this respect. The text of Article 5(3) indicates that the Administrator will only allow such an extension in exceptional cases. This interpretation is confirmed by the Introduction to NAI Arbitration Rules, stating under 6.6:

> 'It should be noted that a request for extension of the time limit of 14 days set for the filing of the short answer (in international arbitration 28 days, see Article 5(2)) will be granted only under exceptional circumstances. The policy of the NAI is to appoint the arbitrator or arbitrators as promptly as possible.'

In practice the Administrator seems to adhere to a more relaxed policy, if an extension is requested for on the basis of substantive arguments. In doing so the NAI practice may be considered in line with international practice, since the ICC Secretariat grants almost routinely extensions of time for the filing of the answer by the respondent.[93]

Parties normally wish to file the short answer within the timeframe set by Article 7(4) (as possibly extended pursuant to Article 5(2) in an international arbitration or pursuant to Article 5(3) following a request for an extension). However, the NAI Rules do not provide for a sanction if the respondent does not timely file the short answer. Given that the short answer, as the request, serves as an introduction to the arbitral procedure and is only aimed at providing the

---

[92] In Art. 1(g), an 'international arbitration' is defined as: 'an arbitration in which at the moment of commencement of arbitration as referred to in Articles 6 and 42b of these Arbitration Rules, at least one of the parties is domiciled or has its seat, or, in the absence thereof, has its actual residence outside the Netherlands'.

[93] Derains and Schwartz, 2005, 67.

Administrator the necessary information for appointing the arbitrators, the respondent's failure to file the short answer will not forfeit its right to set out its defence and submit a statement of defence, once the arbitrators have been appointed. As will be discussed below (see Article 23), the arbitral tribunal must ensure the equal treatment of the parties and give each party an opportunity to substantiate its claims and defences and to present its case. The mere lack of the short answer cannot limit the tribunal's obligations and responsibilities in this respect.

Some respondents request the Administrator for an extension of time for filing the short answer, for example because the respondent has not yet retained counsel, but at the same time respond to the substance of the request. Practice shows that the Administrator may deny the request for an extension of time and consider the respondent's reply as the short answer. In this event, as well as in the event that the respondent does not file its short answer within the period set by Article 7(4) at all, the respondent runs the risk that the Administrator will not have the benefit of the respondent's view when determining the advance on costs and the names of possible arbitrators that will appear on the list pursuant to Article 14. Apart from that, such decision of the Administrator is, however, without consequences. In particular, it does not limit the respondent's right to defend its position in the statement of defence after the appointment of the tribunal and to file a counterclaim or a plea as to lack of jurisdiction, if it wishes to do so.

4.   Content of the Short Answer

The short answer, as the request for arbitration, serves as an introduction to the arbitral procedure and is meant primarily to inform the Administrator of the nature and circumstances of the dispute so as to facilitate the designation of the arbitrators. The short answer can also contain the preferences of the respondent with regard to the particulars of the arbitral proceedings (see below). No specific form is prescribed for the short answer. Just as for the request for arbitration, a simple letter will suffice. As mentioned above, the NAI Rules explicitly provide that the filing of a short answer does not prejudice the right of the respondent to submit a statement of defence, once the arbitral tribunal has been constituted (see Articles 8 and 24(1)).

4.1. Defence

As the respondent will have the opportunity to elaborate on its defences in the statement of defence, it will generally depend on the content of the request for arbitration and the circumstances of the case how much the respondent chooses to state in the short answer. There are, however, a few matters on which the respondent should comment in the short answer, because the respondent is not allowed to do so at a later stage.

4.2. Preference for Number of Arbitrators, Place of Arbitration, Further Particulars as to Arbitral Procedure

If the parties did not agree on the number of arbitrators or the place of arbitration in the arbitration agreement, the short answer should contain the respondent's preferences, if any, in this respect (see Article 7(2)), in order to allow the Administrator to take these preferences into account when composing the list of possible arbitrators. The short answer should also include any comments the respondent may have as to other particulars of the arbitral procedure, such as the method of appointment (if the parties agreed on a method of appointment different from the list-procedure), the nomination of an arbitrator (if the parties agreed to nominate arbitrators themselves), the language of the arbitration and, as a practical matter, any preferences as to the qualifications of the arbitrators favoured by the respondent. The respondent may also include prior agreements between the parties on witness statements, the possibility of a statement of reply and rejoinder, or – failing such agreements – the respondent may indicate its preferences in this respect.

4.3. Counterclaim(s)

In the short answer, the respondent may introduce a counterclaim (Article 7(3)), provided that the respondent's counterclaim falls under the same arbitration agreement (see also Article 25(2)). It is not possible for the respondent to introduce a counterclaim against a co-respondent; this will have to be done by means of a claim for indemnity (see Article 41(3)). The wording of Article 25(2) also precludes counterclaims that are based on other arbitration agreements between the same parties, even if such counterclaim is closely related to the principal claim or another counterclaim. In these cases the respondent in principle has no other option than to initiate separate arbitration proceedings and subsequently seek consolidation. Practice shows that other solutions may also be explored, for example by requesting the Administrator to appoint the same arbitrators in all arbitrations. Although it is recommended that the existence of a counterclaim is known as early as possible in the proceedings (especially in view of the selection and appointment of the arbitrator(s)), the respondent is not obliged to introduce counterclaim(s) in the short answer, but may also do so at a later stage, (but, in principle, no later than) in the statement of defence (see Article 25(1)).[94] The arbitral tribunal, in exceptional circumstances, may approve the introduction of the counterclaim at a later stage after the statement of defence. We do not know of examples of arbitral tribunals allowing such late counterclaims. Amendments to counterclaims are, however, a common feature (see the comments on Article 34). Such amendments can sometimes be far-reaching. The difference

---

[94] This is different under, for example, the ICC Rules, where any counterclaim(s) made by the respondent must be filed with its answer to the request for arbitration (see Art. 5(5) ICC Rules).

between a new counterclaim and an amendment to an existing counterclaim may be difficult to establish. Practice indicates that arbitral tribunals are more reluctant to accept fully new claims than to allow a substantial amendment to a claim already made.

If the respondent decides to submit a counterclaim in the short answer, the requirements of Article 6(3)(c)-(e) apply accordingly to the counterclaim (see Article 7(3)). Hence, the respondent must provide a brief description of the dispute giving rise to the counterclaim (Article 6(3)(c)), as well as a clear description of what is claimed (Article 6(3)(d)). To the extent possible, the description of the relief sought by the respondent should include an indication of any amounts claimed, in order for the Administrator to fix the administration costs due by the respondent in relation to its counterclaim (see Article 57(3)). In the event of a counterclaim, the short answer must also contain a reference to the arbitration agreement, a copy of which must be submitted with the short answer (Article 6(3)(e)). This arbitration agreement will in principle be the same as the one submitted by the claimant with the request for arbitration, given that a counterclaim is only admissible if it falls within the scope of the arbitration agreement on which the request for arbitration is based (see Article 25(2), mentioned in Article 7(3)). For this reason a simple reference to the arbitration agreement already submitted with the request for arbitration will normally suffice.

Contrary to, for example, the ICC Rules,[95] the NAI Rules do not provide for the submission of a short answer by the original claimant as a reply to the counterclaim raised by the respondent in its short answer. The request for arbitration and the short answer only serve as an introduction to the arbitration and to ensure that parties will have (and will be given) sufficient opportunity to respond to each other's claims once the arbitrators have been appointed. The original claimant can, however, express its views on the counterclaim and a possible plea as to lack of jurisdiction in a simple letter. Given the nature of the short answer we see no reason why the original claimant should be prevented from doing so. The legal relevance of such letter is of course limited, if not non-existent.

Counterclaims by the original claimant in response to the respondent's counterclaims are non-existent features. If a counterclaim gives rise to further claims, the original claimant should use its right to amend its claims on the basis of Article 34.

4.4. Plea as to Lack of Jurisdiction

Unlike some other arbitration rules,[96] the NAI Rules do not require the respondent to raise any objections that it may have to the jurisdiction of the arbitrators in the short answer. The Administrator does not formally examine whether the parties

---

[95] See Art. 5(6) ICC Rules.

[96] See, for example, Art. 15(3) ICDR Rules.

have agreed to arbitration under the NAI Rules. It is up to the arbitral tribunal to decide on any plea as to lack of jurisdiction raised by the respondent. A respondent wishing to raise a plea as to lack of jurisdiction must do so in a timely manner, and not later than in the statement of defence, or, failing such statement, before any written or oral defence. In this respect, Article 9(2) explicitly provides that the short answer does not constitute a defence. For the sake of procedural economy, however, it is recommended (also by the NAI) that the respondent raises a plea as to lack of jurisdiction in the short answer.

In practice, the Administrator will try to avoid processing a request for arbitration, if an arbitration agreement is manifestly absent or if the arbitration agreement clearly refers to arbitration with another institute or clearly does not refer to the NAI Rules. It is regarded as good practice to inform a claimant if the request for arbitration is clearly based on a misunderstanding. This practice is, however, only of an informal nature and the Administrator will only contact the claimant in clear-cut cases. In other cases, or if the claimant wishes the jurisdiction to be examined by arbitrators, the Administrator will proceed with processing the request for arbitration by forwarding the same to the respondent and by initiating the nomination of arbitrators.

Thus, in short, the NAI Rules do not include a formal mechanism like Article 6(2) of the ICC Rules, which Article stipulates that the ICC Court must determine whether it is *prima facie* satisfied that an arbitration agreement exists that refers to arbitration under the ICC rules before a tribunal is constituted. The obvious disadvantage of the NAI not having such a mechanism is that defendants may be dragged into a procedure before an arbitral tribunal that may take months and may be costly, even in cases where it is rather self evident that the tribunal, once constituted will have to conclude that it lacks jurisdiction. It is therefore very important that the Administrator of the NAI takes seriously the informal role of contacting the claimant in such case to discuss the perceived lack of jurisdiction with the claimant. Relevant experience shows that this informal mechanism can be very effective.

ARTICLE 8 – PURPOSE OF REQUEST FOR ARBITRATION AND SHORT ANSWER

The request for arbitration and the short answer serve as an introduction to the arbitral procedure. They do not prejudice the right of the parties to submit a statement of claim and a statement of defence, respectively, in accordance with the provisions of Article 24. To the extent that the Administrator is involved in the determination of the number and/or the appointment of the arbitrator(s), he shall draw the required information from the request for arbitration and the short answer.

---

1.   General Comments

This article lays down the aforementioned principle that the request for arbitration and the short answer serve (only) as an introduction to the arbitral procedure and do not prejudice the right of the parties to raise further defences and (counter)claims at a later stage in the arbitral proceedings, in the statement of claim and statement of defence. As also indicated above, the information in the request and the short answer is meant primarily to inform the Administrator of the nature and circumstances of the dispute so as to facilitate the appointment of the arbitrators (to the extent that the Administrator is involved in determining the number of the arbitrators and/or their appointment). The principle laid down in Article 8 also explains why the request and the short answer are not exhaustive in the sense that the parties would be barred from raising claims, pleas or defences that have not been raised in the request or the short answer. By the same token changes to the claims and the counterclaims compared to those described in the request for arbitration and the short answer are not regarded as amendments of claims within the meaning of Article 34.

ARTICLE 9 – PLEA AS TO LACK OF ARBITRATION AGREEMENT

1. A party who participated in the appointment of the arbitrator(s) in the manner provided in the third section shall not be barred from raising the plea that the arbitral tribunal lacks jurisdiction on the ground that there is no valid arbitration agreement.
2. A respondent who appears in the arbitral proceedings and wishes to raise the plea that the arbitral tribunal lacks jurisdiction on the ground that there is no valid arbitration agreement shall raise this plea before submitting any defence. Accordingly, this plea shall be raised ultimately in the statement of defence or, in the absence thereof, prior to the first written or oral defence. For the purpose of this paragraph, the short answer referred to in Article 7 shall not be deemed to constitute a defence.
3. If a respondent fails to raise this plea before submitting any defence, as provided in the previous paragraph, he shall be barred from doing so thereafter in the arbitral proceedings or in proceedings before a court unless the plea is made on the ground that the dispute is not capable of settlement by arbitration.
4. A plea that the arbitral tribunal lacks jurisdiction shall be decided by the arbitral tribunal.
5. An arbitration agreement shall be considered and decided upon as a separate agreement. The arbitral tribunal shall have the power to decide on the validity of the contract of which the arbitration agreement forms part or to which the arbitration agreement is related.

6. A plea that the arbitral tribunal lacks jurisdiction shall not preclude the NAI from administering the arbitration.

1. General Comments

It is a generally accepted principle, also under Dutch law, that the arbitral tribunal has the authority to rule on its own jurisdiction (competence-competence). Hence, it is at the arbitral tribunal's discretion to decide on a plea as to lack of jurisdiction raised by the respondent. Article 9 lays down how and when a plea as to lack of jurisdiction of the arbitral tribunal must be raised, and what the powers of the arbitral tribunal are in this respect.

2. Pleas as to the Lack of Jurisdiction of the Tribunal

Pursuant to Article 9(2), a respondent wishing to invoke the lack of a (valid) arbitration agreement referring disputes to NAI arbitration, must do so in a timely manner. At the latest, a plea as to lack of jurisdiction must be raised in the statement of defence, or, failing such statement, before any written or oral defence. The participation of the respondent in the appointment of the arbitrators is not considered implicit acceptance of their jurisdiction and hence, does not prevent the respondent from raising the plea as to lack of jurisdiction (see Article 9(1)).

Article 9(6) provides that a plea as to lack of jurisdiction does not preclude the NAI from administering the arbitration.

If the respondent does not timely (i.e. in the statement of defence or, as the case may be, prior to the first written or oral defence) raise a plea as to lack of jurisdiction of the arbitral tribunal, Article 9(3) provides that the respondent forfeits the right to do so later in the arbitral proceedings or in proceedings before a court, unless the plea is made on the ground that the dispute is not capable of being settled by arbitration (lack of arbitrability). Whether a dispute is capable of being settled by arbitration will depend on the (mandatory) arbitration law of the country in which the arbitration is seated.

> See for the issue of arbitrability under Dutch law, Part I, Chapter 2, Section 2, and the comments on Article 3.

3. Tribunal Decides on its Own Jurisdiction (Competence-Competence)

Article 9(4) provides that a plea as to lack of jurisdiction shall be decided by the arbitral tribunal. This provision lays down the internationally accepted principle of competence-competence (also referred to as *Kompetenz-Kompetenz*), which means that the arbitral tribunal is competent to decide on its own jurisdiction.[97]

---

[97] The principle of competence-competence is also laid down in: Art. 21(1) UNCITRAL Rules, Art. 15(1) ICDR Rules, Art. 23.1 LCIA Rules, Art. 6(2) ICC Rules.

Irrespective of the applicable decision standard, the arbitral tribunal must always decide on its jurisdiction in accordance with the rules of law.[98] The principle of competence-competence prevents a party from being able to intentionally delay the arbitral proceedings by challenging the jurisdiction of the tribunal before the courts.

> In two different cases in which the claimant had initiated both arbitral proceedings and proceedings before a state court, the The Hague District Court and the Groningen District Court ruled that the principle of competence-competence entails that the court has to refrain from a decision on its competence to hear the claim for as long as the dispute is pending before an arbitral tribunal.[99] In both cases the claimant had chosen to initiate the arbitral proceedings prior to addressing the state courts. The outcome of the cases could have been different, if the claimant had done this the other way around. Whenever a state court is addressed and a plea as to lack of jurisdiction is introduced on the ground that the case should be resolved by arbitration, the state court has to deal with this defence in order to establish its own jurisdiction. In our view state courts cannot refuse rendering a full-fledged decision in this respect simply because the defence relates to arbitration. The principle of competence-competence entails that arbitrators can decide on their own jurisdiction, even if accepting jurisdiction implies that the jurisdiction of the state courts is denied by the tribunal, and even if the result of the arbitral tribunal's assessment would be that it has no jurisdiction at all. However, the principle of competence-competence does not prevent state courts from performing their own tasks and assessing their own jurisdiction in full, whenever they are requested to do so.

The parties will first have to await the tribunal's decision on its jurisdiction before being able to challenge the tribunal's competence before the courts (if the arbitral tribunal decided it is competent to hear the claim) or to bring the claim before the courts (if the arbitral tribunal decided that it lacks jurisdiction). For avoidance of doubt, it is thus mentioned that the competence-competence principle does not mean that the arbitral tribunal also has the last and final say on the issue of jurisdiction: the state courts will have that last and final word.

If the arbitral tribunal decides that it is competent to hear the claim, such decision will normally be laid down in an interim arbitral award (following which the arbitration will continue), but may also be given in a (partial) final arbitral award. The NAI Rules do not oblige the tribunal to rule on a jurisdictional plea prior to considering the merits of the case and issuing a final award. However, if the respondent only submits a plea as to the lack of jurisdiction, this will force the arbitral tribunal to rule on such jurisdictional plea prior to considering the merits of the case. From a perspective of procedural economy, an early decision on jurisdiction has the advantage of avoiding the possibly

---

[98] Burg. Rv, 2006 (H.J. Snijders), Art. 1052 DCCP, note 1.

[99] See Groningen District Court 13 Oct. 2004, BR 2005, 162 and TvA 2006, 144-145, with an annotation by B.C. Punt; The Hague District Court 19 May 2004, BR 2004, 632.

unnecessary devotion of time and energy to the merits of the case for as long as there is a possibility that the tribunal may hold that it does not have jurisdiction. If the decision that the tribunal has jurisdiction is laid down in an interim award, an action for the setting aside of the decision on jurisdiction in the interim award can only be initiated together with an action for the setting aside of a later (partial) final award, since interim awards cannot be challenged separately in setting aside proceedings. This means that the parties will have to continue the arbitral proceedings before they may challenge the competence of the arbitral tribunal before the courts. If on the other hand the arbitral tribunal denies its jurisdiction, the claimant has in principle no other option than to initiate legal proceedings before the competent state court or – as the case may be – arbitration under the arbitration rules that have been established to be applicable.

It is a matter of discussion whether or not a declaration by the tribunal that it lacks jurisdiction can be given in the form of an arbitral award.[100] An argument pleading against this is that it would be illogical to assume that a valid arbitral award can be rendered when the decision of the arbitral tribunal implies the exact opposite, i.e. that the tribunal lacks jurisdiction and hence, is not competent to render an award.[101] A practical argument pleading in favour of this is that the respondent who successfully raises a plea as to lack of jurisdiction of the tribunal will feel the need for an enforceable award insofar as the decision as to costs is concerned. Should the tribunal take the view that it is not competent to render any decision, other than to decide that it lacks jurisdiction, then that tribunal would not have the power to decide that the costs of the procedure and defendant's costs should be borne by claimant. This seems an undesirable result, especially in those cases where the attempt to have a dispute decided in arbitration is frivolous (as mentioned above, given the lack of a formal mechanism like provided by Article 6(2) ICC Rules, even such frivolous cases may take months and turn out to be costly). In practice most arbitral tribunals seem to adopt the practical approach by simply giving the declaration in the form of an arbitral award. On point case law from Dutch state courts is not available.

The NAI Rules provide for a construction to circumvent the above discussion, which, however, requires the cooperation of all parties involved. As stated in para. 7.3 of the Introduction to NAI Arbitration Rules, the parties may conclude a separate arbitration agreement to which the NAI Rules will apply in respect of the issue of jurisdiction. A standard form for this purpose can be obtained from the Administrator. By entering into such a separate arbitration agreement, the parties

---

[100] See for example Meijer, 2008, para. 11.4.4.4; O.L.O. de Witt Wijnen, 'Noot TvA inzake het scheids-rechterlijk vonnis van onbevoegdheid: Een beetje zwanger kan alleen bij wet', TvA 2000, 67-70, and 'Naschrift bij het artikel van prof. mr. H.J. Snijders "Een beetje zwanger kan niet, maar een beetje bevoegd wel" ', TvA 2000, 151; Burg. Rv, 2006 (H.J. Snijders), Art. 1052 DCCP, note 5.

[101] See the Introduction to the NAI Arbitration Rules, para. 5.3.

cover a situation that is generally considered an imperfection in the law. If no separate arbitration agreement is made, the NAI is not precluded nevertheless from administering the arbitration pursuant to Article 9(6).

> Article 1052 DCCP contains a similar provision on the jurisdiction of the arbitral tribunal, except for Article 1052(3) DCCP, which provides – in addition to the NAI Rules – that a party who cooperated in appointing the arbitrators is barred from raising the plea as to lack of jurisdiction, either in the arbitration or before a state court, on the ground that the arbitral tribunal has been composed in violation with the applicable rules (see Article 1052(3) DCCP). However, Article 1027(4) DCCP provides, similar to Article 9(1) that a party who cooperated in appointing the arbitrators is not prevented from raising the plea that the arbitral tribunal lacks jurisdiction on the ground that there is no valid arbitration agreement. Article 1052(3) DCCP only applies, if the parties cooperate in appointing the arbitrators without raising any objections. The party that cooperates reluctantly after raising complaints will not forfeit its right to raise the plea as to lack of jurisdiction. In addition, cooperation in appointing the arbitrators does not bar the right to raise a plea as to lack of jurisdiction on the ground that the arbitral tribunal has been composed in violation with the applicable rules, if an even number of arbitrators has been appointed. Such appointment being in conflict with public order can be challenged in any event (see Part III, Chapter 1 in regard of Article 1065(1)(e) DCCP).
>
> If the arbitral tribunal decides that it lacks jurisdiction, the state courts will regain jurisdiction, unless the parties agreed otherwise (either before or after the declaration by the tribunal that it lacks jurisdiction) (see Article 1052(5) DCCP).

If the declaration that the arbitral tribunal lacks jurisdiction is given in the form of an arbitral award, such award constitutes a final award, which is subject to a possible challenge in setting aside proceedings.

4.   Separability of the Arbitration Agreement

Article 9(5) embodies the principle of separability of the arbitration agreement.[102] The first sentence of Article 9(5) provides that the agreement to arbitrate has to be considered and decided upon as a separate agreement. The second sentence of Article 9(5) states that the arbitral tribunal has the power to decide on the validity of the contract of which the agreement to arbitrate forms a part or to which the arbitration agreement relates.

The separability (also referred to as the autonomy) of the arbitration agreement entails that the arbitral tribunal has to decide on the validity of the main contract (e.g., a sale and purchase agreement) separately from the validity of the arbitration agreement concluded in relation to and/or included in the main contract. The essential function of the principle of separability is evident: this

---

[102] This principle is also laid down in: Art. 21(2) UNCITRAL Rules, Art. 6(4) ICC Rules, Art. 15(2) ICDR Rules, Art. 23.1 LCIA Rules.

principle prevents the tribunal from undermining its own jurisdiction by declaring the main agreement null and void, terminated or otherwise invalid and thus ensures that an arbitral award holding that the main contract is invalid, is considered valid. In other words: the mere fact that the main contract may be invalid does not suffice to invalidate the arbitration agreement contained therein. However, this does not prevent the arbitral tribunal from finding the arbitration agreement also to be invalid, if the relevant facts and circumstances specifically support such a finding. Unlike the ICC Rules[103] the NAI Rules do not explicitly provide that the arbitral tribunal shall continue to have jurisdiction, if it is established that the main contract is non-existent.[104] It is assumed, however, that the same rule applies pursuant to the principle of separability.[105]

Article 9(5) reproduces verbatim the text of Article 1053 DCCP.

---

[103] Art. 6(4) ICC Rules.

[104] Neither does the DCCP.

[105] See Burg. Rv, 2006 (H.J. Snijders), Art. 1053 DCCP, note 1 for a summary of the discussion whether under Dutch law, the principle of separability also applies in the case of non-existence of the main contract.

APPOINTMENT OF ARBITRATORS
(Articles 10-19)

The provisions of the NAI Rules on the appointment of arbitrators can be divided into three types of provisions: (i) a group of mandatory general provisions (Articles 10, 11, 15, 16), (ii) a group of articles from which the parties are free to derogate (Articles 12-14) and (iii) a group of articles on the release, challenge and replacement of arbitrators (Articles 17-19).

The NAI Rules in this section contain a number of principles that are fundamental to the NAI arbitration process. Most importantly, the NAI Rules allow parties autonomy with regard to the (method of) appointment of the arbitral tribunal. The parties are free to agree on the number of arbitrators and the method of appointment and they are also free to designate the arbitrator(s) of their choice without regard to a panel of approved arbitrators, although the Administrator may refuse to administer the arbitration if one or more of the arbitrators who were appointed by the parties, in the opinion of the Administrator, do not offer sufficient safeguards for a sound arbitration. Although the NAI Rules have much in common with other arbitration rules concerning the appointment of arbitrators, the NAI Rules contain a few distinctive features, of which the most important is the list-procedure of Article 14. Furthermore, contrary to most other arbitration rules, the NAI Rules contain a separate procedure for the challenging of an arbitrator (Article 19).

ARTICLE 10 – IMPARTIALITY AND INDEPENDENCE OF ARBITRATORS

1. The arbitrator shall be impartial and independent. He may not have close personal or professional relationship with a co-arbitrator or with any of the parties. He may not have any direct personal or professional interest in the outcome of the case. He may not, prior to his appointment, disclose his opinion on the case to one of the parties.

> 2. In the course of the proceedings an arbitrator shall not have any contacts with a party concerning matters regarding the proceedings unless he has obtained prior consent of the other parties and, if the tribunal consists of more than one arbitrator, of the co-arbitrators.

1. General Comments

It is a general rule in (international) arbitration that all the arbitrators, including those chosen and/or appointed by the parties,[106] must be impartial towards any of the parties and carry out their functions impartially and without bias.[107] The same applies to the secretary to the arbitral tribunal. Most arbitration rules contain provisions on the impartiality and independence of arbitrators.[108] Article 19 states that an arbitrator may be challenged if there is reasonable doubt about the arbitrator's impartiality and independence.

> The Dutch arbitration act does not contain a similar single provision on impartiality and independence, but Article 1033 DCCP – like Article 19 of the NAI Rules – states that an arbitrator may be challenged if there is reasonable doubt about the arbitrator's impartiality and independence.

Examples from Dutch case law on Article 1033 DCCP (see above) will be used in order to further define the (practical) meaning of the requirements of independence and impartiality as mentioned in the NAI Rules. The comments on this article will also be relevant for Articles 11 (disclosure in case of doubt as to impartiality and independence) and 19 (challenge of arbitrator in case of reasonable doubt as to his impartiality or independence).

2. Definitions of Impartiality and Independence (Article 10(1))

Article 10(1) specifies the requirements of independence and/or impartiality for an arbitrator, by stating that an arbitrator: (i) may not have a close personal or professional relationship with a co-arbitrator or with any of the parties, (ii) may not have any direct personal or professional interest in the outcome of the case and (iii) may not, prior to his appointment, disclose his opinion on the case to one of the parties. These requirements are discussed separately below.

At the outset, it is important to note that according to standard case law in the Netherlands the *outward appearance of partiality* may – under certain

---

[106] See for an example under Dutch arbitration law: Amsterdam Court of Appeal 13 Feb. 1994, NJ 1996, 8 in which the court emphasized that also a party-appointed arbitrator has to be independent and impartial.

[107] See for example Derains and Schwartz, 2005, 116.

[108] See for example Art. 7(1) ICC Rules, Art. 7(1) ICDR Rules, Art. 5.2 LCIA Rules and Art. 22(a) WIPO Arbitration Rules.

circumstances – also be relevant when establishing whether there is sufficient cause to challenge an arbitrator on the basis of Article 1033 DCCP,[109] whereas the outward appearance of partiality is insufficient for the setting aside of an arbitral award (see Article 1065 DCCP, note 6 in Part III, Chapter 1). Thus different tests have to be met, depending on whether the arbitrator's impartiality is assessed in the context of either a challenge of the arbitrator or the arbitral award in setting aside proceedings.

Furthermore, the IBA Guidelines[110] may serve as a tool in order to further define the concepts of impartiality and independence. The IBA Guidelines contain General Standards, a Red List of those circumstances affecting impartiality and independence that cannot be waived by the parties, a Red List of those circumstances that may be waived, an Orange List of circumstances that should be disclosed by an arbitrator, and that may or may not affect his impartiality or independence depending on further specifics and circumstances of the case at hand, and a Green list of circumstances that do not even need to be disclosed. Although the IBA Guidelines have no binding effect, they are relied upon in arbitrations and court proceedings and there seems to be a tendency to rely on these guidelines for establishing good practice in international arbitration. The IBA Guidelines therefore constitute a point of view that cannot be ignored. The IBA Guidelines are the more relevant, since the list of prohibitions in Article 10 is rather arbitrary and the IBA Guidelines provide a much more detailed picture of possible relationships that affect or are likely to affect an arbitrator's impartiality.

Finally, it should be noted from the outset that the foregoing only relates to the notion of impartiality when discussed and assessed in the context of disputes aimed at either challenging an arbitrator or the setting aside of an arbitral award. In practice, the Administrator and arbitrators may adhere to a much stricter policy. The Administrator will try to avoid appointing an arbitrator when the arbitrator's impartiality may become an issue. In addition, some arbitrators tend to withdraw from a case as arbitrator, whenever their impartiality is challenged. The Administrator's and the arbitrator's policy to be on the safe side can easily lead to a more stringent policy than strictly necessary. Yet it is desirable in practice to be on the safe side, most certainly at the outset of the case, so as to avoid that the procedure is disrupted by challenges or even to avoid that a later award is set aside. On the other hand, the caution applied should not serve to allow a party to disqualify an arbitrator that the party does not like by making frivolous allegations as to his perceived lack of independence.

---

[109] HR 18 Feb. 1994, NJ 1994, 765 (Nordström/Nigoco). See also HR 29 Jun. 2007, RvdW 2007, 630.
[110] See <www.ibanet.org>.

2.1. Close Relationship

Especially part (i) of the definition, which prohibits an arbitrator from having a close personal or professional relationship with a co-arbitrator or with any of the parties, may lead to disagreement between parties in the circumstances of a particular case. For example, the article does not clarify whether only 'close relationships' existing at the time of the appointment of the arbitrator and during the arbitration are relevant, or that past relationships – that have ended prior to the appointment of the arbitrator – may also lead to a proscribed 'close relationship'. The article also does not make clear whether a close relationship with a party includes that party's counsel. In this respect, the ICC Rules may serve as decisive guidance as to the meaning of the notion of 'close relationship' under the NAI Rules. The ICC Court requires all prospective arbitrators to disclose (see Article 7(2) ICC Rules):

> '*inter alia*, whether there exists any *past or present* relationship, *direct or indirect*, with any of the parties, *their counsel*, whether financial, professional or of another kind (. . .)'.[111]

We contend that the same applies under Article 10(1) of the NAI Rules. This is confirmed by case law, where the notion of impartiality was construed in line with the above-mentioned requirement.[112] The mere fact that an arbitrator personally knows (the counsel of) a party, does not necessarily establish a close relationship. This may be different if the arbitrator regularly sees (the counsel of) a party on a personal basis.[113] We note that in Dutch arbitration practice, especially in the larger cases, it is not at all uncommon that the parties' counsel and one or more arbitrators have personal or professional relations of some sort that might qualify as 'close'. The Dutch arbitration community is simply not large enough to prevent this altogether. In these cases, it seems advisable for arbitrators to widely disclose yet to not necessarily conclude that doubts as to the lack of independence or impartiality are justified. Parties and their counsel often accept such arbitrators in case of a clear disclosure.

2.2. Interest in the Outcome of the Case

Part (ii) of the definition prohibits an arbitrator from having a direct personal or professional interest in the outcome of the case. Such interest – or at least the

---

[111] Derains and Schwartz, 2005, 121-122 (emphasis added).

[112] See for example President (*voorzieningenrechter*) of the Amsterdam District Court 29 Dec. 1988, TvA 1989, 103-106. The President of the Amsterdam District Court ruled that it is not only the (close) relationship between the arbitrator and the parties that is relevant, but also the relationship between the arbitrator and counsel to the parties.

[113] Orange List of the IBA Guidelines, Section 3.3.6 contains the following relationship between an arbitrator and a counsel: 'A close personal relationship exists between an arbitrator and a counsel of one party, as demonstrated by the fact that the arbitrator and the counsel regularly spend considerable time together unrelated to professional work commitments or the activities of professional

appearance thereof – is amongst others assumed, if the arbitrator is simultaneously acting as counsel in proceedings in which the same or similar issues are at stake. There is an obvious risk that the arbitrator may be reluctant to decide contrary to the position that he is defending as counsel in other proceedings. To put it differently, there is a risk that the arbitrator may be inclined to generate case law in favour of his client.[114]

On the other hand, case law seems to indicate that a (possible) arbitrator can regain his impartiality by withdrawing as counsel from the conflicting case.[115] On this basis it can be assumed that the impartiality of a possible arbitrator is sufficiently secured, if he discloses his position as counsel and offers to withdraw from the case, if any of the parties indicates to have a problem with this position. It should be noted however that both the parties, the NAI as well as the arbitrator concerned might in such a case be better off if the arbitrator withdrew from the case or declined appointment. The mere fact that strictly speaking an arbitrator could hold on to his position as counsel and accept an appointment, does not mean that this would also be the most desirable option for the parties and the proceedings to follow.

2.3. Disclosing an Opinion on the Case

According to part (iii) of the definition, an arbitrator may not, prior to his appointment, disclose his opinion on the case to one of the parties. In this respect, communications between a party and a person whom it wishes to nominate are, to a certain extent, inevitable, especially in cases where the parties agreed to nominate the arbitrators themselves. Communications between parties and prospective arbitrators about the arbitrator's qualifications, background and even on his general views are universally regarded as acceptable.[116] However, a prospective arbitrator may lose his impartiality or independence if he – prior to his appointment – discusses the merits of the case with one of the parties. Although it should in principle be possible to provide the arbitrator with information on the nature of the dispute and the issues at stake in general terms, the prospective arbitrator is advised to refrain from making any comments at all about the merits of the case.[117] The above does not apply to an arbitrator who has previously published a general opinion concerning an issue which also arises in the arbitration (but this opinion is not focused on the case that is being arbitrated).[118]

[   ] associations or social organizations.' Orange List of the IBA Guidelines, Section 3.4.3 contains a similar relationship between an arbitrator and a party and others involved in the arbitration.

[114] President (*voorzieningenrechter*) of The Hague District Court 18 Oct. 2004, TvA 2005, 106-109.

[115] President (*voorzieningenrechter*) of The Hague District Court 5 Oct. 2004, TvA 2005, 109-111.

[116] Derains and Schwartz, 2005, 131; IBA Guidelines Green list, Section 4.5.1.

[117] Waivable Red List of the IBA Guidelines, Section 2.1.1 contains the following relationship of the arbitrator to the dispute: 'The arbitrator has given legal advice or provided an expert opinion on the dispute to a party or an affiliate of one of the parties.'

[118] See also Green List of the IBA Guidelines, Section 4.1.1. This may be different if the arbitrator has publicly advocated a specific position regarding the case that is being arbitrated, whether in a published paper or speech or otherwise (Orange List of the IBA Guidelines, Section 3.5.2).

3. Article 10(2)

According to Article 10(2), an arbitrator may not have contacts with one of the parties without the other party being present concerning matters regarding the proceedings. An exception to this rule has been made when the arbitrator has obtained prior consent of the other parties and the co-arbitrators (if any).[119] Although this article primarily appears to address contacts with regard to procedural or practical matters, an arbitrator obviously is also not allowed to discuss the merits of the case with one of the parties during the arbitration (see also note 2). With the modern means of communication there is actually no need for one-to-one contacts between the arbitral tribunal and the parties. There is no reason not to set up a telephone conference or e-mail discussion, if the arbitral tribunal feels the need to discuss an issue with one of the parties. Having contact with only one of the parties without the other party being involved, can easily lead to the arbitrator losing his appearance of impartiality. There have been successful challenges on this ground in the past. In order to avoid discussion on this point, it is advisable that the arbitral tribunal (or the chairman of the arbitral tribunal, with consent of the other arbitrators) always speaks to the parties jointly (in a conference call or otherwise).

4. Standards for Arbitrator's Examination of Evidence

Apart from Article 10(1) and (2), an arbitrator must ensure that he remains impartial and independent during the arbitral proceedings. An arbitrator may not show prejudice, for example by giving his view on the merits of the case at the start of a hearing.

According to case law of the Dutch Supreme Court[120] the rules of impartiality and independence dictate that an arbitrator cannot gather evidence himself outside the parties. The Supreme Court ruled that arbitrators should in principle restrict themselves to the examination of evidence. They may use their specific expertise to resolve the dispute, but if this were to require them to conduct their own inquiry, they may only do so if the parties have given them explicit permission to base their judgments on their own findings. If an arbitrator himself conducts an examination of the facts, he may later have to weigh his own conclusion against those of a party-appointed expert contesting the validity of the findings of the arbitrator. Such party may justifiably doubt that the arbitrator will be impartial towards the conclusions of the party-appointed expert and not favour his own conclusion.

---

[119] The principle that no party or anyone acting on its behalf may have any ex parte communication relating to the case with any arbitrator or any candidate for appointment as arbitrator is also laid down in other arbitration rules. See for example Art. 7(2) ICDR Rules and Art. 21 WIPO Arbitration Rules.

[120] HR 29 Jun. 2007, NJ 2008, 177. See for a discussion of this judgment also *Global Arbitration Review*, The European & Middle Eastern Arbitration Review 2008, 56.

As a result of this judgment of the Dutch Supreme Court, arbitrators – and especially arbitrators who have been selected and appointed for their specific expertise – may only conduct their own inquiry with the explicit approval of the parties. Failing such approval, the impartiality and independence of the investigating arbitrator is at stake.

On the basis of the present status of Dutch case law it is clear that any arbitrator conducting his own investigation in regard of the facts, without the prior explicit consent of the parties, loses his appearance of impartiality. It could be argued that the same applies to the other arbitrators, composing the arbitral tribunal, if the arbitral tribunal renders a decision on the basis of the outcome of the first arbitrator's investigation. If the other arbitrators are aware of the fact that the first arbitrator has been conducting his own investigation outside the parties, but nevertheless choose to rely on his findings, it seems reasonable that the other arbitrators share the first arbitrator's lot. In general, it is arguable that any arbitrator who resolves a dispute on the basis of information that has been obtained irregularly, loses his appearance of impartiality. If, for example, an arbitrator relies on a letter that has not been produced by one of the parties, but has been acquired by himself on his own initiative, this affects his appearance of impartiality. The same goes for arbitrators who are relying on expert opinions that have been generated in the absence of the parties. Accordingly, the habit of some arbitrators to organize a pre-meeting with the tribunal-appointed expert prior to the hearing set for examining this same expert raises serious questions. The Dutch Supreme Court's approach logically leads to the conclusion that an arbitral tribunal's decision that is based on the outcome of the investigations by arbitrators in the absence of the parties and without the parties' prior explicit consent, does not only entail that the arbitral tribunal's awards are likely to become subject to challenges in setting aside proceedings on the basis of Article 1065(1)(e) DCCP, but also that the arbitrators' appearance of impartiality is no longer secured.

The above applies to investigations in regard of the facts. It is not clear what the Dutch Supreme Court's approach will be in regard to issues of law, including issues of foreign law. State courts in the Netherlands are supposed to apply the law ex officio pursuant to Article 25 DCCP. This rule does not only apply to Dutch law, but is generally assumed to cover foreign law as well, although the state courts may require the parties to advise on the contents of the applicable foreign law and may draw the appropriate conclusions, if a party fails to do so.[121] There is, however, no similar provision in the Dutch arbitration act or in the NAI Rules. It is even more ambiguous what the proper approach should be in international arbitrations, where it may even be difficult to establish which law has to be regarded as foreign law, taking into account the various

---

[121] See M.V. Polak 2008 (T&C Rv), Introductory notes to Book 1, Title 1, Section 7 DCCP, note 1(b).

nationalities involved and where the parties may stem from jurisdictions that are not familiar with the approach solicited by Article 25 DCCP.[122]

5. Secretary to the Arbitral Tribunal

Article 10 also applies to the secretary to the arbitral tribunal.

ARTICLE 11 – DISCLOSURE IN CASE OF DOUBT AS TO IMPARTIALITY AND INDEPENDENCE

1. If a person invited to be appointed as arbitrator believes that he might be challenged, he shall so notify the person by whom he has been invited, such notice to be in writing and to state the probable grounds for such challenge.
2. If the person referred to in paragraph (1) has already been appointed as arbitrator, he shall also send the Administrator the notice as referred to in that paragraph, if the invitation relating to his appointment was not made by the Administrator. The Administrator shall send copies of the notice to the parties and, if the arbitral tribunal is composed of more than one arbitrator, to the other arbitrators.
3. If pending the arbitration proceedings an arbitrator believes that he might be challenged, he shall so notify in writing the probable grounds for such challenge, and the Administrator shall send copies of the notice to the parties and, if the arbitral tribunal is composed of more than one arbitrator, to the other arbitrators.

1. Disclosure Before the Commencement of the Proceedings

According to Article 11(1), the (prospective) arbitrator has a duty to disclose the existence of grounds which may give rise to a challenge.[123] On the basis of Article 19, an arbitrator may be challenged if circumstances exist that give rise to justifiable doubt as to his impartiality or independence.[124]

---

[122] See in this respect also G. Kaufmann-Kohler, 'The Arbitrator and the Law: Does He/She Know It? Apply It? How? And a Few More Questions', *Arbitration International* 21, No. 4 (2005), 631-638.

[123] For example, Art. 7(2) ICC Rules provides that a prospective arbitrator shall sign a statement of independence and disclose in writing any facts or circumstances which might be of such nature as to call into question the arbitrator's independence in the eyes of the parties. The same is provided by Art. 5.3 LCIA Rules. The language of the ICC provision differs from the more conventional wording in other arbitration rules, such as the NAI Rules, to disclose all circumstances likely to give rise to justifiable doubts as to the arbitrator's independence (see Art. 7(1) ICDR Rules, Art. 9 UNCITRAL Rules).

[124] See the comments on Art. 10 for a definition of the impartiality and independence of an arbitrator.

The notice given by the prospective arbitrator is relevant, since a challenge cannot be based on grounds that have been revealed by the arbitrator on the basis of Article 11, unless the relevant party notifies the challenge within one week – or two weeks in international arbitrations – after receipt of the arbitrator's notice (see Article 19(3)).

> Article 1034(1) DCCP contains a similar provision on disclosure before the commencement of the arbitral proceedings.

2.   Disclosure Pending the Arbitral Proceedings

If pending the arbitral proceedings an arbitrator believes that he might be challenged (for example because possible grounds for a challenge only became known to him during the arbitral proceedings or because a new relationship gave rise to a possible ground for a challenge), he must notify in writing such grounds to the Administrator. The Administrator must also send copies of the notice to the parties and, if the arbitral tribunal is composed of more than one arbitrator, to the other arbitrators.

Article 11(3) makes explicit the continuing nature of the arbitrator's obligation to disclose during an arbitration. In practice, this means that an arbitrator will have to be attentive to any new relationships that may arise with the parties, their counsel or others during the course of the arbitration.[125] This provision can be particularly burdensome for arbitrators that are associated with a professional organization, such as major law firms and accounting firms and other groups of professional experts. New assignments can easily give rise to a ground for challenge. Many professional organizations accept appointments as arbitrator only after careful consideration of possible future conflicts. Occasionally, however, arbitrators seek their release from their mandate as arbitrator, in order to clear the road for a new assignment. The Administrator and the other parties often have no other option than to accept the arbitrator's release. Under the circumstances the arbitrator's behaviour may be regarded as breach of contract and can result in the arbitrator forfeiting his right to fees.

> Article 1034(2) DCCP contains a similar provision on disclosure during the arbitral proceedings.

3.   Comments on the Disclosed Information

Contrary to – for example – Article 7(2) of the ICC Rules, Article 11 does not give the parties (or the other members of the arbitral tribunal) the opportunity to comment on the disclosed information. In practice however, parties will be given the opportunity to comment on the disclosed information. This will also provide

---

[125]   Derains and Schwartz, 2005, 138.

the Administrator with information on whether the disclosed information gives rise to an objection of one of the parties.

4. Secretary to the Arbitral Tribunal

Article 10 also applies to the secretary to the arbitral tribunal.

ARTICLE 12 – NUMBER OF ARBITRATORS

---

1. If the parties have not agreed on the number of arbitrators, the number shall be determined by the Administrator after the filing of the short answer or, in the absence thereof, after expiration of the period of time for filing the short answer.
2. The Administrator shall determine that the number of arbitrators be one or three, taking into account the preference of the parties, the amount of the claim and of the counterclaim, if any, and the complexity of the case.
3. If the parties agreed on an even number of arbitrators, the latter shall appoint an additional arbitrator who shall act as the chairman of the arbitral tribunal. If within two weeks[*] after acceptance of their mandate, the arbitrators fail to agree on the additional arbitrator, the latter shall, at the request of either party, be appointed in accordance with the list-procedure provided in Article 14.

[*] This period of time is doubled in an international arbitration (art. 5(2)).

---

1. Agreement by the Parties (Article 12(1))

The parties may (and it is advisable to do so) agree on the number of arbitrators (Article 12(1)).[126] This can be done either in the arbitration agreement (or the *compromis*) or by separate agreement. If the parties have agreed on the number of arbitrators, this number should be mentioned in the request for arbitration (see Article 6(3)(h)). Absenting such agreement, a preference for the number of arbitrators may also be included in the request for arbitration and/or the short answer (see Articles 6(3)(j) and 7(2)).

> If the arbitration is seated in the Netherlands, the parties have to take Article 1026 DCCP into account that states that an arbitral tribunal must consist of an odd number of arbitrators (see note 3). See also Article 12(3).

---

[126] If it is to be expected that a dispute may arise that only involves a small amount, it may be advisable not to arrange for the number of arbitrators yet, leaving open the possibility that for such cases only one arbitrator is appointed.

2.   Number Determined by the Administrator (Article 12(2))

If the parties have not agreed on the number of arbitrators, the number will be determined by the Administrator after the filing of the short answer or, in the absence thereof, after expiration of the period of time for filing the short answer. The number of arbitrators determined by the Administrator will be either one or three. The Administrator will take into account the preference of the parties (indicated in the request for arbitration and the short answer; see Articles 6 and 7), the amount of the claim and the complexity of the case. According to the Introduction to NAI Arbitration Rules, the number of arbitrators will in general be three if the material interest of the case exceeds EUR 150,000. In practice, the Administrator will often apply a higher threshold.

3.   Even Number of Arbitrators (Article 12(3))

The designation of one or three arbitrators is the general rule in international arbitration.[127] In practice, parties rarely agree on more than three arbitrators. However, in some jurisdictions, such as England, the law permits the constitution of an arbitral tribunal composed of an even number of arbitrators.[128] It is therefore possible – mainly in international arbitrations – that parties have agreed on two (or another even number of) arbitrators. As the NAI – in accordance with Article 1026(1) DCCP (see below) – may not agree on an arbitral tribunal to consist of an even number of arbitrators, Article 12(3) provides that the two arbitrators will have to appoint an additional arbitrator who will act as the chairman of the arbitral tribunal. In this respect, Article 12(3) stipulates that if within two weeks after acceptance of their mandate, the arbitrators fail to agree on the additional arbitrator, the latter shall, at the request of either party, be appointed in accordance with the list-procedure provided in Article 14.

> Article 1026(1) DCCP states that the arbitral tribunal must consist of an odd number of arbitrators and may also consist of one arbitrator. As this article is (internal) public policy,[129] the parties may not deviate from this provision. Article 1026(3) DCCP contains the same provision as the first sentence of Article 12(3): if the parties agreed on an even number of arbitrators, the latter shall appoint an additional arbitrator who shall act as the chairman of the tribunal. Article 1026(4)

---

[127]   See for example Art. 8(1) ICC Rules.

[128]   There has been criticism in the Netherlands on the impossibility to appoint an even number of arbitrators. See A.J. van den Berg, *Hoe gastvrij is Nederland voor de internationale arbitrage?* Oration Erasmus University Rotterdam (Deventer, Kluwer, 1990).

[129]   Parliamentary History TK 1983-1984, 18.464, No. 3, 36. In the Parliamentary History with regard to Art. 1076 DCCP, which article deals with the enforcement of arbitral awards in the Netherlands, it has been noted that a arbitral award that has been rendered outside the Netherlands by an even number of arbitrators (according to the law of the country in which the arbitral award has been rendered), may be recognized and enforced in the Netherlands, because this would not be contrary to international public policy. An arbitral award that has been rendered by an even number of arbitrators in the Netherlands may not be enforced in the Netherlands, as this is contrary to Dutch public policy.

DCCP provides that if the arbitrators cannot agree on the additional arbitrator, the latter shall be appointed at the request of either party by the President (*voorzieningenrechter*) of the District Court, unless the parties have agreed otherwise. Such agreement is included in Article 12(3), which provides that such arbitrator shall be appointed in accordance with the list-procedure of Article 14.

According to Article 1026(2) DCCP, the parties may ask the President of the District Court to decide on the number of arbitrators, if parties have not agreed on a method of deciding the number of arbitrators, or if the method as agreed on by the parties has not been executed (for example, because the Administrator does not decide on the number of arbitrators according to this agreed method) and the parties cannot yet agree on the number of arbitrators.

ARTICLE 13 – METHOD OF APPOINTMENT AS AGREED BY THE PARTIES

1. If the parties agreed on a method of appointing the arbitrator(s) other than the list-procedure provided in Article 14, the appointment shall take place as agreed by the parties, subject to the provisions of the following paragraphs.

2. If such method of appointment is not complied with wholly or in part within the period of time agreed to by the parties, or, in the absence of such period of time, within four weeks[*] after commencement of the arbitration, the appointment of the arbitrator(s) shall take place in accordance with the list-procedure in Article 14.

3. If one or more of the arbitrators who were appointed by the parties themselves do not, in the opinion of the Administrator, offer sufficient safeguards for a sound arbitration, the Administrator may refuse to administer the arbitration, unless the parties agree to the replacement of such arbitrator in accordance with the list-procedure provided in Article 14.

[*]   This period of time is doubled in an international arbitration (Art. 5(2)).

1.   Method of Appointment as Agreed by the Parties

According to Article 13(1), the parties are free to agree on a method of appointment other than the list-procedure provided in Article 14. The claimant will have to indicate the agreed method of appointment (if different from the list-procedure) and/or the names and address details of the arbitrator(s) in the request for arbitration (see Article 6(3)(f)).[130] The respondent will most likely also indicate this in the short answer. For example, the parties may agree on the appointment

---

[130]   See also Art. 1027 DCCP.

by a third party other than the Administrator. Furthermore, the parties may agree on the situation that each party may appoint its own arbitrator and these two arbitrators will appoint the chairman of the arbitral tribunal, or the chairman will be appointed by a third party, such as the Administrator or the President (*voorzieningenrechter*) of the District Court or any other third party. The parties may also agree on a different method of appointment during the arbitral proceedings, even if the arbitration clause were to lead to the appointment of arbitrators on the basis of the list-procedure.

Parties may also agree (beforehand or during the arbitral proceedings) on the arbitrator or arbitrators. The claimant must indicate the names and address details of the arbitrator(s) in the request for arbitration (see Article 6(3)(f) and, for the number of arbitrators Article 6(3)(h)).[131] We would not recommend the nomination of specific individuals in arbitration clauses covering future disputes. There is a considerable chance that such arrangements will result in a deadlock situation. For example, the specific individuals may no longer be available once a dispute has arisen. Furthermore their situation may have substantially changed. A change of profession may for instance take away the very reason for the parties to agree on his nomination. In addition, practice shows that the parties often refrain from agreeing on an adequate fall back scenario for the event that the nominated individuals are no longer available. All these arguments against the nomination of specific individuals do of course not apply in case of an ad hoc arbitration agreement in regard of an already existing dispute.

> According to Article 1027(1) DCCP, the parties may agree on the method of appointment of the arbitrator(s). Article 1028 DCCP provides in this respect that if one of the parties has a privileged position with regard to the appointment of arbitrator(s), the other party may request the President (*voorzieningenrechter*) of the District Court within one month after the commencement of the arbitration to appoint the arbitrator(s). A party is deemed to have a privileged position if this party has paramount influence in appointing the arbitrator. This article is of mandatory law and will therefore also apply in the case of NAI arbitration when the arbitration is seated in the Netherlands (see also Article 64, which provides that in this event the President of the Rotterdam District Court has jurisdiction).

2.   Periods of Time

The parties may also agree on a period of time for the appointment. A period of two months normally suffices. If the parties reside in different countries a slightly longer period of three months may be advisable, although it is arguable that the international nature of a dispute is no longer a sound reason for applying longer terms. If the parties do not comply (wholly or in part) with the method of appointment within the period of time agreed to by the parties, or, in the absence

---

[131] Ibid.

of such period of time, within four weeks after commencement of the arbitration, the appointment of the arbitrator(s) shall take place in accordance with the list-procedure in Article 14 (Article 13(2)). The parties may extend this period of time, based on an agreement on the period of time for the appointment of arbitrators as provided for in Article 13(2). The parties must inform the Administrator of their agreement.

A consequence of this provision may be that a party that – on further considerations – chooses not to comply with the agreed method to appoint arbitrators, will be able to have the appointment of the arbitrators take place in accordance with the list-procedure of Article 14 just by allowing the time period to expire. If, however, the agreed method of appointment boils down to the nomination of one arbitrator by each party and only one party fails to timely nominate its arbitrator, its seems logical that the other party's nomination remains valid. Accordingly, we contend that under these circumstances only the failing party's arbitrator should be appointed on the basis of the list-procedure of Article 14. If it is agreed that the third arbitrator shall be nominated by a third party other than the Administrator, good practice requires the Administrator to live up to this agreement and to leave the appointment of the third arbitrator to the agreed third party. The parties' agreement should be respected whenever possible. In addition, the Administrator should not allow one party to frustrate the parties' agreement, if the other party indicates that it still has an interest in maintaining the agreement.

> Article 1027(2) DCCP provides that the arbitrator(s) must be appointed within two months after commencement of the arbitration. This time limit will be three months if at least one of the parties lives or has its actual residence outside the Netherlands.[132] If the arbitrator(s) have not been appointed within this time period, they will be appointed, at the request of one of the parties, by the President (*voorzieningenrechter*) of the District Court (Article 1027(3) DCCP; see also Article 64 that provides that the President of the Rotterdam District Court will have jurisdiction). However, the parties may shorten or lengthen these periods of time (see also Article 13(2)). This article is not of mandatory law.

3. Refusal of the Administrator to Administer the Arbitration

If the parties agree to the appointment of an arbitrator without following the list-procedure, it may be advisable to confer with the NAI concerning the arbitrator, especially when the parties have some doubts about the person of the arbitrator. This would be especially apt as the Administrator may refuse to administer the arbitration if one or more of the party-appointed arbitrators themselves, in the opinion of the Administrator, do not offer sufficient safeguards for a sound arbitration. The parties may agree to the replacement of such arbitrator in accordance with the list-procedure provided in Article 14 (Article 13(3)). The NAI

---

[132] The Draft Bill proposes deletion of the exception for non-Dutch parties, by extending the time limits to three months.

Rules do not specify the grounds for such refusal by the Administrator. However, the Administrator will take into account the arbitrator's availability and ability to conduct an arbitration in accordance with the NAI Rules.[133] Among the issues that may arise with respect to an arbitrator's ability to conduct a sound arbitration – although these are not strict requirements according to the NAI Rules – is the fact that an arbitrator must have an adequate working knowledge of the language(s) of the arbitration. Furthermore, the Administrator may take into account the legal training of an arbitrator, the arbitrator's expertise in the commercial or technical field that is the subject of the arbitration as well as expertise in arbitration. That being said, in practice the Administrator only checks whether the arbitrator has no conflict and does not check for any other qualifications of arbitrators that have been selected by the parties.

ARTICLE 14 – LIST-PROCEDURE

1. As soon as possible after receipt of the short answer referred to in Article 7 or, on the absence thereof, after expiration of the period of time for filing of short answer, the Administrator shall communicate to each of the parties an identical list of names. If one arbitrator is to be appointed, the list shall contain not less than three names; if three arbitrators are to be appointed, the list shall contain not less than nine names.

2. Each party may delete from this list the names of persons against whom he has overriding objections, and number the remaining names in the order of his preference.

3. If a list is not returned to the Administrator within 14 days* after its dispatch to a party, it will be assumed that all persons appearing on it are equally acceptable to that party for appointment as arbitrator.

4. As soon as possible after receipt of the lists, or failing this, after expiration of the period of time referred to in the previous paragraph, the Administrator shall, taking into account the preferences and/or objections expressed by the parties, invite one or three persons from the list, as the case may be, to act as arbitrator.

5. If and to the extent that the lists which have been returned show an insufficient number of persons who are acceptable as arbitrator to each of the parties, the Administrator shall be authorized to invite directly one or more other persons to act as arbitrator. The same shall apply if a person is not able or does not wish to accept the Administrator's invitation to act as arbitrator, or if there appear to be other reasons precluding him from acting as arbitrator, and there

---

[133] See for example also Art. 9(1) of the ICC Rules.

remain on the lists an insufficient number of persons who are acceptable as arbitrator to each of the parties.

6. If the arbitral tribunal is composed of three arbitrators, the arbitrators shall choose a chairman from amongst themselves, if necessary, in accordance with the provisions of Article 16(3).

7. If the parties agreed only to the appointment of arbitrator(s) by the NAI, without referring to arbitration by the NAI or arbitration in accordance with the NAI Rules, such appointments shall take place in accordance with the provisions of this article unless the parties agreed to another method of appointment by the NAI.

8. For the application of the provisions of this article, the Administrator preferably shall draw the names of persons from the General Panel of Arbitrators which is established, expanded and amended by the NAI.

9. The appointment of the arbitrator(s) in accordance with the provisions of this article shall take place within two months[*] after commencement of the arbitration.

[*] This period of time is doubled in an international arbitration (Art. 5(2)).

1. Background

Article 14 contains the main distinctive feature of the NAI Rules: the list-procedure for the appointment of arbitrators. This method of appointment for arbitrators was introduced in the United States by the American Arbitration Association and has been adopted by the NAI. The UNCITRAL Rules[134] and the WIPO Arbitration Rules[135] also provide for a list-procedure for the appointment of the sole or presiding arbitrator, but only when the parties or, as the case may be, the two party-appointed arbitrators are unable to agree on the sole or third arbitrator to be appointed.

> This article is in line with Article 1027(1) DCCP, which provides that the parties may also assign the appointment of the arbitrator(s) to a third party.

2. List-Procedure

According to this list-procedure, after the receipt of the short answer, the Administrator shall send to the parties an identical list with the names of possible arbitrators. If one arbitrator is to be appointed, the list shall contain not less than three names; if three arbitrators are to be appointed, the list shall contain

---

[134] See Arts 6(3) and 7(3) UNCITRAL Rules.
[135] See Art. 19 WIPO Arbitration Rules.

not less than nine names. Each party will have 14 days to consider the list and to delete from this list the names of persons against whom it has overriding objections, and number the remaining names in the order of its preference. It is advisable not to delete too many names, as this may lead to the Administrator appointing the arbitrators himself without giving the parties further opportunity to choose arbitrators from a (new) list.

The Administrator will appoint the arbitrator or arbitrators on the basis of the lists returned by the parties. If a list is not returned to the Administrator within 14 days after it has been sent to a party, it will be assumed that all persons appearing on it are equally acceptable to that party for appointment as arbitrator. In practice, the Administrator will always call the party to check on whether the party has in fact received the list from the NAI.

The names on the list are preferably chosen from the General Panel of Arbitrators from the NAI (see Article 14(8)). This list presently contains approximately 300 individuals who have sufficient expertise and experience. Candidates for this General Panel of Arbitrators may be recommended by (individual) members of the Executive Board. Upon such recommendation or at the request of a candidate, a form requesting information such as personal details, expertise, experience and knowledge of languages is sent to the candidate. After evaluation and approval of the candidate's application by the Executive Board and if no member of the Executive Board exercises its veto against the candidate, this candidate's name is placed on the General Panel of Arbitrators. This list is divided into several areas of specialization. If the General Panel of Arbitrators does not include individuals with the appropriate qualifications or if such individuals are not available, the Administrator may select possible arbitrators who are not on the General panel of Arbitrators. According to the Introduction to the NAI Arbitration Rules, this General Panel of Arbitrators forms part of the 'know how' of the NAI and is therefore not publicly available.

The prospective arbitrators are not informed of the fact that the NAI Administrator has placed their names on the list of possible arbitrators, which is sent to the parties. In addition, persons listed are not informed of the parties' deletions on the list and/or comments thereto (if any) either. The Administrator will only check the prospective arbitrator's availability after the relevant arbitrators have been selected during the list-procedure.

If the lists which the parties have returned show an insufficient number of individuals who are acceptable as arbitrator to each of the parties, the Administrator is authorized to invite directly one or more other individuals to act as arbitrator without further consulting the parties. However, the Administrator may also send the parties an additional, second list from which the parties may delete names and number the remaining names in the order of their preference. The Administrator is used to appoint as many arbitrators as possible on the basis of the first list and will normally initiate the extended list-procedure for selecting the missing number of arbitrators only.

The NAI Rules stipulate that the appointment of arbitrators must take place within two months after commencement of the arbitration. This period of time is four months in the case of an international arbitration. Late appointment of the arbitrators is basically without legal effect. The appointment will be effective, despite the delay. The only consequence of a delay beyond the two-month period – or as the case may be four-month period – is that either party may turn to the President (*voorzieningenrechter*) of the District Court with the request to appoint the arbitrators, if the place of arbitration is situated in the Netherlands.

> According to Article 1027(3) DCCP, if the appointment of the arbitrator(s) did not take place within the time period mentioned in Article 1027(2) DCCP, the arbitrator(s) shall be appointed, at the request of either party, by the President (*voorzieningenrechter*) of the District Court. This article applies when the arbitration is seated in the Netherlands. It is unclear what happens if the appointment of arbitrator(s) does not take place within the two-month time period mentioned in Article 14(9) when the arbitration is seated outside the Netherlands. That will depend on the applicable (mandatory) law of the country in which the arbitration is seated.

3. No Reference to NAI Arbitration or NAI Rules

If the parties agreed only on the appointment of arbitrator(s) by the NAI, without referring to arbitration by the NAI or arbitration in accordance with the NAI Rules, such appointments shall take place in accordance with the provisions of this article unless the parties agreed to another method of appointment by the NAI (Article 14(7)). This provision can be used by the parties to appoint the NAI as Appointing Authority under the UNCITRAL Rules.

See also Article 57(7), which provides that if parties have agreed only on the appointment of arbitrators on the basis of Article 14(7), half of the administration costs will be due from the claimant requesting the arbitration.

ARTICLE 15 – LETTER OF APPOINTMENT; ACCEPTANCE OF MANDATE; NOTICE OF APPOINTMENT TO PARTIES

---

1. The appointment of the arbitrator(s) in accordance with the provisions of Article 13 and 14 shall be confirmed by the Administrator by a letter of appointment addressed to the arbitrator(s).
2. An arbitrator shall accept his mandate in writing. The signing and returning to the Administrator of a copy of the letter of appointment will suffice for this purpose.
3. Simultaneously with the dispatch of the letter of appointment, the Administrator shall notify the parties in writing of the appointment.

---

1. General Comments

The Administrator shall confirm the appointment of the arbitrator(s) according to Article 13 and 14 by a letter of appointment addressed to the arbitrator(s) (Article 15(1)). Simultaneously, the Administrator shall notify the parties in writing of the appointment (Article 15(3)). Article 15(3) does not provide that a copy of the letter of appointment must be sent to the parties. However, in all cases, the Administrator will send a copy of this letter to the parties.

An arbitrator shall accept his mandate in writing, for which the signing and returning to the Administrator of a copy of the letter of appointment will suffice (Article 15(2)). The article does not provide for time limits in regard of the letter of appointment, the letter to the parties or the acceptance of the mandate by the arbitrators. However, practice shows that all this takes place rapidly, shortly after the appointment of the arbitrators on the basis of Article 13 or 14.

2. Contractual Relationship between (i) the Parties and the Arbitrators, (ii) the NAI and the Parties and (iii) the NAI and the Arbitrators

The contractual relationship between (i) the parties and the arbitrators, (ii) the NAI and the parties and (iii) the NAI and the arbitrators has been discussed in detail in Part I, Chapter 1, Section 6.

> Article 1029 DCCP equally provides that the arbitrator will accept his mandate in writing.

Article 16 – Nationality of Arbitrator

1. No person shall be precluded from appointment as arbitrator by reason of his nationality, except as provided in the following paragraphs.
2. In an arbitration between parties of different nationality, if an arbitral tribunal composed of one arbitrator is to be appointed in accordance with the list-procedure provided in Article 14, each of the parties may require that this arbitrator be of a nationality other than that of any of the parties.
3. In an arbitration between parties of different nationality, if an arbitral tribunal composed of three arbitrators is to be appointed in accordance with the list-procedure provided in Article 14, each of the parties may require that the arbitrator who will act as the chairman of the arbitral tribunal be of a nationality other than that of any of the parties.

4. Such request shall be communicated to the Administrator, by the claimant in the request for arbitration referred to in Article 6, and by the respondent in the short answer referred to in Article 7.

1. General Rule – Exceptions

Following from Article 1023 DCCP, this article provides as a general rule that no person may be precluded from an appointment as arbitrator by reason of his nationality (Article 16(1)).[136] Under the NAI Rules, two exceptions have been made to this general rule. Both exceptions apply in the case of an international arbitration and only apply at the request of (one of) the parties. Firstly, if a sole arbitrator is appointed according to the list-procedure, each of the parties may require that the sole arbitrator be of a different nationality than that of any of the parties (Article 16(2)). Secondly, if an arbitral tribunal composed of three arbitrators is to be appointed according to the list-procedure, each of the parties may require that the chairman of the arbitral tribunal be of a different nationality than that of any of the parties (Article 16(3)). These exceptions provide the parties with the opportunity to rule out a possible advantage for a party to have a sole arbitrator with the same nationality deciding the dispute or acting as chairman of the arbitral tribunal, while the other party does not. These requests must be made in the request for arbitration or the short answer (Article 16(4)). Requests as meant in Article 16(2) are made in international arbitrations on a regular basis. Even in the absence of such request, the Administrator may avoid appointing an arbitrator with the nationality of one of the parties at its own initiative. A preference for the nationality of the chairman may also be included in the request for arbitration or the short answer.

Article 16(2) does not block the appointment of fellow-countrymen as co-arbitrators. The parties cannot prevent a co-arbitrator to be of the same nationality as the counterparty, unless this has been agreed by the parties. It can be assumed, however, that the Administrator will avoid composing the arbitral tribunal with two co-arbitrators of whom only one has the nationality of one of the parties. It seems logical to adhere in principle to a policy of appointing both co-arbitrators with a nationality other than that of the parties or assuring that both parties' nationality is reflected in the arbitral tribunal. Adhering to such a policy is of course difficult in multi-party arbitrations.

---

[136] Article 6.1 LCIA Rules provides that where the parties are of different nationalities, a sole arbitrator or the chairman of the arbitral tribunal shall not have the same nationality as any party, unless the parties who are not of the same nationality as the proposed appointee all agree in writing otherwise. Art. 6.2 LCIA Rules provides that the nationality of parties shall be understood to include that of controlling shareholders or interests. In respect of the nationality of a sole arbitrator or the chairman, see also Art. 9(5) ICC Rules, Art. 6(4) UNCITRAL Rules and Art. 20 WIPO Arbitration Rules.

The NAI Rules do not grant the parties other options for blocking the appointment of an arbitrator because of certain qualifications or the lack thereof. The parties' possible other preferences can only be enforced if these preferences affect the arbitrator's appearance of impartiality and independence and a ground for challenging the arbitrator applies.

ARTICLE 17 – RELEASE FROM MANDATE

1. An arbitrator who has accepted his mandate may, at his own request, be released therefrom either with the consent of the parties or by the Administrator.
2. An arbitrator who has accepted his mandate may be released therefrom by the parties jointly, without a request thereto from the arbitrator himself being necessary. The parties shall promptly notify the Administrator of such release.
3. An arbitrator who has accepted his mandate and who has become de jure or de facto unable to perform his mandate may, at the written request of a party, be released from his mandate by the Administrator.
4. In the cases referred to in paragraphs (1) and (3), the Administrator shall not release an arbitrator from his mandate until the parties have been given the opportunity to express their views in writing to the Administrator.

1. Release from Mandate by Arbitrator's own Request (Article 17(1))

An arbitrator may be released from his mandate at his own request, either with the consent of the parties or the Administrator (Article 17(1)). In practice, the arbitrator will first request the parties to release him from his mandate (according to Article 17(2)) and only if (one of) the parties do not agree to this request, will he ask the Administrator. In deciding on such a request, the Administrator will have discretionary powers. However, if the arbitrator does no longer wish to act as an arbitrator, it is difficult for the Administrator to force him to do so. The Administrator may informally put pressure on the arbitrator in an attempt to change his mind.

Although the NAI Rules do not elaborate on the possible grounds for the evaluation of such a request, it can be assumed that a release is acceptable only on the basis of a valid reason, such as a serious illness or an extended stay abroad. From a practicable point of view, however, the Administrator and the parties have only limited means to effectively force an arbitrator to continue. Although an arbitrator that is seeking his release for convenience only runs the risk of being liable for breach of contract, the exposure is normally limited due to the exclusion of liability in Article 66. Nevertheless, it seems reasonable to assume that the arbitrator forfeits his rights to fees, unless he clearly has been of service to the parties in the arbitral proceedings, for instance by rendering an interim award.

The Administrator will not release the arbitrator from his mandate until the parties have been given the opportunity to express their views in writing to the Administrator (Article 17(4)).

> Article 1029(2) DCCP contains a similar provision. On the basis of this article, also the President (*voorzieningenrechter*) of the District Court may release the arbitrator from his mandate. As this article is of mandatory law, this will also apply in the case of an NAI arbitration seated in the Netherlands.

2. Release from Mandate by the Parties Acting Jointly (Article 17(2))

On the basis of Article 17(2), an arbitrator may also be released from his mandate by the parties acting jointly. A request thereto from the arbitrator is not necessary. The NAI Rules do not mention specific circumstances for the release from mandate by the parties acting jointly. Under the Dutch arbitration act, it is generally accepted that parties may jointly release an arbitrator from his mandate for any reason. The same applies to a release on the basis of the NAI Rules. As arbitration is based on the parties' agreement, it seems only logical that the parties are free to release the arbitrator from his mandate, if they mutually agree to do so. If a party does not agree to the release of an arbitrator, the party that wishes the arbitrator released may request the Administrator to release the arbitrator from his mandate on the basis of Article 17(3).

> Article 1029(3) DCCP provides that an arbitrator may be released from his mandate by the parties acting jointly. Under Dutch law it may also be considered relevant that any assignment can be terminated by the principal for convenience pursuant to Article 7:407 DCC.

3. Release from Mandate by the Administrator at the Request of a Party (Article 17(3))

An arbitrator may also be released from his mandate by the Administrator, at the request of one of the parties, if he has become de jure or de facto unable to perform his mandate. For example, an arbitrator is legally unable to perform his mandate if he is placed under legal restraint. An arbitrator may be factually unable to perform his mandate if he is seriously ill or on an extended stay abroad. Also in this case, the Administrator shall not release an arbitrator from his mandate until the parties have been given the opportunity to express their views in writing to the Administrator. It has to be assumed that the arbitrator will also have the opportunity to comment on such request of the party.

The possibility for a party to make such a request should be used with caution and should only be used in manifest cases in which the other party only refuses to cooperate in order to frustrate the proceedings.

> Article 1029(4) DCCP contains a similar provision. On the basis of this article, also the President (*voorzieningenrechter*) of the District Court may release the arbitrator from his mandate. As this article is of mandatory law, this will also apply in the case of an NAI arbitration seated in the Netherlands.
>
> Contrary to the NAI Rules, the DCCP contains a provision on the termination of the arbitral tribunal's mandate (see Article 1031 DCCP). Article 1031(1) DCCP provides that the parties may agree to terminate the mandate of the arbitral tribunal. Article 1031(2) DCCP stipulates that the President of the District Court may – at the request of one of the parties – terminate the mandate of the arbitral tribunal if, despite repeated reminders, the arbitral tribunal carries out its mandate in an unacceptably slow manner. According to this article, in these circumstances, the jurisdiction of the court shall revive, unless the parties have agreed otherwise.
>
> This termination of the arbitral tribunal's mandate has to be distinguished from the release from mandate from a single arbitrator as provided for in Articles 1029 DCCP and 17 NAI Rules. The release from a single arbitrator from his mandate does not terminate the mandate of the arbitral tribunal, as an arbitrator who is released from his mandate will be replaced on the basis of Articles 1030 DCCP and 18 NAI Rules.
>
> In NAI arbitrations seated in the Netherlands, it is possible to terminate the arbitral tribunal's mandate on the basis of this article.

4. Consequences of Release from Mandate

If an arbitrator is released from his mandate, he shall be replaced by another arbitrator. The specifics of such replacement are dealt with in Article 18.

ARTICLE 18 – REPLACEMENT OF ARBITRATOR

---

1. An arbitrator who, for whatever reason, is released from his mandate shall be replaced by a new arbitrator. The new arbitrator shall be appointed in accordance with the list-procedure provided in Article 14 unless the parties have agreed to another method of replacement. The same applies in case of death of an arbitrator.

2. Until replacement has taken place, the arbitral proceedings shall be suspended by operation of law. After replacement, the arbitral proceedings shall continue from the stage they had reached unless the arbitral tribunal deems a reconsideration of the matter, wholly or in part, justified.

---

1.   Replacement of an Arbitrator

Article 18(1) provides that an arbitrator who, for whatever reason, is released from his mandate (on the basis of Article 17) shall be replaced by a new arbitrator. The new arbitrator will be appointed according to the list-procedure of Article 14, unless the parties have agreed to another method of replacement (beforehand or when the situation arises). Article 18(1) specifically refers to another method of *replacement.* This seems to indicate that the mere fact that the released arbitrator was by virtue of the parties' agreement nominated by another method than the list-procedure, does not lead to the conclusion that his replacement shall occur on the basis of the same method. In this respect the NAI Rules provide for a method different from that in the UNCITRAL Rules and the ICC Rules. Pursuant to Article 13 of the UNCITRAL Rules the substitute arbitrator 'shall be appointed pursuant to the procedure provided for in Articles 6 to 9 that was applicable to the appointment or choice of the arbitrator being replaced'. Article 12(4) ICC Rules leaves it to the discretion of the ICC Court whether or not to follow the original nominating procedure. Also the DCCP refers to the appointment method that was applied to the original appointment. We consider in particular the provision of the UNCITRAL Rules more in line with what the parties are likely to expect. We contend that the Administrator should adhere to the parties' agreement as much as possible by applying the agreed matter. Depending on the specific wording of the agreement there may of course be room to construe the parties' agreement in regard of the appointment procedure extensively to the effect that it includes the possible appointment of a substitute arbitrator as well. In any event we would favour the Administrator to consult the parties prior to initiating the list-procedure for appointing the substitute arbitrator.

The separate agreement to a method of replacement may be entered into beforehand or as the situation arises.

The above also applies in case of an arbitrator's death (and also in this case after the release from mandate).

> The possibility of a separate agreement for the replacement is in line with Article 1030 DCCP, which provides that an arbitrator who is released from his mandate will be replaced according to the rules that were applicable to the original appointment, but that the parties may agree otherwise. Contrary to Article 1030 DCCP, according to the NAI Rules, the arbitrator will not (always) be replaced according to the rules that were applicable to the original appointment.

2.   Effect on Prior Proceedings

According to Article 18(2), the arbitral proceedings will be suspended until replacement of the arbitrator has taken place. This means that submissions will not be filed, hearings will not be held and the arbitral tribunal will not render an (partial) award or give an order. The suspension of the arbitral proceedings will end when a replacing arbitrator has been appointed. After the suspension of the arbitral proceedings has ended, the arbitral tribunal will have to determine new procedural rules (new dates etc.).

In the event that an arbitrator has been replaced, it will need to be determined whether, and if so, to what extent any part of the arbitration needs to be repeated. Article 18(2) states that, after replacement, the proceedings will continue from the stage they had reached, unless the arbitral tribunal deems a reconsideration of the matter, wholly or in part, justified.

The NAI Rules do not specify the consequences of a 'reconsideration' of the matter. Most rules simply provide for a possible repetition of prior *hearings*.[137] Article 12(4) of the ICC Rules is broader in scope, by stating that the arbitral tribunal may decide whether any prior *proceedings* will be repeated. Article 18(2) seems to follow this broader approach. The question may arise as to whether it is appropriate for the new arbitral tribunal to reopen matters that may already have been the subject of an interim or partial award. As Derains and Schwartz state there is no 'legitimate basis upon which a newly constituted Arbitral Tribunal could choose, without the parties' agreement, to reopen proceedings that had already been the subject of a partial award regarded as final under the law applicable to the arbitral proceedings, although prior decisions of a purely interlocutory or interim nature could conceivably be revisited, if necessary.'[138]

In practice, it is likely that, after the replacement of an arbitrator, an arbitral tribunal will have to address the question as to whether to repeat any hearings (for example, for the examination of witnesses or oral arguments) conducted before the appointment of the new arbitrator. Arbitrators may not be inclined to do so because of the additional costs of repeated hearings, especially in international arbitrations. Detailed reports of the hearings – possibly verbatim by use of court reporters – could help to avoid the need for new hearings.

> Article 1030(3) DCCP contains a similar provision on the suspension of arbitral proceedings and provides that the parties may agree otherwise. This article also mentions that the proceedings will continue from the stage they had reached unless the parties have agreed otherwise, but does not mention a possible reconsideration of the matter by the arbitral tribunal.

ARTICLE 19 – CHALLENGE OF ARBITRATOR

1. An arbitrator may be challenged by a party in accordance with the provisions of this article, if circumstances exist that give rise to

---

[137] See for example Art. 11(2) ICDR Rules, Art. 14 UNCITRAL Rules and Art. 34 WIPO Arbitration Rules. According to Art. 14 UNCITRAL Rules, any previous hearings must be repeated if the chairman or a sole arbitrator has been replaced. If a co-arbitrator has been replaced, the arbitral tribunal is required to decide whether such a repetition is necessary.

[138] Derains and Schwartz, 2005, 202-203.

justifiable doubts as to his impartiality or independence, including the requirements of Article 10(1) and (2).

2. An arbitrator may also be challenged on grounds that existed prior to his appointment.

3. The challenge and the grounds therefore shall be notified in writing by the challenging party to the challenged arbitrator, the other party, the Administrator and, if the arbitral tribunal is composed of more than one arbitrator, the other arbitrators. Said notification shall be made within one week* after receipt of the notification referred to in Article 11 or, in the absence thereof, within one week* after the challenging party became aware of the grounds for the challenge.

4. If the challenge is not made in accordance with the provisions of the previous paragraph, the right to bring a challenge on these grounds shall be barred thereafter in the arbitral proceedings or in proceedings before a court.

5. The arbitral tribunal may suspend the arbitral proceedings as of the day of receipt of the notification from the challenging party.

6. Withdrawal by a challenged arbitrator shall not be interpreted as acceptance of the grounds for the challenge.

7. If the challenged arbitrator does not withdraw within two weeks* after the day of receipt of the notification from the challenging party, the Executive Board shall promptly decide in writing on the merits of the challenge. The Executive Board may give the challenged arbitrator and the parties the opportunity to be heard. The decision shall be communicated by the Administrator to the parties and the arbitrator(s).

8. If the Executive Board rejects the challenge, the challenging party may bring the grounds for the challenge before the court.

9. If the challenged arbitrator withdraws or if the challenge is upheld by the Executive Board or by the court, the arbitrator shall be replaced in accordance with the provisions of Article 18(1). The provisions of Article 18(2) shall apply accordingly.

10. If the challenged arbitrator is domiciled or has his actual residence outside the Netherlands, the period of time mentioned in paragraph (7) shall be doubled, regardless of whether the arbitration is international or not.

* This period of time is doubled in an international arbitration (Art. 5(2)).

1. Possible Grounds for the Challenge of an Arbitrator

An arbitrator may be challenged if circumstances exist that give rise to justifiable doubts as to his impartiality or independence, including the requirements of Article 10 (Article 19(1)). Reference is made to the comments on Article 10, where examples of such grounds from Dutch case law and literature have been given. It is advisable for a party to be very cautious when considering challenging an arbitrator. An unsuccessful attempt to challenge an arbitrator may have a negative result on the course of the proceedings for the challenging party, although one would expect a professional arbitrator being able to accept that challenges are part of the game and nothing personal, just as the parties and their counsel have to accept that a negative decision by the arbitral tribunal cannot automatically be held against the arbitrator.

> Article 1033(1) DCCP contains a similar provision. As mentioned in the comments on Article 10, under Dutch procedural law, the *outward appearance* of partiality may be sufficient to challenge an arbitrator as it raises justifiable doubts as to his impartiality or independence. However, once the (partial) final arbitral award has been rendered, justifiable doubts with regard to the arbitrator's impartiality or independence are not sufficient to have the arbitral award set aside. Setting aside of an award could only occur if there are facts and/or circumstances that prove that an arbitrator has not been impartial or independent in rendering his decision or if there is such serious doubt as to the impartiality or independence of the arbitrator that – also taking into account the other circumstances of the case – it would be unacceptable for the losing party to reconcile itself to the award. See for a more elaborate discussion on the setting aside of awards in the Netherlands, Part III, Chapter 1.

2. Grounds that Arose Prior to Appointment

Article 19(2) provides that a challenge may also be made on grounds that existed prior to the appointment. This article does not distinguish between grounds that existed prior to the appointment that the party was aware of and such grounds that the party only became aware of after the appointment.

The provisions of Article 19 reveal that the initiative is with the arbitrator. It is the arbitrator's responsibility to disclose circumstances that may give rise to debate in regard of his impartiality and independence. There is basically no obligation of the parties to conduct an investigation on their own initiative in regard of the prospective arbitrator's curriculum vitae and existing relationships. The parties can simply await the arbitrator's disclosure and challenge an arbitrator on the basis of such information, even if the information was already in the public domain. This system is in line with international arbitration practice and is to be preferred above another system, since any obligation of the parties to actively establish the absence of circumstances that could give rise to a challenge, brings about the need to consult the prospective arbitrators and discuss with them the dispute in at least some detail. Although one-to-one contacts between the parties and the arbitrators do not inevitably result in the arbitrator losing his appearance of impartiality and independence, a system that forces the parties involved to make contacts that can easily affect the impartiality and the independence of the arbitrators is undesirable. The starting point is therefore that the parties can await the arbitrators' disclosures and base a challenge on the information then revealed, even if the relevant information was already known to them. An exception may apply, in cases where a party's conduct shows that it was aware of the information and accepted the arbitrator's appointment after all. The parties can actually arrange for this situation to come into existence by revealing relevant information that could give rise to a challenge to the other party. When the parties have agreed on an appointment method in the context of which the co-arbitrators are nominated by each of the parties, it is not uncommon to provide the other party with a curriculum vitae of the prospective arbitrator together with the nomination. It can be assumed that any information included in the curriculum vitae can no longer be used for challenging an arbitrator, unless such challenge is made swiftly after receipt of the nomination. Article 19(3) provides in that respect for a time limit of one week in national arbitrations and two weeks in international arbitrations.

> Article 1033(2) DCCP provides that if the arbitrator was appointed by a party, that party may challenge the arbitrator only on grounds of which the party became aware after the appointment of the arbitrator. This could also include grounds that existed prior to the appointment of the arbitrator, but that the challenging party was at that time unaware of.
>
> In the Draft Bill, it is proposed to explicitly stipulate that parties may agree otherwise. In the Explanatory Notes, Article 19(2) is specifically mentioned as such an agreement between parties.
>
> Also, Article 1033(3) DCCP provides that if the arbitrator was appointed by a third party (for example the arbitration institute) or by the President (*voorzieningenrechter*) of the District Court, a party may not challenge the arbitrator if the party resigned itself to the appointment, unless the party became aware of the grounds for challenging the arbitrator after his appointment.

3.   Procedural Requirements

The procedure for challenging an arbitrator is set out in Article 19(3)-(10). The challenge shall be notified in writing by the challenging party to the challenged arbitrator, the other members of the arbitral tribunal, the other party, and the Administrator. The notification must include the grounds for the challenge and be made within one week after receipt of the notification of disclosure (Article 11) or, in the absence thereof, within one week after the challenging party became aware of the ground(s) for the challenge.[139]

---

[139] See for example NAI Executive Board 18 Jun. 2005, TvA 2006, 23-26 (the challenge was inadmissible because the one-week period of Art. 19(3) had lapsed).

A ground for a challenge may arise during a hearing. Although the article is tacit in this regard, it is advisable to request a suspension of the hearing in order to discuss the matter with the client and then mention such ground during the hearing. In this case, the hearing will probably be suspended, unless the arbitral tribunal finds it very likely to assume that the challenge is unjustified (see Article 19(5)).

Article 19(4) provides that if a party does not meet the aforementioned requirements, the party no longer has the right to bring a challenge on these grounds in the arbitral proceedings or in court proceedings.

According to Article 19(5), the arbitral tribunal may suspend the arbitral proceedings as of the date of the receipt of the challenge. The arbitral tribunal has discretionary powers in this respect. A challenge as such has no suspensive effect. The arbitral tribunal may decide to continue the proceedings and will normally do so, if it feels that the challenge is basically part of a strategy aimed at frustrating the arbitral proceedings. However, in practice most arbitrators do suspend the proceedings, until the challenge has been decided. Such practice must be valued favourably, in particular since any decisions and orders given by the arbitral tribunal after the challenge will be critically judged, if the challenge turns out to be successful. The arbitral tribunal may also decide to continue the arbitral proceedings (including the continuation of a hearing during which a challenge has been notified) on the basis of procedural arguments. In this event, the arbitral tribunal will have to take into account all relevant circumstances, such as the phase of the proceedings.[140]

A challenged arbitrator may decide to withdraw from the arbitral proceedings after he has been challenged by one of the parties. Article 19(6) gives the challenged arbitrator an 'easy way out' by stipulating that the withdrawal of the arbitrator shall not be interpreted as acceptance of the grounds for the challenge.

If the challenged arbitrator does not withdraw within two weeks after the day of receipt of the notification of the challenging party, the Executive Board of the NAI shall decide promptly on the merits of the challenge (Article 19(7)). If the challenged arbitrator is domiciled or has his actual residence outside the Netherlands, the time period mentioned will be doubled, regardless of whether the arbitration is international or not (Article 19(8)). The Administrator will inform the Executive Board of the NAI of the challenge. The challenge will typically be heard by a panel of three members of the Executive Board. They will allow the arbitrator and the other party to respond to the challenge and will call for a hearing. Some arbitrators prefer not to attend such hearings in order to allow the parties to freely discuss the grounds for challenge. Subsequent to the

---

[140] HR 29 Jun. 2007, RvdW 2007, 630.

hearing the Executive Board will render a reasoned decision. The decision is not published, but is sent to the parties and the arbitrators only.

> The procedure for a challenge under the Dutch arbitration act is described in Article 1035 DCCP (see note 4).

4.   Challenge before the District Court

According to Article 19(8), if the Executive Board rejects the challenge the challenging party may bring the grounds of the challenge before the Rotterdam District Court. The (mandatory) law of the country in which the arbitration is seated determines before which court the challenging party will have to bring the grounds of the challenge.

> This article is based on Article 1035 DCCP on the challenge before the President (*voorzieningenrechter*) of the District Court. The fact that parties have agreed to a specific method of challenging arbitrators (for example the NAI Rules), does not exclude the right of parties to ask for a decision from the President of the District Court on this issue, either parallel to or after the specific method of challenge, such as provided for in the NAI Rules. In fact a party who wants to turn to the President of the District Court should do so without delay, since it will forfeit its right if the applicable time limit is not adhered to. Article 1035 DCCP applies regardless of whether the challenging party first brings the grounds for its challenge before the Executive Board of the NAI according to Article 19 NAI Rules. Accordingly, the right to challenge will extinguish if the request for challenge is not filed with the President of the District Court within four weeks after the date of receipt of the notification (see Articles 19(1) NAI Rules and 1035(1) DCCP, as well as Article 64 NAI Rules). Thus Articles 19(1) NAI Rules and 1035 DCCP provide for a complex and confusing system of conflicting challenging procedures. Not only should the challenging party file two requests for challenge almost at the same time. In addition, there is no coordination whatsoever between the two procedures. In fact, the challenge of an arbitrator is likely to end in a bizarre race between the Executive Board of the NAI and the President of the District Court where the parties and the arbitrators simply have to wait which forum is going to render a decision first and subsequently to what extent the other forum will take the first decision into account. In order to avoid this highly undesirable situation either the NAI Rules or the DCCP should be altered at short notice.
>
> In the Draft Bill, the inclusion of a provision is proposed that will stipulate that if a third party (an arbitral institution, such as the NAI) has decided that the challenge is either inadmissible or unfounded, the challenging party will not have the right to bring the challenge before a court. However, the Explanatory Notes mention that there is no consensus among the members of the working group, as some members are of the opinion that the challenging party must always have the opportunity to have a court decide on the decision of the third party, as some of these institutions (but explicitly not the NAI) do not give reasons for a decision on a challenge.
>
> A decision from the President (*voorzieningenrechter*) of the District Court is not subject to appeal (Article 1070 DCCP).

5. Effect on Proceedings

If the challenged arbitrator withdraws or if the challenge is upheld by the Executive Board or by a court, the arbitrator shall be replaced in accordance with the provisions of Article 18(1). The arbitral proceedings will continue in accordance with the provisions of Article 18(2). See also the comments on Article 18.

6. Secretary to the Arbitral Tribunal

Article 19 applies accordingly to the secretary to the arbitral tribunal.

PROCEDURE (Articles 20-42)

ARTICLE 20 – ARBITRATION FILE AND COMMUNICATIONS

1. Simultaneously with the communication of the letter of appointment referred to in Article 15, the Administrator shall transmit the arbitration file to the arbitral tribunal.
2. After transmission of the arbitration file to the arbitral tribunal, the parties shall send their communications and other written submissions directly to the arbitral tribunal. A copy of every communication or written submission shall be sent simultaneously to the Administrator. The same applies to communications from the arbitral tribunal to the parties.

1. Transmission of the File

The letter of appointment constitutes a turning point in the arbitral proceedings: before the letter of appointment, it is the Administrator who is charged with communicating with the parties and decides on procedural issues, whereas after the letter of appointment has been sent, it is the arbitral tribunal who is in charge of the proceedings.

In order to allow the arbitral tribunal to take the lead in the proceedings, Article 20(1) of the NAI Rules provides that simultaneously with the letter of appointment, the Administrator will transmit the arbitration file to the arbitral tribunal. Although Article 20(1) provides that the arbitration file is transmitted to the *arbitral tribunal*, it will in fact be transmitted to the individual arbitrators, together with the letter of appointment of each individual member of the arbitral tribunal. In cases with more than one arbitrator, the arbitration file should, in our view, be transmitted to all of the arbitrators at the same time. In practice however, if two arbitrators have been appointed, the Administrator often sends the file to those arbitrators even though the third arbitrator has not yet been appointed. If the arbitral tribunal has requested the Administrator to arrange for a secretary to the arbitral tribunal (see the comments on Article 39), the Administrator will also send the selected secretary a letter of his or her appointment and a copy of the arbitration file.

At the moment the arbitration file is transmitted to the arbitral tribunal, it will generally consist of the request for arbitration and the short answer. The arbitration file sent to the arbitrators generally does not include the correspondence between the Administrator and (one of) the parties, such as the acknowledgement of receipt of the request for arbitration (see Article 6(6)), the invitation of the Administrator to the respondent to file a short answer (see Article 7(1)), the letter with which the Administrator has forwarded a copy of the short answer to the claimant (see Article 7(5)) and any other correspondence, such as, for example, a request of the respondent for an extension of time for filing the short answer. The arbitration file that is sent to the arbitral tribunal will in any event not contain the correspondence regarding the selection and the appointment of arbitrators, such as the list with names of arbitrators that the parties return to the Administrator when the list-procedure is followed (see also the comments on Article 14). These communications are dealt with on a confidential basis and will not be disclosed to the arbitral tribunal.

It follows from Article 20(1) that the arbitral tribunal does not see the submissions made by the parties in the arbitration (the request for arbitration and the short answer) until the arbitration file is transmitted to it. Although the request for arbitration and the short answer may be brief and are meant primarily to inform the Administrator of the nature and circumstances of the dispute (see the comments on Articles 6 and 7), it is good to realize when drafting these submissions, that they are also the first to be read by the arbitrators so that the arbitrators can get an idea of the dispute and determine the procedural order.

2.   Communications and Other Written Submissions

From the moment the arbitration file has been transmitted to the arbitral tribunal, it is the tribunal which is in charge of the arbitration and determines the course of the proceedings (see also the comments on Article 23). That is why Article 20(2) requires the parties to correspond directly with the arbitral tribunal when the arbitration file has been transmitted to it. If the arbitral tribunal is assisted by a secretary (see Article 39(1)), the arbitral tribunal may request the parties to send all correspondence and submissions to the secretary, either with or without a copy to the individual arbitrators. In the latter case, the secretary will be charged with forwarding the documents received from the parties to the individual members of the tribunal.

As set out in the comments on Article 1 above, the Administrator is charged with the responsibility of safeguarding the quality of NAI arbitrations and for that purpose closely monitors the arbitration process. In order to allow the Administrator to do so, Article 20(2) also requires that the Administrator be copied on all direct communications or written submissions, either from (one of) the parties to the arbitral tribunal or from the arbitral tribunal to the parties. In practice, copies of correspondence or other submissions will usually be sent to the NAI Secretariat, marked for the attention of the Administrator.

The NAI Rules lack a provision on sending a copy of communications and other written submissions to the other party. However, the parties will in practice be obliged to send a copy of all communications and submissions to (counsel for) the other party. If the parties are represented by a lawyer, this obligation may also follow from the lawyer's professional rules of conduct. It is also very common that the arbitral tribunal, once the arbitration file has been transmitted to it, establishes the procedural rules with which the parties have to comply during the arbitration, in a procedural order (either of its own accord or after a procedural meeting with the parties as provided for by Article 23(4)). These procedural rules usually include that a copy of all correspondence to the arbitral tribunal and all submissions must be sent simultaneously (also) to the other party.

ARTICLE 21 – REPRESENTATION OF AND ASSISTANCE
FOR PARTIES

---

1. The parties may appear before the arbitral tribunal in person, be represented by a practising lawyer or be represented by any other person expressly authorized in writing for this purpose. The parties may be assisted in the arbitral proceedings by any persons they may choose.
2. If a party is to be represented at a hearing by a practising lawyer or by an authorized representative, he shall so notify in writing the arbitral tribunal and the other party as soon as possible after the date of the hearing is determined. If the request for arbitration referred to in Article 6, or the short answer referred to in Article 7, was filed by a practising lawyer or by an authorized representative, said notification shall be deemed to have taken place.

---

1.   Representation and Assistance

Article 21(1) entitles the parties to appear before the arbitral tribunal in person. Hence, there is no requirement in NAI arbitration that a party be represented by a practising lawyer (*advocaat*), although this is almost always the case in practice. In the context of Article 21(1) (and Article 1038(1) DCCP; see below), 'appear' is understood to mean any participation in the arbitral proceedings.[141] It does not only refer to a personal appearance before the arbitral tribunal during a hearing, but also includes, for example, the filing of written submissions, such as the statement of claim or the statement of defence.

---

[141]   Vademecum Arbitrage, 2002 (W. ten Cate), 21-22; G.J. Meijer 2008 (T&C Rv), Art. 1038 DCCP, note 1(a).

Article 21(1) also entitles the parties to be represented in the arbitral proceedings by a practising lawyer (*advocaat*) or by any other person expressly authorized in writing for this purpose. The person, not being a lawyer, presenting himself as being authorized to represent a party in the arbitration, may be requested by the arbitral tribunal to submit the required authorization in writing. It is not necessary for a lawyer to be expressly authorized, as his or her authority is assumed. Powers of attorney are not a common feature in NAI arbitrations. Also, foreign lawyers may act as a lawyer as meant in Article 21(1) and it must be assumed that they will then be treated as equal to Dutch lawyers. Although the parties may act in person in the arbitration, they will usually be represented by counsel in NAI arbitrations. In practice, the fact that parties are represented by counsel does not mean that the parties themselves are not expected to attend hearings or meetings with the arbitral tribunal. It is standard practice in arbitration that the parties themselves – or to be more precise representatives of the parties that are familiar with the dispute and authorized to speak on behalf of the relevant legal entities – attend hearings, irrespective of whether they are represented by counsel. Usually, the arbitral tribunal will expect that the hearing be attended by one or more representatives of the parties that are fully informed about the case, so that it can ask questions to the parties directly, if necessary. In this respect, Article 33 authorizes the arbitral tribunal to order the personal appearance of the parties at any stage of the proceedings (see also the comments on Article 33).

The second sentence of Article 21(1) entitles the parties to be assisted in the arbitral proceedings by any person of their choice. This assistance is to be distinguished from the above-mentioned legal representation and relates, for example, to assistance in the arbitration by party-appointed experts, such as an accountant, a tax adviser or a technical specialist.

> Article 21(1) NAI Rules reproduces almost verbatim the text of Article 1038(1) and 1038(2) DCCP, which are both considered to be of mandatory law. Therefore, the parties' right to act in person cannot be validly excluded by the parties or in arbitration rules, nor can the parties' right to be represented by a lawyer (or by any other person expressly authorized in writing).

2. Notification

Article 21(2) states that if a party is to be represented at a hearing by a practising lawyer (*advocaat*) or by an authorized representative, it shall so notify the arbitral tribunal and the other party in writing as soon as possible after the date of the hearing is determined. Given that Article 21(2) also provides that this notification is deemed to have taken place if the request for arbitration or the short answer was filed by a practising lawyer or by an authorized representative, the practical relevance of this article is limited. In practice, the request for arbitration and the short answer will almost always be filed by the parties' counsel, so that there is usually no need for a separate notification as required by Article 21(2). This may be different in the (occasional) event that a party retains outside counsel at a later stage in the arbitral proceedings (after the request for arbitration or the short answer has been filed) or if a party retains an additional or local counsel in the course of the arbitration who then takes over from the counsel that originally filed the request for arbitration or the short answer. However, even if there is no need for a separate notification as referred to by Article 21(2) because the request for arbitration or the short answer was filed by a practising lawyer or by an authorized representative, it is still recommended to provide the arbitral tribunal prior to a hearing with the names of the persons who will be attending the hearing on behalf of a party, and to also mention the capacity in which these persons will be attending the hearing. Usually, the parties will also be requested by (the secretary to) the arbitral tribunal to provide this information in advance in light of the practical arrangements that have to be made for the hearing (location, number of seats, etc.).

ARTICLE 22 – PLACE OF ARBITRATION

1. If the place of arbitration is not agreed to by the parties, the place shall be determined by the arbitral tribunal as soon as possible after receipt of the arbitration file. The arbitral tribunal shall notify the parties and the Administrator in writing of the place so determined.
2. The arbitral tribunal may hold hearings, deliberate, and examine witnesses and experts at any other place, within or outside the Netherlands, which it deems appropriate.

1. Relevance of the Place of Arbitration

Although parties may not always be aware of this, the choice of the place of arbitration is one of the most important choices to be made, particularly in an international setting. Although an NAI Arbitration may take place anywhere in the world, the place of arbitration in the vast majority of NAI arbitrations is in the Netherlands. The place of arbitration is a legal concept that determines, first of all, the applicable arbitration law.

> If the arbitration is seated in the Netherlands, Article 1073(1) DCCP provides that Title 1 of the Dutch arbitration act contained in Book IV of the DCCP (Articles 1020-1073 DCCP) is applicable. An exception applies only for those provisions that are not of mandatory law and from which the parties have deviated (in their arbitration agreement or subsequently, by additional agreement).
>
> Article 1037 DCCP relates to the place of arbitration. The first sentence of Article 22(1) NAI Rules is similar to the first sentence of Article 1037(1) DCCP. The second sentence of Article 1037(1) DCCP provides that the place of arbitration determines also where the arbitral award shall be made. Furthermore, the

place of arbitration determines with which District Court the arbitral award must be deposited (see Article 1058(1)(b) DCCP) and consequently also where setting aside proceedings must be initiated (see Article 1064(2) DCCP) and where a request for execution of the award must be filed if the award is to be executed in the Netherlands (see Article 1062(1) DCCP).

The place of arbitration does not force the arbitral tribunal to actually hold hearings and other sessions in the country where the place of arbitration is located. Article 22(2) explicitly stipulates that hearings may be held in other places within or outside the Netherlands and in fact hearings in other places and even in other countries are a common phenomenon, as it is in international arbitration. Accordingly, the place of arbitration does not restrict in any way hearings by telephone conferences or other modern means of communication.

If the parties opt for a place of arbitration outside the Netherlands, it is important to realize that this automatically entails the applicability of the arbitration law of the country in which the arbitration is seated. When choosing a place of arbitration outside the Netherlands, the parties should therefore carefully consider the local law regarding recourse against arbitral awards, as well as mandatory local rules which, if violated, could cause an arbitral award to be set aside. In this respect, it is noted that the NAI Rules are not necessarily in line with the mandatory rules of arbitration law of countries other than the Netherlands. What parties should also assess, is the extent to which, under the applicable arbitration law, local courts are likely to assist or to interfere in arbitral proceedings. Finally and perhaps most importantly, if the parties consider choosing a place of arbitration outside the Netherlands, they should verify whether the country in which the arbitration under consideration is seated, has ratified the New York Convention or any other international convention on the recognition and enforcement of arbitral awards. In order to allow actual enforcement of the award, the same conventions should be adhered to by the country or countries in which execution of the award might be sought.

The Netherlands is a party to the New York Convention.

2. Party Agreement

It follows from Article 22(1) that it is primarily up to the parties to determine the place of arbitration, either in their arbitration agreement or in a subsequent additional agreement. Given the possible consequences attached to the choice of the place of arbitration (see note 1), it is recommended that the parties agree on the place of arbitration in their arbitration agreement. If the parties have agreed on the place of arbitration, the claimant has to mention the place of arbitration in the request for arbitration (see Article 6(1)(i)). As the place of arbitration is one of the additional matters that may be provided for in the model arbitration clause recommended by the NAI (see also the comments on Article 1(e)), parties will often mention the place of arbitration in their arbitration agreement (if they agreed on one). At the same time, however, it is not unusual that parties agree on the place of arbitration at a later stage, at the commencement of the arbitral proceedings. Thus, the parties themselves keep control over the choice of the place of arbitration. Absenting a choice of the parties, the place of arbitration will be determined by the arbitral tribunal (see note 3).

Sometimes it is not clear whether the parties have agreed on a place of arbitration or what they have agreed on this subject. Some arbitration clauses provide that any dispute will be resolved under the 'Rules of the Netherlands Arbitration Institute in Rotterdam'. Such wording leaves open the question whether the parties meant to choose Rotterdam as the place of arbitration, or merely referred to Rotterdam as the city where the NAI is seated. If the parties do not agree on the interpretation of the arbitration clause, the arbitral tribunal will decide and determine the place of arbitration.

3. Tribunal's Criteria for Determining the Place of Arbitration

Lacking an agreement of the parties, the place of arbitration shall be determined by the arbitral tribunal as soon as possible after receipt of the arbitration file (Article 22(1)). The arbitral tribunal will subsequently inform the parties and the Administrator of the place determined.

When determining the place of arbitration, the arbitral tribunal will, insofar as possible, take into account any preferences of the parties with regard to the place of arbitration. If the parties have not agreed on the place of arbitration at the commencement of the arbitration, they are expected to make their preferences in this respect known in the request for arbitration and the short answer (see Articles 6(3)(j) and 7(2) respectively).

In a national setting where the place of arbitration is in the Netherlands, it usually does not matter what place within the Netherlands is chosen as the place of arbitration, given Article 22(2) which provides that hearings etc. may be held at any place the arbitral tribunal deems appropriate. There may be circumstances, however, in which it does matter what place within the Netherlands is chosen as the place of arbitration. These circumstances include the situation where the arbitral tribunal is composed of arbitrators who are an active District Court judge in the Netherlands. In that event, the place of arbitration should preferably be chosen in another district. If not, conflicts with the District Court organization may arise, should the parties wish to address the state courts during or in relation to the arbitration (e.g., if there is a challenge of one of the arbitrators or proceedings to set aside the award), the court will be able to have judges handle the case who are not the direct colleagues of the arbitrator/judge involved.

In determining the place of arbitration, the arbitral tribunal may, especially in an international setting, also take other factors into consideration, such as the neutrality of a place (if the parties are of different nationalities, the tribunal might wish to avoid situating the place of arbitration in either of the parties' country of origin), the applicable law or the language agreed upon by the parties (this might make certain locations more appropriate than others) as well as the local laws and conventions on (international) arbitration of a country (which may limit, for example, the arbitrability of some matters or allow local courts to intervene in the arbitral process). If the arbitral tribunal intends to select a place of arbitration outside the Netherlands, it is important to assess whether until that moment, the arbitral procedure was conducted in accordance with the arbitration laws of the country of the intended place of arbitration. In order to avoid arbitral awards being set aside, it is particularly important that the composition of the arbitral tribunal (including the number of arbitrators of which it consists) satisfies the applicable arbitration law.

> Article 22(1) NAI Rules is based on Article 1037(1) DCCP. Article 1037(2) DCCP provides for the situation that the place of arbitration has not been determined by the parties, nor by the arbitral tribunal. In that event, the place that the tribunal mentioned in the arbitral award is considered to be the place of arbitration. However, this situation is not expected to occur in NAI arbitrations, given the monitoring of the arbitral procedure by the Administrator.

4. Changing the Place of Arbitration

The question may arise, in exceptional circumstances, whether the place of arbitration can be changed, once it has been established. Neither the NAI Rules nor the Dutch arbitration act prohibits such change.[142] Notwithstanding this, parties should, in our view, be extremely reluctant in changing the place of arbitration during the arbitral proceedings and they should only change the place of arbitration if that is absolutely necessary. Changing the place of arbitration to a place in a different country might lead to complicated procedural issues (such as with regard to execution and enforcement, if there are multiple arbitral awards with different places of arbitration). Changing the place of arbitration may also increase the risk of the arbitral award(s) being set aside.

5. Place for Hearings, Deliberations, Witness and Expert Examinations

Article 22(2) introduces a distinction between the place of arbitration, which is a legal concept, and the physical places where hearings and meetings can be held. According to Article 22(2), the arbitral tribunal may hold hearings, deliberate and examine witnesses and experts at any other place than the place of arbitration, within or outside the Netherlands, which it deems appropriate. It is

---

[142] Vademecum Arbitrage, 2002 (W. ten Cate), 40. Snijders is of the view that once the place of arbitration has been determined, it should not be possible to change it, given the importance of the place of arbitration and the possibility of conflicting procedural rules (Burg. Rv, 2006 (H.J. Snijders), Art. 1037 DCCP, note 1).

not uncommon for hearings and meetings to be held at locations other than the place of arbitration, which will usually be done for reasons of convenience. For example, the place of arbitration may be distant geographically from the parties or the arbitrators. It may also be that none of the parties or the arbitrators is located or has an office in the place of arbitration, in which case it is practical that the hearing be held, for example, at the offices of the chairman of the tribunal, at the offices of the NAI in Rotterdam or even at the offices of the counsel of one of the parties (although it is recommended in that case that the arbitral tribunal verifies that all the parties have consented to this; see also the comments on Article 26). Also the Peace Palace in The Hague is available for hearings in arbitrations and is considered to be a good venue for international arbitrations by both parties and arbitral tribunals. Furthermore, it may be efficient to hear certain witnesses where they reside instead of having them come to a hearing. Finally, it can be efficient to have a hearing near the object of the dispute (e.g., a building or plant).

Unlike Article 14(2) of the ICC Rules, Article 22(2) of the NAI Rules does not require the arbitral tribunal to consult with the parties before deciding to conduct a hearing or meeting at a location other than the place of arbitration. However, the arbitral tribunal will probably do so in practice if the location envisaged might give rise to objections of the parties.

Article 22(2) NAI Rules reproduces verbatim the text of Article 1037(3) DCCP.

ARTICLE 23 – PROCEDURE IN GENERAL

1. The arbitral tribunal shall ensure the equal treatment of the parties. It shall give each party an opportunity to substantiate his claims and to present his case.

2. The arbitral tribunal shall determine the manner in which, and the periods of time within which, the procedure shall be conducted, taking into account the provisions of these Rules, arrangements, if any, between the parties, and the circumstances of the arbitration.

3. The arbitral tribunal shall ensure that the arbitral procedure takes place with due dispatch. It may, at the request of a party or on its own motion, extend in exceptional cases a period of time fixed by it or agreed to by the parties.

4. At the request of a party, or on its own motion, the arbitral tribunal may, after receipt of the arbitration file or at a later stage of the proceedings, hold a meeting with the parties to discuss the course of the proceedings and/or to specify further the factual and legal issues in dispute.

1.   General Comments

Article 23 sets out some basic principles as to the arbitration procedure. The NAI Rules themselves only provide the framework for conducting the proceedings. They set requirements to ensure that the basic principles of due process are complied with (such as the right to a hearing and a reasonable opportunity to present one's case), but it is mostly up to the parties and the arbitral tribunal to determine the procedural rules and to structure the proceedings, subject only to the NAI Rules and possible mandatory provisions of the applicable arbitration law.

2.   Principles of Equal Treatment and Hearing Both Sides

Article 23(1) contains two basic procedural principles of due process that the arbitral tribunal must apply, i.e. the principle of equal treatment of the parties and the obligation to give each party an opportunity to substantiate its claims and to present its case (the principle of hearing both sides or *audite et alteram partem*). The principle of equal treatment entails that both parties will have to be heard to the same extent. The principle of hearing both sides involves the parties' right to be notified of the other party's claims and their substantiation, to respond to statements of the other party and to express their views on the information on which the award will be based.

In practice, the principles of equal treatment and hearing both sides will entail that both parties are equally given the opportunity to respond to each other's statements. However, given that the exchange of statements and written submissions cannot extend indefinitely, the respondent (either in the principal action or in the counterclaim) will have the last word. Therefore, if the respondent submits a counterclaim with the statement of defence, the claimant (also respondent in the counterclaim) must be given the opportunity to respond to the counterclaim. Also, if the claimant is given the opportunity to submit a memorial of reply, the respondent must be given the opportunity to submit a memorial of rejoinder. If the parties are given the opportunity to comment on evidence, the arbitral tribunal must always hear both sides (usually in the order that the claimant goes first, and then the respondent). The obligation to hear both sides does not only apply for the exchange of written submissions, but also for hearings, meetings or conference calls with the arbitral tribunal.

Furthermore, the principles of due process entail that the arbitral tribunal may not hear a party in the absence of the other party, unless the other party has been given the opportunity to attend. This does not only apply for actual hearings, but includes telephone conferences and the like. The arbitral tribunal may also not communicate about the case with a party or its counsel outside the arbitral proceedings (see also Article 10(2)).

The importance of the principles of due process may not be underestimated. A substantial violation of these principles may lead to the refusal of the recognition and enforcement of the arbitral award under the New York Convention, for the reason that a party was unable to present its case (Article V(1)(b) New York Convention) and for the violation of public policy (Article V(2)(b) New York Convention). Also, a violation of the principles of due process will be a ground for setting aside the award in many jurisdictions.

Article 23(1) NAI Rules reproduces practically verbatim the text of Article 1039(1) DCCP. The basic principles laid down in these articles can be found also in Article 15 of the UNCITRAL Rules and Article 18 of the UNCITRAL Model Law. A substantial violation of the principle of equal treatment and hearing both sides may – under Dutch arbitration law – result in the arbitral award being set aside (Article 1065(1)(e) DCCP) and in refusal of the recognition and enforcement (Articles 1063(1) and 1076 DCCP), on the basis that the manner in which the award was made violates public policy (see Article 1065 DCCP, note 6 in Part III, Chapter 1, and the comments on Articles 1063 and 1076 DCCP in Part III, Chapter 3).

3. The Course of the Proceedings

Article 23(2) provides that the arbitral tribunal determines the manner in which, and the periods of time within which, the procedure shall be conducted, taking into account the provisions of the NAI Rules, arrangements, if any, between the parties, and the circumstances of the arbitration. By providing that the arbitral tribunal shall take any arrangements of the parties into account when determining the course of the proceedings, Article 23(2), in principle, gives priority to any agreements on procedure that the parties may reach. The parties may, for example, agree in advance that they will be given the opportunity for a second round of written submissions, following the submission of the statement of claim and the statement of defence (see Article 24(2)), or that they will have the right to submit post-hearing briefs. They may also agree on deadlines for their submissions or on a complete procedural timetable. The latter may also include a deadline for rendering an award (although it is questionable whether the arbitral tribunal will be bound by such arrangements and it is, in our view, not to be recommended to agree on such deadlines for the arbitral tribunal, given that missing such a deadline might be a ground for setting aside or refusal of enforcement of the award).[143] If the arbitral tribunal fails to conduct the proceedings in accordance with the parties' agreement, this may be a ground for setting aside an award (under Dutch arbitration law, but also in many other jurisdictions).

The autonomy of the parties to decide on the course of the proceedings is, however, not unlimited. The arrangements made by the parties, first of all, may not violate any rules of mandatory law that apply to the arbitral proceedings. The arbitrators should be attentive to the mandatory rules of the place of arbitration, since a violation of these rules may constitute a ground for setting aside an award.

---

[143] See the example of the enforcement of an award made in the Netherlands that was refused by the French courts for this reason, mentioned by A.J. van den Berg, 'New York Convention of 1958: Refusals of Enforcement', *ICC International Court of Arbitration Bulletin* 18, No. 2 (2007), 35.

Secondly, the arbitral tribunal is authorized to deviate from any arrangements of the parties if it finds these arrangements otherwise incorrect or unjustified (for example if the arrangements between the parties lead to an unacceptable delay of the proceedings). However, the arbitral tribunal should use its authority to deviate from the parties' agreements with restraint and it is recommended that the arbitral tribunal discuss any intended deviations with the parties before actually determining the order of the proceedings. There is a remarkable area of tension between on the one hand the parties' autonomy and on the other hand the responsibility of the arbitral tribunal to determine the procedural order pursuant to Article 23(2). The more detailed the parties' agreement in regard of the procedural order is, the more likely it will be that the arbitral tribunal finds itself in a position where it feels that it can no longer perform its responsibilities. Normally arbitrators will find an acceptable solution for all parties involved in consultation with the parties. In exceptional cases where neither the parties nor the arbitral tribunal is willing to give in, the only way out may be that the arbitrators are relieved from their mandate, either at their own initiative or at the parties' motion. Under normal circumstances, however, taking into account that arbitration is primarily based on the parties' agreement and that the parties' autonomy is regarded as the overriding principle of arbitration, arbitrators should exercise restraint in ignoring the parties' mutual wishes.

The manner in which the procedure is conducted and the applicable terms will usually be determined by the arbitral tribunal at the outset of the arbitration (once the arbitration file has been transmitted to it), either on its own motion or after a meeting (or conference call) with the parties as provided for by Article 23(4) (see note 6). The arbitral tribunal may also send the parties a suggested procedural order and ask for the parties' comments. The course of the proceedings and the applicable rules will be laid down in a procedural order or in a simple letter from the arbitral tribunal to the parties. In an 'average' arbitration, the claimant and respondent will be given the opportunity to submit a statement of claim and a statement of defence, respectively. Subsequently, there may be a second round of written submissions (memorials of reply and rejoinder; see Article 24(2)). Then, a hearing will take place where the parties may orally elaborate on their contentions and present their case. Also, witnesses, if any, may be heard at this hearing or at a separate hearing. After the hearing, the arbitral tribunal will draft an award (which may, of course, either be a final or an interim award, or a combination of both).

As the arbitral tribunal might determine the order of the proceedings on its own motion after the arbitration file has been transmitted to it, it is recommended that the parties inform the arbitral tribunal of any procedural arrangements made between them by means of the request for arbitration and the short answer. The parties are also advised to indicate any preferences as to the terms for filing the statement of claim and statement of defence. In this respect, it may be advisable to mention actual dates (which can be tentative) instead of terms. Although it is not how it should be done in our view, in practice arbitrators sometimes determine that the respondent is required to file its statement of defence within a certain period of time *from the date of receipt* of the statement of claim. This may cause serious timing problems for the respondent if the claimant decides to file its statement of claim four weeks before the deadline, as some claimants tend to do, when knowing that this will leave their opponent with a serious timing problem due to other obligations. This problem may be avoided if the parties agree on (or the tribunal sets) specific dates for their submissions.

4.   Due Dispatch

The arbitral tribunal is expected to see to it that the proceedings are conducted without undue delay. Article 23(3) therefore requires the arbitral tribunal to ensure that the arbitral procedure takes place with due dispatch. The Introduction to NAI Arbitration Rules states the obvious: the length of an arbitral procedure primarily depends on the size and the complexity of the case and also on the conduct of the parties and their counsel. According to the NAI,[144] an NAI Arbitration takes approximately nine months, from the initial application to the final decision. This might be true for 'average' arbitrations. In large and more complex cases, however, it easily takes one to two years before a final award is available. In this respect NAI arbitration is not different from arbitration under the rules of other arbitration institutes.

   Unlike the ICC Rules, which provide for the possibility of replacement of one or more arbitrators if the arbitration is not completed in a timely manner,[145] the NAI Rules do not provide for sanctions if the arbitral tribunal does not satisfy its obligation under Article 23(3). Sanctions may be provided, however, by mandatory provisions of the applicable arbitration law.

> Article 1031(2) DCCP, which is of mandatory law, stipulates that at the request of one of the parties, the mandate of the arbitral tribunal may be terminated by the President (*voorzieningenrechter*) of the District Court or by a third party that has been appointed by the parties, if, despite repeated reminders, the arbitral tribunal executes its mandate in an unacceptably slow manner. See also the comments on Article 17 NAI Rules above. Article 1031(2) DCCP is hardly ever used. In a recent case, a request to terminate the mandate of the arbitral tribunal on the basis of Article 1031(2) DCCP was denied on the ground that the arbitral tribunal was not given the reminder notice as required, leaving unanswered the question whether the time that has lapsed since the hearing without an arbitral award having been rendered (over seven months), was too long.[146]

5.   Extensions of Time

Article 23(3) furthermore provides that the arbitral tribunal is authorized to extend in exceptional cases a period of time fixed by it or agreed to by the parties, either on its own motion or at the request of a party. Although Article 23(3)

---

[144]   <www.nai-nl.org>.

[145]   See Arts 12(2) and 24 ICC Rules.

[146]   Rotterdam District Court, 2 Dec. 2008, LJN: BH1633.

suggests that the arbitral tribunal will only grant extensions of time *in exceptional cases*, arbitrators will, in practice, often grant a request for an extension of time, especially if the other party agrees to the extension or if the party requesting the extension indicates the reasons for it. The refusal to grant an extension of time may raise the question whether the relevant party's right to be heard is effectively respected. A refusal might therefore give rise to a challenge of the tribunal's award in setting aside proceedings, which most arbitral tribunals eagerly try to avoid. A request for an extension of time may be denied, however, if the extension were to lead to undue delay of the arbitral proceedings (as a result of which the arbitral tribunal violates its obligation to ensure that the arbitral procedure takes place with due dispatch (Article 23(3)) or if the extension were to jeopardize, for example, the date set for the hearing.

6.   Meetings

According to Article 23(4), the arbitral tribunal may, at the request of a party or on its own motion, hold a meeting with the parties to discuss the course of the proceedings or to establish in more detail the factual and legal issues in dispute. Such a meeting (which can also be held in the form of a telephone or video conference) is likely to have a less formal character than a hearing where the parties present their case and where witnesses and experts may be heard. In the 'average' arbitration, a procedural meeting will usually not be necessary, as the NAI Rules provide a sufficient framework for a standard arbitration. In large and complex arbitrations, however, it may be useful to arrange for a procedural meeting after receipt of the arbitration file by the arbitral tribunal. In such meeting, procedural matters may be discussed and agreed upon. In general, it is not uncommon to use a procedural meeting to agree on a procedural order that more or less resembles the provisions one would normally find in Terms of Reference under the ICC Rules. Examples of such matters are: the procedural timetable, including the number of written submissions, deadlines for the written submissions (see Article 24), whether the parties are expected to present written witness statements with their submissions, whether document requests are possible, the date of the hearing (see Article 26), the venue of the hearing (see Article 22(2)) and the manner in which notices and submissions must be sent (see Articles 4 and 20). The procedural arrangements made during the meeting will usually be laid down by the arbitral tribunal in a procedural order. Article 23(4) also allows the arbitral tribunal to hold a procedural meeting at a later stage of the arbitral proceedings. In complex arbitrations or in arbitrations involving multiple claimants or respondents, it may be useful to hold a procedural meeting prior to an actual hearing in order to discuss the general purpose and structure of the hearing (such as the time available for the oral pleadings (e.g., each party gets 30 minutes for oral pleadings and 10 minutes for rebuttal), the possibility of examination of witnesses or experts at the hearing, the order in which witnesses and/or experts will be examined, the time available for (cross-)examination by the other party etc.).

ARTICLE 24 – EXCHANGE OF MEMORIALS

1. Unless the parties have agreed otherwise, the claimant and the respondent shall be given the opportunity by the arbitral tribunal to submit a statement of claim and a statement of defence, respectively.
2. Unless the parties have agreed otherwise, it is at the discretion of the arbitral tribunal whether a memorial of reply and a memorial of rejoinder shall be submitted. The same applies to any further written submissions of the parties.
3. The provisions of this article shall apply to a counterclaim accordingly.

1.   Statement of Claim and Statement of Defence

Article 24(1) provides for the submission of a statement of claim by the claimant and a statement of defence by the respondent, in which they can fully present their case. Unless the parties have agreed otherwise, the arbitral tribunal is obliged to give the claimant and the respondent the opportunity to submit a statement of claim and a statement of defence, respectively.

As set out in the comments on Articles 6 and 7 above, the request for arbitration and the short answer serve only as an introduction to the arbitral procedure and are meant primarily to inform the Administrator of the nature and circumstances of the dispute so as to facilitate the appointment of the arbitrators and to determine the amount of administration costs due. Article 8 explicitly provides that the request for arbitration and the short answer do not prejudice the right of the parties to submit a statement of claim and a statement of defence in accordance with Article 24. Hence, the statement of claim and the statement of defence will generally be the first written submissions of any substance. The statement of claim and the statement of defence are also possibly the only written submissions of the parties before a hearing takes place, so it is important that they contain a full description and substantiation of the parties' claims and defences, respectively. For the respondent, it is particularly important to realize that the statement of defence is, in principle, the last opportunity to raise a plea as to lack of jurisdiction of the arbitral tribunal (see Article 9(2)) or a counterclaim (see Article 25).

As to the structure of the written submissions, the statement of claim will generally include an introduction, a description of the relevant facts against the background of the legal issues at stake, an offer to produce (additional) evidence (see also below) and a clear description of the claimant's claims. If the respondent raised a counterclaim in the short answer, it is in our view recommended that the claimant replies to this counterclaim in the statement of claim, even though the claimant will have another opportunity to respond to the counterclaim in the statement of defence in respect of the counterclaim (see also Article 24(3)). Except for the description of the claims, the statement of defence may be structured more or less in the same way as the statement of claim (i.e. introduction, description of facts, respondent's defences and relevant legal issues, conclusion that claimant's claims must be fully or partially dismissed).

Generally, both the statement of claim and the statement of defence will be accompanied by supporting evidence, in the form of exhibits, expert reports or written witness statements (see also the comments on Article 28). The statement of claim and the statement of defence generally also include an offer to produce (additional) evidence. Depending on the circumstances of the case, an offer to produce evidence should be as concrete as possible. If possible, the parties should, for example, mention the names of the persons that could be examined as witnesses (if written witness statements are submitted with the statement of claim or statement of defence, this is already clear from these statements) and also indicate the relevance of their (anticipated) witness statements. If the procedural rules determined by the arbitral tribunal or agreed by the parties allow for the possibility of requests for production of documents, the statement of claim or statement of defence may also contain such a request.

As briefly mentioned above, the parties are free to derogate from Article 24(1). They may renounce the right to submit a statement of claim and a statement of defence. Although this will rarely be done in practice, the parties might agree to use the request for arbitration and the short answer to fully present their case and to renounce the right to submit a statement of claim and a statement of defence, if a decision on the merits is urgently required. It is also noted that the arbitration will be conducted differently if the respondent, in its statement of defence, raises the plea that the arbitral tribunal lacks jurisdiction (see the comments on Article 9). In that event, the claimant will generally first be given the opportunity to comment on the issue of jurisdiction in a written submission, following which the arbitral tribunal may determine that a hearing should be held on this issue. Subsequently, the arbitral tribunal will decide on its jurisdiction and the proceedings on the merits will only continue if the arbitral tribunal decides that it is competent to hear the claim.

2. Memorial of Reply, Memorial of Rejoinder and Further Written Submissions

As mentioned in the comments on Article 23 above, the parties are free to agree on a second (or even a third) round of written submissions, following the submission of the statement of claim and the statement of defence. If the parties have not made specific arrangements in this respect, Article 24(2) provides that it is at the discretion of the arbitral tribunal to decide whether the parties will be given the opportunity to file a memorial of reply and a memorial of rejoinder, or any other further written submissions. The claimant might aim for a second round of written submissions if the respondent, in the statement of defence, raised defences that the claimant would rather rebut in writing than orally at the hearing. The claimant itself might also wish to raise additional arguments prior to the hearing. The arbitral tribunal might order the submission of memorials of reply and rejoinder if, for example, it finds that certain issues have not yet been discussed sufficiently in the statement of claim and the statement of defence. Whether or not the arbitral tribunal orders a second round of written submissions will in practice also depend on the personal preference of the arbitrator(s). As a general rule, an arbitral tribunal will comply with a request for a further round of written submissions if the parties agree. However, if a date has already been set for the hearing and a further round of written submissions will jeopardize the date set, the arbitral tribunal might be more reluctant, given that it is usually difficult to find a new date at relatively short notice on which all parties involved are available for a hearing. On the other hand, depending on the circumstances and the grounds given by the requesting party, the arbitral tribunal's refusal to give the opportunity to file a further written submission, may also give rise to a challenge of the arbitral award in setting aside proceedings.

3. Counterclaim

According to Article 24(3), the provisions of Article 24(1) and 24(2) apply accordingly to a counterclaim. This means that the same order of exchanging documents will apply in the case of a counterclaim of the respondent. If the respondent files a counterclaim with its statement of defence (see also the comments on Article 25), the original claimant (who is at the same time the respondent in the counterclaim action) will be given the opportunity to respond to this counterclaim in a statement of defence regarding the counterclaim. If further memorials are to be submitted, the memorials regarding the principal action and the counterclaim may be combined in one memorial, which will then be titled, for example, memorial of rejoinder in the principal action and memorial of reply in the counterclaim action.

In the Dutch jurisdiction, counterclaims are normally dealt with in an exchange of written submissions – normally combined with written submissions in regard of the claim – that will eventually result in the original claimant submitting a statement of rejoinder in respect of the counterclaim. In international arbitrations there seems to be a tendency to limit the number of submissions and to omit the statement of rejoinder by the original claimant in regard of the counterclaim. Such practice seems to be acceptable in cases where the claim and the counterclaim are closely related and cover the same issue. This is particularly the case where the claim and the counterclaim actually address the same issues, but only propagate opposite conclusions. Under these circumstances a separate statement of rejoinder in the counterclaim would primarily result in a repetition of arguments and would basically provide the original claimant with an additional turn to run its arguments. Under normal circumstances, however, we would consider a procedural order which deprives the original claimant of the right to submit a statement of rejoinder in the counterclaim as questionable against the background of the principle of equal treatment and the right to be heard.

4. Deadlines and Time Limits

The NAI Rules do not provide for deadlines for the submission of statements or for the exchange of further memorials. This means that time limits may be determined by the parties or, in the absence of an agreement of the parties, will be determined by the arbitral tribunal, subject to the requirements of due process (which means that the parties should be given equal terms; see also the comments on Article 23(2)) and taking into account the obligation of the tribunal to ensure that the arbitral proceedings must be conducted with due dispatch (see Article 23(3)). In an 'average' NAI arbitration, the parties are usually given six or eight weeks for the submission of the statement of claim and the statement of defence. Shorter terms might be set for the submission of further memorials. In complex arbitrations, the arbitral tribunal will be inclined to set longer terms (e.g., three or four months) and the parties themselves may also request the arbitral tribunal to do so. See the comments on Article 23(3) for the way in which the arbitral tribunal usually handles requests for an extension of time. It is not always clear what the consequences will be of missing a deadline set by the arbitral tribunal or agreed on between the parties. If a submission is only one or two days late, most arbitral tribunals will be inclined to accept the submission anyway, in order to avoid complaints regarding a violation of the principles of due process, either in the arbitration or in setting aside proceedings. For the same reasons, the arbitral tribunal will ordinarily give a party who completely missed a deadline, one final opportunity to file the submission before it is found inadmissible. In the event that the arbitral tribunal does refuse to admit a submission filed after the deadline, this omission might be cured by presenting the contents of the submission at a hearing, to which the parties are, in principle, entitled (see also the comments on Article 26). The parties' right to be heard may also become an issue, if the arbitrator and the other party are confronted for the first time with statements and arguments at a hearing. In such cases most arbitrators are likely to arrange for a solution where the party who missed the deadline for the submission is given another opportunity to present its case in writing, before a hearing takes place.

ARTICLE 25 – COUNTERCLAIM

1. A counterclaim that is not raised, at the latest, in the statement of defence or, in the absence thereof, that is not brought forward in the first written or oral defence, cannot be raised at a later stage in the same arbitral proceedings, except in exceptional circumstances as determined by the arbitral tribunal.
2. A counterclaim is admissible if it falls under the same arbitration agreement as that on which the request for arbitration is based, or if the same arbitration agreement is expressly or tacitly made to apply to it by the parties.

1.   Counterclaim – Admissibility

The respondent has the right to pursue its own claims against the claimant in the same arbitral proceedings. According to Article 25(2), a counterclaim is admissible if it falls under the same arbitration agreement as that on which the request for arbitration is based, or if the same arbitration agreement is expressly or tacitly made to apply to it by the parties.

By requiring that the counterclaim falls under the *same* arbitration agreement as the claim in the principal action, Article 25(2) seems more stringent than strictly necessary. In our view, it should be sufficient that the counterclaim is governed by an arbitration agreement – possibly a different arbitration agreement than the one applying to the claim in the principal action – which provides for arbitration under the NAI Rules.[147] This does not necessarily have to be the same arbitration agreement as for the claim in the principal action, as there may be multiple contractual relationships between the parties with identical arbitration agreements.

If the counterclaim does not fall under the same arbitration agreement as that pursuant to which the arbitral tribunal is competent to hear the claim in the principal action, Article 25(2) allows the parties to agree, either expressly or tacitly, that the same arbitration agreement also applies to the counterclaim. If the counterclaim is not covered by the same arbitration agreement as the claim in the principal action, the claimant is not very likely to agree to the analogous application of the arbitration agreement to the counterclaim, as this will allow the respondent to extend the scope of the arbitration, whereas it would otherwise be forced to initiate separate arbitral proceedings to pursue its own claim. Should the parties agree that the same arbitration agreement that applies to the principal action, be applied to the counterclaim, it is advised that the parties agree to this explicitly, in order to avoid possible problems with the

---

[147] This view is shared by Ten Cate, see Vademecum Arbitrage, 2002 (W. ten Cate), 53.

enforcement and execution of the award in respect of the counterclaim (for instance because it is argued by the original claimant that the arbitral tribunal lacks jurisdiction for the counterclaim after all). This being said, it must be assumed that the claimant has at least tacitly agreed to the counterclaim being dealt with in the same arbitration, if a counterclaim is submitted and the claimant refrains from raising the defence that the counterclaim does not fall under the same arbitration agreement. In addition, it should be noted that the provisions with regard to a plea as to lack of jurisdiction also apply to a counterclaim. If the claimant in the principal action wishes to raise the plea that the arbitral tribunal lacks jurisdiction in respect of the counterclaim on the ground that there is no valid arbitration agreement, it must do so before submitting any defence in respect of the counterclaim (see Article 9(2)), i.e. in the statement of defence in the counterclaim action or in a separate memorial. If the original claimant fails to timely raise this plea, it is barred from doing so at a later stage. Consequently, the arbitral tribunal will have jurisdiction to hear the counterclaim.

> If the claimant forces the respondent to initiate new arbitral proceedings for its (counter)claim as set out above, the respondent may aim for consolidation of the arbitrations pursuant to Article 1046 DCCP, when the place of arbitration is in the Netherlands and the possibility of consolidation has not been excluded in (one of) the arbitration agreement(s). For consolidation, see also the comments on Articles 1(e) and 41 NAI Rules.

2. Counterclaim – When to Raise

Article 25(1) provides that as a general rule, a counterclaim must be raised, at the latest, in the statement of defence. In the absence of a statement of defence, the respondent must raise a counterclaim in its first written or oral defence. A statement of defence may be absent in case the respondent initially failed to appear in the arbitral proceedings or if the parties agreed to renounce the right to submit a statement of claim and a statement of defence (see the comments on Article 24(1)). Should it be necessary to raise a counterclaim during a hearing as the first opportunity for an oral defence, it is recommended that the respondent also sets out the counterclaim in writing and, if possible, presents the written counterclaim to the arbitral tribunal and to the other party at the beginning of the hearing.

A counterclaim may be raised at a later stage in the arbitral proceedings only in exceptional circumstances, as determined by the arbitral tribunal. This may occur if the circumstances that give rise to a counterclaim did not occur until after the statement of defence was filed, for example if an amendment of claim by the claimant (which, according to Article 34(1), may be raised until the beginning of the final hearing or the final memorial admitted by the tribunal) gives rise to a counterclaim of the respondent. Should there be uncertainty about the necessity of a counterclaim at the time the statement of defence must be filed, we would recommend that the respondent files the counterclaim with the statement of defence anyway, as the counterclaim, once filed, may be amended or increased until the beginning of the final hearing or, in the absence of a hearing, in the final memorial admitted by the arbitral tribunal, and may be decreased at any time (see also the comments on Article 34).

It will depend on the nature of the counterclaim and the circumstances of the case (such as applicable law) whether it is actually necessary to raise a counterclaim as referred to in Article 25. If the respondent claims to have a claim against the claimant, this claim may be set-off against the claim that the claimant purports to have against the respondent. Whether in that case, an actual counterclaim is necessary, will depend on the applicable law. Some legal systems provide for the possibility of set-off by way of defence. Even if this is the case, it may be advisable to submit the relevant claim as a counterclaim, if the claim is rather complex. From a practical point of view, arbitrators may be reluctant to hear a complex claim by way of defence, although strictly speaking there is no reason not to assess a counterclaim in full, if it is only presented by way of defence. Dutch arbitrators may be inspired in this respect by Article 6:136 of the DCC, pursuant to which the defence that the principal claim has been set off against another claim may be rejected, if the validity of the latter cannot be easily established. Although it is uncertain whether this rule of evidence, which is part of Dutch substantive law, also applies in arbitration (see also Article 27, note 1),[148] some arbitrators may be inclined to take the same approach from a practical point of view.

ARTICLE 26 – HEARING

1. The arbitral tribunal shall give the parties an opportunity to elaborate on their contentions orally at a hearing unless the parties agree to forego such opportunity.
2. The arbitral tribunal shall determine the day, time and place of the hearing and shall give the parties adequate advance notice thereof. The same shall apply to any further hearing that the arbitral tribunal may, at its discretion, deem necessary.
3. The arbitral tribunal may allow other persons than those mentioned in Articles 21, 29, 30 and 31, to attend the hearing unless a party raises objections thereto.

---

[148] See Fung Fen Chung, 2004, 82 et seq.

1.   Right to a Hearing

Article 26(1) lays down the parties' right to present their case and to elaborate on their contentions during a hearing, following the exchange of memorials. The parties may renounce their right to a hearing, if they wish to conduct a documents-only arbitration (Article 26(1)). If they wish to do this, it is required that such renunciation be done explicitly and unambiguously, taking into account that the NAI Rules explicitly instruct the arbitral tribunal to hold a hearing and some arbitrators take the view that the hearing is the most significant part of the arbitral proceedings for gathering information on which to base their decision and may therefore be reluctant to refrain from it.

> Article 1039(2) DCCP, which is of mandatory law, provides that the arbitral tribunal shall give the parties the opportunity to give an oral explanation of their contentions, either at the request of one of the parties or on its own accord. As Article 1039(2) does not provide that the parties may agree otherwise, Article 1039(2) DCCP prohibits parties to agree on *not* having a hearing. However, this only applies prior to the commencement of the arbitral proceedings, i.e. the parties cannot agree in advance (in the arbitration agreement) that no hearing will take place. It is, however, generally accepted that parties are allowed to renounce the right to a hearing after the commencement of the arbitration.[149] Article 26(1) of the NAI Rules is considered to contain the possibility of such renunciation and is therefore not contrary to Article 1039(2).

2.   Hearing – What to Expect

As follows from Article 26(1), the hearing following the exchange of memorials is meant primarily to offer the parties the opportunity to elaborate orally on their contentions. Although not all arbitral tribunals adhere to this rule, it may be considered best practice for arbitrators to inform the parties in advance what the procedural order during the hearing will be. Normally hearings in NAI arbitrations will closely resemble the typical hearing in state court proceedings. Accordingly, the hearing is primarily aimed at allowing the parties to orally elaborate on their written submissions with the only exception that the available time is much longer than in state court hearings. The parties will usually be given the opportunity to plead their case, following which the parties will both be given the opportunity of a rebuttal of the other party's statements. Although witnesses and/or experts may be heard during the same hearing, arbitral tribunals in NAI arbitrations seem reluctant to do so and are inclined to schedule a separate hearing for the examination of witnesses or experts (see also the comments on Articles 29-31).

The structure of a hearing may, however, be different in international arbitrations, as well as in large and complex national arbitrations. The NAI Rules allow for the hearings to be held in line with international practice, including examination and cross-examination of witnesses and experts. In general, the

---

[149] G.J. Meijer 2008 (T&C Rv), Art. 1039 DCCP, note 3.

arbitral tribunal and the parties are free to gear the hearings to their needs. The NAI Rules in principle do not raise any barriers in this respect.

As follows from Article 23(1), each party must have a sufficient opportunity to present its case and the arbitral tribunal must therefore ensure that the party that begins (usually the claimant) does not deprive the other party of the time that it reasonably needs to present its case.

In the Dutch jurisdiction, the production of pleading notes is common and most arbitrators expect the parties to provide them with pleading notes setting out the relevant party's oral elaborations in detail. To date it is even considered good practice to submit the pleading notes directly in advance of the oral elaborations. The submission of post-hearing briefs is not common in national arbitrations. Nevertheless arbitral tribunals and parties are free to agree on such briefs, if they wish to do so. Furthermore, it is not uncommon to arrange for post-hearing briefs in international arbitrations. Also court reporters are an uncommon phenomenon in national arbitrations. We are in fact not aware of the use of court reporters in a national arbitration. However, again it is not uncommon to arrange for court reporters in international arbitrations.

3.   Date, Time and Place of the Hearing

According to Article 26(2), it is the arbitral tribunal that fixes the day, time and physical place of the hearing (or further hearings that the arbitral tribunal may, at its discretion, deem necessary). The arbitral tribunal is required to give the parties adequate advance notice thereof.

Although the language of Article 26(2) suggests otherwise, hearing dates will in practice be determined by the arbitral tribunal in consultation with the parties.

According to Article 26(2), the arbitral tribunal will also determine the location of the hearing. As noted in respect of Article 22(2) above, hearings may be held at any place the arbitral tribunal deems appropriate. Most commonly, the location of the hearing will be determined depending on where the parties and the individual arbitrators reside and on the facilities needed (number of rooms, e.g., hearing room and separate break-out rooms, audiovisual requirements, secretarial assistance, court reporters, etc.). If the hearing is to take place in Rotterdam, the facilities of the NAI can be used. It is recommended, however, that arrangements be made by the arbitral tribunal well in advance, as the available rooms and facilities of the NAI are limited. In international arbitrations, the Peace Palace in The Hague is regularly chosen as venue for hearings.

4.   Persons Attending the Hearing

The arbitral proceedings – and mainly the hearings – are assumed to be confidential and therefore not open to the public. This principle of confidentiality is, however, not embedded in the NAI Rules, as it is not in most other arbitration rules. Article 26 may be considered as one of the few exceptions of provisions that seem to be based on a principle of confidentiality. Article 26(3) limits the individuals that are, in principle, admitted to the hearing to the following (categories of) individuals: the parties themselves, their lawyers or authorized representatives and other assistants (see Article 21), witnesses (and, if applicable, their counsel; see Article 29), party-appointed experts (see Article 30) and tribunal-appointed experts (see Article 31). The arbitral tribunal may allow individuals other than those mentioned above to attend the hearing, unless a party raises objections thereto. Although not mentioned by Article 26(3), it is evident that the secretary to the arbitral tribunal (if there is one; see Article 39(1)) is also allowed to attend hearings.

Given the privacy of hearings in arbitral proceedings, it is customary that all those present identify themselves at the beginning of a hearing by stating their name and position. For this purpose, the arbitral tribunal will appreciate (and will most commonly also request) receiving from each party in advance a list with the names of the individuals who will be attending the hearing on its behalf (see also the comments on Article 21(2)).

Although party-appointed experts are explicitly mentioned as category of individuals that are typically allowed to attend the hearing, this is not to say that they will be allowed to attend hearings at all times. It may be assumed that party-appointed experts will only have access, if they have produced an expert report during the previous stages of the arbitral proceedings. Experts that only attend a hearing for the purpose of responding to possible questions of the arbitral tribunal are likely to be refused, if the other party timely raises objections.

The presence of potential witnesses may also be a problem, if one of the parties intends to have them heard at a later stage of the arbitral proceedings (see Article 29, note 2).

5. Report of the Hearing

The NAI Rules do not require that minutes be taken of the hearing and as a consequence, no minutes are taken in 'average' NAI arbitrations. It is, however, advisable that the arbitration file contains at least some record of what was discussed during the hearing. If there is a secretary to the arbitral tribunal, the parties may request the secretary to keep notes during the hearing (which the secretary or one of the arbitrators will generally already do on his or her own motion). In a recent case, a party summoned the arbitrators to submit the informal hearing notes made by the secretary to the tribunal, which were not submitted to the parties, as it wanted to use these notes in setting aside proceedings. The Amsterdam Court of Appeal ordered the tribunal to submit the notes, but allowed the arbitrators – under the supervision of an independent third party – to delete those parts of the notes that did not relate to the facts of the hearing, for instance those relating to the deliberations by the arbitrators about the case.[150]

---

[150] Amsterdam Court of Appeal, 2 Dec. 2008, NJF 2009, 39. Note that Supreme Court appeal is pending.

If the parties wish to have a more precise reporting of the hearing, they may arrange for sound recording or for a verbatim transcript of the hearing by court reporters. It is recommended, however, to discuss these wishes with the arbitral tribunal prior to the hearing, as sound recordings and court reporters are not often found in NAI arbitrations.

ARTICLE 27 – EVIDENCE IN GENERAL

> Unless the parties have agreed otherwise, the arbitral tribunal shall be free to determine the admissibility, relevance, materiality and weight of evidence as well as the allocation of the burden of proof.

1. Evidence in General

Article 27 provides that the arbitral tribunal is free to determine the admissibility, relevance, materiality and weight of evidence as well as the allocation of the burden of proof, unless the parties have agreed otherwise.[151] Therefore, the arbitral tribunal is not bound by the procedural rules of evidence that apply in state court proceedings. In practice, however, most arbitral tribunals seem to adhere to the same basic rules. This does not change the fact that complicated questions may arise as to the weighing of evidence and the allocation of the burden of proof. The chances of the arbitral tribunal encountering complicated issues regarding evidence are equally substantial in NAI arbitration as in any other arbitration. It is, for example, already a difficult question whether an arbitral tribunal is obliged to apply rules of evidence following from the applicable substantive law chosen by the parties, if the parties authorized the arbitral tribunal to make its award in accordance with the rules of law.[152] Then again this question may be of little relevance in practice, since the arbitral tribunal's decisions in this respect will not be subject to review by state courts in setting aside proceedings (see also Article 1065 DCCP, note 4, in Part III, Chapter 1). Consequently, some arbitrators may be inclined to allow themselves more freedom in deciding issues of evidence, knowing that their decision cannot effectively be challenged by the parties.

> Article 27 of the NAI Rules is in line with Article 1039(5) DCCP, which provides that the rules of evidence to be applied are at the discretion of the arbitral tribunal, unless the parties have agreed otherwise. However, it is generally accepted that under Dutch law, arbitral tribunals should apply the same rules of evidence as a court would apply, when deciding on its competence and hence, on the validity of

---

[151] Unlike the NAI Rules, Art. 24(1) UNCITRAL Rules and Art. 19(1) ICDR Rules explicitly provide that each party shall have the burden of proving the facts relied on to support its claim or defence.

[152] G.J. Meijer 2008 (T&C Rv), Art. 1039 DCCP, note 6(b); Fung Fen Chung, 2004, 82 et seq.

the arbitration agreement.[153] It is thus assured that arbitrators are applying the same test as would apply in setting aside proceedings.

The principle of party autonomy dictates that the parties may agree on the rules of evidence to be applied by the arbitral tribunal. If the parties made use of this opportunity, the arbitral tribunal should, in principle, adhere to the parties' agreement. It is for instance not uncommon to refer to the IBA Rules of Evidence in order to obtain more certainty as to rules of evidence that the arbitral tribunal is going to apply. Reference to the IBA Rules of Evidence can be regarded as a useful addition to the NAI Rules, particularly in international arbitrations in the context of which there is a need for document production or other forms of disclosure. As with most continental law systems, discovery and similar forms of disclosure are an unknown phenomenon under Dutch law. Although it is generally accepted that any form of disclosure can be introduced in NAI arbitrations on the basis of Article 28 NAI Rules, the NAI Rules do not provide any guidance as to specific rules that arbitral tribunal should apply, when assessing requests for disclosure.

The IBA Rules of Evidence have been prepared by a Working Party of the IBA and have been issued as a resource to parties and to arbitrators in order to enable them to conduct the evidence phase of international arbitration in an efficient and economical manner. The IBA Rules of Evidence contain provisions for, inter alia, the presentation of documents, witnesses and experts, as well as for the admissibility of certain evidence and the conduct of evidentiary hearings. The IBA Rules of Evidence reflect procedures in use in many different legal systems (both United States/United Kingdom practices and continental practices) and they may therefore be particularly useful when the parties come from different legal cultures. In the Foreword to the IBA Rules of Evidence, it is recommended that the parties add the following additional language to their arbitration clause if they wish to adopt the IBA Rules of Evidence in their arbitration clause: 'In addition to the NAI Rules, the parties agree that the arbitration shall be conducted according to the IBA Rules of Evidence'. Obviously, the parties may also adopt the IBA Rules of Evidence, in whole or in part, at a later stage, when the arbitration is underway, or they may vary them. Some arbitrators prefer referring to the IBA Rules of Evidence as guidelines only, apparently with the objective to retain more room for manoeuvre. Although no rule prohibits such approach, using the IBA Rules of Evidence as mere guidelines obviously provides the parties with less certainty as to the rules of evidence that the arbitral tribunal is likely to use.

Also, the UNCITRAL Notes on Organising Arbitral Proceedings could be a practical tool for finding guidance in organizing the matter of proof in arbitral proceedings.[154] The purpose of these non-binding Notes is to assist arbitration

---

[153] Burg. Rv, 2006 (H.J. Snijders), Art. 1039 DCCP, note 5. See also Fung Fen Chung, 2004, 76 et seq., who is not convinced that arbitrators, when deciding a plea as to lack of jurisdiction, are required to apply the same rules of evidence as a court would apply in determining the existence and validity of the arbitration agreement.

[154] See <www.uncitral.org/pdf/english/texts/arbitration/arb-notes/arb-notes-e.pdf>.

practitioners by listing and briefly describing questions on which appropriately timed decisions on organizing arbitral proceedings may be useful. The Notes have been prepared with a particular view to international arbitrations and may be used irrespective of whether the arbitration is administered by an arbitration institute.[155]

Dutch arbitrators in national arbitrations are likely to apply the rules of evidence that apply in state court proceedings, even though the arbitral tribunal is not bound by those rules. It is generally assumed that there is no need for more specific rules of evidence in national arbitrations, unless the parties wish to have absolute certainty on the rules of evidence that will be applied by the arbitral tribunal.

ARTICLE 28 – PRODUCTION OF DOCUMENTS

1. Except as otherwise agreed by the parties, the memorials mentioned in Article 24 shall be accompanied by, to as large an extent as possible, the documentary evidence relied on by the parties.
2. The arbitral tribunal shall have the power to order the production of specific documents which it deems relevant to the dispute.

1. Supporting Written Evidence

Article 28(1) stipulates that the memorials referred to in Article 24 (meaning: the statement of claim and statement of defence and possible further written submissions, if any) will be accompanied, to as large an extent as possible, by the documentary evidence relied on by the parties. Although Article 28(1) provides that the parties may agree otherwise, this is rarely done in practice. It is recommended that the parties indeed submit the relevant documentary evidence with the first round of written submissions, as there may not be a further round of submissions. That being said, it does not frequently occur in practice that the arbitral tribunal actually refuses to admit documents as evidence that have been submitted shortly before or even at the hearing. In that event, the arbitral tribunal must see to it, however, that the other party has sufficient opportunity to respond to the contents of the documents submitted (see also the comments on Article 23(1)). If it cannot be expected that the other party will respond to the documents presented at the hearing (for example after a short break), the arbitral tribunal may allow that party to comment on the evidence submitted in writing after the hearing.

There is no provision with regard to the form in which the documents must be presented. Absenting an agreement of the parties on the production of documents, the arbitral tribunal may decide on the manner in which evidence is to be presented

---

[155] See also A.J. van den Berg (ed), *Yearbook Commercial Arbitration*, Vol. XXII (The Hague, Kluwer Law International, 1997).

(possibly in a procedural meeting, see Article 23(4)). The arbitral tribunal will usually expect that the documentary evidence on which each party relies, will be presented to it in the form of exhibits which are contained in one or more binders, numbered consecutively (for example C-1, C-2 etc. for the exhibits of the claimant and R-1, R-2 etc. for the exhibits of the respondent), separated by dividing pages and listed in a structured index. If a large number of documents are (expected to be) submitted, the arbitral tribunal might request the parties to file the exhibits also in digital form, possibly in a searchable format. Written evidence may also include expert opinions or witness testimonies in written form (as a signed witness statement or as a sworn affidavit). The party submitting witness or expert evidence in written form should, however, be prepared that the other party or the arbitral tribunal may require the relevant witness or expert to attend a hearing before the tribunal for oral questioning (see also the comments on Articles 29 and 30).

2.   Production of Documents Ordered by the Arbitral Tribunal

Article 28(2) authorizes the arbitral tribunal to order the production of specific documents which it deems relevant to the dispute. The arbitral tribunal may order the production of documents on its own motion, but may also do so following a request of one or more of the parties.

The arbitral tribunal cannot force a party to actually submit the documents that it was ordered to produce, but if a party refuses to comply with the arbitral tribunal's order, the arbitral tribunal may deduce the conclusions that it deems appropriate (see also Article 42). It goes without saying that those conclusions will usually not be in favour of the party refusing to produce documents. In addition, a number of national laws, including Dutch law, allow the arbitral tribunal to impose a penalty (*dwangsom*), for the time that the requested documents are not produced. Furthermore, under Dutch law, a party's refusal to produce the requested documents may have a counterproductive effect, even after the final award has been rendered. A party that wilfully withholds evidence or documents that may have been relevant for the decision of the arbitral tribunal, risks revocation of the arbitral award pursuant to Article 1068(1)(c) DCCP (see also Article 1068 DCCP, note 5 in Part III, Chapter 2). It is probably for all these reasons that non-compliance with an order of the arbitral tribunal to produce documents is rare in practice.

The wording of Article 28(2) provides only limited guidance as to the circumstances that may give rise to the production of documents. In fact, Article 28(2) hardly sets any limits in this respect. However, the following limitations apply in any event. Firstly, the arbitral tribunal is only authorized to order the production of documents *by the parties*. It cannot order third parties to produce evidence. The production of documents by third parties should be enforced by a state court if the applicable law provides for that. Under circumstances, there may also be a possibility of obtaining documents from a third party by requesting the arbitral tribunal to order the other party to retrieve the necessary documents from the relevant third party (if necessary by taking appropriate legal action). For example, such order may be considered, if the documents are held by a subsidiary of one of the parties. Secondly, the arbitral tribunal will generally not order, on its own motion or at the request of a party, the production of a wide range of unspecified documents, but only specific documents that it deems relevant or that have been requested by the other party. In this respect the arbitral tribunal is likely to apply criteria that more or less resemble those in the IBA Rules of Evidence, even if these rules have not been explicitly agreed upon by the parties or referred to by the arbitral tribunal in a procedural order, because there seems to be growing tendency to regard the IBA Rules of Evidence as best practice in international arbitrations. Thirdly, by the same token arbitrators are likely to apply restrictions similar to those contained in Article 9(2) of the IBA Rules of Evidence, even if these rules do not explicitly apply. Accordingly, it may be assumed that arbitral tribunals will generally be reluctant or will refuse to order the production of documents that are legally privileged or commercially or technically confidential or sensitive. Also, arbitrators may refuse to order the production of documents if it constitutes an unreasonable burden for the party that is ordered to produce the documents, or if the party that is ordered to produce certain documents is able to show that those documents have been lost or destroyed.[156] In respect of the notion of legal privilege, it is important to note that Dutch law does not provide for a doctrine of legal privilege. Even without such doctrine the arbitral tribunal may consider certain documents to be legally privileged, for instance because they are regarded as legally privileged pursuant to the laws of one of the parties or any other laws relevant to the dispute. Without a doctrine of legal privilege, it is, however, difficult to predict what specific approach the arbitrators are likely to choose.

> Article 28(2) of the NAI Rules is based on Article 1039(4) DCCP, which also provides that the arbitral tribunal may order the production of documents.

3. Production of Documents at the Request of a Party

The NAI Rules do not provide for the possibility for a party to request documents or evidence directly from the other party. However, as mentioned above, a party may request the arbitral tribunal to use its authority under Article 28(2) to order the production of specific documents which the arbitral tribunal (also) deems relevant to the dispute.

---

[156] See 'Document production in international arbitration', 2006 Special Supplement to *ICC International Court of Arbitration Bulletin*, and the 'Commentary on the new IBA Rules of Evidence in international commercial arbitration' by the IBA Working Party, published in *Business Law International*, 2000, Issue 2.

ARTICLE 29 – WITNESSES

---

1. The arbitral tribunal shall determine the day, time and place of the examination of witnesses, as well as the manner in which the examination shall proceed unless the parties agreed to a manner of examination. The parties shall be notified in writing in a timely manner of this day, time and place.

2. A party who wishes to have a witness examined shall notify the arbitral tribunal and the other party in a timely manner of the witness' name and the subject matters of the witness' testimony.

3. The arbitral tribunal shall decide whether a witness shall be examined under oath or on affirmation.

4. The arbitral tribunal shall decide whether, and in what form, the examination shall be recorded.

5. If the arbitral tribunal is composed of more than one arbitrator, it shall be authorized to designate one of its members to examine witnesses. In such case a written report of the examination of the witnesses shall be made.

---

1.   General Comments

Witness examination is a common phenomenon in NAI arbitrations as it is in proceedings before the state courts. Having said this, it should be noted that witness examination does not play a role that is equally significant as in Anglo-Saxon law systems. In fact, most arbitrations are concluded without any witnesses being heard. There seems to be a tendency to rely on written evidence only and witness testimonies are regarded as a form of evidence that is potentially unreliable.

This does not change the fact that there may be a stage in the arbitral proceedings where it becomes necessary to examine the witnesses on whose testimony the parties have relied in their written submissions in order to prove certain facts or to clarify certain issues that are deemed relevant for the arbitral tribunal's decision. The arbitral tribunal may set out in an interim award or in an order which facts it deems relevant and which party has the burden of proof in that respect. However, this is not always done in practice, so that the parties should also ensure that the witnesses, whose testimonies they are to rely on, are examined to see if their testimony can be relevant for the outcome of the case.

Article 29 authorizes the arbitral tribunal to examine witnesses during a hearing. Witnesses can be examined either at the hearing following the exchange of written submissions, or at a separate evidentiary hearing. As mentioned above in the comments on Article 26, arbitrators in NAI arbitrations are generally inclined to schedule separate hearings for the examination of witnesses.

If witnesses are heard, this is normally done in a way that is quite different from Anglo-Saxon examination and cross-examination. Such examination and cross-examination is only conducted in international arbitrations, if at all. In national arbitrations, the parties normally take a much less active role. Normally the arbitral tribunal takes the lead in examining the witnesses.

Occasionally, the arbitrators prefer to hear potential witnesses informally *ad informandum*, without formally hearing them as witnesses. If both parties agree, we see no harm in such practice. However, if any of the parties wishes the relevant individual to be properly heard as witness, the arbitral tribunal should respect such wish and should refrain from pushing the parties to accept a less informal approach. The arbitral tribunal should also see to it that the principle of hearing both sides is respected and that the parties get sufficient opportunity to hear other witnesses on the same subject.[157]

2. Identification of Witnesses to be Heard

Article 29(2) provides that a party who wishes to have a witness examined, shall notify the arbitral tribunal and the other party in a timely manner of the witness' name and the subject matter(s) of the witness' testimony. This article seems to suggest that it is, in principle, up to the parties to decide which and how many witnesses will be examined. It is assumed, however, that in exceptional circumstances, the arbitral tribunal may refuse to hear one or more witnesses proposed by the parties if this is justified by the circumstances of the case (for example, if a party attempts to frustrate the proceedings by calling a disproportionate number of witnesses or if the proposed witnesses may also be heard at a later stage of the proceedings).[158] The arbitral tribunal, however, will have to exercise restraint in using this authority, as a refusal to hear a witness may violate a party's right to be heard (see Article 23(1)) and may give rise to a challenge in setting aside proceedings.[159] The arbitral tribunal should, in principle, refrain from refusing a witness because of its doubts as to the witness' reliability, for example because of a special relationship between the witness and one of the parties. The weighing of the evidence should be conducted on the basis of the witness testimony. The arbitral tribunal should not deprive a party of the right to produce the evidence it deems necessary, because again this could constitute a violation of the relevant party's right to be heard. The same goes for possible witnesses who have attended previous hearings. Although the arbitral tribunal may negatively assess this fact when weighing the witness testimony, it should not refuse to examine the witness

---

[157] See HR 25 May 2007, NJ 2007, 294 (Spaanderman/Anova Food). On this decision, see also M.H. de Boer, 'Kroniek arbitragerecht', *Tijdschrift voor Civiele Rechtspleging* 2008, 137-141.

[158] See for example NAI 6 Apr. 2000 and NAI 1 Aug. 2003, TvA 2004, 20-21 (para. 5.3).

[159] See also Art. 20(3) of the ICC Rules, which also states that the arbitral tribunal *may* decide to hear witnesses.

at all, because again this could constitute a violation of the relevant party's right to be heard.

> Article 1039(3) DCCP provides that the arbitral tribunal *may* – at the request of either party – allow parties to examine witnesses, which implies that the arbitral tribunal has the authority to reject the hearing of a proposed witness. As stated above, this authority should, however, be used with restraint, given that the refusal to examine a witness may violate principles of due process.

Although the NAI Rules do not include a provision that explicitly allows the arbitral tribunal to examine witnesses at its own initiative, it may be assumed that it follows implicitly from Article 29(1) that the arbitral tribunal has the authority to do so. This authority may be relevant, for example, if the parties fail to call a key witness that the arbitral tribunal wishes to examine.

3.   Summoning of Witnesses

Although the NAI Rules provide for witnesses to be summoned to appear, such summoning normally does not take place. Most parties are inclined to rely on witnesses who have declared their willingness to appear and therefore summoning is normally not necessary. Summoning of witnesses is in practice the exception. In case of summoning the following applies.

Once the witnesses to be examined have been identified and a date for the hearing has been set, the relevant witnesses must be summoned to appear before the arbitral tribunal. In arbitration, it is usually sufficient to summon a witness by registered letter. If possible, it is recommended to contact the witness in advance and to announce that the witness can expect to receive a formal invitation to testify at the hearing. In addition, it is advised to ask the witness in advance for dates on which he or she is unable to attend a hearing so that the arbitral tribunal can take this into account when setting a date.

It follows implicitly from Article 29(2) that it is the responsibility of the party relying on the statement of a witness to summon that witness to appear before the arbitral tribunal at the date set for the (evidentiary) hearing. Article 29(2) also requires that party to timely notify the arbitral tribunal and the other party of the witness' name (and although not mentioned by Article 29(2), in practice also the witness' place of residence) and the subject matters of the witness' testimony. What can be considered as timely in this respect will depend on the circumstances of the case. As a general rule, however, the notification to the arbitral tribunal and the other party should be given at least one week before the hearing, but preferably longer.[160] It must be assumed that the information required by Article 29(2) regarding the subject matters of the witness' testimony may be

---

[160] Article 25(2) UNCITRAL Rules provides that the names and addresses of the witnesses shall be communicated to the tribunal and the other party at least 15 days before the hearing. Art. 20(2) ICDR Rules contains a similar provision.

brief, as a party obviously cannot be required to run ahead of the witness' testimony.

4. Assistance of State Courts in Examination of Witnesses

Under the NAI Rules, arbitrators do not have the power to compel the appearance of persons who do not wish to be heard, nor to compel a witness to give testimony. The authority of the arbitral tribunal is limited to drawing negative inferences from the refusal of a witness to appear or to answer certain questions for the party relying on the witness' statement or the party who has the power to force the witness to appear (for example if the witness is an employee of one of the parties). However, many jurisdictions (including the Netherlands) provide for the possibility for the party who wishes to have an unwilling witness examined, to solicit the assistance of the state courts in obtaining testimony.

> Under Article 1041(2) DCCP, a party may request the arbitral tribunal for permission to petition the President (*voorzieningenrechter*) of the District Court (the Rotterdam District Court, see Article 64 of the NAI Rules) to appoint a judge before whom the examination of a witness can take place when a witness refuses to appear before the arbitral tribunal or refuses to give testimony. According to Article 1041(2) DCCP, the examination shall take place in accordance with the rules that apply in state court proceedings (i.e. Articles 163-184 DCCP). Article 1041(2) DCCP provides that the arbitrator(s) shall be given the opportunity to attend the examination of the witness. The arbitrators will have the opportunity to ask questions to the witness, albeit through the intermediary of the court judge appointed for the examination. Although not explicitly provided for in Article 1041(2), the parties and their counsel are, in our view, entitled to attend the examination of the witness by the District Court judge and as with regular witness examination, the parties' counsel should be given the opportunity to ask questions. As soon as possible after the unwilling witness has been examined, the court clerk shall send the arbitral tribunal and the parties a copy of the record of the examination (Article 1041(3) DCCP). Article 1041(4) provides that the tribunal may suspend the arbitral proceedings until it has received the record of the examination, which the arbitral tribunal will usually do in practice, unless the suspension causes unacceptable delay.

5. Time and Place of Examination

The arbitral tribunal determines day, time and place for examining witnesses, unless the parties agreed otherwise (Article 29(1)). Even without an explicit agreement between the parties, the arbitral tribunal will ordinarily consult with the parties before actually setting day, time and place of examining witnesses in order to avoid that a date is set for the hearing on which the parties or the witnesses to be examined are unavailable.

> Similar to Article 29(1) of the NAI Rules, Article 1041(1) DCCP stipulates that the arbitral tribunal determines time and place of the hearing and the manner in which the examination will proceed.

6.   Manner of Witness Examination

The NAI Rules allow the parties to determine the manner of witness examination (see Article 29(1)). The parties may agree, for example, on Anglo-American examination and cross-examination, including the submission of depositions, following the examination of the relevant witness by the parties' counsel in the presence of only a court reporter. The parties may also agree on the applicability of procedural rules that include provisions on the examination of witnesses, such as the IBA Rules of Evidence.

Absenting an agreement of the parties on the manner of examination, the arbitral tribunal will determine the way in which the witnesses are examined. If the parties have not agreed on a specific manner of examination, arbitrators in NAI arbitrations will generally be inclined to hear witnesses in the way it is done before the state courts in the Netherlands. In that event, the arbitral tribunal will take the lead in questioning the witness. If there is more than one arbitrator, the chairman will ordinarily do the questioning and if he does not have any further questions, he will give the other arbitrators the opportunity to ask questions, if any. Subsequently, the parties (or their counsel) will be given the opportunity to pose questions to the witness (most commonly the party who has summoned the witness goes first).

> Although not stated explicitly, it is generally accepted under Dutch law that parties may also agree to a manner of examination themselves.[161]

7.   Oath and Affirmation

Article 29(3) provides that it is at the discretion of the arbitral tribunal to decide whether a witness, before giving testimony, shall be required to affirm that he or she is telling the truth either by taking an oath (*eed*) or making an affirmation (*belofte*). In practice, however, it is the relevant witness who effectively determines whether he will take the oath or render its testimony on affirmation. Occasionally, arbitral tribunals, both in national and international arbitrations, refrain from examining witnesses under oath.[162] If the arbitral tribunal decides that a witness should be examined under oath (or on affirmation, if the witness so prefers), the administration of the oath should take place in accordance with the applicable statutory provisions, if any, of the place of arbitration (i.e. the *Eedswet 1971* in the Netherlands).[163] If the arbitral tribunal wishes to examine a witness under oath and the witness refuses to affirm in any way that he or she is telling the

---

[161]   Fung Fen Chung, 2004, 182-183.
[162]   Fung Fen Chung, 2004, 197.
[163]   Burg. Rv, 2006 (H.J. Snijders), Art. 1041 DCCP, note 1.

truth, the only remedy for the arbitral tribunal is to draw therefrom the conclusions that it deems appropriate.

> The provisions of Article 1041(2) DCCP concerning unwilling witnesses (see note 4) do not apply if a witness refuses to affirm before arbitrators that he or she is telling the truth. Hence, there is no recourse to the state courts and the only remedy that arbitrators have, is to draw from the witness' refusal the conclusions that they deem appropriate.[164]

8. Witness' Right of Refusal to Testify

Witnesses appearing before the arbitral tribunal might refuse to answer certain questions by invoking a right of refusal to testify (*verschoningsrecht*). If a witness invokes a right of refusal to testify, the arbitral tribunal will have to decide whether this is justified.

> Article 165 DCCP enumerates the reasons for which a person may be exempted from the obligation to testify, which broadly include a right of refusal to testify for only a limited number of professionals who have a confidentiality obligation towards their clients. These professionals include lawyers, civil law notaries, doctors and clergymen. A right of refusal to testify relates to specific questions only. If such right applies, the witnesses may refuse to answer questions in regard of the subject matter for which the right of refusal to testify exists. The witness is, however, not entitled to refuse to appear as a witness at all. Article 165 DCCP also provides a right of refusal to testify for persons who have a family relationship with a party.

Absenting a right of refusal to testify, invoking an obligation of confidentiality cannot justify leaving questions unanswered. Also, the fact that the answers of a witness might have a negative impact on the position of one of the parties in the arbitration does not release the witness from the obligation to testify.

As stated above, the NAI Rules do not provide arbitrators with the power to compel a witness to give testimony. If the witness continues to refuse to testify or to answer certain questions, many jurisdictions (including the Netherlands) provide for the possibility of soliciting the assistance of state courts in obtaining testimony.

> As set out in more detail in note 4 above, Article 1041(2) DCCP allows a party to request the arbitral tribunal for permission to petition the President (*voorzieningenrechter*) of the District Court (of Rotterdam, see Article 64 of the NAI Rules) to appoint a judge in order to examine a witness if a witness refuses to appear before the arbitral tribunal or refuses to give testimony. Thus, if a witness invokes a right of refusal to testify and the arbitral tribunal considers this to be unjustified, either party can solicit the assistance of the state court. The state court's exam-

---

[164] Burg. Rv, 2006 (H.J. Snijders), Art. 1041 DCCP, note 1; Fung Fen Chung, 2004, 195-196.

ination is conducted in accordance with the rules of the DCCP (see the comments relating to Article 1041(2) DCCP in note 4 above).

9. Recording of Witness Examination

According to Article 29(4), it is at the discretion of the arbitral tribunal to decide whether the examination shall be recorded and, if so, in what form. Especially if witnesses are heard informally, the arbitral tribunal during a standard hearing may not always find it necessary to record the witness statements in full. However, it is in our view highly recommended that witness examinations always be recorded in some form. Particularly in international arbitrations, witness examinations are often recorded by sound recording or by verbatim transcripts made by a court reporter. Should the parties prefer a specific form of recording, they are advised to discuss their preferences with the arbitral tribunal. The tribunal will usually try to take these preferences into account as much as possible.

Article 29(5) provides that if the arbitral tribunal is composed of more than one arbitrator, it is authorized to designate one of its members to examine witnesses. This will usually be done for reasons of efficiency and costs. If the witnesses are examined by only one of the members of the arbitral tribunal, the arbitrator is obliged to make a written report of the examination of the witnesses (which allows the other arbitrators to read the witness testimony themselves when making the award). In our view, the hearing of witnesses by only one of the arbitrators is not recommended, in particular not in larger arbitrations. Preferably all arbitrators have to see and hear the witnesses themselves. In addition, the presence of all arbitrators allows the parties to see the arbitrators' response to statements made by the witnesses and the way they behave and react (e.g., who pays attention and asks the right questions and who does not). This may be relevant to assess the possible outcome of the case (which may be relevant to decide whether a party might not be better off with a settlement).

> Article 29(5) is based on Article 1039(3) DCCP, which also allows the arbitral tribunal to designate one of its members to examine witnesses.

10. Costs

The costs incurred by a witness to give testimony (e.g., travel and accommodation expenses, loss of income etc.) shall primarily be borne by the party relying on the testimony of this witness. Depending on the circumstances, the winning party might be able to recover part of these costs from the losing party as reasonable costs necessarily incurred in the arbitration (see also Section 6 on Costs). However, it is up to the arbitral tribunal to decide on costs.

ARTICLE 30 – EXPERTS (PARTY-APPOINTED)

A party shall be free to submit the opinion of an expert consulted by him. If the party submitting the expert opinion or the other party so requires, or if the arbitral tribunal so determines, the party submitting the opinion shall call the expert to appear at a hearing to further explain his opinion, unless the arbitral tribunal shall determine a different method of calling such expert witness.

---

1. Party-Appointed Experts

As a means of providing evidence on specific issues, a party may wish to rely on an expert and submit a report or opinion of a party-appointed expert as written evidence. Article 30 allows the parties to submit as supporting evidence the opinion or report of an expert, for example with the statement of claim or statement of defence. No permission of the arbitral tribunal is required for the submission of such a written expert opinion.

If an expert opinion has been submitted, either party may require or the arbitral tribunal may determine that the party who has submitted the expert opinion, will call the expert to appear at a hearing for further testimony (Article 30, second sentence). The wording of Article 30 indicates that, if a party requests for an expert to be heard, the examination of the expert is compulsory. The NAI Rules do not stipulate what will be the consequences if the submitting party refuses to call the expert or if the expert refuses to appear. Again it is assumed that the arbitral tribunal may draw the conclusions that it deems appropriate (see also the comments on Article 42).

At the hearing, the expert is expected to further explain his opinion. In that context, the parties and the tribunal may ask questions about the expert's conclusions and the method and information used in arriving at those conclusions. Article 30 also provides that the arbitral tribunal may determine a different method of examining an expert witness. Instead of a hearing, the arbitral tribunal may, for example, allow the other party to submit questions to the expert in writing, or order a simple meeting between the parties and the party-appointed expert(s). In practice, an expert report presented by a party will often provoke the other party to engage its own expert. The arbitral tribunal shall ensure that both parties are provided sufficient opportunity to reply to the expert reports presented, either before or at a hearing.

Article 1039(3) provides that the arbitral tribunal may allow a party, at its request, to call an expert to a hearing. The authority of the arbitral tribunal to decide upon a request of a party to call an expert, relates to the examination of an expert at a hearing only. The parties are free to submit opinions or reports of party-appointed experts.

The NAI Rules do not preclude a so-called confrontation of expert witnesses where both parties' experts are present and are examined by the arbitral tribunal or the parties in the presence of the other party's expert.

As a general rule, the costs incurred for an opinion of a party-appointed expert shall be borne by the party that has engaged the expert. Depending on the circumstances, it might be possible for the winning party to recover part of the costs from the losing party as reasonable costs necessarily incurred in the arbitration (see also Section 6 on Costs).

ARTICLE 31 – EXPERTS (TRIBUNAL-APPOINTED)

1. The arbitral tribunal may appoint one or more experts to give advice. The arbitral tribunal may consult the parties as to the terms of reference for the expert.
2. The arbitral tribunal shall promptly communicate to the parties a copy of the appointment and the terms of reference of the expert.
3. If a party fails to provide an expert with the information required by him or fails to give him the necessary cooperation, the expert may request the arbitral tribunal to order that party to do so.
4. Promptly upon receipt of the expert's report, the arbitral tribunal shall communicate a copy of this report to the parties.
5. The parties shall be given an opportunity to comment in writing on the expert's report within a period of time set by the arbitral tribunal.
6. A party may request the arbitral tribunal to examine the expert at a hearing. If a party wishes to make such request, he shall so inform the arbitral tribunal and the other party promptly upon receipt of the expert's report. The arbitral tribunal shall give each party, so if requested, an opportunity of presenting his own experts at the same hearing. Article 29(5) shall apply accordingly.
7. The arbitral tribunal shall not be obligated to follow the expert's advice if it is not in conformity with its own convictions.

1.   Tribunal-Appointed Experts

Article 31(1) affirms the power of the arbitral tribunal to appoint experts to report on matters which are relevant to the issues in dispute and as to which independent expertise is necessary. As it will strongly depend on the circumstances of the case and the composition of the arbitral tribunal which expertise is needed, the NAI Rules do not place any restrictions on the types of experts the arbitral tribunal may appoint. Hence, the arbitral tribunal may appoint technical, financial or even legal experts if this is deemed necessary.

Tribunal-appointed experts are to be distinguished from party-appointed experts as referred to in Article 30. Unlike party-appointed experts, tribunal-appointed experts shall be and remain impartial and independent of the parties throughout the arbitral proceedings (see also note 2 on the appointment of experts).

Tribunal-appointed experts are also to be distinguished from experts that have been appointed as arbitrator. When it is clear from the outset of an arbitration that the subject of the arbitration will require expert knowledge in a particular field, the parties may consider appointing an expert in that specific field of expertise as an arbitrator. This may have the advantage that the arbitral tribunal itself will have the necessary expertise, so that there is no need to appoint a further expert, which is often costly and will prolong the duration of the arbitration. On the other hand, there is also the risk that the arbitral tribunal will rely solely on the expertise of the 'expert arbitrator' for its decision, whereas it may be difficult for the parties to get a feel for the 'expert arbitrator's' considerations and possible misunderstandings. Practice shows that the appointment of an expert arbitrator may result in debates within the arbitral tribunal outside the presence of the parties. Normally, one would expect the arbitral tribunal to come back to the parties with any significant issues that have arisen during internal discussions. However, it may not always be clear to the arbitral tribunal which issues are actually considered to be significant by the parties.

2.   The Appointment of Experts; Terms of Reference

Although Article 31(1) provides that the arbitral tribunal *may* consult the parties as to the terms of reference for the expert, it is in fact common practice that the arbitral tribunal consults with the parties prior to appointing an expert. The arbitral tribunal will usually not only discuss the terms of reference with the parties, but also the identity of the expert and the associated costs. Although it is not a strict requirement for the arbitral tribunal to consult with the parties on the appointment of the expert, the arbitral tribunal will in practice not impose an expert on the parties against whom they have overriding objections.

Identifying a suitable expert can be a difficult matter, especially in highly specialized fields where there may only be a small number of people having the required level of expertise. Even though this is not stated explicitly in the NAI Rules, tribunal-appointed experts must be impartial and independent, just like arbitrators. In order to ensure the required impartiality and independence, it is recommended that the arbitral tribunal (either on its own motion or at the request of the parties) requests the expert, before accepting appointment, to issue a statement of his or her impartiality and independence and to disclose any (current or former) commercial ties or business relationships with the parties, any family relationships with the parties or with employees or managers within the parties' groups of companies, or any other facts or circumstances that may raise doubts as to the expert's impartiality or independence (such as personal or business relationships with a party's counsel).[165] If the intended expert is not able to issue a statement of impartiality and independence or if he or she discloses facts or circumstances that may lead to one of the parties objecting to his or her appointment, the arbitral tribunal will most commonly refrain from appointing this person as an expert. In fact, appointing an expert who is lacking impartiality and independence should be avoided and the arbitral tribunal should refrain from relying on such expert's expertise when rendering its decision. However, it is not evident what the consequences are if the arbitral tribunal fails to comply with these rules. The rules in regard of challenging arbitrators and challenging arbitral awards do not apply equally to tribunal-appointed experts. It can be argued that the lack of impartiality and independence of a tribunal-appointed expert eventually results in the arbitral tribunal losing its own appearance of impartiality and independence, if it assumes the expert's findings when rendering a decision. Accordingly, a lack of impartiality and independence of the tribunal-appointed expert may eventually result in the arbitrators being challenged or their final awards being set aside.

Once the expert to be appointed has been identified, the arbitral tribunal will have to establish the terms of reference of the expert, containing the precise nature of the expert's mission. The expert may have a variety of different missions, ranging from answering specific questions of the arbitral tribunal to determining, for example, the cause of damages that may be the subject of the dispute. As stated above, it is common practice that the arbitral tribunal consults with the parties on the terms of reference. This consultation may be done during a hearing, meeting or telephone conference with the arbitral tribunal (see also the comments on Article 23(4)), but the arbitral tribunal might also give the parties the opportunity to comment on, for example, the questions to be posed to the expert in writing (e.g., in additional memorials; see also Article 24(2)). Apart from the expert's mission, the terms of reference may include issues such as the expert's anticipated costs and any additional deposit required (see also the comments on Article 59), a possible exoneration of the expert's liability, etc.

After the terms of reference have been established and the expert has been appointed, the arbitral tribunal will promptly communicate to the parties a copy of the appointment and the terms of reference (Article 31(2)).

---

[165] Article 6(2) of the IBA Rules of Evidence requires all tribunal-appointed experts to submit a statement of his or her independence to the tribunal and the parties *before* accepting an appointment in the proceedings.

3. The Conduct of the Expertise Procedure

After appointment by the arbitral tribunal, the expert will begin his mission in accordance with the terms of reference. The concrete activities of the expert will strongly depend on the circumstances of the case. In most cases, the expert will be requested to produce a written expert report, answering the questions posed by the tribunal and/or setting out his views as to one or more specific technical, financial or legal issues.

To fulfil his mission, the expert may need information from the parties or access to documents or goods, property or a site for inspection. Upon the appointment of the expert, the arbitral tribunal will as a practical matter usually request the parties to cooperate with the expert and to provide the expert with any information required. To ensure that the expert will receive the necessary cooperation from the parties, Article 31(3) provides that the expert may require the arbitral tribunal to order a party to provide him with information or to provide him with the necessary cooperation, if a party fails to do so upon his request. Should a party disregard such an order by the arbitral tribunal, the tribunal may draw from that the conclusions that it deems appropriate (see also the comments on Article 42). Given that the expert will not always be familiar with the conduct of arbitral proceedings, it is recommended that the arbitral tribunal instructs the expert (and that the parties themselves also ensure) that the expert does not communicate with one of the parties without sending the other party a copy of the communication and that the expert does not meet with one of the parties without the other party being present, as this would violate the principles of due process, in particular the principle of hearing both sides.

Once the expert has finalized his research, he will usually report his findings to the arbitral tribunal in the form of a written expert report. Promptly upon receipt of the expert's report, the arbitral tribunal shall communicate a copy of this report to the parties (Article 31(4)).

4. Parties' Comments Following the Expert's Report

After the expert has sent his report to the arbitral tribunal, the parties shall be given the opportunity to present their views on the expert's findings. Pursuant to Article 31(5), the parties are entitled to comment on the expert's report in writing within a period of time set by the arbitral tribunal (often in consultation with the parties). In practice, the parties are frequently given the opportunity to comment on a draft expert report before a final version is sent to the arbitral tribunal.

Besides the opportunity of commenting in writing, Article 31(6) provides for the possibility of an examination of the tribunal-appointed expert at an evidentiary hearing. Either party may request the arbitral tribunal for such examination. If a party wishes to make a request for examination of the expert at a hearing, it shall inform the arbitral tribunal and the other party 'promptly upon receipt of the expert's report' (Article 31(6)). Promptly in this respect should in our view be understood to mean as soon as possible after the parties have received the expert's report and have had a reasonable opportunity to review its contents and to determine whether it is necessary to question the expert at a hearing. Article 31(6) seems to indicate that the examination of the tribunal-appointed expert is compulsory, if requested by either of the parties. If the tribunal-appointed expert is examined during a hearing, the arbitral tribunal shall give each party, if so requested, the opportunity of presenting its own experts at the same hearing (Article 31(6)). This will allow the parties to bring the necessary expertise to the hearing to question the tribunal-appointed expert on the points at issue. If the arbitral tribunal is composed of more than one arbitrator, it is authorized to designate one of its members to examine the experts at the hearing (although this is usually not to be recommended in our view). In such case a written report of the examination of the experts shall be made (see Articles 31(6) and 29(5)). Obviously, this is also recommended if the entire arbitral tribunal is present.

5.   Arbitral Tribunal is not Bound by an Expert's Advice

A tribunal-appointed expert should not be regarded as an additional arbitrator. This is confirmed by Article 31(7), which provides that the arbitral tribunal is not obliged to follow the expert's advice if it is not in conformity with its own convictions. Hence, it is the arbitral tribunal that decides the case, not the expert. A tribunal-appointed expert should therefore not participate in the arbitral tribunal's deliberations, nor meet with the arbitral tribunal outside the presence of the parties. Meeting with the expert in the absence of the parties would also violate the parties' right to be heard.

Although the report of the expert is of probative value only and does not bind the arbitral tribunal, reports of tribunal-appointed experts will, in practice, be accorded a great deal of weight, given the independence and impartiality of the expert and the fact that the arbitral tribunal that appointed the expert will usually not have the necessary expertise itself to decide on certain issues. Obviously, a prerequisite for according such weight to the report of a tribunal-appointed expert is that the report has been drafted carefully and that the principles of due process have been properly observed.

6.   Costs

The fees and expenses of any expert appointed by the arbitral tribunal will form part of the costs of the arbitration as referred to in Article 56 and will therefore in principle be borne by the losing party (see also the comments on Section 6). During the arbitration, the costs of a tribunal-appointed expert will be paid from the deposit for costs paid by the claimant (or, in case of a counterclaim, also by the respondent) (see Article 59(2)). If an expert is appointed by the arbitral tribunal, the Administrator will usually require payment of an additional deposit by (one of) the parties to cover the costs of the expert (see Article 59(4)). Some arbitrators prefer to arrange for the report to be paid directly by the parties, which is compatible with the NAI Rules.

> The wording of Article 31 of the NAI Rules strongly resembles Article 1042 DCCP, which contains a similar provision regarding the appointment of experts by the arbitral tribunal.

ARTICLE 32 – SITE INSPECTION

If the arbitral tribunal deems it appropriate, it may order a site inspection. The parties shall be given the opportunity to be present at the inspection.

1. Site Inspection by the Arbitral Tribunal

In some situations, it may be very useful for the arbitrators to see with their own eyes what the dispute between the parties is actually about. For these situations, Article 32 provides that the arbitral tribunal may order a site inspection, which includes not only the inspection of a site, but also the inspection of any property, building, plant, machinery or other goods. Although the wording of Article 32 suggests that a site inspection is only possible on the arbitral tribunal's own motion, the parties are always free to request or to suggest to the arbitral tribunal that a site inspection be held. If the parties jointly request the tribunal for a site inspection and can explain the relevance of it, it is highly unlikely that such a request would be refused. The timing and arrangement for the inspection will normally be determined by the arbitral tribunal in consultation with the parties.

The second sentence of Article 32 provides that the parties shall be given the opportunity to be present at the inspection. This provision finds its basis in the principles of due process, in particular the principle of hearing both sides (see also the comments on Article 23). Having a site inspection without the parties being present also raises serious questions as to the appearance of impartiality and independence of the arbitrators and could give rise to a challenge of the arbitrators (see comments on Article 10). If the arbitral tribunal inspects a site, the parties (including, if applicable, their representatives, and possibly also party-appointed experts) should be given the opportunity to attend the site visit in order to provide explanations, to answer possible questions and to respond to any comments made by the arbitral tribunal or the other party during the site visit.

ARTICLE 33 – ORDER FOR APPEARANCE IN PERSON OF PARTIES

At any stage of the proceedings the arbitral tribunal may order the parties to appear in person for the purpose of providing information or attempting to arrive at a settlement.

1. Personal Appearance of the Parties

As stated above in relation to Article 21, it is common practice that parties them-selves (or party representatives if the party is a legal entity) attend hearings before the arbitral tribunal, irrespective of whether they are represented by counsel. Should the parties not wish to attend a hearing in person voluntarily, Article 33 provides the arbitral tribunal with the authority to order the parties, at any stage of the proceedings, to appear before the tribunal in person. The purpose of the personal appearance of the parties may be to provide information or to attempt to arrive at a settlement. In the case of legal entities, a 'personal' appearance includes the appearance of a person who is legally authorized to represent the entity and who is preferably also aware of the substance of the matter.

The arbitral tribunal may order the parties to appear before it in person at a hearing that has been specifically scheduled for the purpose of, for example, providing information, but the tribunal may of course also use the authority granted to it by Article 33 in the context of any other hearing. Obviously, the arbitral tribunal will only have to use the authority granted to it by Article 33 if it is aware in advance that a party may not or will not appear at the hearing.

If a party that has been duly summoned to appear at a hearing in person ignores an order by the arbitral tribunal, the arbitral tribunal may draw from that the conclusions that it deems appropriate (see also the comments on Article 42). Hence, depending on the circumstances, the arbitral tribunal may draw negative inferences from a party's failure to appear in person. Also, if a party fails to appear in person without a valid excuse, the arbitral tribunal will have the power to proceed with the hearing. However, arbitrators will normally be inclined to be relatively indulgent, given their obligation to ensure that the parties have an opportunity to be heard, to substantiate their claims and defences and to present their case (see also the comments in relation to Article 23(1)).

2. Attempt at a Settlement

Article 33 allows the arbitral tribunal to order a personal appearance of the parties not only for the purpose of providing information, but also for the purpose of attempting to arrive at a settlement. The arbitral tribunal may also initiate a settlement attempt during a regular hearing (e.g., the hearing following the sub-mission of the statement of claim and the statement of defence, or a witness hearing). Whether an arbitral tribunal will aim for a settlement during a hearing will strongly depend on the individual preferences of the arbitrators (the chairman in particular). Some arbitrators will always investigate the possibility of a settlement during a hearing, others will just hear the parties' pleadings and head directly for an award. In the majority of NAI arbitrations, however, the arbitral tribunal will at some stage during the proceedings advance the possibility of a settlement, usually by giving its – strictly preliminary – views on the parties' claims and defences at the end of a hearing. Although parties will normally profit from a settlement in terms of costs and duration of the arbitration, it is sometimes difficult to avoid receiving the impression that arbitrators may be trying to direct the parties towards a settlement so that they do not have to draft a final award.

The possibility of an attempt to arrive at a settlement by the arbitral tribunal may seem contradictory to international views that the arbitral function should be separate from the conciliatory function. For example, Article 19 of the UNCITRAL Conciliation Rules states that 'the parties and the conciliator undertake that the conciliator will not act as an arbitrator (. . .) in any arbitral or judicial proceedings in respect of a dispute that is the subject of the conciliation proceedings'.[166] However, the suggested contradiction does not exist: arbitrators may also attempt to arrive at a settlement, provided, however, that they do not lose sight of the requirements of impartiality and independence (see Article 10). This is even more so as the arbitral tribunal will have to render (impartially and independently) an award if the attempt at a settlement fails and a settlement cannot be reached.

If the attempt to arrive at a settlement is successful and the parties reach a settlement during the arbitration, Article 54 authorizes the arbitral tribunal to render an arbitral award on agreed terms, meaning that at the parties' joint request, the tribunal may record the contents of the settlement agreement in an arbitral award. See also the comments on Article 54.

3. Conduct and Recording of Appearance before Tribunal

Article 33 does not provide for the possibility mentioned in Articles 29(5) and 31(6) that the arbitral tribunal, if it consists of more than one arbitrator, designates one of its members to lead the hearing or meeting. Although we would generally not recommend this, it should in our view be possible that also a hearing on the basis of Article 33 be conducted by one of the arbitrators, unless the parties have agreed otherwise or object to it.

The NAI Rules are tacit as to the recording of a hearing or meeting with a personal appearance of the parties. As for all hearings, it is, however, advisable that a report be made of the hearing or meeting with the arbitral tribunal, either by the secretary to the arbitral tribunal or a court reporter.

Article 33 NAI Rules reproduces verbatim the text of Article 1043 DCCP.

ARTICLE 34 – AMENDMENT OF CLAIM

1. A party may amend or increase a claim or counterclaim, as the case may be, at the latest at the beginning of the final hearing or, in the absence of a hearing, at the latest in the final memorial admitted by the arbitral tribunal. Thereafter, such shall no longer be allowed

---

[166] Burg. Rv, 2006 (H.J. Snijders), Art. 1043 DCCP, note 1.

except in exceptional circumstances as determined by the arbitral tribunal. A party may at all times decrease his claim or counterclaim, as the case may be.

2. The other party may object to an amendment or increase if this unreasonably hinders his defence, or if this causes unreasonable delay of the proceedings. The arbitral tribunal shall hear the parties and promptly decide on the objections raised by the other party.

3. In case of default of a party as provided in Article 36, the arbitral tribunal shall give in writing the defaulting party an opportunity to comment on the amendment or increase.

1.   Amendment of a (Counter)Claim during the Arbitration

Article 34 sets forth the general principle that a claimant (including a claimant in the counterclaim action) has the right to amend its claim (or counterclaim, as the case may be) during the arbitral proceedings. Roughly, three types of amendments can be distinguished. The first is an increase of the claim, which is usually merely an increase of the amount claimed, but may also be the introduction of an additional claim. The second is an amendment of the claim, which may be a change of the nature of the claim, but which is mostly a change of the grounds for the claim. The third type is a decrease of the claim. The claimant may, for example, drop one of its claims or decrease the amount of its claim.

Although Article 34 is tacit on the manner in which an amendment, increase or decrease of claim must be presented, it is recommended that this is done in writing, so that it forms part of the arbitration file and discussions as to the scope of the amendment are avoided as much as possible.

As regards amendments and increases of claims, a respondent is advised to always be attentive to hidden amendments of (the grounds for the) claim, as it is sometimes in the interest of a claimant not to bring forward an amendment of its claim(s) too obviously, in the hope that the respondent will not notice and will not raise objections. For the claimant, the risk attached to this strategy is of course that the arbitral tribunal will also not notice the amendment of (the grounds for) the claim.

2.   Increase and Amendment of (the Grounds for) a Claim

Article 34(1), in principle, allows the increase or the amendment of (the grounds for) a claim until the beginning of the final hearing or, in the absence of a hearing, until the final written submission admitted by the arbitral tribunal. The rationale behind this rule is that thereafter, the respondent is deemed to have insufficient opportunity to properly respond to the amendment of claim. After (the beginning of) the final hearing or the final written submission accepted by the arbitral tribunal, an increase or an amendment of claim will no longer be allowed, except in exceptional circumstances as determined by the arbitral tribunal. For example, an increase or amendment may be considered acceptable by the tribunal if it is based on circumstances that did not occur until after the final hearing or submission and if the amended or increased claim is in line with the rest of claimant's claims and does not give rise to further discussions (which will rarely be the case). To be on the safe side, a change of claim should generally be presented as soon as possible during the arbitration. Although Article 34(1) allows the introduction of new claims or counterclaims until the final hearing or final submission, it is not advisable to wait until then if not necessary. Eleventh-hour amendments of a claim will not be appreciated by the arbitral tribunal and the other party, especially if it turns out that the amendment or increase of claim could have been presented earlier.

Article 34 of the NAI Rules differs from the provisions as to the amendment of claims in the ICC Rules. Unlike the NAI Rules, the ICC Rules are fairly strict as to the admissibility of new claims or counterclaims after the Terms of Reference have been drawn up. Article 19 of the ICC Rules provides that after the Terms of Reference have been signed, no party shall make new claims or counterclaims which fall outside the limits of the Terms of Reference unless it has been authorized to do so by the arbitral tribunal, which shall consider the nature of such new claims or counterclaims, the stage of the arbitration and other relevant circumstances.

Article 34(2) allows the respondent to object to an increase or amendment of claim (not to a decrease of claim; see note 3) on the ground that the increase or amendment unreasonably hinders its defence or causes unreasonable delay of the proceedings. The respondent may, for example, be unreasonably hindered in its defence if the increase or amendment of claim requires the respondent to conduct further research or fact finding that takes more time than reasonably available for the arbitration. If the respondent raises objections to an increase or amendment of claim, Article 34(2) requires the arbitral tribunal to hear the parties and to decide promptly on the objections raised. For reasons of efficiency and costs, it must be assumed that the arbitral tribunal does not necessarily have to 'hear' the parties at a hearing, but may also give the parties the opportunity to comment on the objections raised by the other party in writing.

With regard to the admissibility of an amendment or increase of claim, arbitral tribunals will generally be indulgent and will be quite reluctant to dismiss an amendment or increase of claim, given that arbitrations usually are one-instance only and it would not be very efficient to force the claimant to commence separate arbitral proceedings for its increased or amended claim. Against this background, the respondent who is confronted with an amendment or increase of claim is advised not to merely raise objections to the amendment or increase as such (insofar as it has any), but also to request the arbitral tribunal for sufficient time to prepare a response to the amended or increased claim, especially if the amended claim has been presented during a hearing. The principle of hearing both sides requires the arbitral tribunal to give the respondent sufficient opportunity for a response. Hence, if the arbitral tribunal decides that an amendment or increase of the claim or counterclaim is permitted, the other party must be given the opportunity to comment on the amended or increased part of the (counter)claim (see also the comments on Article 23(1)).

Article 34(3) requires the arbitral tribunal to inform a defaulting party as meant in Article 36 in writing and to give it the opportunity to comment on the amendment or increase of the claim. The purport of this provision is to avoid that a party that has not participated in the arbitration is confronted with an award without knowing the claims and the grounds for it. The arbitral tribunal should therefore take all reasonable measures to ensure that the defaulting party is informed of the amended or increased claim.

3. Decrease of a Claim

The final sentence of Article 34(1) contains the generally accepted rule that a party may at all times decrease its claim (or counterclaim, as the case may be). The provisions of Article 34(2) do not apply in the case of a decrease of claim. Therefore, no objections against the decrease can be made by the other party. Article 34(3) also does not apply in the case of a decrease of the claim. The rationale behind this is that a decrease of claim will be to the advantage of the defaulting party, so that there is no necessity for the defaulting party to be invited to comment on the decrease of the claim.

It is assumed that the claimant cannot avoid an award for costs by decreasing its claim in the course of the arbitration. In that event, the arbitral tribunal might, depending on the circumstances, put a decrease of the claim on par with a rejection of (the relevant part of) the claim, when rendering a decision on costs.

4. Consequences of Amendments of Claim for Administration Costs and the Deposit for Costs

The amount of administration costs due by the claimant (or by the respondent in the case of a counterclaim) is determined based on the value of the claim in accordance with the relevant schedule fixed by the Governing Board (see also the comments on Article 57). If a claim or counterclaim is increased, Article 57(4) provides that additional administration costs shall be due from the claimant or the respondent, respectively. Whether additional administration costs will actually be due will depend on whether the amount of the claim falls in a higher scale as a result of the increase. For example, if the claim amounted to EUR 1,000,000 and is increased by EUR 900,000, the claim will still fall in the scale for claims between EUR 1,000,000 and EUR 2,000,000, so that the administration costs should remain the same. If additional administration costs are due, the Administrator will collect these additional costs from the claimant (or in the case of a counterclaim, the respondent). It is assumed that Article 57(5) also applies if there is an increase of the claim or counterclaim. If the claimant (or in the case of a counterclaim, the respondent) fails to pay the additional administration costs due with 14 days (28 days in an international arbitration) after a second reminder in writing by the Administrator, the increased part of the claim (or counterclaim) shall be deemed to have been withdrawn (see also the comments on Article 57).

Since Article 57(4) only refers to the increase of a claim or counterclaim, it may be assumed that the amendment of the grounds for a claim will generally not affect the amount of administration costs due.

The NAI Rules do not provide for a refund of administration costs if there is a decrease of the claim or counterclaim. It may therefore be worthwhile to carefully consider the amount in dispute when introducing a claim or counterclaim, especially if the amount in dispute is just above or below the limits of the applicable scale of the schedule for administration costs (see also the comments on Article 57). If the amount of the claim cannot yet be established with certainty at the commencement of the arbitration, it may be wise to stay within the limits of the lower scale of claim amounts and increase the claim later in the arbitration, if necessary.

The amount of the claim not only determines the amount of administration costs due, but it may also be taken into account by the Administrator when determining the arbitrators' fees (see Article 58(1)). The NAI Rules do not provide for the possibility of adjusting the arbitrators' fees if there is an increase, amendment or decrease of the claim or counterclaim. Given that the fees of the arbitrators are determined also based on other circumstances (such as the complexity of the case and the time spent by the arbitrators; see Article 58(1)), it is generally unlikely that an increase, amendment or a decrease of the claim will lead to an adjustment of the arbitrators' fees. This may be different, however, if the claim is raised substantially. A substantial increase of the financial interest may justify a higher hourly rate of the arbitrators. In addition, the amendment or increase of claim may result in additional work for the arbitrators (e.g., because it necessitates an additional hearing) or in an extension of the duration of the arbitration. For all these reasons, the Administrator may require the claimant (or the respondent in the case of a counterclaim) to pay an additional deposit on the basis of Article 59(4) (see also the further comments on Article 59).

ARTICLE 35 – WITHDRAWAL OF REQUEST FOR ARBITRATION

1. The claimant may withdraw his request for arbitration so long as the respondent has not submitted a statement of defence as referred to in Article 24 or, in case the arbitration does not take place on the basis of written submissions, so long as a hearing has not been held.

2. Thereafter, withdrawal of the request for arbitration shall be possible only with the express consent of the respondent, without prejudice to the provisions of Articles 57(5) and 59(6).

3. The withdrawal shall be confirmed in writing to the parties by the Administrator and, after its appointment, by the arbitral tribunal through the intermediary of the Administrator.

1. General Comments

Circumstances may arise during the arbitration which lead the claimant to withdraw its request for arbitration. For example, the claimant may wish to withdraw its claim even before the arbitration file has been transmitted to the arbitral tribunal if the dispute between the parties has been resolved. Also at a later stage during the arbitration, there may be reasons why the claimant wishes to withdraw its claim.

Article 35 lays down the principle that the claimant may withdraw its request for arbitration at any point during the arbitration. It depends, however, on the stage in which the request for arbitration is withdrawn whether the claimant needs the respondent's permission for the withdrawal.

Article 35(1) provides that the claimant may withdraw its request for arbitration without the respondent's permission being required, so long as the respondent has not submitted a statement of defence or, if no written submissions are foreseen, so long as there has not been a hearing. The reason that no permission of the respondent is needed if the request for arbitration is withdrawn prior to the statement of defence (or, lacking a statement of defence, prior to the first hearing) will be that it is assumed that the respondent has not yet incurred costs in relation to the arbitration. In our view, however, whether this assumption is correct is called into doubt. If the claimant withdraws the request for arbitration a week before the deadline for the statement of defence, the respondent will have done all the work for the preparation of the defence and will thus have incurred costs. That in this situation, the claimant is nevertheless entitled to withdraw its claim without the respondent's permission and without any compensation for the respondent's costs is, in our view, a gap in the NAI Rules. It would be more suitable to use the date of submission of the statement of claim as the relevant date after which the withdrawal is only permitted with the consent of the respondent or upon reimbursement of respondent's costs. If the claimant withdraws its request for arbitration before the arbitration file is transmitted to the arbitral tribunal, half of the administration costs paid will be reimbursed (see Article 57(6)). After that, no administration costs will be refunded if the request for arbitration is withdrawn.

The fact that the respondent will have incurred costs for the preparation of a written submission or a hearing, entails that after the submission of the statement of defence (or after a hearing, as the case may be), the claimant can only withdraw the request for arbitration with the express consent of the respondent (see

Article 35(2)). In that event, the respondent may wish to withhold its consent unless the claimant compensates the respondent for the costs incurred in the arbitration. If the respondent withholds its consent for the withdrawal of the request for arbitration, the claimant can always decrease its claims to zero on the basis of Article 34(1), final sentence. As noted above in the comments on Article 34, however, the claimant cannot avoid an order to pay costs this way.

Article 35(2) makes clear that the requirement of the respondent's consent for the withdrawal does not apply if the claim is deemed to have been withdrawn because the claimant failed to timely pay the administration costs due (see Article 57(5)) or the deposit for costs required (see Article 59(6)). The withdrawal on the basis of these articles is intended as a sanction to ensure timely payment of the administration costs and the deposit due and it would not be effective if the respondent could hinder the withdrawal (in the unlikely event that the respondent would want to do so) by withholding its consent.

Article 35(3) requires that the withdrawal be confirmed in writing to the parties by the Administrator and, after its appointment, by the arbitral tribunal through the intermediary of the Administrator.

The question may arise as to whether a claimant that has withdrawn its request for arbitration is entitled to initiate new arbitral proceedings on the same dispute at a later stage. As the arbitration in which the request for arbitration is withdrawn by the claimant does not result in a final arbitral award, it should in our view be possible for the claimant to re-commence arbitral proceedings on the same issues if necessary. However, the reason why the request is withdrawn is relevant in this respect. If the request for arbitration is withdrawn because the parties have settled their dispute amicably, the claimant will probably be barred by the settlement agreement from bringing the same claim again. Also if there is no settlement, but the claimant has explicitly waived its rights or renounced its claims, the claimant will be barred from initiating new arbitral proceedings on the same issues.

ARTICLE 36 – DEFAULT

1. If the respondent, without showing good cause, fails to submit within the period of time set by the arbitral tribunal a statement of defence as referred to in Article 24, the arbitral tribunal may render an award forthwith.
2. This award shall be rendered in favour of the claimant unless the arbitral tribunal considers the claim to be unlawful or unfounded. Before rendering the award, the arbitral tribunal may require the claimant to produce evidence in support of one ore more of his contentions.
3. Paragraphs (1) and (2) shall apply accordingly if a hearing takes place, whether or not preceded by an exchange of memorials, and the respondent, although duly notified, fails to appear without showing good cause.

4. If the claimant, without showing good cause, fails to submit, within the period of time set by the arbitral tribunal, a statement of claim as referred to in Article 24, the arbitral tribunal may terminate the arbitral proceedings by means of an award. The same shall apply if the claimant, after submitting the statement of claim, fails to comply with an order of the arbitral tribunal to duly explain his claim within the period of time set by the arbitral tribunal.

5. The provisions of this article shall apply accordingly to a counterclaim.

1. Default of Respondent

The first three paragraphs of Article 36 deal with default of the respondent. It follows from Article 36 that in the NAI Rules, default covers those situations not only in which the respondent does not participate in the arbitral proceedings at all, but also in which the respondent does participate in the arbitration at first, but later on fails to submit a statement of defence or to attend a hearing without showing good cause.

Article 36(1) provides that the arbitral tribunal is entitled to render an award forthwith if the respondent fails to timely submit a statement of defence without showing good cause.

Article 36(1) reproduces almost verbatim Article 1040(2) DCCP.

According to Article 36(3), the same applies if the respondent, although duly notified, fails to appear at a hearing without showing good cause, irrespective of whether the hearing was preceded by written submissions. Based on the wording of Article 36(3), read in conjunction with Article 36(1) and 36(2), this could be understood to mean that if the respondent does not appear at a hearing without a valid excuse, the arbitral tribunal may consider this to be a renouncement of the defence presented in any prior written submissions.[167] This interpretation is contrary to most other arbitration rules, which allow the arbitral tribunal to proceed with the arbitration if one of the parties fails to appear at a hearing without a valid excuse[168] and to make the award on the basis of the submissions filed and the evidence presented until then. Therefore, it is our view that the rule of Article 36(3) should be understood to mean that the arbitral tribunal has to take into account any defences presented by the respondent before that hearing when determining whether the claim is not unlawful or unfounded. A different interpretation would violate the relevant party's right to be heard and the principle that rights or claims cannot be waived implicitly or by the mere failure to act. There is

---

[167] See in this respect, an arbitral award to be published in TvA 2009, Issue 2.

[168] See for example Art. 21(2) ICC Rules, Art. 28(2) UNCITRAL Rules and Art. 23(2) ICDR Rules.

the more reason for this restrictive interpretation of Article 36(3), if the provision should be understood to cover not only the hearing that is normally scheduled after submission of the statement of claim and the statement of defence, but also any other hearing that the arbitral tribunal may have ordered.

The NAI Rules do not provide any guidance as to what may constitute a 'good cause', but it may be assumed that the respondent has to come up with a valid excuse why the respondent was not in the position to file the statement of defence within the timeframe set by the arbitral tribunal or to appear at a hearing. It will be at the discretion of the arbitral tribunal to decide what constitutes a sufficiently good reason for the respondent's failure to submit a statement of defence or to appear at the hearing. It is also at the tribunal's discretion to decide whether or not it will forthwith render a default award. The arbitral tribunal is not obliged to render a default award immediately (for example, the tribunal may also require the claimant to produce evidence first; see note 2). If the tribunal decides not to render a default award, the proceedings may remain pending until a decision is made by the tribunal as to the further course of the proceedings.

According to Article 36(2), the award referred to in Article 36(1) will be rendered in favour of the claimant, unless the arbitral tribunal considers the claim to be unlawful or unfounded. Before rendering the award, however, the arbitral tribunal may require the claimant to produce evidence in support of one or more of its contentions.

Article 36(2) reproduces verbatim the text of Article 1040(3) DCCP.

The English translation of Article 36(2) differs slightly from the Dutch text, which provides that the award shall be rendered 'wholly or partially' in favour of claimant. The arbitral tribunal is thus at liberty to award the claimant's claim only in part.

The provision of Article 36(2) also differs from other arbitration rules in instructing the arbitral tribunal to render an award in favour of the claimant, unless the arbitral tribunal considers the claim to be unlawful or unfounded. Other arbitration rules merely provide that the arbitral tribunal has the power to proceed with the arbitration.[169] In most cases both types of provisions are likely to have the same result, i.e. an award in favour of the claimant.

As to the criterion 'unlawful or unfounded' in Article 36(2), this criterion is the same as in Article 1040(3) DCCP and appears to be derived from the provisions in the DCCP that apply to state court proceedings.[170] The claim may be unlawful if it violates, for example, mandatory law that the arbitral tribunal should apply ex officio. In the practice of state courts, claims are rarely rejected on the ground that they are considered to be unlawful or unfounded. In arbitral

---

[169] See for example Arts 6(3) and 21(2) ICC Rules, Art. 15(8) LCIA and Art. 28 UNCITRAL Rules. See also Derains and Schwartz, 2005, 289 (comments on Art. 21(2) ICC Rules).

[170] Article 139 DCCP provides that if the respondent does not appear in court although it was duly summoned, the court will award what is claimed, unless the court considers the claim to be unlawful or unfounded.

practice, however, arbitral tribunals will generally be much more reluctant to render a default award in favour of the claimant because their award may be vulnerable to attack if it can be established by the defaulting party that it was not given a reasonable opportunity to participate or to present its case.

Article 36 is tacit as to what will happen if the respondent fails to file other written submissions than the statement of defence. Lacking an explicit provision to this effect, there seems to be no room for application of the compelling provision of Article 36(2), instructing the arbitral tribunal to render an award in favour of the claimant. However, it can be assumed that the arbitral tribunal may draw from this failure the conclusions that it deems appropriate (see also the comments on Article 42). The failure to submit other written submissions than the statement of defence is therefore likely to have negative effects. Whether this will eventually result in an award in favour of the claimant is, however, dependent on the circumstances, since the arbitral tribunal still has to consider the respondent's defences in the statement of defence.

2. Default of Claimant

Article 36(4) deals with default of the claimant, meaning that the claimant, after commencing the arbitration, disappears or fails to proceed with its claim. In order for this to occur, the claimant will also have had to pay the administration costs due and the required deposit, because if the claimant fails to do so, the claims shall be deemed to have been withdrawn (see the comments on Articles 57(5) and 59(6)). Article 36(4) provides that if the claimant, without showing good cause, fails to submit, within the period of time set by the arbitral tribunal, a statement of claim, the arbitral tribunal may terminate the arbitration proceeding by means of an award. The same applies if the claimant, after submitting the statement of claim, fails to comply with an order of the arbitral tribunal to duly explain its claim within the period of time set by the arbitral tribunal. It must be assumed that such order by the arbitral tribunal will only be issued if the initial statement of claim submitted by the claimant did not explain or support the claimant's claims *at all*. If the statement of claim did not sufficiently explain the claimant's claims, this will most likely result in the dismissal of the claims by lack of substantiation, not by default.

Default of the claimant rarely occurs in practice, given that the claimant is the party who took the initiative for the arbitration in the first place. An award terminating the arbitral proceedings due to default of the claimant is even rarer. Not only will the claimant in practice avoid default by requesting an extension of the deadline for filing the statement of claim, but arbitral tribunals will generally also be reluctant to terminate the arbitration at such an early stage of the proceedings if the claimant fails to timely submit the statement of claim.

The arbitral tribunal has a discretionary power in terminating arbitral proceedings by rendering a default award. The tribunal may also decide to keep the arbitration pending, awaiting possible further action by the claimant.[171] A default award as referred to in Article 36(4) will generally not contain a decision on the merits (for which the tribunal will not have sufficient information, lacking a (proper) statement of claim), but only a simple declaration by the arbitral tribunal that the arbitration has been terminated.[172] A default award will generally refer to the reminders and notices that the tribunal has sent to claimant. Also, the award may contain an order for the claimant to pay the costs of the arbitration (although the NAI Rules are tacit in this respect).[173]

The question may arise whether the claimant is barred from filing its claim again if the arbitral tribunal has terminated the arbitral proceedings by means of an award on the basis of Article 36(4). Since such an award will not contain a decision on the merits, it is generally assumed that termination of the arbitral proceedings on the basis of Article 36(4) does not prevent the claimant from filing its claim again.[174] Obviously, claimant may be barred from doing so at a later stage due to limitation of its claims.

> Article 36(4) of the NAI Rules is based on Article 1040(1) DCCP, which contains a similar provision.

3. Applicability in Case of Counterclaim

Article 36(5) provides that the provisions of Article 36 apply accordingly in the case of a counterclaim. That entails that the arbitral tribunal may render an award in favour of the claimant in the counterclaim action (i.e. the respondent in the principal action) if the respondent in the counterclaim action (i.e. the claimant in the principal action) fails to submit, without showing good cause, a statement of defence in respect of the counterclaim within the timeframe set by the arbitral tribunal (see Article 36(1) and 36(2)). It also entails that the arbitral tribunal may terminate the arbitral proceedings (which is to be understood: in respect of the counterclaim) by means of an award (see Article 36(4)). Again, however, default of the respondent is rare in arbitration and default of the claimant is even rarer. In addition, arbitrators will generally be reluctant to award claims in the case of default of the respondent or to terminate the arbitral proceedings in the case of default of the claimant, given that this may give rise to proceedings to set aside the award on the ground that the arbitral award violates fundamental principles of due process, such as the principle of hearing both sides.

---

[171] G.J. Meijer 2008 (T&C Rv), Art. 1040 DCCP, note 1.

[172] A default award on the basis of Art. 36(4) NAI Rules may be comparable to an 'order for the termination of the arbitral proceedings' as referred to in Art. 28(1) UNCITRAL Rules. See also Burg. Rv, 2006 (H.J. Snijders), Art. 1040 DCCP, note 1.

[173] See Burg. Rv, 2006 (H.J. Snijders), Art. 1040 DCCP, note 1.

[174] This is based on literature concerning Art. 1040(1) DCCP, which contains a similar provision as Art. 36(4) NAI Rules. See Burg. Rv, 2006 (H.J. Snijders), Art. 1040 DCCP, note 1; G.J. Meijer 2008 (T&C Rv), Art. 1040 DCCP, note 1(c).

ARTICLE 37 – SUMMARY ARBITRAL PROCEEDINGS
AFTER THE APPOINTMENT OF THE ARBITRAL
TRIBUNAL ON THE MERITS

1. If the place of arbitration is situated within the Netherlands, the arbitral tribunal is authorized, at the request of a party, in case where, considering the interests of the parties, an immediate provisional measure is urgently required, to make an award in summary arbitral proceedings at any stage of the proceedings. This includes the authority to order the provision of security on behalf of the party who requests it, in a form to be determined by the arbitral tribunal, regarding any claim or counterclaim, as well as regarding costs related to the arbitration on the merits.

2. The request shall be submitted to the arbitral tribunal in a separate memorial; simultaneously, a copy of the memorial shall be sent to the other party and to the Administrator. The memorial shall contain a clear description of the requested provisional measure, the reasons for the claim and for the purported urgency. The evidence on which the claim is based shall be submitted together with the memorial, in so far as they have not yet already been submitted in the proceedings.

3. The arbitral tribunal shall determine immediately the day, time and place of the hearing for the claim referred to in the second paragraph and shall promptly notify the parties in writing thereof. Further submission of written memorials shall only take place if the arbitral tribunal so determines.

4. If the arbitral tribunal determines that the case is not sufficiently urgent or is too complicated to be decided by a provisional decision, it may reject the claim either wholly or partially and determine that it shall be decided in the arbitration on the merits.

5. A decision as referred to in the first paragraph shall be regarded as an arbitral award in the sense of Article 1051(3) of the Code of Civil Procedure. The provisions of Section Five of these Rules also apply.

6. The provisional decision shall in no way prejudice the final judgment of the arbitral tribunal with regard to the merits of the case.

7. The submission of a claim based on this article does not preclude a party from requesting a court to grant interim measures of protection.

1.   General Comments

In Article 37, the NAI Rules provide for summary arbitral proceedings subsequent to the appointment of an arbitral tribunal in proceedings on the merits. This form of summary proceedings may be regarded as an interim application (*incident*) in arbitral proceedings on the merits.[175]

The type of summary proceedings arranged for in Article 37 is comparable to a distinct and second form of summary arbitral proceedings governed by Articles 42a-42o (see Section 4A). A further distinction can be made between summary proceedings in state courts (see Article 37(7)) and expedited or fast-track arbitral proceedings on the merits. Further comments on this distinction are made in the introductory notes to Section 4A, to which we refer.[176]

Summary arbitral proceedings prior to proceedings on the merits, i.e. before an arbitral tribunal on the merits is appointed (Articles 42a-42o), are more prevalent than proceedings on the basis of this Article 37.

Summary arbitral proceedings on the basis of Article 37 are only available if the place of arbitration is in the Netherlands (Article 37(1)). This ensures the applicability of Article 1051 DCCP (Article 37(5) of the NAI Rules), which is the primary reason for this condition. Article 1051 DCCP provides that Articles 1049-1068 DCCP apply to arbitral summary awards arising out of proceedings on the basis of Article 37.

The rationale for the inclusion of the provision in Article 37 in the NAI Rules is considered to be the following.[177] The provision enables an arbitral tribunal dealing with a case on the merits to provide immediate provisional measures in a (partial) summary award that is enforceable in a fashion similar to a (partial) final award (as per Article 1051(3) DCCP and reflected in Article 37(5) of the NAI Rules; see on the enforcement of arbitral awards Part III, Chapter 3). This distinguishes the outcome of proceedings on the basis of this Article 37 from mere orders and interim awards.

2.   Proceedings

The NAI Rules do not provide for an elaborate set of procedural guidelines for these summary proceedings (as compared to Articles 42a-42o). Consequently, the arbitral tribunal has considerable discretion in designing the proceedings,

---

[175] See, inter alia, an article by J.L.W. Sillevis Smitt, the president of the NAI at the time of the introduction of summary arbitral proceedings into the NAI Rules. J.L.W. Sillevis Smitt, 'Het NAI introduceert het arbitraal kort geding: een toelichting', TvA 1997, 124.

[176] See also, in detail, B.C. Punt, 'Spoedarbitrages', TvA 2008, 85-94.

[177] Snijders questions the relevance of the provision for summary proceedings in Art. 37 (Burg. Rv, 2006 (H.J. Snijders), Art. 1051 DCCP, note 1). He argues that the Dutch arbitration act should be revised to enable arbitral interim awards (rendered in proceedings on the merits) to be enforceable. This would do away with the remaining, and admitted, usage of this provision: that is, using a summary arbitral award instead of an interim award and enforcing such summary arbitral award by application of Art. 1051(3) DCCP.

including written submissions (if any), time limits and various other procedural arrangements. Arbitral tribunals should invite parties to comment on proposed procedural arrangements and parties should not hesitate to provide input on their own motion.

Standard proceedings on the basis of Article 37 being an interim application in proceedings on the merits, tend to take the following format. The claimant in summary proceedings, which may also be the respondent in proceedings on the merits, is expected to submit a statement of claim setting out a description of the provisional measures requested (for examples, see Section 4A, introductory notes, note 2), the reasons for the claims made and also, in particular, the urgency of the respective claims (see Article 37(4) and, in detail, the introductory notes to Section 4A). If time permits, the respondent may be invited to submit a written reply prior to the hearing. It is unlikely that a further round of written submissions will be permitted prior to the hearing. Subsequent to the submission of a statement of claim, and subject to the submission of additional written briefs, a hearing will be scheduled by the tribunal (Article 37(3)). Thereafter, the tribunal will inform the parties of the period of time within which it will make its (partial) award[178] (Articles 37(5) and 43(1)).

In terms of structuring the proceedings, and deviating from the standard track provided for in the NAI Rules, the tribunal will be guided by the need to resolve the dispute as soon as possible, given the urgency involved and summary nature thereof. Tribunals are also entitled to request, or grant the opportunity to, the parties to submit limited post-hearing memorials.

Article 37(2) provides that the statement of claim must be included in a separate submission and that this submission must be supplemented by evidence supporting the claims made and sent to both the NAI Administrator and the counterparty simultaneously. Given that the respondent may very well oppose the claim in summary proceedings by arguing that the claims are not urgent and that the case is too complex to be decided in summary proceedings, a claimant is well advised to be both brief and clear in the description of the issues and to anticipate this defence. A respondent on the other hand may have a tactical advantage in preserving arguments for an oral hearing.

Insofar as the hearing is concerned, it may be helpful, subject to tactical considerations, to bring party representatives, potential witnesses or experts to the hearing in order to produce evidence and offer the tribunal an opportunity to ask questions to such persons.

3. Nature of Claims that may be Brought in Summary Arbitral Proceedings

The type of claims that may be brought in summary arbitral proceedings are described in Section 4A, introductory notes, note 2.

---

[178] This (partial) award does not yet have to include a decision on costs (Art. 49(3)).

An objective of initiating summary proceedings under this Article 37 may be that a party seeks to obtain security regarding one of its claims in the proceedings on the merits and/or the costs for the proceedings on the merits.[179] Independent summary proceedings governed by Articles 42a-42o do not provide for the provision of such security because an arbitral tribunal dealing with the case on the merits is considered to be more capable of doing so and because it may also be premature to make such request in summary proceedings prior to proceedings on the merits.[180]

Proceedings on the basis of Article 37 may also be combined with a request for the issuance of an order on the basis of Article 38.[181]

4.   Parallel Summary Proceedings in State Courts

Parties may also bring (summary) proceedings in state courts parallel to summary arbitral proceedings. Such is not precluded by the DCCP (Articles 1022(2) and 1051(2) DCCP) and is further discussed in the introductory notes to Section 4A. However, the initiation of summary proceedings in state courts in parallel with proceedings on the basis of Article 37 is only likely to be successful, and desirable, if and when a party desires to obtain security in a form that can not be granted by an arbitral tribunal, such as pre-judgment attachments or garnishments.

A state court that has to decide whether to decline hearing the case in summary proceedings and refer the claimant to ongoing proceedings on the basis of Article 37 will consider that an arbitral tribunal is already constituted and is both able to deal expediently with the case and is likely to possess the desired expertise (if any) (see also the introductory notes to Section 4A).

5.   No Res Judicata Effect

Article 37(6) provides that an arbitral award resulting from these summary arbitral proceedings shall 'in no way prejudice the final judgment of the arbitral tribunal with regard to the merits of the case'. The consequence thereof is that (partial) final arbitral awards in summary proceedings do not have res judicata effect (see also the comments on Article 51). The same applies to binding final decisions (*bindende eindbeslissingen*) in interim awards (*tussenvonnissen*), i.e. decisions that are both explicit (*uitdrukkelijk*) and unconditional (*zonder voorbehoud*) and relate to a matter in dispute between the parties (*geschilpunt*). Binding final decisions also do not bind the arbitral tribunal in deciding on the merits of the case (see also the comments on Article 44).[182]

---

[179] See NAI 2 Mar. 2007, TvA 2008, 32 in which the tribunal held that the conditions applicable in the state courts regarding a claim for an advance of sums due are equally applicable.

[180] See for example NAI 23 Apr. 2002, TvA 2003, 21-24.

[181] See NAI 31 Mar. 2005, TvA 2006, 20-21.

[182] It can be argued that the Supreme Court has decided in HR 20 Jun. 2003, NJ 2004, 569 (Milieutech) that this doctrine of the so-called binding final decisions in interim awards also applies in arbitration.

However, and notwithstanding the absence of res judicata, arbitral tribunals seem to be reluctant to decide otherwise in proceedings on the merits, even if the further debate between the parties in the proceedings on the merits reveals that significant facts and circumstances have not been taken into account in making the summary award.

ARTICLE 38 – PROVISIONAL MEASURES OTHER THAN IN SUMMARY ARBITRAL PROCEEDINGS

---

1. Without prejudice to the power provided in Article 37, the arbitral tribunal, at the request of a party, at any point in the proceedings, may provisionally make any decision or take any measure regarding the object of the dispute which it deems useful or necessary.
2. The decision or measure shall be made or taken, respectively, in the form of an order of the arbitral tribunal.
3. The decision or measure shall in no way prejudice the final judgment of the arbitral tribunal with regard to the merits of the case.
4. The request does not preclude a party from requesting a court to grant interim measures of protection or from applying to the President of the District Court for a decision in summary proceedings.

---

1. General Comments

Article 38 provides arbitral tribunals dealing with a case on the merits with the mandate to issue orders regarding the object in dispute between the parties in addition to interim awards. These measures may be distinguished from (partial) final awards on the merits, (partial) final summary awards and interim awards and typically relate to procedural matters such as the production of documents and evidentiary issues.[183]

The orders to which Article 38(2) refers are not awards in the sense of Article 1051(3) DCCP. Consequently, these orders cannot be enforced through exequatur proceedings.

Article 38 is particularly relevant when the arbitration is seated outside the Netherlands. In such matters Articles 37 and 42a-42o do not apply and can thus not be used as basis for rendering interim measures. In such arbitrations an arbitral tribunal only has the power to render interim measures on the basis of Article 38. The object of providing for provisional measures in arbitral proceedings seated

---

[183] The distinction between orders, interim awards, partial awards and partial final awards has, insofar as the context of the Netherlands is concerned, recently been discussed in an article by J.J. van Haersolte-van Hof & J. Drok, 'Vonnissen en orders – een Nederlands perspectief', TvA 2007, 131-138; G.J. Meijer 2008 (T&C Rv), Art. 1049 DCCP, note 3.

outside the Netherlands is one of the primary reasons for including this Article 38 in the NAI Rules.[184]

> Article 1049 DCCP, which provides for the type of measures that can be ordered in arbitration, does not make explicit reference to orders. The Draft Bill introduces a new provision in Article 1043b(4) DCCP that is inspired by this Article 38. The proposed Article 1043b(4) DCCP will provide a new basis for orders and interim awards.[185] The former are not enforceable, whereas the latter will be treated as awards and may thus be enforceable.

Article 38(3) is comparable to Article 37(6) and provides that orders do not bind tribunals dealing with the case on the merits. Reference is made to the comments on Article 37(6) (see Article 37, note 5).

Article 38(4) provides that parallel proceedings may be initiated in the state courts. This is in line with Articles 1022(2) and 1051(2) DCCP, which apply if the arbitration is seated in the Netherlands and could be used to obtain, notably, a pre-judgment attachment (see also Article 42l, note 2).

Parties may try to circumvent the non-enforceability of an order issued on the basis of this Article 38 through intervention of state courts in summary proceedings.[186] Such could be done by requesting a state court in summary proceedings to render a judgment in accordance with the order. This option may, however, not be effective, if the relevant party is in need for an enforceable award outside the Netherlands and it is not likely that the award of the Dutch state court in summary proceedings will be recognized in the country in which enforcement is sought.

Chapter IVa, Article 17(2) of the revised UNCITRAL Model Law may be used as source of inspiration with respect to the measures that may be taken by means of an order.[187] These measures include orders to: (a) preserve a status quo pending determination of the dispute; (b) take action that would prevent, or refrain from action that is likely to cause, current or imminent harm or prejudice to the arbitral proceedings; (c) provide a means of preserving assets out of which a subsequent award may be satisfied; and (d) preserve evidence that may be relevant and material to the resolution of the dispute.

---

[184] J.L.W. Sillevis Smitt, 'Het NAI introduceert het arbitraal kort geding: een toelichting', TvA 1997, 125.

[185] See the explanatory note to Art. 1043b(4) in the Draft Bill, which can be found at <www.arbitrage-wet.nl/1043B_4.html>.

[186] J.L.W. Sillevis Smitt, 'Het NAI introduceert het arbitraal kort geding: een toelichting', TvA 1997, 125.

[187] Such is also suggested by Van Haersolte-van Hof and Drok: J.J. van Haersolte-van Hof & J. Drok, 'Vonnissen en orders – een Nederlands perspectief', TvA 2007, 131-138.

ARTICLE 39 – TRIBUNAL SECRETARY; TECHNICAL ASSISTANCE

1. At the request of the arbitral tribunal, the Administrator shall arrange for the presence of a lawyer who acts as the secretary to the arbitral tribunal. The provisions of Articles 10, 11 and 19 shall apply accordingly to the secretary.
2. The arbitral tribunal may request the Administrator to arrange for technical assistance in the arbitral proceedings.

1.   Secretary to the Tribunal

Various administrative services (e.g., secretarial services, correspondence, arranging of hearing rooms) may need to be procured for the arbitral tribunal to be able to carry out its functions efficiently. Although the Administrator and the NAI Secretariat may provide some of the required assistance to the arbitral tribunal, the arbitral tribunal may have to engage a secretary to the arbitral tribunal if it needs more than occasional administrative support. An arbitral tribunal in need of such support, pursuant to Article 39(1), may request the Administrator to arrange for the presence of a lawyer who will act as the secretary to the arbitral tribunal. The NAI has a pool of trained secretaries at its disposal from which the Administrator may select a secretary. The NAI also regularly organizes courses for lawyers who occasionally act as secretary to an arbitral tribunal.

The NAI does not routinely assign secretaries to the arbitral tribunal in arbitrations which it administers. It is entirely at the discretion of the arbitral tribunal to decide whether a secretary will be engaged. Some arbitrators frequently engage secretaries to the arbitral tribunal, at least in certain types of cases, whereas others normally conduct proceedings without them. The need for a secretary may also depend on the field of expertise of the arbitrators involved. As Article 39(1) requires the secretary to the arbitral tribunal to be a lawyer, it may provide for the efficient and proper conduct of the arbitral proceedings if a secretary is appointed when there is a sole arbitrator who is not legally trained, or in the event that there are more arbitrators, none of whom is a legal professional. Also, the appointment of a secretary may be cost-effective, as the secretary, whose hourly rate is well below that of the arbitrators, may carry out tasks that otherwise would have to be done by one of the arbitrators.

The secretary to the arbitral tribunal carries out his or her tasks under the direction of the arbitral tribunal and will usually provide administrative and organizational assistance to the arbitral tribunal in relation to the arbitral proceedings. The NAI Rules do not define the role and responsibilities of the secretary and these may vary depending on the circumstances. There may be more weight given to the secretary's role and responsibilities in the event that there is a sole arbitrator who is not a legal professional. Generally, however, the secretary will be the first person to contact for the parties to discuss practical issues concerning the organization of the arbitration. The secretary will also take care of correspondence on behalf and under the direction of the arbitral tribunal and take minutes of hearings or witness examinations. The secretary may also facilitate communications between the individual arbitrators. In practice, some arbitrators request the secretary to prepare a first draft of the arbitral award.

Whatever tasks the secretary is charged with, the arbitral tribunal at all times remains in charge of and responsible for the arbitral proceedings. The secretary does not form part of the arbitral tribunal (see Article 1(f)) and the situation where the secretary – who is not chosen by the parties, but appointed by the Administrator – becomes the 'fourth arbitrator' should be avoided.[188] In this respect, we refer to the UNCITRAL Notes on Organizing Arbitral Proceedings, which note:

> 'To the extent the tasks of the secretary are purely organizational (e.g., obtaining meeting rooms and providing or coordinating secretarial services), this is usually not controversial. Differences in views, however, may arise if the tasks include legal research and other professional assistance to the arbitral tribunal (e.g., collecting case law or published commentaries on legal issues defined by the arbitral tribunal, preparing summaries from case law and publications, and sometimes also preparing drafts of procedural decisions or drafts of certain parts of the award, in particular those concerning the facts of the case). Views or expectations may differ especially where a task of the secretary is similar to professional functions of the arbitrators. Such a role of the secretary is in the view of some commentators inappropriate or is appropriate only under certain conditions, such as that the parties agree thereto. However, it is typically recognized that it is important to ensure that the secretary does not perform any decision making function of the arbitral tribunal.'[189]

For ICC arbitrations, the Secretariat of the ICC Court has issued the Note on the appointment of administrative secretaries by arbitral tribunals,[190] which deals inter alia with the duties of the secretary and the responsibility of the arbitral tribunal for the secretary's work. The directions of the ICC Court as to the duties

---

[188] For a discussion on the role and responsibilities of the secretary in NAI arbitrations, see: M.P.J. Smakman, 'De rol van de secretaris van het scheidsgerecht belicht', TvA 2007, 2-7; P. Sanders, 'De secretaris van het scheidsgerecht', TvA 2007, 93-97; F.D. von Hombracht-Brinkman, 'Er zijn secretarissen en secretarissen! Reactie op het artikel van prof. mr. P. Sanders, "De secretaris van het scheidsgerecht" ', TvA 2008, 53-54.

[189] UNCITRAL Notes on Organizing Arbitral Proceedings, para. 27, see <www.uncitral.org/pdf/english/texts/arbitration/arb-notes/arb-notes-e.pdf>.

[190] Published in the *ICC International Court of Arbitration Bulletin* 6, No. 2 (Nov. 1995), 77-78.

of the secretary are fairly strict: the duties of the secretary must be strictly limited to administrative tasks and the secretary may not influence in any manner whatsoever the decisions of the arbitral tribunal. These strict rules do not apply in NAI arbitrations, however, although in NAI arbitrations, it is recognized that the secretary should refrain from taking an active part in the decision-making process.

Article 39(1) provides that Articles 10, 11 and 19 (relating to impartiality and independence, disclosure and challenge of arbitrators) apply accordingly to the secretary to the arbitral tribunal. That entails that the secretary, like arbitrators, is required to be impartial and independent. The secretary may not have close personal or professional relationships with any of the parties and may not have any direct personal or professional interest in the outcome of the case (see also the comments on Article 10). Although Article 10 does not allow arbitrators to have a close professional relationship with a co-arbitrator, the secretary having a professional relationship with one or more of the arbitrators seems more accepted in practice. If one of the arbitrators is a lawyer, frequently one of his associates is appointed as secretary to the arbitral tribunal.

Pursuant to Article 11, the secretary also has a duty to disclose the existence of grounds which may form the basis for a challenge. On the basis of Article 19, (also) the secretary to the arbitral tribunal may be challenged if circumstances exist that raise justifiable doubts as to the secretary's impartiality or independence. Although challenge of a secretary is rare in practice, a secretary is sometimes challenged. In that event, the challenge of the secretary will usually coincide with the challenge of one or more of the arbitrators.

2. Technical Assistance

Besides the need for administrative support, the arbitral tribunal may also need technical assistance in relation to the arbitral proceedings (especially hearings), such as laptops, beamers, printers, sound recording systems, a court reporter or other technical equipment or support. According to Article 39(2), the arbitral tribunal may request the Administrator to arrange for such technical assistance. In practice, technical assistance (for which costs will be charged; see note 3) will usually only be requested from the Administrator if a hearing takes place at the offices of the NAI in Rotterdam. If the hearing takes place at another location, it will mostly be the parties or (the secretary to) the arbitral tribunal that arrange for any technical equipment needed.

3. Costs of a Secretary and Costs of Technical Assistance

The costs of a secretary to the tribunal are considered disbursements of the arbitrators and will be paid from the deposit for costs paid by the claimant and/or the respondent (see Article 59(2)). The costs of a secretary are determined by the Administrator at the end of the arbitration. The Administrator then requests the secretary to provide a statement of the hours spent on the arbitration and any costs incurred.

The costs of technical assistance provided by the Administrator on the basis of Article 39(2) will also be paid from the deposit for costs (see Article 59(2)).

ARTICLE 40 – LANGUAGE

1. The arbitral proceedings shall be conducted in the language or languages as agreed by the parties or, in the absence of such agreement, in the language or languages determined by the arbitral tribunal.

2. Until such time as the arbitral tribunal has determined the language or languages as referred to in paragraph (1), the Administrator may, at the request of the other party or on his own motion, require a party to provide translations of his submissions and documents in a language which the other party understands and in such form and within such period of time as the Administrator shall determine.

3. Without prejudice to the provisions of paragraphs (1) and (2), if any notice, submission or document is written in a language which the Administrator or the arbitral tribunal does not understand, the Administrator and, after its appointment, the arbitral tribunal may require the party from whom such notice, submission or document emanates to provide a translation in such language, in such form and within such period of time as the Administrator or the arbitral tribunal, as the case may be, shall determine.

4. At the request of the arbitral tribunal, the Administrator shall arrange for the presence of an interpreter at the hearing.

1. Party Agreement

The governing principle of Article 40 is that the parties may choose the language or languages to be used in the arbitral proceedings. The language chosen by the parties should be used in any correspondence with the arbitral tribunal and the Administrator, in any written submissions filed and also during oral hearings.

As stated in the comments on Article 1(e), the parties may wish to stipulate in the arbitration agreement the language or languages of the arbitration, in order to avoid uncertainties in that respect at the beginning of the arbitration. It is useful to know in advance what the language of the arbitration will be, as this may be relevant when choosing counsel or selecting arbitrators for appointment, drafting the request for arbitration or assessing whether the arbitration is likely to involve significant translation and interpreters' costs. If the parties have agreed on the language of the arbitration in their arbitration agreement or subsequently, it is advisable for the claimant to mention this in the request for arbitration (and/or for the respondent to mention this in the short answer), as this is relevant information for the Administrator to know when composing the list with the names of possible arbitrators (see also the comments on Articles 6(3)(k) and 14). The use of multiple languages in arbitration should be considered only if this is absolutely necessary, as this can be problematic and can significantly increase costs (see also note 3).

2. Absence of Agreement; Arbitral Tribunal's Criteria for Determining the Language of the Arbitration

Like many other arbitration rules,[191] Article 40(1) empowers the arbitral tribunal to determine the language or languages to be used in the proceedings, lacking an agreement of the parties. If the parties have been unable to agree on the language of the arbitration, they may want to consider mentioning their preferences concerning language in the request for arbitration and the short answer so that the arbitral tribunal can take these preferences into account when deciding on the language of the arbitration.

The NAI Rules do not provide guidelines as to the language of the arbitration to be determined by the arbitral tribunal, absenting a choice of the parties. In determining the language or languages of the arbitration, the arbitral tribunal will have to consider all relevant circumstances of the case. Although the language of the contract (usually including the arbitration agreement) is considered an important factor for the arbitral tribunal to take into account when making its decision,[192] it is not decisive and other circumstances may be equally or even more important. These other circumstances may include, for example, the nationality and language skills of the persons involved in the arbitration (i.e. the arbitrators, the parties, their legal counsel and possible witnesses to be examined), the applicable law, the place of arbitration, and the language of relevant evidentiary documentation.

As to the language skills of NAI arbitrators, practically all arbitrators are Dutch native speakers, who are often also fluent in English. The general list

---

[191] See for example Art. 16 ICC Rules, Art. 17(1) UNCITRAL Rules and Art. 17(3) LCIA Rules.

[192] Art. 16 ICC Rules provides that the arbitral tribunal shall determine the language of the arbitration, due regard being given to all relevant circumstances, *including the language of the contract*. Art. 17(1) LCIA Rules provides that unless the parties agree otherwise, the initial language of the arbitration shall be the language of the arbitration agreement. Lacking an agreement by the parties, the arbitral tribunal shall, according to Art. 17(3) LCIA Rules, decide upon the language of the arbitration, taking into account the *initial language of the arbitration* and other circumstances it deems relevant. Art. 40 WIPO Arbitration Rules provides that unless otherwise agreed by the parties, the language of the arbitration shall be the language of the arbitration agreement, subject to the power of the arbitral tribunal to determine otherwise, having regard of any observations of the parties and the circumstances of the arbitration. A similar provision can be found in Art. 14 ICDR Rules.

of arbitrators also contains many names of arbitrators who have a command of German or French. There are arbitrators on the list who are fluent in other languages as well. If required because of a specific need for language skills, the Administrator will appoint foreign native speakers as arbitrators who are not on the general list of arbitrators. The Administrator is likely to do so, if the arbitration agreement stipulates that the arbitration shall be conducted in a foreign language and the arbitrators – or some of them – should be native speakers.

3.   Multiple Languages

As evident from Article 40(1), which refers to 'language or languages', the parties may agree or the arbitral tribunal may determine that the arbitration be conducted in more than one language.

Arbitration agreements providing that the arbitration will be conducted in two languages may raise problems of interpretation. It should be clear from the arbitration agreement whether the parties are free to use either one of the two languages, or whether both languages must be used by both parties at all times. Obviously, the latter option will be very costly, as all submissions will have to be made in two languages, the parties will have to address the arbitrators in two languages at a hearing (with the assistance of interpreters) and all evidence (including witness examinations) will need to be translated. The use of more than one language is not to be encouraged in most cases. Not only will it significantly increase costs, it may also complicate the appointment of arbitrators as it may be difficult to find qualified arbitrators who have a command of the languages selected. Also, awards may have to be drafted in the languages specified, which may create the risk of inconsistent texts. In general, the use of more than one language should be considered only when this would reduce rather than increase time and costs. If the parties have agreed or the arbitral tribunal has determined that the arbitration will be conducted in two (or more) languages, the parties and the arbitral tribunal should consider agreeing on practical means to avoid duplication. In those cases where the members of the arbitral tribunal are fluent in all applicable languages, submissions may not need to be translated. Consideration should also be given to avoiding having procedural orders and awards in more than one language. If preparing these in more than one language cannot be avoided, the parties are well advised to agree that only one version will be binding.

4.   Documentary Evidence in a Language Other than the
Language of the Arbitration

Even if only one language is chosen as the language of the arbitration, multiple language issues may arise with respect to written evidence submitted. Some documents annexed to the statement of claim and statement of defence or later submissions may not be in the language of the proceedings. For example, the language of the arbitration may be English and an exhibit on which a party relies may be in Spanish. Bearing in mind the needs of the proceedings and economy, it may be considered whether the arbitral tribunal should order that any of those documents or parts thereof should be accompanied by a translation in the language of the proceedings. If possible, the parties are advised to try to agree in advance (for example, during a procedural conference with the arbitral tribunal; see Article 23(4)) how translations of any evidentiary documents are to be dealt with. To avoid unnecessary translation costs, it may be advisable to agree that only those parts of exhibits or evidentiary documents need to be translated on which a party directly relies in its submissions. Also, minimizing the need for certified translations will reduce costs. Such certified translations might only be required when translation issues emerge from unofficial translations.

5.   Role of the Administrator

As set out above, the language of the arbitration will be determined by the arbitral tribunal if the parties were unable to agree on the language. However, as the arbitral tribunal is not appointed until after the request for arbitration and the short answer have been filed, there is uncertainty at the commencement of the arbitration concerning the language in which the request for arbitration and the short answer have to be filed. Absenting a choice of the language by the parties, the request for arbitration might be filed in a language that the future respondent does not understand. For these situations, Article 40(3) provides the Administrator with the authority to require a party to provide translations of its submissions and documents (such as the request for arbitration, the short answer and possible evidentiary documents) in a language that the other party understands, until the arbitral tribunal (has been appointed and) has determined the language of the arbitral proceedings. The Administrator may also determine the form in which and the period within which such translation has to be provided.

Against the same background, Article 40(3) provides that if any notice, submission or document is written in a language which the Administrator does not understand, the Administrator may require a translation in such language, in such form and within such period of time as the Administrator shall determine. Article 40(3) grants the same authority to the arbitral tribunal. It is not very likely, however, that the arbitral tribunal will receive submissions etc. in a language that it does not understand once the language of the arbitration has been determined. The relevance of Article 40(3) will therefore be limited in practice after the arbitral tribunal has been appointed.

6.   Interpreters

Depending on the language(s) of the arbitration and the language skills of the arbitrators and the parties, interpreters may need to be arranged to be present at hearings. Article 40(4) provides that the arbitral tribunal may request the Administrator to arrange for the presence of an interpreter at the hearing. The costs of such an interpreter will be paid out of the deposit for costs paid by the claimant and/or the respondent (see Article 59(2)). In practice, arrangements for interpreters are often made by the parties jointly, instead of by the Administrator at the request of the arbitral tribunal. In the event the parties themselves arrange for an interpreter, the costs of the interpreter will not be paid from the deposit, but have to be paid by the parties directly. The parties may then wish to make arrangements as to which party will (initially) pay for the services of the interpreter. If both parties require an interpreter, they may agree to share these costs equally. The parties may also agree that the costs of an interpreter shall be included in the award for costs by the arbitral tribunal and shall thus be borne by the losing party.

ARTICLE 41 – THIRD PARTIES

1. A third party who has an interest in the outcome of arbitral proceedings to which these Rules apply may request the arbitral tribunal for permission to join the proceedings or to intervene therein.
2. Such request shall be filed with the Administrator in six copies. The Administrator shall communicate a copy of the request to the parties and to the arbitral tribunal.
3. A party who claims to be indemnified by a third party may serve a notice of joinder on such a party. A copy of the notice shall be sent without delay to the arbitral tribunal, the other party and the Administrator.
4. The joinder, intervention or joinder for the claim of indemnity may only be permitted by the arbitral tribunal, having heard the parties and the third party, if the third party accedes to the arbitration agreement by an agreement in writing between him and the parties to the arbitration agreement. On the grant of request for joinder, intervention or joinder for the claim of indemnity, the third party becomes a party to the arbitral proceedings.
5. In case of a request or notice as referred to in paragraphs (1) and (3), respectively, the arbitral tribunal may suspend the proceedings. After the suspension, the proceedings shall be resumed in the manner as determined by the arbitral tribunal, unless the parties have agreed otherwise.
6. The provisions on the costs of the arbitration contained in the sixth section shall apply accordingly to a third party who has acceded to the arbitration agreement in accordance with the provisions of paragraph (4).

1.   Participation of Third Parties in Arbitral Proceedings

Article 41 deals with the participation of third parties in the arbitral proceedings. There are several ways in which third parties may become a participant in the arbitration, none of which occurs often in practice because it requires the consent of both the parties in the arbitration and the third party. A party may wish to intervene in an arbitration between two other parties voluntarily, by means of joinder (*voeging*) or intervention (*tussenkomst*), or a party may be forced to participate in the arbitration to indemnify (*vrijwaren*) one of the parties in the arbitration (mostly the respondent). Article 41(1) and 41(2) relate to joinder and intervention, whereas Article 41(3) relates to a claim for indemnity. The provisions of Article 41(4), 41(5) and 41(6) apply to all types of third-party intervention.

> Article 41 of the NAI Rules has been copied almost literally from Article 1045 DCCP, which contains a similar provision on the participation of third parties in the arbitral proceedings.

2.   Joinder and Intervention

Article 41(1) provides that a third party who has an interest in the outcome of the arbitral proceedings, may request the arbitral tribunal to join the proceedings or to intervene therein. A prerequisite for joinder or intervention is that the third party is aware that arbitral proceedings are pending before an arbitral tribunal, which will not always be the case, given the confidential nature of arbitral proceedings. The request for joinder or intervention to the arbitral tribunal must be filed with the Administrator (which implies that the third party also knows that the NAI Rules apply to the arbitral proceedings), who will forward a copy of the request to each of the parties and to the arbitral tribunal (see Article 41(2)). Against this background, the request has to be filed in six copies (Article 41(2)).

One of the conditions that must be satisfied for the arbitral tribunal to allow a request for joinder or intervention is that the third party has 'an interest in the outcome of the arbitral proceedings' (see Article 41(1)). An imminent loss of rights, a prejudice or the risk of conflicting decisions will usually qualify as such an interest in the outcome of the arbitral proceedings. The difference between joinder and intervention is to be found in the nature of this interest. If the third party wishes to take its own position in the proceedings, exercise its own rights or institute its own claims (for example, if a third party claims to be the owner in proceedings between two other parties with respect to a right of ownership), it needs to intervene. If the third party does not wish to take its own position but only wishes to support one or more parties (on the same side) in the arbitration in its claim or defence (e.g., a guarantor who wants to assist its debtor in the arbitral proceedings), it needs to join the proceedings.

3. Joinder for the Claim of Indemnity

Unlike the joinder or intervention of a third party on the basis of Article 41(1), the initiative of a claim for indemnity comes from one of the parties in the arbitration. If, for example, the respondent is a contractor who is confronted with a claim of its principal, the contractor may be indemnified by a subcontractor. According to Article 41(3), a party (in the arbitral proceedings) who claims to be indemnified by a third party may serve a notice of joinder on that third party. A copy of the notice shall be sent without delay to the arbitral tribunal, the other party in the arbitral proceedings and the Administrator. A joinder for the claim of indemnity is frequently encountered in arbitrations related to the construction industry. Although Article 41(3) suggests that the permission of the arbitral tribunal is not required for a joinder for the claim of indemnity, this is not the case. The permission of the tribunal for participation of a third party in the proceedings is also required in the case of a joinder for the claim of indemnity (see Article 41(4) and note 5).

4. Prerequisite: Arbitration Agreement

As set out in the comments on Article 1(e), the submission of a dispute to arbitration requires an agreement to arbitrate or arbitration agreement. Therefore, a third party may only participate in the arbitration if it also is or becomes a party to the applicable arbitration agreement. Against this background, Article 41(4) provides that a joinder, intervention or joinder for the claim of indemnity may only be permitted by the arbitral tribunal if the third party accedes to the arbitration agreement that applies between the parties already involved in the arbitration.

The third party is required to accede to 'the arbitration agreement by an agreement in writing between him and the parties to the arbitration agreement' (see Article 41(4)). This requirement is in our view unnecessary burdensome for a number of reasons. Firstly, it would suffice if all parties involved are a party to an arbitration agreement providing for arbitration in accordance of the NAI Rules, without the additional requirement that all parties are signatories to one and the same arbitration agreement. This is in fact the arrangement provided for by the Arbitration Rules of the Arbitration Council for the Construction Industry.[193] Although the requirement of one single arbitration agreement is sound from a theoretical point of view, it often turns out to be a show stopper, since it gives any party involved the opportunity to frustrate the participation of the third party even without cause. In practice therefore the NAI Rules provide for a

---

[193] See <www.raadvanarbitrage.nl/overdesite/index.htm>. Arts 15(4) and 16(3) of the Arbitration Rules of the Arbitration Council for the Construction Industry – provide for 'accession in advance', which means that the requirement of a written agreement has been satisfied if the acceding third party 'concluded' an arbitration agreement with one of the parties in the arbitration that refers to the same arbitration rules that provide for joinder, intervention or joinder for the claim of indemnity.

system where there is in fact little room for the participation of third parties by way of joinder, intervention or indemnification. Secondly, the requirement of an 'agreement in writing' constitutes a deviation from Article 1(e), which entails that an instrument in writing is only required for the purpose of proving the existence of the arbitration agreement. Article 41(4) thus prevents to proceed with a joinder, intervention or indemnification, if the parties' submissions show that all parties agree to the participation of the third party, but the parties failed to lay down such agreement in a multiparty-agreement. The latter restriction may be circumvented by assuming that the required 'agreement in writing' is contained implicitly in the parties' submissions.

As set out above in respect of Article 1(e), an arbitration agreement may not only be in the form of a submission agreement (*compromis*), in which the parties agree to submit an existing dispute to arbitration, but also of an arbitration clause referring possible future disputes to arbitration. Consequently, the intervening third party may already be a party to the arbitration agreement by an arbitration clause included in a contract between the third party and the parties in the arbitration. In that event, a separate written agreement between the third party and the original parties in the arbitration does not seem necessary.[194]

The requirement of a written agreement between the intervening third party and the parties to the arbitral proceedings entails that the participation of the third party will only be permitted if all parties in the arbitral proceedings agree. As a result, third party participation does not often occur in arbitral proceedings.

5. Tribunal Decides on Participation of Third Party

The arbitral tribunal decides on the course of the proceedings after receipt of a request from a third party for joinder or intervention (Article 41(1)) or a notice of joinder from one of the parties in the arbitration (Article 41(3)). If such request or notice is received, Article 41(5) allows the arbitral tribunal to suspend the proceedings (i.e. the main proceedings) to decide on the participation of the third party in the proceedings.

Before taking a decision as to whether a third party will be allowed to participate in the proceedings, the arbitral tribunal is required by Article 41(4) to hear the parties and the third party. This requirement intends to avoid as much as possible that disputes arise regarding the participation of the third party after it has acceded to the arbitration agreement and the proceedings. Although Article 41(4) refers to 'hearing' the parties and the third party, in practice the parties will be given the opportunity to comment on the participation in writing, and then, only if necessary, followed by an oral hearing (which facilitates an interactive

---

[194] It is generally accepted under Dutch law that a written agreement between a third party and the original parties in the arbitration as meant in Art. 1045(3) DCCP is not required if the third party was already a party to the applicable arbitration agreement. Given that Art. 41 NAI Rules has been copied from Art. 1045 DCCP, this will also apply for the requirement of a written agreement in Art. 41(4) NAI Rules.

discussion between the arbitral tribunal, the parties and the third party about the consequences of the possible participation of the third party in the proceedings).

As set out above, the joinder, intervention or joinder for the claim of indemnity may only be permitted by the arbitral tribunal if the third party accedes in writing to the arbitration agreement from which the tribunal derives its competence (Article 41(4)). In the case of joinder and intervention on the basis of Article 41(1), the arbitral tribunal may in addition refuse the third-party's participation if it does not have an interest in the outcome of the proceedings (see note 2).

Even if all applicable conditions have been satisfied, the arbitral tribunal may still refuse the third-party's participation in the proceedings. A reason for refusal may be that the joinder or intervention will cause unacceptable delay to the main proceedings, which the tribunal must ensure takes place 'with due dispatch' (see Article 23(3)).[195] The delay that may result from third-party participation is also the reason that the provisions of Article 41 do not apply in summary arbitral proceedings (see Articles 42a(3), second sentence, and 42j). Another reason for refusal may be that the joinder or intervention will overly complicate the proceedings. Whether this is the case will also depend on the stage that the proceedings are in at the time a request for joinder or intervention is submitted.

Article 1045 DCCP contains provisions setting similar requirements as Article 41.

Article 1046 DCCP, providing for the consolidation of separate arbitral proceedings may provide an acceptable solution, if the participation of a third party is not allowed (either because not all parties cooperate in concluding the required written agreement for the accession of the third party, or because the arbitral tribunal refuses the participation for another reason). In this case, the relevant party has no other option than to initiate separate arbitral proceedings. Under Dutch law, these proceedings may be consolidated with the 'main' proceedings in which the participation of the third party was refused. Article 1046 DCCP provides for the possibility to consolidate arbitral proceedings that are pending in the Netherlands and that have a subject matter that is connected with that of other arbitral proceedings pending before an arbitral tribunal in the Netherlands. Consolidation of arbitrations concerning the same subject may limit the risk of conflicting decisions. Pursuant to Article 1046 DCCP, a request for consolidation must be filed with the President (*voorzieningenrechter*) of the Amsterdam District Court. The President may order the consolidation in full or in part. In the case of a consolidation, the parties shall in consultation with each other appoint the arbitrators who will decide in the consolidated proceedings. In the case of full consolidation, the mandate of the arbitrators that had already been appointed in the separate arbitrations is terminated.

The parties may for various reasons exclude the possibility of consolidation on the basis of Article 1046 DCCP, but the NAI Rules do not include this exclusion. Therefore, unless the parties have agreed on such exclusion in addition to the NAI

---

[195] A joinder for the claim of indemnity was refused for reasons of delay in: NAI 19 Dec. 1987, TvA 1988, 16-17.

Rules (see also the comments on Article 1(e) of the NAI Rules), NAI arbitral proceedings may be consolidated with other arbitral proceedings in the Netherlands (which do not necessarily have to be arbitral proceedings under the NAI Rules).

6. Consequences of Accession of a Third Party

The second sentence of Article 41(4) provides that if the arbitral tribunal permits the participation of a third party in the arbitral proceedings, the third party becomes a party to the arbitral proceedings. Although the text of Article 41(4) suggests otherwise, we take the view that the third party does not become a party in the main arbitral proceedings in the case of a joinder for the claim of indemnity.[196]

If the proceedings had been suspended by the arbitral tribunal pending a decision regarding the third-party participation, Article 41(5) provides that the proceedings will be resumed in the manner as determined by the arbitral tribunal, unless the parties have agreed otherwise (which will often not be the case in advance, but the parties may make arrangements in this respect when the occasion arises, for example by agreeing on the order in which submissions will be filed). Depending on the stage the original proceedings were in and depending on the nature of the third-party participation (joinder, intervention or joinder for the claim of indemnity), the arbitral tribunal will have to determine a new order of the proceedings. The third party will generally have to be offered the opportunity to file a written submission to set out its position (in the case of joinder), its claim (in the case of intervention) or its defence (in the case of joinder for the claim of indemnity). In addition, the third party should generally be given an opportunity to present its case orally at a hearing. The original parties in the arbitration should also be given the opportunity to respond to the allegations of the third party.

7. Costs

Pursuant to Article 41(6), the provisions on the costs of the arbitration included in Section 6 of the NAI Rules apply accordingly to a third party who has acceded to the arbitration agreement in accordance with the provisions of Article 41(4). This means that a third party, depending on the nature of its participation, may be required to pay administration costs (Article 57) and/or an additional deposit for the fees and disbursements of the arbitrators (Article 59). Also, there may even be

---

[196] This view is also taken by Snijders (Burg. Rv, 2006 (H.J. Snijders), Art. 1045 DCCP, note 5). Meijer (G.J. Meijer 2008 (T&C Rv), Art. 1045 DCCP, note 5), however, seems to take the position that Art. 1045(4) DCCP (which is similar to Art. 41(4) NAI Rules) differs from the provisions for a claim for indemnity before state courts (where the main proceedings and the proceedings regarding the claim for indemnity are two separate proceedings).

circumstances in which the third party is required to bear (part of) the costs of the arbitration (Article 61).

ARTICLE 42 – NON-COMPLIANCE OF A PARTY WITH PROVISIONS CONTAINED IN SECTION FOUR

If a party does not comply, or complies insufficiently, with any provision contained in this section, or with an order, decision or measure issued by the arbitral tribunal pursuant to this section, the arbitral tribunal may draw therefrom the conclusions it deems appropriate.

1. Consequences in Case of Non-Compliance with Provisions of Articles 20-42 or with Orders of the Arbitral Tribunal

Article 42 provides the arbitral tribunal with the authority to do or to decide what it deems appropriate in case a party ignores or does not comply with the provisions of Section 4 (Articles 20-42). The same applies if a party does not comply, or complies insufficiently, with an order, decision or measure issued by the arbitral tribunal.[197] By providing that the arbitral tribunal 'may draw the conclusions that it deems appropriate', Article 42 seems to refer to conclusions concerning the substance of a case, rather than to procedural consequences. However, Article 42 intends to cover both. For example, not only may the arbitral tribunal draw an adverse inference in respect of evidence which a party failed to produce upon request of the arbitral tribunal, but it is also allowed to ignore the contents of a written submission which is filed after the deadline set by the arbitral tribunal (although the arbitral tribunal will generally be reluctant to apply sanctions if this happens, due to the risk of proceedings to set aside an award in case of a violation of the principle of hearing both sides). For further examples of situations in which the arbitral tribunal may use the authority granted to it by Article 42, see the comments on Articles 28, 30, 31(3), 33 and 36 above. In general, the arbitral tribunal should apply Article 42 prudently and with restraint, after advising the resisting party of the risks of refusing to comply with the provisions of the NAI Rules or with an order, decision or measure of the arbitral tribunal.

---

[197] Article 56(d) WIPO Arbitration Rules contains a provision similar to Art. 42 NAI Rules, which stipulates that if a party without showing good cause, fails to comply with any provision or requirement under the Rules or any direction given by the tribunal, the tribunal may draw the inferences therefrom that it considers appropriate.

SUMMARY ARBITRAL PROCEEDINGS
(Articles 42a-42o)

This section deals with one of the two forms of summary arbitral proceedings (*arbitraal kort geding*). This type is provided for in Articles 42a-42o (Section 4A) of the NAI Rules. The other type of summary arbitral proceedings involves summary arbitral proceedings that are initiated subsequent to the appointment of the arbitral tribunal dealing with the case on the merits, as provided for in Article 37 (see the comments on that Article).

Because the type of summary proceedings governed by Section 4A is frequently used, it warrants a somewhat more extensive set of introductory notes. These introductory notes relate to the distinction between these summary proceedings and other types of proceedings, situations in which it is advisable to opt for summary proceedings, the application of mandatory and non-mandatory provisions of the DCCP in summary arbitral proceedings, further proceedings and the application of fundamental procedural principles of due process.[198]

The NAI Rules only provide for this type of summary arbitral proceedings, as per the amendment of the rules on 1 January 1998, which amendment took immediate effect.[199] In the past 10 years more than 100 cases have been dealt with in summary arbitral proceedings (in the last couple of years about 15 per year).[200] The NAI Rules do not require parties who wish to initiate summary arbitral proceedings to enter into a separate agreement to that effect.[201]

---

[198] See also, for an excellent overview, B.C. Punt, 'Spoedarbitrages', TvA 2008, 85-94.

[199] The validity of the immediate application of these provisions as per Art. 67 has not been challenged in published arbitral case law or proceedings to set aside an award.

[200] This information is derived from the annual reports of the Netherlands Arbitration Institute.

[201] Such is the case in respect of the ICC pre-arbitral referee proceedings, for which a separate agreement between the parties is required. The ICC Rules itself do not contain provisions for summary arbitral proceedings. See also Derains and Schwartz, 2005, 297-298. As to the use of the ICC pre-arbitral referee proceedings, see E. Gaillard & P. Pinsolle, 'The ICC Pre-arbitral Referee: First Practical Experiences', *Arbitration International* 20, No. 1 (2004), 1-19.

1. Distinction Between Summary Arbitral Proceedings and other Types of Proceedings

A series of proceedings are discussed in the paragraphs below. First of all, a distinction is made between summary arbitral proceedings (*kort geding procedures*) and proceedings on the merits (*bodemprocedures*). Secondly, a distinction is made between different types of summary proceedings. Thirdly, a few comments are made on summary arbitral proceedings and summary proceedings in state courts.

1.1. Distinction Between Summary Arbitral Proceedings and Arbitral Proceedings on the Merits

While arbitral proceedings on the merits will result in an award on the merits, summary arbitral proceedings result in a summary award. A summary award does not bind an arbitral tribunal dealing with the case on the merits.

The NAI Rules provide in Article 42j for the equal application of substantial parts of Section 4 ('Procedure') of the NAI Rules (Articles 20-42) on arbitral procedure to summary arbitral proceedings. However, these provisions may, and will, be deviated from in summary proceedings, to the extent the tribunal is required to deal with the case expediently.

The NAI Rules also provide that, upon the joint request of the parties, an arbitral tribunal in summary arbitral proceedings may render an award on the merits (Article 42l(3)). The distinction between summary proceedings and proceedings on the merits is further blurred by the fact that proceedings on the merits may, to a significant extent, adopt characteristics that are commonly associated with summary proceedings, notably by an arbitral tribunal or the parties providing for shorter time limits. The NAI Rules thus leave room for proceedings on the merits to borrow from characteristics typically associated with summary proceedings.

1.2. Different Types of Summary Arbitral Proceedings and Hybrid Proceedings

The NAI Rules contain two distinct forms of summary arbitral proceedings in Articles 37 and 42a-42o, respectively. In addition, the NAI Rules permit parties to design mixed or hybrid proceedings that borrow elements from summary proceedings but are, in a formal sense, proceedings on the merits. Furthermore, the NAI Rules also include a provision that allows arbitral tribunals dealing with a case on the merits to order provisional measures (Article 38).

The first type of summary arbitral proceedings is available if an arbitral tribunal dealing with proceedings on the merits is in place. This is provided for in Article 37 and has been discussed above (see comments on Article 37).

The second type of summary proceedings is governed by Articles 42a-42o and is discussed in this section. These provisions govern summary proceedings separate from proceedings on the merits and are, when compared to Article 37, used most often. The relationship between these two forms of summary arbitral proceedings is set out in Article 42a(2), which is discussed below.[202]

The NAI Rules also permit parties to conduct what may be described as mixed or hybrid proceedings. These proceedings borrow from summary proceedings but are proceedings on the merits and can take the form of expedited or fast-track proceedings by applying shorter time limits for both submissions and the issuance of an award. In addition, parties can agree to dispense with written memorials and/or witness examinations.[203] Although parties are, in principle, at liberty to agree upon their own procedural arrangements, doing so may result in complications. These complications can arise from the fact that such arrangements form part of the mandate of an arbitral tribunal. Consequently, a deviation from that mandate – for example when the agreed time limits and/or procedural arrangements prove unworkable – may very well require an additional agreement by the parties that can be difficult to obtain when the parties are in dispute.

By the same token, summary proceedings can be turned into mixed or hybrid proceedings by designing and agreeing upon more extended summary proceedings by conducting written pleadings (see also Article 42g(2)) or full blown witness or expert examinations. Also, parties can jointly request the arbitral tribunal in summary proceedings to render a decision on the merits (Article 42l(3)).

A final distinction can be made with proceedings under in Article 38. This article provides an arbitral tribunal with the mandate to issue provisional measures in the form of an order (*opdracht*) during the course of arbitral proceedings (see, in more detail, the comments on Article 38).

1.3. Summary Arbitral Proceedings and Summary Proceedings in Regular State Courts

A further distinction can be made between summary arbitral proceedings and summary proceedings in regular state courts. Summary arbitral proceedings are based on Article 1051 DCCP. Summary proceedings in state courts are provided for in Article 254 DCCP.[204]

Summary proceedings are very much part and parcel of the legal culture in the Netherlands and are widely applied. The availability and frequent use of summary

---

[202] This distinction has been noted and confirmed by an arbitral tribunal dealing with summary arbitral proceedings on the basis of Art. 37, in NAI 2 Mar. 2007, TvA 2008, 99-100.

[203] Given that the NAI Rules do not contain a separate arrangement for fast-track proceedings on the merits, the parties should agree on shorter time limits themselves or approach the NAI and/or, subsequent to its appointment, the arbitral tribunal to provide for a fast-track regime. In the context of the Netherlands, reference may be made to fast-track provisions in the Arbitration Rules of the Royal Netherlands Soccer Association (KNVB) in Arts 68-70 and the Arbitration Council for the Construction Industry in Art. 14(1) of its Arbitration Rules of 27 May 2006.

[204] Which is further developed in case law and supplemented by a set of uniform procedural arrangements for summary proceedings known as *Procesreglement Kort Geding* effective as per 1 Jan. 2008.

proceedings in state courts provided an important impetus for the introduction of a provision for summary proceedings in the NAI Rules. It is also the reason why Article 1051 of the DCCP makes explicit reference to Article 254 DCCP and that quite a few elements of the provisions in Articles 42a-42o can, or are to be, interpreted by reference to the practice of summary proceedings in state courts (as will also appear from the discussion of specific articles in this section).

The provision for, or even prior or parallel conduct of, summary arbitral proceedings under the NAI Rules does preclude parties from initiating summary proceedings in state courts.[205]

Article 1022(2) and 1051 DCCP arrange the correlation between summary arbitral proceedings and summary proceedings in Dutch state courts. Pursuant to Article 1022(2), the existence of an agreement to arbitrate in summary arbitral proceedings must be invoked by the respondent, if such respondent is unwilling to accept the jurisdiction of state courts in summary proceedings. The courts will not consider this point ex officio (Article 1051(2) DCCP). Furthermore, the President (*voorzieningenrechter*) of the District Court, in his discretion, may retain jurisdiction notwithstanding the parties' choice of summary arbitral proceedings.[206] In making this discretionary decision, courts will consider the urgency of the matter and the time required from the initiation of summary arbitral proceedings to the moment of completion of exequatur proceedings,[207] as well as the fact that the nature of the dispute may or may not call for specific expertise of an arbitrator (instead of a judge) such as knowledge of technical intricacies and/or applicable trade usages.[208] If the President of the District Court retains jurisdiction even though a party has requested that the case be referred to summary arbitral proceedings, such decision is open to appeal. Such an appeal is, however, not open if the President of the District Court decides that the case should be arbitrated in summary arbitral proceedings (Article 1051(4) DCCP).

2. When to Opt for Summary Arbitral Proceedings

Whether to opt for summary arbitral proceedings is a question that only arises if the place of arbitration is in the Netherlands. The provisions in Articles 42a-42o (and also Article 37) are available only if the arbitration is seated in the

---

[205] Art. 1022(2) DCCP provides that 'An agreement to arbitrate does not bar a party from requesting a conservatory measure from the [state] courts or from addressing the President of the District Court in summary proceedings in accordance with Article 254 DCCP; who will rule in such matters in observance with Article 1051 DCCP'.

[206] A recent example is contained in a decision by the President of the Dordrecht District Court on 13 Apr. 2006, NJF 2006, 336. See also Amsterdam Court of Appeal 3 Feb. 2000, TvA 2003, 68-69 with an annotation by W.D.H. Asser.

[207] See, recently, The Hague District Court 16 Oct. 2007, NJF 2008, 139 and also Burg. Rv, 2006 (H.J. Snijders), Art. 1051, note 2.

[208] See for a somewhat critical view in this respect an annotation by W.D.H. Asser under Amsterdam Court of Appeal, 3 Feb. 2000, TvA 2003, 69.

Netherlands (Article 42a(4)).[209] The primary reason for this condition in the NAI Rules is that an award in summary arbitral proceedings is only enforceable as an arbitral award on the basis of Article 1051(3) DCCP if the arbitration is seated in the Netherlands (Article 1073(1) DCCP). Although such is not provided for in the NAI Rules, the application of summary arbitral proceedings is not inconceivable if the place of arbitration is outside the Netherlands. We do not recommend applying the NAI provisions on summary arbitral proceedings if the place of arbitration is outside the Netherlands, however, if such is considered prior consultation with the NAI is strongly advised. This follows from the fact that Section 4A, modelled as it is on summary proceedings in Dutch state courts (see e.g., Article 42a(1)), refers explicitly and implicitly to the norms and conditions reflected in Article 254 DCCP, which deals with summary proceedings in Dutch state courts.

Whether summary arbitral proceedings are expedient depends on various circumstances. Generally, the more complex and less urgent a case is, the more likely that an arbitral tribunal will not be willing to deal with the case in summary proceedings (see Article 42k).

The primary use of summary arbitral proceedings arises in scenarios demanding an urgent resolution of a dispute by means of a (provisionally) enforceable arbitral award. The urgency must be of such magnitude that regular arbitral proceedings cannot be conducted in due time (see Article 42a, note 2, regarding timing).

Cases that have been dealt with in summary arbitral proceedings cover a wide range of subjects and include intervention in takeovers, claims to pay monetary sums (*geldvorderingen*),[210] post-merger disputes regarding escrow agreements, specific performance of agreements,[211] performance of previous arbitral awards,[212] blocking the transfer of shares as a form of security[213] and suspension of share trading. These types of cases are comparable with the sort of cases litigated in summary proceedings in Dutch state courts.

The complexity of a case is a circumstance that is also relevant in deciding whether to grant a request in summary proceedings: if a case is too complex to be

---

[209] If the parties have omitted to make any prior determination of the place of arbitration, Art. 42a(4) provides that the place of arbitration is Rotterdam.

[210] See, inter alia, NAI 28 Feb. 2007, TvA 2008, 19-22 and NAI 18 Apr. 2002, TvA 2003, 19-21. In both cases the norms applicable to claims for monetary sums (*geldvorderingen*) in summary proceedings in the state courts were applied to the same claims in summary arbitral proceedings. See also, NAI 28 Jul. 1999, TvA 2000, 11-14 applying a three-pronged test in order to decide whether or not to grant a claim for monetary sums.

[211] See, for example, NAI 15 Oct. 1998, TvA 1999, 11-14; NAI 2 Dec. 2003, TvA 2005, 8-11 and NAI 12 May 2005, TvA 2006, 22-23.

[212] See NAI 27 Mar. 2000, TvA 2001, 8-10.

[213] See for an example of a case in which this claim was unsuccessful but entertained: NAI 23 Nov. 2001, TvA 2002, 63-66.

dealt with in summary proceedings, the request can be denied. In this respect, a distinction can be made between procedural complexity and complexity of the nature of the case. From the decided matters outlined above, which are often complex by nature and require decisions with a significant impact, it may be concluded that arbitral tribunals will not lightly decide that a case is too complex to be dealt with in summary arbitration, albeit that this is also subject to the aptitude and attitude of an individual arbitral tribunal.[214] Procedural constraints in summary proceedings may be of greater concern when deciding whether to opt for summary arbitral proceedings. After all, if summary proceedings are aborted at some point due, for example, to the fact that the case requires more elaborate consideration of evidence and/or other factual matters than can typically be accommodated in summary proceedings, considerable time and money may be wasted. In cases where such complexity is to be expected, parties should be cautious not to rush into commencing summary arbitral proceedings, and only do so if the urgency is so apparent that the arbitrators can be convinced that the complexity of the matter and/or potential procedural hiccups should not stand in the way of an award in summary proceedings.

3. Application of Provisions of the DCCP in Summary Arbitral Proceedings

Article 1051 DCCP is a mandatory provision and applies if the parties have agreed to summary arbitral proceedings. It provides a limitation on the use of summary arbitral proceedings: arbitrators are only empowered to decide in summary arbitral proceedings within the constraints of Article 254 DCCP, which article governs summary proceedings in state courts.

Pursuant to Article 1051(3) DCCP, Articles 1049-1068 DCCP that are designed for proceedings on the merits also apply to summary proceedings, albeit that their application is influenced by the summary nature of the proceedings. Consequently, by operation of law an arbitral award in summary proceedings is put on an equal footing to an arbitral award rendered in proceedings on the merits. Consequently it can be enforced in a similar fashion – although this is somewhat controversial (see further the comments on Article 42l). Other provisions that also apply to summary arbitral proceedings include those with respect to the required deposit of an arbitral award, awards containing a settlement, provisional enforceability of awards, arbitral appeal and the setting aside of arbitral awards.

Arbitrators in summary arbitral proceedings must observe fundamental due process norms (*fundamentale beginselen van behoorlijk procesrecht*) in the same way as they must in arbitral proceedings on the merits. They are first and

---

[214] This also applies in the context of summary proceedings on the basis of Art. 254 DCCP, as has been noted in a recent standard work on Dutch Procedural Law: H.J. Snijders, C.J.M. Klaassen & G.J. Meijer, *Nederlands burgerlijk procesrecht* (Deventer, Kluwer, 2007), No. 336.

foremost required to (ex officio) ensure that the parties are treated equally and receive a fair hearing.[215] A breach of due process rules may result in setting aside of the award in summary arbitral proceedings on the basis of Article 1065(1)(c) and/or (e) DCCP (see Article 1065 DCCP, note 4 and 6 in Part III, Chapter 1). The particularities of summary arbitral proceedings may bring about that the effectuation of the right to be heard is limited to the possibility to present the case during the hearing, depending on the nature of the case and the urgency of the matter, whereas in proceedings on the merits parties are commonly given the opportunity to file and respond to submissions in writing.

Parties that have already pursued a claim in summary proceedings in state courts will not be permitted to bring the same claim in summary arbitral proceedings, absent a change of facts that justifies such second proceedings on the same matter.[216]

4. Further Proceedings after Issuance of an Award in Summary Arbitral Proceedings

Neither the DCCP nor the NAI Rules requires the commencement of arbitral proceedings on the merits subsequent to the issuance of an award in summary arbitral proceedings.[217] Consequently, a successful claimant may choose to enforce an arbitral award obtained in summary arbitral proceedings without the initiation of arbitral proceedings on the merits.

Parties can agree on arbitral summary appeal proceedings as a second instance after the issuance of an arbitral award in summary arbitral proceedings. In practice, we have not observed any arbitral appeal in NAI summary arbitral proceedings, perhaps because it is hardly if ever agreed on in arbitration agreements under the NAI Rules, or because parties choose to conduct arbitral proceedings on the merits instead. If the parties have made a general provision in their arbitration agreement that provides for an arbitral appeal, such provision will probably not be interpreted to also provide for an appeal in summary arbitral proceedings. Parties should use specific wording to that effect if they wish to agree to arbitral appeal in summary proceedings.[218]

---

[215] Articles 1036 and 1039(1) DCCP, Art. 6 ECHR, Art. 23(1) NAI Rules (see the comments on this article). The latter article also applies to summary arbitral proceedings, pursuant to Art. 42j.

[216] NAI 16 Dec. 2005, TvA 2007, 11-15 is an example thereof. See also Burg. Rv, 2006 (H.J. Snijders), Art. 1022, note 4.

[217] See also Introduction to NAI Arbitration Rules, para. 9.2.

[218] Parliamentary History TK 1983-1984, 18.464, No. 3, 20; G.J. Meijer 2008 (T&C Rv), Art. 1051 DCCP, note 5(c).

ARTICLE 42A – IN GENERAL, RELATIONSHIP WITH
ARTICLE 37 PROCEDURE

1. In cases where, considering the interests of the parties, an immediate provisional measure is urgently required, a request for such measures may be heard and decided in summary arbitral proceedings, in accordance with the provisions of this section.
2. If, however, an arbitration between the same parties has been commenced and the appointment of the arbitrators has been confirmed by the Administrator in accordance with Article 15(1), the provisions of this Section do not apply and the special procedure prescribed in Article 37 of these Rules is to be followed.
3. The provisions of Section One and Sections Five through Seven apply to the procedure referred to in the first paragraph without exception. The provisions of Sections Two through Four apply only in so far as reference is made to them in this Section.
4. The provisions of this Section apply if the place of arbitration in situated within the Netherlands. If the parties have not determined the place of arbitration, Rotterdam will be the place of arbitration, for the purpose of the application of the provisions of this Section.

1. General Comments

This provision determines the place of summary arbitral proceedings vis-à-vis both the DCCP and the NAI Rules.

The wording of Article 42a(1) is derived from Article 254 DCCP. This provision in the DCCP, and case law relating thereto, governs summary proceedings in Dutch state courts and is considered to be a primary source of reference for summary arbitral proceedings as well. This notion is further supported by Article 1051(1) DCCP, which governs summary arbitral proceedings and makes explicit reference to this Article 254 DCCP.

Article 254(1) DCCP reads as follows:

> 'In all urgent matters in which, given the respective interests of the parties, an immediate, provisionally enforceable measure is required, the President of the District Court is competent to order such.'

2. Requirements for Application

Article 42a makes clear that summary arbitral proceedings on the basis of Section 4A of the NAI Rules are only available, if the following requirements have been met:

– the arbitration is seated in the Netherlands;

– an arbitral tribunal (if any) has not yet received a confirmation of its appointment by the Administrator; and
– considering the interests of the parties, an immediate provisional measure is urgently required.

These requirements will be dealt with, in turn, below.

2.1. Place of Arbitration in the Netherlands

Article 42a(4) confirms (as noted in the introductory notes to this section), that Section 4A of the NAI Rules only applies if the parties have seated the arbitration in the Netherlands.[219] The primary reason for this condition is that a location in the Netherlands ensures that Article 1051(3) DCCP applies, which provides for the status of an arbitral award in summary proceedings. If the parties have failed to provide for a place of arbitration, Article 42a(4) acts as a default and provides for Rotterdam as the place of arbitration.

2.2. No Arbitral Tribunal in Arbitral Proceedings on the Merits

Article 42a(2) regulates how Articles 42a-42o relate to summary arbitral proceedings conducted before an arbitral tribunal dealing with the case on the merits (see the introductory notes to this section). Pursuant to this provision Articles 42a-42o only apply if an arbitral tribunal (if any) dealing with the case on the merits has not received a confirmation of its appointment by the Administrator of the NAI (Article 15(1)).[220] As soon as the appointment of the arbitral tribunal in the proceedings on the merits has been confirmed, the parties will only have recourse to summary arbitral proceedings on the basis of Article 37.

2.3. Further Requirements Pursuant to Article 42a(1)

The further requirements set out in Article 42a reflect the wording of Article 254(1) DCCP. However, explicit reference to this provision and case law thereon of the Dutch state courts is not made. Nevertheless, most arbitrators acting in summary arbitral proceedings on the basis of Articles 42a-42o tend to use such case law as guidance when determining the scope of their mandate and the interpretation of the notions of (i) interests of the parties, (ii) immediate provisional measure and (iii) urgency, all as mentioned in Article 42a(1), and discussed below. Accordingly, summary arbitral proceedings on the basis of Article 42a-42o may, for example, be effectively used for debt-collection on

---

[219] See, for example, NAI 2 Dec. 2003, TvA 2005, 8-11.

[220] See for a decision on precisely this point, recently, NAI 2 Mar. 2007, TvA 2008, 99-100.

the same flexible terms as debt-collection in summary proceedings in the Dutch state courts the (*incasso kort geding*).[221]

(i) Interests of the parties. To a considerable extent, this criterion tends to be amalgamated in the assessment of the urgency (*spoedeisendheid*) of claims made (see below under (iii)), and is thus not often applied separately.[222]

Arbitral tribunals are required to make a provisional assessment (if possible) of the merits of the case in connection with weighing the interests of the parties. However, this does not entail making an assessment of the chances of success in terms of the outcome of proceedings on the merits.[223] By the same token, a tribunal will assess the consequences of not granting the claims made including the availability of alternative causes of action for the claimant.

When considering the interests of the parties in the context of summary proceedings, the tribunal should address whether the effects of an award in summary proceedings are reversible, i.e. can they be undone if a tribunal dealing with the case in proceedings on the merits comes to a different conclusion. However, irreversibility does not prevent a particular claim from being granted in summary (arbitral) proceedings per se.[224] Insofar as a claim for the payment of monetary sums is concerned, which is an important use of summary proceedings in Dutch state courts, a tribunal will also have to assess the recoverability (*restitutierisico*) of sums ordered to be paid in proceedings on the merits from the party to whom they are paid pursuant to an award in summary proceedings.

(ii) Immediate provisional measure. On the basis of the analogy with regular summary proceedings, the tribunal will have to weigh the legal basis of the claims, the effect of granting the claims made and the proportionality thereof. In the Dutch tradition of summary proceedings, state courts are authorized to exercise considerable discretion in drafting provisions that are ordered. This probably entails a wider mandate for arbitral tribunals as well when compared

---

[221] This arrangement has been subject to criticism in light of the pattern of expectations of international parties that may not be aware of this Art. 254 DCCP and case law relating thereto: G.W. van der Bend & M.A. Leijten, 'Het incasso kort geding bij het Nederlands Arbitrage Instituut', *Ars Aequi* 51 (2002): 553-558. Note that the Netherlands Supreme Court has held that arbitration rules that are applied in an international arbitration must be interpreted also in light of international practice. This has been held in a decision of 17 Jan. 2003, and can also be argued to apply in the context of summary arbitral proceedings (HR 17 Jan. 2003, NJ 2004, 384). See, however, also NAI 28 Feb. 2007, TvA 2008, 19-22 for an application of both Art. 1051 of the DCCP and the provisions regarding summary arbitral proceedings in an international arbitration.

[222] A similar process occurred in the 2006 amendment of Ch. IV A to the UNCITRAL Model Law. This chapter no longer provides for a separate and distinct condition of urgency in relation to provisional measures and makes the existence or absence of urgency part and parcel of the required weighing of the parties' interests.

[223] W. Hugenholtz, *Hoofdlijnen van het Nederlands burgerlijk procesrecht*, edited by W.H. Heemskerk (Den Haag, Elsevier, 2006), No. 131.

[224] The Netherlands Supreme Court has ruled that a court dealing with a case in summary proceedings may render a judgment with effects that are irreversible; HR 11 Feb. 1994, NJ 1994, 651.

to arbitral proceedings on the merits, albeit that such has not yet been tested in proceedings to set aside an award rendered in summary proceedings.[225]

Furthermore, the provision that is requested to be ordered must have a provisional character. Consequently, tribunals will not grant declaratory relief or permanently establish legal rights (*constitutief vonnis wijzen*). This is also reflected in Article 42m. However, this does not imply that a particular measure cannot be ordered if and when some of the consequences thereof are de facto not reversible.[226]

(iii) Urgency. This criterion does not pose a high threshold in summary proceedings in the Dutch state courts.[227] Given the analogy with the norms applicable in state proceedings, this also applies to summary arbitral proceedings.

A claimant will have to state that, and explain why, each of its respective claims is urgent enough for him not to await the outcome of proceedings on the merits.[228] The same applies to counterclaims. An assessment of the urgency of the claims will be made at the time of the issuance of an award. See also the comments on Article 42k in this respect.

In respect of claims for sums due (*geldvorderingen*) that are not, or hardly, contestable, urgency is generally accepted easily.[229]

2.4 Further Analogy with Summary Proceedings in State Courts

The Parliamentary History to Article 1051 DCCP indicates that the analogy with summary proceedings in state courts may go further than Article 254 DCCP outlined above. In particular, Article 256 DCCP is also relevant. This article provides that claims made in a case that is not suited to be dealt with in summary proceedings may be rejected. This provision is applied ex officio by the courts,

---

[225] See B.C. Punt, 'Spoedarbitrages', TvA 2008, 89.

[226] By way of illustration, summary proceedings in state courts can, and frequently do, result in lifting attachments. Also orders, aimed at transferring goods or shares in a company, can be issued in summary proceedings.

[227] This is also expressed by the working group for the revision of the Dutch arbitration act in its comments on a new Art. 1043b DCCP, which provision replaces Art. 1051 DCCP. In the context of the ICC pre-arbitral referee procedure, the need to be able to demonstrate urgency seems to depend upon the nature of the remedy sought, E. Gaillard & P. Pinsolle, 'The ICC Pre-arbitral Referee: First Practical Experiences', *Arbitration International* 20, No. 1 (2004), 1-19, para. I.a. See also, and with nuances in respect of monetary impact of claims, the new Chapter IV A of the UNCITRAL Model Law and the column of F.J.M. de Ly, 'Internationale Arbitrage', TvA 2007, 125-129.

[228] In respect of typical ancillary claims such as for costs, the requirement of urgency will not have to be specifically addressed, HR 15 Jun. 2007, RvdW 2007, 583. A distinct assessment of the urgency of claims made is also evident from a case in which the state courts have been asked to render an award in summary proceedings notwithstanding an agreement that provides for summary arbitral proceedings, The Hague District Court 16 Oct. 2007, NJF 2008, 139.

[229] See for a recent example NAI 22 Mar. 2007, TvA 2008, 100.

albeit restrictively.[230] Cases that may fall in this category may be those in which either the relevant facts are unclear, or the consequences of granting the claims made cannot be adequately assessed (see in further detail, the introductory notes to this section).[231] Arbitrators dealing with summary arbitral proceedings on the basis of Section 4A of the NAI Rules are likely to apply the same test when assessing the requirements set out in Article 42a(1). In addition, the considerations referred to in Article 256 DCCP may lead to application of Article 42k.

The assessment of the above requirements is part of the mandate of an arbitral tribunal (as per Articles 1036 and 1051(1) DCCP). A serious non-compliance with these requirements may result in a challenge of the summary award in setting aside proceedings (based on Article 1065(1)(c) DCCP; see the comments on this article in Part III, Chapter 1).

3. Party Autonomy

Since parties are free to choose whether to agree to summary arbitral proceedings, parties are also at liberty to limit the availability of summary arbitral proceedings. A limitation may be considered by international parties that do not feel comfortable with exposing themselves to the initiation of summary proceedings. Such discomfort may arise due to unfamiliarity with the Netherlands regime for summary proceedings, which arbitrators may use as reference (in particular the use of summary proceedings for debt collection).[232]

4. Equal Application of NAI Rules Relating to Proceedings on the Merits

Article 42a(3) provides for the equal application to summary arbitral proceedings of a number of provisions of the NAI rules that apply to proceedings on the merits.

Article 42a(3) provides that Sections 1 (Articles 1-5), 5 (Articles 43-55), 6 (Articles 56-62) and 7 (Articles 63-67) of the NAI Rules apply equally to proceedings on the merits. Insofar as Sections 2 (Articles 6-9), 3 (Articles 10-19) and 4 (Articles 20-42) of the NAI Rules are concerned, Article 42a(3) provides that such provisions *only* apply to the extent that explicit reference is made thereto in Section 4A. Such explicit reference is made to Articles 6 (in Articles 42e and 42f); 9(3), 9(6) (in Article 42h); 10, 11, 15(2), 15(3), 17-19 (in Article 42f(3));

---

[230] HR 24 Feb. 2006, NJ 2007, 37.

[231] An example of a claim in summary arbitral proceedings being rejected is contained in NAI 2 Dec. 2003, TvA 2005, 8-11 in which it was held that the claim required an investigation into the facts, including witness examination, to a degree that, according to the arbitrator, proved to be unfeasible in the summary proceedings.

[232] The ICC Rules for pre-arbitral referee procedure also provide for an agreement by the parties to alter the mandate of an arbitral tribunal in Art. 2.1.1.

26(3) (in Article 42g); and 20, 21, 22(2), 23(1), 23(3), 27-36, 39, 40 and 42 (in Article 42j).

Consequently, and subject to further and more detailed provisions in Articles 42b-42o, parties conducting summary arbitral proceedings may have recourse to the provisions referenced by Article 42a(3). The nature of summary proceedings in terms of speed and its inherently more informal character entails that the referenced provisions may have to be applied somewhat more flexible in summary arbitral proceedings than one would expect in proceedings on the merits.

ARTICLE 42B – COMMENCEMENT

1. Summary arbitral proceedings as meant in this Section commence by the filing of a request for summary arbitral proceedings with the NAI Secretariat. It shall be deemed to have commenced on the day the request is received by the NAI Secretariat.
2. The request shall be filed in two copies and shall be accompanied by the exhibits on which the claimant bases his claim.
3. The request may also be commenced by rapid written communication on the condition that after the commencement the claimant promptly transmits any exhibits in duplicate to the Administrator.

1. General Comments

This article provides for the commencement (*aanhangig maken*) of summary arbitral proceedings. Such is done by filing a formal request for summary arbitral proceedings, accompanied by any exhibits that support the claims made (Article 42b(1) and (2)), with the NAI Secretariat.

The exact moment of commencement of summary arbitral proceedings is, primarily, relevant in the context of pre-judgment attachments. Given that summary arbitral proceedings do count as proceedings on the merits that have to be initiated within a time set by the state court that grants leave for a pre-judgment attachment (*conservatoir beslag*), the moment of commencement of summary proceedings is important. In addition, the commencement of the summary arbitral proceedings can be relevant to stop possible statutory or contractual limitation periods. Furthermore, state courts will take the filing of summary arbitral proceedings into account when either of the parties seeks to commence parallel proceedings in the state courts. The state court that is addressed will have to decide whether or not to defer to summary arbitral proceedings that have already commenced (see the introductory notes to this section, note 1).

Before the actual filing of a request, as described in Article 42b(1), claimants are well advised to contact the Administrator of the NAI. Doing so will enable the Administrator to commence preparations for the appointment of an arbitrator in advance of receipt of the official documentation. Such will speed up the process.

The formal commencement occurs upon the receipt by the NAI Secretariat of the request for arbitration. The claimant will have to comply with Article 42b(2) and file two copies of the request with the NAI and also send a copy to the respondent (in advance of communications by the NAI to the respondent and as per Article 42d).

2.   Means of Filing

In standard cases, a claimant sends or couriers a written request for arbitration with exhibits to the NAI Secretariat. If this is not possible in view of urgency, Article 42b(3) refers to the use of 'rapid written communication', which is permitted subject to the claimant also forwarding hardcopies of the exhibits in duplicate to the Administrator. In the comments on Article 6(5), above, it has been noted that 'rapid written communication' includes telefax and also e-mail. Until recently, the NAI Secretariat has not been keen on the use of e-mail and tended to put more emphasis on the relatively more certain use of telefax communications. However, the use of e-mail communication is nowadays acceptable, in particular insofar as summary proceedings are concerned, upon prior consultation with the NAI Secretariat.

If a claimant decides or cannot file the exhibits to the request for arbitration simultaneously with the request itself, which may occur if doing so is logistically not feasible, the claimant may do so at a later and more suitable moment. This is in line with practice in Dutch state courts. However, a claimant should avoid prejudicing the rights of the respondent and is well advised to submit a copy of the arbitration agreement simultaneously with the request in any event (see also Article 6(3)(e) that is cross referenced in Article 42c).

Article 42c – Contents of the Request

The request shall contain the information mentioned in Article 6(3) under (a), (b), (c), (d), (e) and (i), on the condition that the brief description of the dispute be accompanied by a description of the reasons for the claim and for the purported urgency.

---

1.   General Comments

This article prescribes the required contents of the request for summary arbitral proceedings. In doing so, it explicitly declares a substantial part of Article 6(3), which applies to proceedings on the merits, applicable to a request for summary proceedings.

2.   Contents of the Request for Summary Proceedings

Article 42c makes clear that the claimant is required to provide a description of both the dispute, the reasons, i.e. the grounds for the claims made, as well as a description of the purported urgency.

The description of the dispute is not required to be elaborate, as is apparent from the text of Article 42c. The description of the dispute will have to be sufficient for an arbitral tribunal to comprehend the essential elements and background of the dispute. The Administrator will, however, decide on the appointment of the arbitrator (Article 42f) on the basis of this description. Consequently, if a claimant would prefer the arbitrator to have certain characteristics and/or experience, the claimant should make this clear in the request and further substantiate this by means of the description of the dispute as contained in the request. However, if the claimant requests that the arbitrator has a particular expertise, he should be aware that the Adminstrator in practice will ask the respondent on its views on the requested expertise. This may potentially lead to a certain delay in the appointment of the arbitrators.

Although the claimant will be able to further develop the grounds for its claims, the claimant is expected to provide a description of such grounds. In this respect, the request for summary proceedings differs from a request for proceedings on the merits as provided for in Article 6. It is not possible to give hard and fast rules with respect to the threshold that has to be met. However, the supportive grounds for the claims will have to be set out.

Finally, a claimant must also explain the urgency of the claims made. This is in line with Articles 42a and 42k NAI Rules and Article 254 DCCP, given that the mandate of arbitral tribunals is limited to urgent matters (see Article 42a, note 2).

Insofar as the contents of the request are concerned, a claimant will have to weigh the potential advantage of not being too elaborate in drafting the request and saving part of its argumentation for a subsequent submission (if determined by the tribunal as per Article 42g) or the oral hearing *against* irritating the arbitral tribunal and/or prejudicing the respondent's rights. A respondent, in turn, should be aware of this potential procedural imbalance and be alert in terms of offering criticism on prejudice caused by the claimant. In addition, a claimant must note that it is quite possible that an arbitral tribunal will not offer another opportunity to submit a written brief (see Article 42g(2)).

ARTICLE 42D – NOTIFICATION OF REQUEST TO RESPONDENT

1. One copy of the request, together with any exhibits shall be promptly and properly notified to each respondent.
2. Proof of the notification to each respondent shall at the latest be submitted at the hearing referred to in Article 42g(1).

1. General Comments

The claimant is obliged to promptly forward one copy of the request to the respondent and to submit proof thereof, ultimately at the hearing (Articles 42d(2) and 42g(1)). The rationale is obviously to make the respondent aware of the request and to allow it to prepare its defence.

Respondents are entitled to due process rights, also in summary proceedings. If a respondent is unable to prepare a response to the claims made due to, notably, the procedural conduct of the claimant, this should be noted by the respondent to the tribunal at the earliest opportunity. Whether this will result in a procedural remedy and/or delay of the proceedings depends on the circumstances of the case and cannot be stated in general terms.

A claimant is not under an obligation to engage a bailiff to serve the request on the respondent.

ARTICLE 42E – CONFIRMATION OF RECEIPT OF REQUEST

The Administrator shall communicate to the parties a written acknowledgement of the receipt of the request, making mention of the date of receipt.

1. General Comments

The acknowledgement of both the receipt itself and the date of such receipt can be important to a claimant. For example, the claimant may be under an obligation to commence proceedings in order to comply with conditions set by a court for granting leave for a pre-judgment attachment or statutory or contractual limitation periods.

Typically, conditions set by state courts in connection with pre-judgment attachments provide for a very last moment when so-called principal proceedings must be commenced. This has been noted above, see Article 42b, note 1.

ARTICLE 42F – APPOINTMENT OF ARBITRAL TRIBUNAL

1. As soon as possible after the receipt of the request, the Administrator shall appoint the arbitral tribunal, consisting of a sole arbitrator, which arbitral tribunal shall decide in summary arbitral proceedings. If the parties have agreed on a method of appointment of the arbitrator or arbitrators, such method shall not apply to the appointment of the arbitral tribunal referred to in the previous sentence, unless the parties have actually agreed upon a method of appointment of a summary proceedings arbitral tribunal.

No person shall be precluded from appointment as arbitrator by reason of his nationality.

2. The appointment of the arbitrator shall be confirmed by the Administrator by a letter of appointment addressed to the arbitrator.

3. Articles 10, 11, 15(2) and (3), 17, 18(2) and 19 apply without exception. In the cases referred to in Articles 18(1) and 19(9), the appointment of the new arbitrator shall take place according to the method provided in the first paragraph of this article.

1. General Comments

This provision for the appointment of a tribunal in summary proceedings differs markedly from the arrangement designed for proceedings on the merits. Consequently, the Administrator is able to dispense with both the list-procedure of Article 14 (see, further, the comments on Article 14) and any specific agreements regarding the appointment of an arbitral tribunal entered into by the parties. The latter is only subject to an explicit arrangement by the parties for the appointment of a specific person to compose an arbitral tribunal in summary proceedings (see note 2).[233]

The objective of this arrangement is, quite clearly, to appoint a tribunal as soon as possible and to avoid undue delay.[234] The NAI's policy is to appoint an arbitral tribunal within 24 hours after the filing of the request for arbitration for summary arbitral proceedings (Article 42b(1)). This is important in view of the urgency of the matter and also in light of state courts' ability to decide on the matter in summary proceedings, notwithstanding the agreement by the parties that includes summary arbitral proceedings such as are being discussed here (see the introductory notes to this section, note 1).

2. Qualifications of Arbitrators in Summary Proceedings

Pursuant to Article 42f(1), the arbitral tribunal in summary proceedings shall consist of a sole arbitrator. The English text version is actually not that clear in this respect, but the parties may agree on a different number of arbitrators. However, if they wish to do so, the parties must make an explicit agreement to that effect and should also explicitly stipulate that such agreement is meant to apply to summary arbitral proceedings. If they simply agree on the number of arbitrators in general terms, the Administrator will ignore such agreement when appointing the arbitral tribunal in accordance with Article 42f(1).

The same goes for the method of appointment and the qualifications of possible arbitrators that the parties have agreed upon. If the parties wish their

---

[233] The unavailability of such persons can, obviously, present complications.

[234] J.L.W. Sillevis Smitt, 'Het NAI introduceert het arbitraal kort geding: een toelichting', TvA 1997, 126.

agreement thereto to equally apply to arbitrators in summary arbitral proceedings, they should explicitly stipulate so. If not, the Administrator will ignore their agreement when appointing the arbitral tribunal.

No person shall be precluded from being appointed as arbitrator in summary arbitral proceedings by reason of his nationality. Accordingly, the provision of Article 16(2), allowing each party to require that a sole arbitrator shall hold a nationality other than that of any of the parties, does not apply in summary arbitral proceedings.

On the basis of published cases and our experience, the NAI will generally appoint very experienced arbitrators in summary arbitral proceedings. These arbitrators include (former and present) Presidents of District Courts or Courts of Appeal who are highly experienced in dealing with summary proceedings. An advantage of appointing members of the judiciary is a general absence of conflicts of interests.

Subsequent to the appointment of the arbitrator complications such as conflicts of interests and replacement of arbitrators may occur although such is unlikely. These are dealt with in a fashion similar to proceedings on the merits, albeit more expediently. This follows from Article 42f(3) that provides for the equal application of a range of provisions that have each been discussed above. Reference is made to the comments given on impartiality and independence (Article 10), disclosure obligations on the part of arbitrators (Article 11), acceptance of mandate (Article 15(2)), notification of appointment to parties (Article 15(3)), release from mandate (Article 17), replacement of the arbitrator (Article 18(2)) and challenge (Article 19). If an arbitrator has to be replaced as a consequence of such complications, the same expedient procedure for the appointment will apply to a new arbitrator (Article 42f(1)).

ARTICLE 42g – HEARING

1. The arbitral tribunal shall determine immediately the day, time and place of the hearing for the claim in summary arbitral proceedings and shall promptly notify the parties in writing thereof.
2. Written memorials are to be filed only if the arbitral tribunal so determines, without prejudice to the provisions of Articles 42h and 42i. Article 26(3) shall apply accordingly.

1. Determination of the Hearing

This provision is designed to enable the summary proceedings to proceed swiftly to an oral hearing. The hearing offers an opportunity to inform the tribunal about the case and enables a tribunal to obtain an explanation of pertinent issues and, for example, parts of the factual/documentary record that are not self-explanatory. In addition, the tribunal may attempt to guide the parties towards a settlement of their dispute.

In terms of procedural and logistical discretion afforded to an arbitral tribunal the proceedings mirror summary proceedings in Dutch state courts.

In practice, parties are invited to submit, at very short notice, a list of dates at which they cannot attend a hearing, but they are well advised to do so proactively in the request for arbitration (claimant), also for the respondent, and/or upon receipt of the request or correspondence from the NAI (respondent), if the claimant has not already submitted this information. If the claimant also submits information on the respondent's availability, such information will be used by the Administrator to select the arbitrator. Subsequent thereto, a hearing will be planned. It is also customary for an arbitral tribunal to organize a pre-hearing conference (possibly in the form of a conference call) in order to determine and agree on basic procedural arrangements such as required time, the hearing, use and submission of pleading notes (i.e. written copies of oral arguments), potential witnesses, a cut-off moment for the submission of (additional) documentary evidence, court reporters etc.

2.   Written Memorials and Practice at the Hearing

The NAI Rules provide that the parties, in principle, will not be given an opportunity to conduct a round of written submissions prior to the oral hearing. However, either party may request the tribunal to grant an opportunity for doing so. A claimant should consider doing so as part of his request for arbitration and the respondent in a letter to the arbitral tribunal. However, in either case, and especially if no round of written pleadings is or can be provided, much weight is placed on the hearing itself.

A hearing generally commences by addressing formalities. At that moment, and on pain of potentially forfeiting the right to do so in proceedings to set aside an award (see Part III, Chapter 1), the parties will have to convey any formal objections that they may have in terms of the proceedings (including the right to an equal hearing and or defence). The same applies to the respondent who, at that stage, will have to invoke efficiencies or absence of an agreement to arbitrate in summary proceedings (albeit that this is generally done in a written submission, as per Article 42h) or the introduction of a counterclaim (Article 42i).

Subsequently, each of the parties will generally be provided the opportunity to present oral argument. In the Netherlands, parties tend to also submit a written version of their oral argument in the form of pleading notes, in advance of the commencement of their oral argument. These pleading notes are considered to be part of the arbitration file and can serve as a source of reference for the tribunal, in particular if court reporters are not present (which is, also, customary in the Dutch jurisdiction). Insofar as the relationship between the oral arguments and the written pleading notes is concerned, parties are allowed to improvise but are also expected not to deviate from the arguments contained in the written pleading notes by leaving out substantial parts, albeit that a deviation – in particular if such is done transparently – is seldom objected to. Adding to the argument included in the written pleading notes is perfectly acceptable. In general, the tribunal will also ask, and allow for, limited questions to witnesses or experts, in particular if such has been announced in a pre-hearing meeting/conference call and if time permits (which it does not in regular state court summary proceedings).

After the hearing, a tribunal may, in principle, render an award. If (either of) the parties desire to submit post-hearing memorials, these may be accepted by the arbitral tribunal, in particular in summary proceedings, if a specific matter requires a further limited round of written debate or instruction by the parties to be decided upon.

3.   Attendance at the Hearing

Article 42g(2) further provides, by referring to Article 26(3), that the arbitral tribunal may permit a wide array of people to attend the hearing. Generally, the parties are expected to inform the arbitral tribunal in advance of the hearing of the identity of the persons that will attend.

The reference to Article 26(3) makes clear that witnesses and experts are allowed to attend the hearing, even without the arbitral tribunal's explicit consent. The arbitral tribunal may also permit the examination of witnesses and experts during the hearing. However, there is also the risk that such examination will be refused. In fact, some arbitrators consider the examination of witnesses and experts to be incompatible with the nature of summary proceedings. There are no fixed rules to determine when the examination of witnesses and experts is likely to be allowed. Much depends on the nature of the dispute, the available time (also in light of the urgency of the matter) and the personal views of the arbitrator.

In the interest of time, the tribunal or the parties may seek to have witnesses and experts heard informally. If this occurs, procedural tactics demand a good understanding of the questions that may be asked and preparation of individuals attending the hearing. It goes without saying that an unconsidered answer to an informal question may be disastrous.

At all times the arbitral tribunal will have to make sure that the requirements of due process, in particular the right to an equal hearing, are observed. Such may be at issue if one of the parties presents witnesses and experts at the hearing without the other party being in a position to respond adequately in view of an inability to duly prepare. Under circumstances it may be inevitable to schedule a second hearing for examining both parties' witnesses and experts.

ARTICLE 42H – PLEA AS TO LACK OF JURISDICTION

If the respondent wishes to raise the plea of lack of jurisdiction of the arbitral tribunal on the ground that there is no valid arbitration agreement, he shall raise this plea before submitting any defence at the very latest at the hearing referred to in Article 42g(1) or, if a memorial is filed prior to that hearing, at the very latest in that memorial. Article 9(3) through (6) applies.

1. General Comments

The requirements for a valid arbitration agreement have been discussed above in Article 1, note 3. These requirements also apply to the agreement in which arbitrators are given the mandate to render an award in summary arbitral proceedings (Article 1051(1) DCCP). The NAI Rules (Articles 37 and 42a-42o) contain such an agreement, although the parties are free to determine otherwise.

Since the submission of written statements prior to a hearing in summary arbitral proceedings is the exception rather than the rule, the plea that there is no valid arbitration agreement, or at least not an agreement for summary arbitral proceedings, will have to be made at the hearing. In view of desired efficiency, this plea should be introduced at the opening of the hearing prior to the commencement of the oral arguments, although it is only required to be raised at some point during the hearing. If this plea is made, it is unlikely that the tribunal will close the hearing immediately. The tribunal will generally proceed and rule on its jurisdiction in an award, after hearing the case in full (see Article 9, note 3).[235]

This Article 42h is also in line with the arrangement for proceedings on the merits as set out in Article 9(2)-(6), which has already been commented on above. Consequently, if the tribunal determines that written statements must be submitted, a plea as to lack of jurisdiction must be included therein. The same applies to a counterclaim statement, if any, submitted pursuant to Article 42i. However, this does not seem to apply to a plea as to lack of jurisdiction on the basis of non-arbitrability (Article 1020(3) DCCP), which may be raised at any stage and in the state courts as well (Article 1052(2) DCCP), most notably in proceedings to set aside an award (Article 1065(1) and (2)). This follows from the public policy nature of such an argument. See in respect of arbitrability, Part I, Chapter 2, Section 2.

ARTICLE 42i – COUNTERCLAIM

The respondent or respondents are entitled to submit a counterclaim in summary arbitral proceedings. The counterclaim shall be made by means of a written memorial which shall be submitted to the arbitral

---

[235] If the respondent does not appear at the hearing, the arbitral tribunal will, inter alia, have to verify whether or not the respondent has been adequately informed and, if required ex officio, whether or not it has jurisdiction to decide on the matter. See NAI 30 Mar. 2007, TvA 2008, 34.

tribunal at the latest at the hearing referred to in Article 42g(1) and copies shall be delivered either by mail or by hand to the claimant and sent to the Administrator.

1.   General Comments

Counterclaims may be submitted and must be made in writing prior to or, at the very latest, at the hearing. Submitting a counterclaim at the hearing itself is not advisable, given that such makes a claimant more likely to be successful in objecting by invoking due process rights. If such an objection is successful, the counterclaim will have to be addressed in separate proceedings.

It follows from case law relating to summary proceedings in state courts that a counterclaim in summary arbitral proceedings must also possess the required urgency.[236] In addition, the tribunal will weigh the interests of the parties in determining whether to grant the counterclaim (see the introductory notes to this section, note 3).

The claimant will typically neither be able nor permitted to respond in writing to the counterclaim. This is in line with the practice in respect of the primary claim, to which a respondent is, in principle, only to respond at the hearing (subject to the tribunal determining that the parties may submit a round of written statements on the basis of Article 42g(2)).

Insofar as the submission of evidence for counterclaims is concerned, the following applies. Although Article 42i does not, explicitly, put a respondent under an obligation to also submit his evidence for a counterclaim at the time of submission thereof, it is advisable, in light of due process requirements, for a respondent to include evidence with the counterclaim memorial or submit such evidence as soon as possible thereafter. This also follows from the applicability of Article 28(1) that governs the production of documents (as per the linking provision in Article 42j).

If a respondent files a counterclaim, a corresponding deposit for costs (see Article 59) will have to be made upon the request of the Administrator. As per Article 42n, this will have to be done either before the hearing, if the counterclaim is filed before the hearing, or immediately after the hearing, if the counterclaim is filed at the hearing.

ARTICLE 42J – PROCEDURE

The provisions of Articles 20, 21, 22(2), 23(1) and (3), 27 through 36, 39, 40 and 42 apply accordingly.

---

[236] HR 4 Dec. 1987, NJ 1988, 344.

1. General Comments

This linking provision provides the arbitral tribunal with the mandate to structure and organize the summary arbitral proceedings in accordance with the required speed.

Consequently, most of the procedural provisions designed for proceedings on the merits and set out in Section 2 of the NAI Rules apply equally to summary arbitral proceedings. To the extent relevant, the provisions that do not apply are replaced by specific arrangements in Section 4A dealing with summary proceedings. The latter include Article 22(1) relating to the place of arbitration and Articles 24-26 that govern the exchange of written statements. The comments on the provisions included in this Article 42j may also be referred to in the context of summary proceedings, subject to the following general caveat: an arbitral tribunal in summary proceedings is expected to be more flexible in making procedural arrangements and proceed more quickly than a tribunal dealing with a case on the merits. Consequently, a tribunal may dispense with measures that would take too much time, such as the examination of witnesses and experts.[237] This is in line with practice in state courts and follows from the nature of summary proceedings and the claims that can be made in summary proceedings.

Insofar as the amendment of claims is concerned, Article 42j also provides for the equal application of Article 34. Given that a party who is confronted with such amendment may object to this if it 'unreasonably hinders his defence, or this causes unreasonable delay of the proceedings', an amendment of claims in summary proceedings should also be communicated as soon as possible, and preferably in advance of the hearing.

ARTICLE 42k – REFERRAL TO ARBITRATION ON THE MERITS

If the arbitral tribunal determines that the case is not sufficiently urgent or is too complicated to be decided by a provisional decision, it may reject the claim either wholly or partially and refer the parties to arbitration on the merits. An arbitration on the merits shall be commenced on the basis of Article 6 of these Rules.

---

1. General Comments

This provision follows logically from Article 42a and arranges for the consequences of a case not meeting the criteria for an award being issued in summary proceedings.

Insofar as the elements 'urgency' and 'too complicated' are concerned, reference is made to the introductory notes to this Section 4A and the comments

---

[237] G.J. Meijer 2008 (T&C Rv), Art. 1051 DCCP, note 4.

on Article 42a. However, the parties may agree to deviate from the standard arrangement and provide otherwise by structuring the summary proceedings into a form that resembles proceedings on the merits in order to suit their preferences. Such agreement could arrange for the availability of additional time and resources for a tribunal to deal with the matter in summary proceedings, in view of matter's complexity.

> Article 256 DCCP contains a similar provision for summary proceedings in the state courts.

ARTICLE 42L – NATURE OF THE DECISION; SECURITY

1. A decision in summary arbitral proceedings is an arbitral award in the sense of Article 1051(3) of the Code of Civil Procedure. The provisions of Section Five of these Rules also apply.
2. The arbitral tribunal shall be authorized to order security in a form determined by it with respect to any claim or counterclaim in summary arbitral proceedings on behalf of the party making such request.
3. The arbitral tribunal may decide on the merits upon joint request of the parties.

   In such case, the award shall specifically mention this request and the decision shall be regarded as an award on the merits to which the provisions of Section Five apply.

1.   General Comments

This article is in line with Article 1051(3) DCCP (discussed in the introductory notes to this Section 4A, note 3) and confirms that Dutch arbitration law deems an award in summary arbitration to be a proper arbitral award.[238] Consequently, such an award is enforceable on the same footing as another arbitral award originating from a tribunal seated in the Netherlands (see also the introductory notes to this Section 4A, note 3).

In addition, Article 42l(1) provides that Section 5 of the NAI Rules, relating to awards, applies. Consequently, the requirements regarding the making, form and contents of arbitral awards apply equally to awards rendered in summary proceedings. However, parties may expect the tribunal to render an award sooner than would be customary in proceedings on the merits. In addition, the notion that the reasoning of a judgment in summary proceedings conducted in a state court is less elaborate than in a judgment in proceedings on the merits may also apply in the context of summary arbitral awards (see Article 49(2)(e)) (see below and Article 1065 DCCP, note 5 in Part III, Chapter 1).

---

[238]   See also Introduction to NAI Arbitration Rules, para. 11.3.

The Dutch arrangement on the status of arbitral awards resulting from summary proceedings will not necessarily be accepted in countries where enforceability of an award rendered in summary proceedings is sought on the basis of Article I of the New York Convention. Section IV.A of the 2006 amendment to the UNCITRAL Model Law may, however, be invoked to support the enforceability of awards giving interim measures obtained in contested cases (i.e. excluding cases in which a respondent does not appear). This follows from Articles 17 H (regarding recognition and enforcement) and 17 I (regarding grounds for refusing recognition and enforcement) of the UNCITRAL Model Law, as amended.[239]

2. Form of Security that May Be Ordered

An arbitral tribunal may order security with respect to claims and/or counterclaims in summary arbitral proceedings, on the basis of Article 42l(2). These forms of security typically include bank guarantees, security rights such as pledges over goods but may not include pre-judgment attachments. The granting of leave for pre-judgment attachments, which is a very common form of security in the Dutch arena, falls outside the scope of arbitrability under Dutch arbitration law and requires a party to bring a case in the state courts.[240] However, an arbitral tribunal may take measures that resemble forms of security that an arbitral tribunal is not permitted to grant. For example, an arbitral tribunal may issue an order or interim award requesting a party to cooperate in effectuating a pre-judgment attachment, or to provide a bank guarantee, on pain of a penalty (*dwangsom*; Article 1056 DCCP).[241] The conditions that apply to the imposition of penalties in state courts also apply if an arbitral tribunal considers imposing a penalty. These conditions are set out in detail in Articles 611a-611i DCCP and are referred to in Article 1056 DCCP.[242]

A further limitation on security that may be ordered exists in respect of security for claims in proceedings on the merits and costs. Pursuant to Articles 42a-42o an arbitral tribunal may neither provide security for claims made in proceedings on the merits nor for costs of such proceedings on the merits (see, however, the comments on Article 37).[243] Such should be done in

---

[239] The text of the revised UNCITRAL Model Law may be retrieved from the UNCITRAL website: <www.uncitral.org/uncitral/en/uncitral_texts/arbitration.html>.

[240] A detailed commentary on this matter is provided by A.I.M. van Mierlo, 'Arbitrage, beslag en executie', TvA 2006, 41-43.

[241] However, Art. 1056 DCCP provides that the lifting, suspension or reduction of penalties imposed by an arbitral tribunal requires the intervention of state courts. See for a detailed discussion of this issue in an (inter)national perspective also P. Sanders, *Het Nederlandse arbitragerecht. Nationaal en internationaal* (Deventer, Kluwer, 2001), 117-121.

[242] A detailed commentary on this arrangement is provided by A.I.M. van Mierlo, 'Arbitrage, beslag en executie', TvA 2006, 39-41.

[243] See also Introduction to NAI Arbitration Rules, para. 11.4.

proceedings in state courts.[244] In respect of costs relating to summary arbitral proceedings and proceedings on the merits, no security can be ordered in proceedings on the basis of Article 42a.[245]

3. Request to Render an Award on the Merits

Parties may jointly request the arbitral tribunal to render an award on the merits as per Article 42l(3). The primary reason for offering this possibility is that the parties may desire to obtain finality in respect of the resolution of their dispute by means of an award that has res judicata effect (Article 1059 DCCP). Since a decision on the merits obtains res judicata effect, it is not subject to further proceedings on the merits like an award in summary arbitral proceedings.

This is in line with a practice in summary proceedings in state courts that is referred to as 'short-circuiting' ('*kortsluiten*'). Although the text of Article 42l(3) seems to express a discretionary power on the part of the tribunal regarding whether or not it will comply with a joint request by the parties to render an award on the merits, it is not likely that the tribunal will decline to grant such a request.

If the parties request the tribunal to apply this Article 42l(3), the tribunal will, however, have to be more extensive in its reasoning of the award than in an award in summary proceedings. This follows from an analogy with practice in the state courts. The requirements regarding the reasoning of arbitral awards are subject to legal development in the Netherlands. Article 1057 DCCP provides, in a fashion similar to Article 49(2)(e), that awards should be reasoned. This is discussed in more detail below (see the comments on Article 1065 DCCP in Part III, Chapter 1). However, it is also held in the Netherlands that a lower standard applies to the reasoning required in summary awards. This follows from the nature of summary proceedings and is argued to also apply to arbitral summary awards, albeit that the requirements regarding the reasoning of an arbitral award are already very marginal which makes it hard to envisage even lower standards being applied to awards in summary arbitral proceedings.[246]

ARTICLE 42M – RELATIONSHIP WITH THE CASE ON THE MERITS

The provisional decision shall in no way prejudice the final decision of the arbitral tribunal that decides on the merits of the case.

---

[244] NAI 23 Nov. 2001, TvA 2002, 63-66; NAI 23 Apr. 2002, TvA 2003, 21-24.

[245] NAI 2 Mar. 2007, TvA 2008, 99-100; NAI 22 Mar. 2007, TvA 2008, 100.

[246] See Burg. Rv, 2006 (H.J. Snijders), Art. 1051 DCCP, note 1.

1.   General Comments

The contents of this provision follow from the nature of summary proceedings and have been discussed in the introductory notes to this section. In short, awards arising from summary arbitral proceedings do not have res judicata effect, albeit subject to the parties requesting and the tribunal granting an award on the merits as per Article 42l(3).

Notwithstanding this general and principled notion, awards by arbitral tribunals in summary proceedings *do* carry authoritative weight and may thus be persuasive in subsequent proceedings on the merits or provide an impetus for settlement negotiations. This is evident, paradoxically, from the very fact that, in the state courts, summary proceedings are quite often not followed up by proceedings on the merits. Given the limited publication of arbitral awards, it is not possible to determine whether this practice also applies to summary arbitral proceedings.[247] In our experience, complex cases in which considerable interests are at stake tend to proceed to a case on the merits.

It is questionable whether penalties (*dwangsommen*) that may be attached by an arbitral tribunal to an award in summary arbitral proceedings, and that are forfeited due to non-compliance, remain payable if an arbitral tribunal dealing with proceedings on the merits overturns the award rendered in summary proceedings. In Dutch case law regarding state court proceedings, this question has been resolved and the penalties remain payable.[248] It has been argued that the application of this rule in arbitration would be unacceptable due to the fact that parties are not always represented by counsel and may not be aware of this.[249] We do not consider this to be persuasive, in particular in sofar as national arbitrations are concerned. In international arbitrations we consider it to be arguable that parties should count on such penalties remaining payable, notwithstanding a subsequent reversal of the summary arbitral award to which penalties are attached, taking into account that a considerable number of legal systems take an approach similar to the Dutch jurisdiction.

ARTICLE 42N – ADMINISTRATION COSTS AND DEPOSIT FOR COSTS

1. The provisions of Section Six apply to summary arbitral proceedings, on the condition that the administrative costs and the deposit for costs must be paid or deposited, respectively, prior to the

---

[247] H.J. Snijders, C.J.M. Klaassen & G.J. Meijer, *Nederlands burgerlijk procesrecht* (Deventer, Kluwer, 2007), 340: 'The meaning and position of summary proceedings in legal practice is exemplified by the fact that in the broad majority of cases no final decision is sought in proceedings on the merits (. . .).'

[248] HR 16 Nov. 1984, NJ 1985, 547; HR 22 Dec. 1990, NJ 1990, 234.

[249] See Burg. Rv, 2006 (H.J. Snijders), Art. 1051 DCCP, note 1.

hearing referred to in Article 42g(1) and if a counterclaim is submitted at the hearing, immediately after the hearing.

2. The arbitral tribunal shall be authorized to suspend the procedure or
to withhold its decision if one of the parties has not complied with
the financial obligations arising from this article. If one party after a
reminder in writing by the Administrator has not complied with its
financial obligations arising from this article, it shall be considered
that the party has withdrawn its claim or counterclaim.

1.   General Comments

This article provides for the equal application of the arrangement relating to costs
that applies to proceedings on the merits. Reference is made to the discussion of
this subject in Section 6.

Insofar as summary proceedings are concerned, payment must be made
before, or in the case of counterclaims, shortly after the hearing. This arrangement is intended to ensure swift payment and to prevent delay of the issuance of
the arbitral award. Sanctions are included in Article 42n(2). See also Article 35,
note 1.

It is safe to assume that the award will not be released if sums are not paid,
subject to payment by either party in default of the counterparty's obstruction. If
an award has not yet been drafted, the case may even be dismissed.[250]

ARTICLE 42o – INTERIM MEASURES OF PROTECTION

The submission of a claim based on this Section does not preclude a
party from requesting a court to grant interim measures of protection.

1.   General Comments

This provision makes clear that parties are and remain entitled to address state
courts in order to obtain interim measures of protection, which measures the
arbitral tribunal is not competent to give (as noted in Article 42l, note 2). The
most important and prevalent interim measures, which has been noted above, is a
pre-judgment attachment (*conservatoir beslag*) that may serve to freeze assets
for the purpose of future recourse.[251] In addition, courts may, ultimately, detain a
person for failing to comply with a judicial order or seal property and/or means of
evidence.

---

[250] See, for example, Rotterdam District Court 25 Jan. 2006, TvA 2007, 32-37.

[251] Arbitrators are not competent to provide leave for a conservatory attachment.

AWARD (Articles 43-55)

ARTICLE 43 – PERIOD OF TIME

---

1. At the end of the hearing referred to in Articles 26, 37(3) and 42g(1), the arbitral tribunal shall inform the parties of the period of time within which it will make its award. If the parties have waived a hearing, as referred to in Article 26, the parties shall be informed after submission of the last memorial. The arbitral tribunal shall be authorized, if necessary, to extend the period of time one or more times. In all cases the arbitral tribunal shall decide with all due despatch.

2. The mandate of the arbitral tribunal shall last until it has rendered its last final award, without prejudice to the provisions of Articles 52 and 53.

---

1.   Period of Time

According to Article 43(1), the arbitral tribunal shall inform the parties at the end of the hearing, or, if the parties have waived a hearing, after submission of the last written statement, of the period of time within which it will make its award. There is no time limit provided in the NAI Rules within which the arbitral tribunal must render the award, but the arbitral tribunal must decide with all due dispatch. The Administrator will (and does see to it that the award is rendered within a reasonable period of time. In general, an award in summary proceedings will be rendered much faster (indeed possibly within a few days)[252] than an award in 'normal' arbitral proceedings (typically ranging from several weeks up to six months). Furthermore, the arbitral tribunal will only render a final award

---

[252] The writing requirement prevents the tribunal from giving an oral judgment (see Art. 49), though it is possible to write an award on the spot or to give the parties an oral account of what the award will contain.

after the arbitral tribunal and the NAI have ensured that sufficient funds have been deposited.

The arbitral tribunal is authorized – if necessary – to extend the period of time one or more times. There is no penalty in the NAI Rules if the arbitrators do not render the award with all due dispatch. However, formally, the parties may release the arbitrator(s) from their mandate or terminate the mandate of the arbitral tribunal (the latter on the basis of Article 1031 DCCP, if the arbitration is seated in the Netherlands). This will not happen often, as it will only lead to additional delay in the arbitral proceedings. Informally, the parties – also through the Administrator – may exert pressure on the arbitral tribunal by writing a letter to the arbitral tribunal in which they request the arbitral tribunal to render the award as soon as possible.

> As mentioned above, under Dutch arbitration law, if the arbitral tribunal proceeds in an unacceptably slow manner, the mandate of the arbitral tribunal may be terminated on the basis of Article 1031(2) DCCP (see the comments on Article 17). See for the consequences of such premature termination for the costs of the arbitration Article 62 of the NAI Rules.

2. Mandate

Pursuant to Article 43(2), the mandate of the arbitral tribunal ends when the arbitral tribunal has rendered its last final award, without prejudice to the provisions of Articles 52 (rectification or correction of the award) and 53 (additional award). The reservation in the last part of this provision entails that the tribunal's mandate revives, if a request for rectification or correction or an additional award is filed.

> On the basis of Article 1058(2) DCCP, the mandate of the arbitral tribunal ends with the deposit of the last final award, without prejudice to the provisions on the rectification and correction of the award and the possibility of an additional award. Article 43(2) does not refer to the 'deposit' of the last final award because the NAI itself deals with such deposit (see Article 50(1)(a) and (b) NAI Rules).

ARTICLE 44 – TYPES OF AWARDS

The arbitral tribunal may render a final award, a partial award, or an interim award without prejudice to the powers of the arbitral tribunal referred to in Articles 37(1) and (5), 42a(1) and 42l.

---

1. Types of Awards

Article 44 indicates the types of awards that may be rendered by the arbitral tribunal: a final award, a partial final award[253] or an interim award. Besides these awards, the arbitral tribunal also has the power to render a decision in summary arbitral proceedings on the basis of the Articles 37(1) and (5), 42a(1) and 42l (see the comments on these articles).

2. Interim Award

An interim award is an award in which the arbitral tribunal does not definitively decide (in the operative part of the decision; the dictum) on the merits of the case. In other words: the arbitral tribunal does not definitively allow or dismiss the claims in the operative part of the decision (the dictum). In an interim award, the arbitral tribunal decides, for example, on the jurisdiction of the arbitral tribunal, on issues relating to the gathering of evidence (such as the decision to allow a party to provide evidence, for example by allowing the examination of witnesses or experts, the appearance in person or a site instruction) or the participation of third parties to the arbitral proceedings. The arbitral tribunal does not need to render a formal interim award on these issues; the arbitral tribunal may also issue an order (often in the form of a letter or an e-mail communication to the parties) on issues that it could have decided in an interim award. However, the arbitral tribunal will often choose to render an interim award on such issues, as this will give the arbitral tribunal the ability to decide on other issues that are disputed by the parties. Also, it may be regarded as a violation of good practice if the arbitral tribunal issues an order in case the parties have agreed to the possibility of appeal, because an order will make the possibility of such an appeal illusory. However, the parties have no effective recourse if the arbitrators neglect this rule. In addition, this issue is not likely to arise in practice, because parties only rarely agree upon appeal in arbitrations.

3. (Partial) Final Award

A final award is an award in which the arbitral tribunal renders a definitive decision in the operative part of the decision on the (counter)claim(s). In other words, in a final award, the arbitral tribunal definitively – partially or wholly – allows or dismisses claim(s).

If the arbitral tribunal only allows or dismisses part of the claim and decides that the decision on the remainder of the claim will be postponed, the final award is a partial final award. The decision on the postponement of the decision on the

---

[253] Although the text of the article speaks of a partial award, it is more accurate to call it a partial final award (the Dutch text of the NAI Rules also contains the term partial final award).

remainder of the claim itself is an interim award. A partial final award is binding in the same arbitral proceedings, unless a partial final award has been set aside.

> Under Dutch law, the doctrine of the so-called 'binding decision' (*bindende eindbeslissing*) has been developed in case law. The binding decision is a decision (usually) in the considerations of the award, which has been given explicitly and without reservations on an issue (factual or otherwise) between the parties. The doctrine entails that an arbitral tribunal may, in principle, not reverse to a binding decision in a previous award.
>
> It is generally accepted in the Netherlands that the doctrine of the binding decision also applies in arbitration. It will also likely apply in NAI arbitrations with a place of arbitration in the Netherlands.

4. Legal Consequences of Distinction

The distinction between the different types of award (see Article 1049 DCCP) has a few consequences under the Dutch arbitration act. In the first place, according to Article 1050(2) DCCP, arbitral appeal – if agreed on by the parties – of a partial final award is only possible together with the last final award, unless the parties have agreed otherwise. According to Article 1050(3) DCCP, arbitral appeal of an interim award is only possible together with an appeal against a partial or complete final award, unless the parties have agreed otherwise. These two provisions lead to the conclusion that – except for a different agreement by the parties – the appeal against an interim award is only possible together with an appeal against a final award.

Furthermore, only a partial or complete final award (that is not open to appeal) may be enforced (Article 1062(1) DCCP). Also, a claim to have an interim award set aside may only be instituted together with a claim to set aside a (partial) final award which is not open to appeal (Article 1064(4) DCCP). Finally, Article 1058(1) DCCP, relating to the requirement to deposit the award, applies only to (partial) final awards.

ARTICLE 45 – DECISION ACCORDING TO RULES OF LAW OR AS
AMIABLE COMPOSITEUR

---

1. The arbitral tribunal shall decide as amiable compositeur unless the parties agreed to authorize it to make its award in accordance with the rules of law.
2. In an international arbitration, the arbitral tribunal shall make its award in accordance with the rules of law unless the parties agreed to authorize it to decide as amiable compositeur.

---

1. Applicable Standards

Article 45(1) stipulates that the arbitral tribunal, in principle, has to decide as amiable compositeur. Article 45(2), however, provides that in the case of an international arbitration,[254] the opposite applies: the arbitral tribunal shall make its award in accordance with the rules of law.

In both cases the parties may agree otherwise. Accordingly, they may choose to stipulate that the arbitral tribunal has to decide in accordance with the rules of law also in national arbitrations. On the other hand they may also authorize the arbitral tribunal in an international arbitration to decide as amiable compositeur.

Regardless of the applicable standard, the arbitral tribunal will have to take into account any applicable trade usages (see Article 47 NAI Rules). The arbitral tribunal will also have to take into account any rules that may lead to having the award set aside if such rules are violated (such as EU competition law or mandatory rules of the applicable arbitration law).[255]

> Article 1054(1) and (3) DCCP provide that the arbitral tribunal shall make its decision in accordance with the rules of law, unless the parties have instructed the arbitral tribunal to decide as amiable compositeur.

2. Amiable Compositeur

It is not easy to determine the contents of a decision as amiable compositeur. It is generally accepted that in this case, the arbitral tribunal is not bound by mandatory or supplementary rules of law. However, in practice the distinction between the two standards in Article 45(1) is foremost food for scientific debate. In the majority of cases it is difficult to tell whether the outcome of the case would be different, if the arbitral tribunal would have applied the other standard.

According to Dutch law, the arbitral tribunal may not decide contrary to public policy. As a result of this, even if the arbitral tribunal has to decide as amiable compositeur, the arbitral tribunal will have to apply mandatory rules of law that are of public policy.[256] If the arbitral tribunal does decide contrary to public policy, this may lead to a refusal to enforce the arbitral award on the basis of Article 1063(1) DCCP as well as to having the award set aside on the basis of Article 1065(1)(e) DCCP.

Despite the starting point of Article 45(1) that the arbitral tribunal has to decide as amiable compositeur, under Dutch arbitration law the arbitral tribunal

---

[254] See, for the definition of 'international arbitration' Art. 1(g), note 5.

[255] Under Dutch law, such rules are for example mandatory rules of Dutch law; ECJ 1 Jun. 1999, C-126/97 (Eco Swiss China Time Ltd v. Benetton International NV), European Court reports 1999; page I-03055; also in: NJ 2000, 339.

[256] ECJ 1 Jun. 1999, C-126/97 (Eco Swiss China Time Ltd v. Benetton International NV), European Court reports 1999; page I-03055; also in: NJ 2000, 339. See for a further discussion also Burg. Rv, 2006 (H.J. Snijders), Art. 1054 DCCP, notes 1-4.

will have to decide in accordance with the rules of law in deciding on the jurisdiction of the arbitral tribunal or on other procedural matters.[257]

3. Rules of Law

The parties may authorize the arbitral tribunal to make its award in accordance with the rules of law (Article 45(1)). In this case, the arbitral tribunal will have to decide according to the rules of law chosen by the parties (see Article 46). This choice of law does not necessarily have to be made in the arbitration agreement and is usually made in the main agreement or the applicable general conditions that contain or refer to the arbitration agreement.

According to Article 46, when there is no choice of law made by the parties – but the parties did agree on a decision in accordance with the rules of law – the arbitral tribunal shall make its award in accordance with the rules of law which it considers appropriate (see Article 46).

ARTICLE 46 – APPLICABLE LAW

If a choice of law is made by the parties, the arbitral tribunal shall make its award in accordance with the rules of law chosen by the parties. Failing such choice of law, the arbitral tribunal shall make its award in accordance with the rules of law which it considers appropriate.

1. General Comments

As mentioned before in the comments on Article 45, if the arbitral tribunal has to decide in accordance with the rules of law and a choice of law has been made by the parties, the arbitral tribunal shall make its award in accordance with the rules of law chosen by the parties. If no choice of law has been made, the arbitral tribunal shall make its award in accordance with the rules of law which it considers appropriate. Under Dutch arbitration law, the arbitral tribunal may make a direct choice of law, without being required to apply international conflict of law rules.

If interpreted literally, the provision of Article 46 implies that if parties have made a choice of law, the arbitral tribunal will automatically have to decide in accordance with these rules of law, even if the parties have not instructed the arbitral tribunal to decide in accordance with the rules of law, in which case the arbitral tribunal is to decide as an amiable compositeur. As this is clearly not the intention of Article 46, it should be read that this article applies only if the parties have instructed the arbitral tribunal to decide in accordance with the rules

---

[257] See Burg. Rv, 2006 (H.J. Snijders), Art. 1054 DCCP, notes 1-4.

of law. Nevertheless, a choice of law is also relevant if the tribunal is required to decide as amiable compositeur, because in practice arbitrators in that case often turn to the applicable law for guidance in their decision. In addition, Article 46 entails that the arbitral tribunal cannot use other laws than that chosen by the parties as guidance.

The applicable rules of law have to be distinguished from the applicable arbitration law. In the case of a NAI arbitration these are the mandatory provisions of arbitration law of the country in which the arbitration is seated and the respective supplementary law, to the extent that the NAI Rules or the parties do not provide otherwise.

Article 1054(2) DCCP contains a similar provision.

ARTICLE 47 – TRADE USAGES

In all cases the arbitral tribunal shall take into account any applicable trade usages.

1. General Comments

As mentioned before in the comments on Article 45, the arbitral tribunal – whether deciding as amiable compositeur or in accordance with the rules of law – will have to take into account any applicable trade usages. In this respect, the arbitral tribunal may look at the UNIDROIT Principles of International Commercial Contracts 2004[258] and the Principles of European Contract Law.[259] Also, an arbitrator may use his specific knowledge in a certain branch.

The requirement that arbitrators 'take into account' trade usages does not mean that they are bound by them. Accordingly, an award which does not comply with (international) trade usages cannot be set aside on that ground.[260]

Article 1054(4) DCCP contains a similar provision.

ARTICLE 48 – DECISION-MAKING; SIGNING OF AWARD

1. If the arbitral tribunal is composed of more than one arbitrator, it shall decide by a majority of votes.

---

[258] See <www.unidroit.org>.

[259] Burg. Rv, 2006 (H.J. Snijders), Art. 1054 DCCP, note 4.

[260] Even the incorrect application of applicable law in itself is insufficient to set aside an arbitral award, see HR 22 Dec. 2006, NJ 2008, 4 (Kers/Rijpma) and the comments on Art. 1065 DCCP in Part III, Ch. 1, so this is a fortiori true for the trade usages, which merely have to be 'taken into account'.

2. If a minority of the arbitrators refuses to sign, the other arbitrators shall make mention thereof beneath the award signed by them. This statement shall also be signed by them.

3. If a minority of the arbitrators is incapable of signing and it is unlikely that this impediment will cease to exist within a reasonable time, the provisions of the previous paragraph shall apply accordingly.

4. No mention shall be made in the award of the opinion of a minority of the arbitrators. In an international arbitration, however, a minority may express its opinion to the other arbitrators and to the parties, in a separate document. This document shall not be deemed to form part of the award.

1. General Comments

Article 48(1) provides that if the arbitral tribunal is composed of more than one arbitrator, it shall decide by a majority of votes.[261] However, most NAI awards rendered by arbitral tribunals composing of multiple arbitrators are unanimous. Even if an award is rendered by a majority of votes, the parties will normally not know. Dissenting opinions are an uncommon phenomenon in the Dutch jurisdiction and arbitrators are expected to keep the internal deliberations of the arbitral tribunal confidential.

The arbitral tribunal's deliberations will usually take place in a meeting, by telephone or via the exchange of drafts of the award. In most cases, one of the members of the arbitral tribunal is designated as the author of the award. The decision process is (and should be) secret.

If a minority of arbitrators is incapable of signing the award and it is unlikely that this impediment will cease to exist within a reasonable time, the other arbitrators will make mention thereof at the end of the award which they sign. This statement will also be signed by them (Article 48(3)). An arbitrator that is factually or legally not capable of performing his mandate (which includes an incapability of signing), may be released from his mandate on the basis of Article 17(3). Subsequently, such arbitrator will have to be replaced on the basis of Article 18. However, on the basis of Article 17(3), such a release may only take place at the request of a party and it is likely that the parties will only become aware of an arbitrator's incapability of signing the award after the award has been rendered, as there is no duty for the arbitral tribunal to inform the parties of a refusal or incapability of signing.

---

[261] Unlike inter alia Art. 25(1) ICC Rules and Art. 61 WIPO Arbitration Rules, the NAI rules do not provide that the award shall be made by the chairman of the arbitral tribunal alone, when there is no majority.

If a minority of the arbitrators refuses to sign, the other arbitrators shall make mention thereof at the end of the award which they sign and also sign this statement (Article 48(2)).

It is generally accepted that any award must be preceded by deliberations among all of the members of the arbitral tribunal, although the NAI Rules are tacit in this regard, as are most other arbitration rules and national laws. The need for deliberations is widely considered to be a requirement of international public policy, and therefore an award made in the absence of proper deliberations may run the risk of being set aside. However, this would not necessarily be the case if an arbitrator has simply refused to participate in the deliberations, while having the opportunity to do so.[262] As a result of this, Article 48(2) may also be applicable if an arbitrator fails or refuses to take part in oral deliberation meetings.

Article 1057(1) and (3) DCCP contain similar provisions on the decision-making.

2. Dissenting Opinion

Dissenting opinions are an uncommon phenomenon in the Dutch jurisdiction. Accordingly, Article 48(4) stipulates that no mention shall be made in the award of the opinion of a minority of the arbitrators. However, in an international arbitration, a minority may express its dissenting opinion to the other arbitrators and to the parties in a separate document, as a dissenting opinion is more common in international arbitrations. Such document is not deemed to form part of the award.[263] As a result, such document cannot be enforced or set aside, nor shall the NAI deposit it.

ARTICLE 49 – FORM AND CONTENTS OF AWARD

1. The arbitral award shall be recorded in writing in four copies and signed by the arbitrator(s), having regard to the provisions of Article 48(2) and (3).
2. The arbitral award shall contain in any case:
    (a) the name and domicile or actual residence of the arbitrator(s);
    (b) the name and domicile, seat or actual residence of the parties;
    (c) a short summary of the procedure;
    (d) a description of the claim and a description of the counterclaim, if any;
    (e) the reasons for the decision given in the award;
    (f) the determination and award of the arbitration costs referred to in Article 61;

---

[262] Derains and Schwartz, 2005, 307.

[263] See, in this respect, HR 5 Dec. 2008, NJ 2009, 6 (Bursa/Güris).

(g) the mention whether, in accordance with the provisions of Article 45, the arbitral tribunal decided in accordance with the rules of law or as amiable compositeur;

(h) the decision;

(i) the place where the award is made, which is at the same time the place of arbitration referred to in Article 22; and

(j) the date on which the award is made.

3. If the award is a decision in summary arbitral proceedings, a partial final award or an interim award, the determination and award of the arbitration costs referred to in the previous paragraph under (f) may be reserved until later in the proceedings.

4. As soon as possible after being signed, the copies of the award shall be communicated to the Administrator.

1. Form and Contents of the Award

Pursuant to Article 49(1), the award must be in writing in four copies and must be signed by the arbitrator(s) (see also Article 48(2) and (3), as well as Article 4(2)).

Furthermore, Article 49(2) indicates the (minimum) requirements as to the contents of the award, of which the most important are that the award contains the decision (Article 49(2)(h)) and the reasons for the decision given in the award (Article 49(2)(e)). Besides the (reasons for the) decision, the award must contain the names and domiciles of the arbitrator(s) and the parties (Article 49(2)(a) and (b)), a short summary of the procedure (Article 49(2)(c)), a description of the (counter)claim (Article 49(2)(d)), the determination and award of the arbitration costs (Article 49(2)(f)), the mention of whether the arbitral tribunal decided in accordance with the rules of law or as amiable compositeur (Article 49(2)(g)), the place where the award is made (Article 49(2)(i)) and the date of the award (Article 49(2)(j)).

1.1. The Names and Domiciles of the Arbitrator(s) and the Parties (Article 49(2)(a) and (b))

Article 49(2)(a) and (b) provide for the identification of the arbitrator(s) and the parties. It is advisable to include the first names or the initials of the arbitrator(s) and the parties (if (one of) the parties are (is a) private person(s)). If a party is a legal entity, it is advisable to include the statutory name, as well as the business name. The same applies to the statutory domicile, as well as the actual domicile of a legal entity.

In the case of a legal succession or a change of name of one of the parties during the arbitral proceedings, the parties have to inform the arbitral tribunal of such succession or change of name. The benchmark in this respect is the rendering of the award. This is important, among other things, so as to avoid possible problems in the enforcement of the award.

1.2. A Short Summary of the Procedure (Article 49(2)(c))

According to Article 49(2)(c), the award must contain a short summary of the procedure. Although not explicitly provided for, it is advisable for the arbitral tribunal to give a comprehensive overview of the procedure, including all submissions exchanged between the parties, the oral hearings, etc. An incomplete summary of the procedure may give a party the impression that the arbitral tribunal has not taken into account all of its arguments and submissions.

1.3. A Description of the Claim and the Counterclaim, If Any (Article 49(2)(d))

According to Article 49(2)(d), the award must contain a description of the claim and the counterclaim, if any. It is also advisable in this regard that the arbitral tribunal fully describes the contents of the claim and the counterclaim; if possible – and in order to avoid confusion – it may literally be reproduced from the request for arbitration, the short answer, or other submissions of the parties.

1.4. The Reasons for the Decision Given in the Award (Article 49(2)(e))

According to Article 49(2)(e), the award must state the reasons upon which the decision given in the award is based. The reasons set forth in the award should demonstrate that the arbitral tribunal has given full consideration to the parties' respective submissions. The existence of reasons in the award enhances the likelihood that the parties will voluntarily abide by the decisions of the arbitral tribunal in the award.[264] Also, a lack of reasoning may be a reason for the award being set aside in various jurisdictions. The same applies to an award in which the reasoning by the arbitral tribunal has been extended to matters that the parties have not been able to discuss in their submissions.

It is obvious that the main claim, as well as the other claims (such as a claim for interest and costs) must be dealt with by the arbitral tribunal, including the arguments supporting this claim. The same applies to the essential defences of the respondent. An essential defence is a defence that, if it is honoured by the arbitral tribunal, may lead to the dismissal of one of the claims of the claimant. If the tribunal does not deal with these claims (also not after a request for an additional award) and defences, the award can be set aside on the basis of a breach of the mandate (Article 1065(1)(c) DCCP; see the comments thereto in Part III, Chapter 1).

---

[264] Derains and Schwartz, 2005, 309.

1.5. The Determination and Award of the Arbitration Costs referred to in Article 61 (Article 49(2)(f))

According to Article 49(2)(f), the award must contain the determination and award of the arbitration costs as referred to in Article 61. According to Article 61(1), the arbitral tribunal shall determine the costs of the arbitration, which will include all the costs mentioned in Articles 56-60: the administration costs, the fees and disbursements of the arbitrators, the costs of legal assistance, as well as all other costs which in the opinion of the arbitral tribunal were reasonably incurred in the arbitration. The Secretariat will assist the arbitral tribunal in determining the costs of the arbitration. See for a further discussion the comments on Article 61.

As a practical matter, Article 49(3) provides that the determination and award of costs may be reserved until later in the proceedings if the award is a decision in summary arbitral proceedings, a partial final award or an interim award.

1.6. The Mention of whether the Arbitral Tribunal decided in accordance with the Rules of Law or as Amiable Compositeur (Article 49(2)(g))

According to Article 49(2)(g), the award must mention whether the arbitral tribunal decided in accordance with the rules of law or as amiable compositeur, in accordance with the provisions of Article 45. According to Article 45(1), the arbitral tribunal has to decide as amiable compositeur, unless the parties agreed to authorize it to make its award in accordance with the rules of law. However, in an international arbitration, the tribunal will make its award in accordance with the rules of law unless the parties agreed to authorize it to decide as amiable compositeur (Article 45(2)).

If the arbitral tribunal has to decide as amiable compositeur (on the basis of Article 45(1)), while the award also contains a decision on the jurisdiction of the arbitral tribunal (which decision in any event has to be made in accordance with the rules of law), it is argued that the arbitral tribunal has to mention explicitly that it had to decide as amiable compositeur, but it decided on the jurisdiction in accordance with the rules of law.

The arbitral tribunal will only have to make such mention once (at the end of the award) and not for every separate decision.

1.7. Decision (Article 49(2)(h))

The award must contain the decision on the basis of Article 49(2)(h). This decision must be included in the operative part of the award. In regard of state courts this flows from standard case law, establishing that (partial) final awards are only those awards that contain final decisions in the operative part of the decision. Case law suggests that the same rule applies to arbitration.[265] The

---

[265] HR 20 Jun. 2003, NJ 2004, 569 (Waterschappen/Milieutech Beheer).

arbitral tribunal is not allowed to award more than what has been claimed by the claimant, as this may be a reason for the award being set aside (see below).

1.8. The Place where the Award is Made (Article 49(2)(i))

The award must contain the place where the award is made. This place is at the same time the place of arbitration as referred to in Article 22. It is therefore quite likely to be different from the place where it was actually deliberated, drafted or signed. See for a more detailed description of the place of arbitration the comments on Article 22.

The place of arbitration is (among other things) of importance with regard to Article 50(1)(b), which article provides that an award rendered in the Netherlands has to be deposited with the office of the clerk of the District Court within whose district the place of arbitration is located. Subsequently, the date of the deposit is of importance for the commencement of the time limit for a request for rectification or correction of the award (Article 52), a request for an additional award (Article 53), as well as for a request for the setting aside of an award on the basis of Article 1065 DCCP. See for a more elaborate discussion on the deposit of the award the comments on Article 50.

1.9. The Date on which the Award is Made (Article 49(2)(j))

According to Article 49(2)(j), the award must contain the date on which the award is made. This article is of importance with respect to Article 51, which provides that an arbitral award shall bind the parties from the day it is rendered (see also the comments on Article 51). For this reason it is advisable for an arbitral tribunal to date the award on the date that the award is sent to the parties (instead of on the date of the last signature by the arbitral tribunal). In practice, the NAI Secretariat will date the award (once the final deposit has been received) and immediately send the award to the parties.

2. Correction

If the requirements in Article 49(2)(a) (names and domiciles of the arbitrators), (b) (names and domiciles of the parties), (i) (place of the award) and (j) (date of the award) are stated incorrectly or are partially or wholly absent, these deficiencies may be corrected on the basis of Article 52(2). Article 52(2) stipulates that if the above-mentioned details are stated incorrectly or are partially or wholly absent, a party may, no later than 30 days after the date of deposit of an award in summary proceedings or a (partial) final award that has been rendered in the Netherlands (see Article 50(1)(b)), request that the arbitral tribunal correct such mistake or omission.

3. The Administrator

As soon as possible after the signing of the award, copies of the award shall be communicated to the Administrator (Article 49(4)). Subsequently, upon receipt of the award, the Administrator shall ensure that a copy of the award is communicated to each of the parties by registered mail (see Article 50(1)(a)). As mentioned before, the Administrator will also ensure that an award in summary proceedings, or a (partial) final award, rendered in the Netherlands will be deposited with the Registry of the District Court within whose district the place of arbitration is located (Article 50(1)(b)).

In practice, the Administrator will, either at the request of the arbitral tribunal or by itself, review the award, mainly in order to verify whether the award satisfies the required formalities. This check does usually not relate to issues of substance as may be the case in the scrutinizing of the award by the ICC Court in ICC arbitrations.

> Article 1057(2) DCCP provides that the award must be in writing and must be signed by the arbitrator(s). Article 1057(4) DCCP indicates minimum requirements as to the contents of the award, of which the most important is that the award must contain the grounds for the decision, unless the award concerns merely the determination of the quality of goods as provided in Article 1020(4) DCCP or the recording of a settlement as provided in Article 1069 DCCP. As this article is of mandatory law, the above will also apply in NAI Arbitration in the Netherlands. The other requirements are similar to the requirements of Article 49 of the NAI Rules.
>
> As mentioned before, an award that does not contain any reasons for the decision may be set aside in the Netherlands on the basis of Article 1065(1)(b) DCCP. Also, an award that contains a decision in which the arbitral tribunal has awarded more than what the claimant has claimed, or differs from the claim of the claimant, may be set aside on the basis of Article 1065(1)(c) (breach of the mandate). See for a more elaborate discussion of this article: Part III, Chapter 1.

ARTICLE 50 – NOTIFICATION AND DEPOSIT OF AWARD

1. Upon receipt of the award, the Administrator, on behalf of the arbitral tribunal, shall ensure that without delay:
   (a) a copy of the award is communicated to each of the parties by registered mail;
   (b) an award in summary proceedings or a final award, or partial final award, rendered in the Netherlands is deposited with the Registry of the District Court within whose district the place of arbitration is located.
2. The Administrator shall inform the parties and the arbitral tribunal as soon as possible in writing of the date of the deposit mentioned in the previous paragraph under (b).
3. A copy of the award shall be kept in the archives of the NAI for a period of 10 years. During this period, parties may request the

Administrator for a certified copy of their award, against payment
of the costs therefor.

1. Notification of the Award

On the basis of Article 50(1)(a), the Administrator shall without delay – and on
behalf of the arbitral tribunal – send a copy of the award to the parties by registered
mail. In certain cases, it may be advisable if the parties agree with the NAI to – for
example – collect the award in person from the NAI at an agreed time or to send the
award by (encrypted) e-mail. This may be wise particularly if the award contains or
might contain information that may lead to considerable fluctuations in the share
price of listed companies, or contains other highly sensitive information.

2. Deposit of the Award

Pursuant to Article 50(1)(b), the Administrator must ensure that an award in
summary proceedings, a final award or a partial final award that is rendered
in the Netherlands is deposited with the office of the clerk of the District
Court within whose district the place of arbitration is located. An interim
award does not need to be deposited. Also, according to this article, awards
that have been rendered outside the Netherlands do not need to be deposited.

The date of deposit is of importance for the commencement of the time limit
for the request for rectification or correction of the award on the basis of Article
52 and the request for an additional award on the basis of Article 53. Furthermore, the date of the deposit is of importance for the commencement of a possible action for having the award set aside. According to Article 1064(3) DCCP,
which is – just as Article 50(1)(b) – applicable to awards that have been rendered
in the Netherlands, the request for setting aside an award has to be made within
three months after the date of deposit the award. However, according to Article
1064(3) DCCP, if the award together with a leave for enforcement is officially
served on the other party, that party may request to have the award set aside
within three months after such service, irrespective of whether the period of
three months mentioned in the preceding sentence of the article has lapsed.
See further Part III, Chapter 1 on the setting aside of an award.

Practice shows that, in some cases, the court clerk's office does provide third
parties with a copy of the deposited award, if they so request. Therefore, in order
to reduce this minor risk, the parties or one of them should request, in writing,
that the court clerk's office maintains confidentiality. In practice, courts have
been receptive to such requests. The parties can also agree that the award shall
not be deposited and that the date on which the award is signed will be the
relevant date for statutory periods of time (e.g. setting aside).

As soon as possible, the parties and the arbitral tribunal will be informed of
the date of the deposit by the Administrator (Article 50(2)). Furthermore, a copy

of the award will be kept in the archives of the NAI for 10 years. Parties may request the Administrator for a certified copy of their award (Article 59(3)).

> Article 1058 DCCP deals with the notification and deposit of the award. The Draft Bill proposes to abolish the requirement for the award to be deposited, with the possibility for parties to agree on the deposit of the award with the office of the clerk of the District Court.

ARTICLE 51 – RES JUDICATA OF AWARD

An arbitral award shall bind the parties from the day it is rendered. By agreeing to arbitration by the NAI or in accordance with the NAI Rules, the parties shall be deemed to have undertaken to carry out the resulting award without delay.

On the basis of Article 51, an arbitral award shall bind the parties as from the day it is rendered. Contrary to – for example – Article 1059 DCCP, the NAI Rules do not provide that only a partial or final award may be binding on the parties (or, in other words, res judicata). This is in line with the New York Convention, which eliminated finality as a condition for the enforcement of awards, as was previously the case under the Geneva Convention of 1927. The New York Convention only requires that the award be binding. See Article V(1)(e) of the New York Convention, which stipulates that recognition and enforcement of an award may be refused, at the request of the party against whom it is invoked, only if that party furnishes proof to the competent authority where the recognition and enforcement is sought that the award *has not yet become binding* on the parties or has been set aside or suspended by a competent authority of the country in which, or under the law of which, that award was made.

A party may invoke the res judicata of an award in court proceedings as well as in arbitral proceedings. For example, a party may invoke the res judicata of an interim award of a partial final award in (continuing) arbitral proceedings.

Furthermore, Article 50 provides that, by agreeing to NAI arbitration or arbitration in accordance with the NAI Rules, the parties shall be deemed to have undertaken to carry out the resulting award without delay. This expresses the general principle that parties are expected to comply with NAI arbitration awards. However, this provision does not go as far as Article 28(6) of the ICC Rules, which explicitly states that parties shall be deemed to have waived their right to any form of recourse insofar as such waiver can validly be made.[266]

> Article 1050(1) DCCP provides that parties may agree on the possibility of arbitral appeal. In practice, parties hardly ever do so. In this respect, Article 1055 DCCP

---

[266] Provisions similar to Art. 26(6) ICC Rules can be found in Art. 26.9 LCIA Rules and Art. 64(a) WIPO Arbitration Rules.

stipulates that, if an appeal is provided for, the arbitral tribunal may declare its award provisionally enforceable in cases in which a court has the power to do so. The arbitral tribunal may also determine that the enforceability is subject to the providing of security.

Article 1059(1) DCCP provides that a partial or final award will have res judicata as from the day on which it is rendered. Article 1059(2) contains a provision on res judicata when arbitral appeal is provided for.

ARTICLE 52 – RECTIFICATION OR CORRECTION OF AWARD

1. No later than 30 days after the date of deposit referred to in Article 50(1)(b), a party may request the arbitral tribunal to rectify a manifest computation or clerical error in an award.

2. If the details referred to in Article 49(2) (a) (b), (i) and (j) are stated incorrectly or are partially or wholly absent from an award, a party may, no later than 30 days after the date of deposit of an award referred to in Article 50(1)(b), request that the arbitral tribunal correct the mistake or omission.

3. This request shall be submitted to the Administrator in writing, in five copies. The Administrator shall communicate a copy of the request to the other party and to the arbitral tribunal.

4. The arbitral tribunal may, also on its own initiative, no later than 30 days after the date of deposit of an award referred to in Article 50(1)(b), make the rectification referred to in paragraph (1), or the correction referred to in paragraph (2).

5. In the event that the arbitral tribunal makes the rectification or correction, it shall record it in a separate document which shall be deemed to form part of the award. This document shall be made in four copies and shall contain:

   (a) the details referred to in Article 49(2)(a) and (b);

   (b) a reference to the award to which the rectification or correction pertains;

   (c) the rectification or correction;

   (d) the date of rectification or correction, provided that the date of the award to which the rectification or correction pertains shall remain conclusive;

   (e) a signature to which the provisions of Article 48 apply.

6. The document referred to in the previous paragraph shall be communicated to the Administrator as soon as possible after it is signed. The Administrator shall communicate it to the parties and deposit it with the Registry of the District Court; the provisions of Article 50

shall apply accordingly. The document shall be attached to the copies of the arbitral award to which it pertains.

7. If the arbitral tribunal denies the request for rectification or correction, it shall inform the parties in writing thereof through the intermediary of the Administrator.

8. In case of an interim arbitral award, the provisions of this article shall apply accordingly, it being understood that the request referred to in paragraphs (1) and (2) may be made no later than 30 days after receipt of the award.

1. Rectification and Correction

Pursuant to Article 52(1) and (4), a manifest computation (such as a miscalculation) or clerical error (such as a mistake in writing) may be rectified at the request of a party or at the arbitral tribunal's own initiative. It has to be an evident error that can be easily rectified.

Both the request of a party for the rectification and the rectification on the initiative of the arbitral tribunal must be made no later than 30 days after the date of the deposit of the award as referred to in Article 50(1)(b). If this 30-day period has expired, a party may request such rectification in summary proceedings (see Article 438(2) DCCP). As there is no deposit in case of a binding advice, the period of time for the rectification of an award expires 30 days after the decision has been received (see Article 3(3)). If an award that has to be deposited on the basis of Article 50(1)(b)[267] has not been deposited or has been deposited with the wrong District Court clerk's office, this 30-day time limit will not commence and therefore, the parties may also file such request after the three-month period mentioned in this article has lapsed, unless parties have agreed otherwise.

If the details referred to in Article 49(2)(a), (b), (i) and (j) are stated incorrectly or are partially or wholly absent from an award, a party may, no later than 30 days after the deposit of the award, request that the arbitral tribunal correct the mistake or omission (Article 52(2)). The arbitral tribunal may also make such correction on its own initiative, no later than 30 days after the date of the deposit of the award. The comments above pertaining to the deposit of the award also apply.

As mentioned above, it is only possible to request the correction of the personal details of the parties and the arbitrator(s), the date of the award and the place of the arbitration. This means that it is not possible to request the arbitral tribunal on the basis of this article to include a decision or a reason for the decision in the award if (a reason for) a decision is (completely) lacking.

---

[267] Pursuant to Art. 50(1)(b), the Administrator must ensure that an award in summary proceedings, a final award or partial final award that is rendered in the Netherlands is deposited with the Registry of the District Court within whose district the place of arbitration is located.

However, it is possible to request an additional award on the basis of Article 53 if the arbitral tribunal failed to make a decision on one or more matters.

The period of time, which is running until 30 days after the date of deposit, reveals that this provision has been drafted with regard to arbitrations where the place of arbitration is located in the Netherlands. The NAI Rules do not stipulate, however, what applies in case the place of arbitration is located outside the Netherlands and therefore a deposit of the arbitral award is not envisaged. The strict wording of Article 52 leaves room for two options: either the possibility of rectification and correction does not exist at all if the place of arbitration is located outside the Netherlands or the right to request for rectification or correction is not subject to any time limit due to an open-ended term. The NAI Rules provide no guidance as to the question what applies. In practice, much will depend on the applicable law, governing the arbitral proceedings. It may very well be the case that the possibility of rectification and correction is arranged for in the applicable arbitration law and that the relevant period of time or the whole arrangement is regarded as being of public order. If this is the case, there may not even be room for the application of a contractual provision such as Article 52.

It has been mentioned in the comments on Article 43(2), that the arbitral tribunal's mandate revives, if a request for rectification or correction is filed. It is arguable that thereafter the mandate of the arbitral tribunal ends with either the rendering of the document that contains the rectification or correction or – in the case of a refusal – the associated communication to the parties.

> Article 1060 DCCP deals with the rectification and/or correction of an award. On the basis of Article 1060(7) DCCP, a request for rectification or correction does not suspend the possibility of the enforcement of the award or of setting it aside, unless the President (*voorzieningenrechter*) of the District Court considers it appropriate to decide otherwise. This also follows from Article 52(5)(d) of the NAI Rules, which provides that the date of the award to which the rectification or correction pertains shall remain conclusive.

2. The Procedure

The request by a party for the rectification or correction of the award must be submitted to the Administrator in writing in five copies and the Administrator will communicate a copy of the request to the other party and to the arbitral tribunal (Article 52(3)). The fact that the Administrator will send a copy of the request to the other party indicates that the arbitral tribunal should hear both parties before deciding on the rectification or correction. Contrary to Article 53(3), however, Article 52 does not explicitly impose such obligation on the arbitral tribunal. Case law in regard of Article 1060 DCCP (the equivalent of Article 52) makes clear that the other party should indeed be heard before the request is decided on. It seems only logical to construe Article 52 in the same way.

If the arbitral tribunal makes the rectification or correction, it will record it in a separate document which will be deemed to form part of the award. This document must contain the personal details of the parties and the arbitral tribunal, a reference to the rectified or corrected award, the rectification or correction, the date of the rectification or correction (provided that the date of the award to which the rectification or correction pertains remains conclusive, which means that such a request does not suspend the possibility (for example) of asking for enforcement of the award or the setting it aside – see also below) and a signature to which the provisions on the signing of the award of Article 48 will apply accordingly. This document will be sent to the Administrator, who will send it to the parties and – if the award has been rendered in the Netherlands – deposit it with the Registry of the District Court (see Article 50). The rectification or correction will be attached to the copies of the arbitral award to which it pertains (see Article 52(5) and (6)).

If the arbitral tribunal refuses a request for rectification or correction, it will inform the parties in writing thereof via the intermediary of the Administrator. Contrary to Article 53(4), a copy of this notification does not have to be deposited with the District Court clerk's office.

3. Interim Award

Article 52(8) provides that the provisions of Article 52 apply accordingly in the case of an interim arbitral award, it being understood that the request for rectification or correction may be made no later than 30 days after receipt of the award. Practically, however, this provision does not seem to have a lot of meaning, as it will be possible to indicate the evident error to the arbitral tribunal (or to the parties) during the (further) course of the arbitral proceedings, in which case a formal request for rectification or correction does not seem to be necessary.

4. No Interpretation of Award

Under the NAI Rules, the arbitral tribunal is not entitled to interpret or explain its award after it has been rendered. This differs from most other arbitration rules, which provide for the possibility of a party requesting the arbitral tribunal to interpret the award.[268]

> Also, Dutch arbitration law does not provide for the arbitral tribunal to interpret or explain the (final) award.[269]

---

[268] See Art. 29 ICC Rules, Art. 30 ICDR Rules and Art. 35 UNCITRAL Rules.

[269] Parliamentary History TK 1985-1986, 18.464, No. 6, 31-32; Burg. Rv, 2006 (H.J. Snijders), Art. 1058 DCCP, note 2.

ARTICLE 53 – ADDITIONAL AWARD

1. If the arbitral tribunal has failed to decide on one or more matters which have been submitted to it, a party may, no later than 30 days after the date of deposit of an award referred to in Article 50(1)(b), request the arbitral tribunal to render an additional award.
2. This request shall be submitted to the Administrator in writing, in five copies. The Administrator shall communicate a copy of the request to the other party and to the arbitral tribunal.
3. Before deciding on the request, the arbitral tribunal shall give the parties the opportunity to be heard.
4. An additional award shall be regarded as an arbitral award to which the provisions of this section shall apply.
5. If the arbitral tribunal rejects the request for an additional award, it shall inform the parties in writing through the intermediary of the Administrator. A copy of this notification, signed by an arbitrator or by the secretary of the arbitral tribunal, shall be deposited with the Registry of the District Court, in accordance with the provisions of Article 50(1)(b). The provisions of Article 50(2) and (3) shall apply accordingly.

1. Additional Award

Article 53 provides a party with the opportunity to request the arbitral tribunal to render an additional award if the arbitral tribunal has failed to decide on one or more matters which have been submitted to it. The intended result of this possibility is to prevent the arbitral award from being set aside on the basis of a breach of mandate if the arbitral tribunal has, for example, overlooked one of many claims of the claimant and has not decided on this claim.[270]

> Under Dutch law, it is not possible to render an additional award if the arbitral tribunal has failed to decide on an essential defence of the other party. This general rule probably also applies if the arbitral award has not been rendered in the Netherlands.[271] In that case, the award may be set aside on the basis of a breach of mandate (see Article 1065 DCCP, note 4 in Part III, Chapter 1). Furthermore, this article does not apply to interim awards, as an interim award does not finally decide on (part of) a claim and there is still the possibility of addition in a later interim award or final award.

---

[270] See for the Netherlands Art. 1065(1)(c) DCCP.

[271] See also Art. 37 UNCITRAL Rules and Art. 30(1) ICDR Rules, which are restricted to 'claims presented in the arbitral proceedings but omitted from the award'. Art. 27.3 LCIA Rules refers to 'claims or counterclaims presented in the arbitration but not determined in any award'.

2. Procedure

The request shall be made within 30 days after the date of the deposit of the award and shall be submitted to the Administrator in five copies. As there is no deposit in case of a binding advice, the period of time for rendering an additional decision expires 30 days after the decision has been received (see Article 3(3)). If an award that has to be deposited on the basis of Article 50(1)(b)[272] has not been deposited or has been deposited with the wrong court clerk's office (which in practice, to our knowledge, does not occur in NAI arbitrations), this 30-day time limit will not commence and therefore, the parties may also file such a request indefinitely (albeit rules of acquiescence, estoppel or periods of limitation might at a certain point come into play).

The Administrator shall communicate a copy of the request to the other party and to the arbitral tribunal (Article 53(1) and (2)). The arbitral tribunal has to give the parties the opportunity to be heard before deciding on the request (Article 53(3)). The arbitral tribunal will likely also give the parties the opportunity to comment in writing on the request. However, this provision is not intended to start a (new) discussion on the merits of the issue that has not been decided on.

If the arbitral tribunal allows the request for an additional award and renders an additional award, the additional award shall be regarded as an (independent) arbitral award to which the provisions of this section apply (Article 53(4)). Therefore, an additional award is independently subject to being set aside or enforcement.

If the arbitral tribunal rejects the request for an additional award, it will inform the parties in writing through the intermediary of the Administrator (Article 53(5)). A copy of this notification, signed by the arbitrator or the secretary to the arbitral tribunal, will be deposited with the office of the clerk of the District Court, if the place of arbitration is situated in the Netherlands (see Article 50(1)(b)).

> Article 1061 DCCP contains provisions on the additional award. The party whose request for an additional award has been unjustly rejected, may ask that the original award be set aside on the basis of Article 1065(1)(c) (breach of mandate), by stating that the original award is incomplete and that a request for an additional award has been unjustly rejected. If an additional award has been rendered, but according to a party the arbitral tribunal has still not decided on one or more matters which have been subjected to them, this party may also ask that the awards (the original award and the additional award) be set aside. It follows from Article 1065(6) that, if the arbitral tribunal has failed to decide on one or more

---

[272] Pursuant to Art. 50(1)(b), the Administrator must ensure that an award in summary proceedings, a final award or partial final award that is rendered in the Netherlands is deposited with the Registry of the District Court within whose district the place of arbitration is located.

matters that have been submitted to it, a claim to have an award set aside on the basis of a breach of mandate may only be initiated if the arbitral tribunal has rendered an additional award or has rejected the request for an additional award.

ARTICLE 54 – ARBITRAL AWARD ON AGREED TERMS

1. If during the arbitral proceedings the parties reach a settlement, the contents thereof may, at their joint request, be recorded in an arbitral award. The arbitral tribunal may deny the request without giving reasons.
2. An arbitral award recording a settlement between parties shall be regarded as an arbitral award to which the provisions of this section apply, provided that:
   (a) notwithstanding the provisions of Article 49(2)(e), the award does not need to contain reasons; and
   (b) the award is also signed by the parties.

1.   General Comments

This article is the only provision in the NAI Rules that deals explicitly with the possibility of a settlement during the arbitral proceedings. According to Article 54(1), an award on agreed terms may only be rendered if this is jointly requested by the parties and the arbitral tribunal agrees to do so.

The arbitral tribunal may deny the request without giving reasons. Circumstances under which an arbitral tribunal may deny such request may be the fact that the settlement would establish an agreement that is contrary to relevant mandatory laws or that is otherwise fraudulent or illegal.

An award on agreed terms is governed by the provisions of this section. However, on the basis of Article 54(2), the award does not need to contain reasons (see Article 49(2)(e)) and the award also has to be signed by the parties.

The parties are under no obligation to record the contents of their settlement in an arbitral award, as they may simply withdraw their claims. However, the conventional reason for seeking an award is to make the terms of the settlement subject to enforcement in the same manner as any other award (on the basis of Article 1062 DCCP or the New York Convention). Ordinarily, an award on agreed terms will bring the arbitration to an end, and therefore needs to set out the costs of the arbitration (see Article 49(2)(f) as well as Article 62 on the costs in case of premature termination of the arbitral proceedings). As an award on agreed terms may also reflect a partial settlement of the dispute, the arbitration may have to continue with regard to the remaining issues.

ARTICLE 55 – PUBLICATION OF AWARD

Unless a party communicates in writing to the Administrator his objections thereto within one month after receipt of the award, the NAI shall be authorized to have the award published without mentioning the names of the parties and deleting any further details that might disclose the identity of the parties.

1. General Comments

As mentioned before, NAI arbitrations are characterized by confidentiality (see Part I, Chapter 1, Section 5). In this respect, Article 55 provides that the NAI is authorized to have the award published without mentioning the names of the parties and with deleting any further details that might disclose the identity of the parties.[273] A party may object to such publication within one month after receipt of the award. A party may also object to the publication of the award before an award has been rendered; the NAI will treat such an early objection as an objection in the sense of Article 55. In particular, the awards are published in the *Tijdschrift voor Arbitrage* (Journal of Arbitration).

Contrary to for example, Article 20(7) of the ICC Rules the NAI Rules do not contain any provisions expressly obliging either the parties or the arbitrators to protect the confidentiality of the arbitration.[274] Parties should consider to include a confidentiality clause in the arbitration agreement or to conclude a separate confidentiality agreement (see Part I, Chapter 1, Section 5 and Article 1, note 3 and Article 6).

If a confidentiality agreement is in place Article 55 still remains operative. Therefore, even if a confidentiality agreement is in place, one of the parties must object to publication if they want to prevent publication pursuant to Article 55. Thus the mere existence of the confidentiality agreement does not prevent the Administrator from using his power provided in Article 55.

---

[273] Contrary to Art. 55 NAI Rules, Art. 30.3 LCIA Rules provides that the LCIA Court does not publish any award without the prior written consent of all parties and the arbitral tribunal.

[274] Article 20(7) of the ICC Rules provides that the arbitral tribunal may take measures for protecting trade secrets and confidential information. See also the WIPO Arbitration Rules, which contain an entire section (Arts 73-76) on confidentiality, not only of the award (Art. 75), but also of the existence of the arbitration (Art. 73) and disclosures made during the arbitration (Art. 74).

COSTS (Articles 56-62)

ARTICLE 56 – COSTS IN GENERAL

The costs of the arbitration shall include the costs referred to in Articles 57, 58 and 60 as well as the other costs which in the opinion of the arbitral tribunal were necessarily incurred in the arbitration.

---

1. General Comments

Article 56 is the first article of Section 6 on Costs and is of a general nature. It provides an arbitral tribunal with a (broad) mandate to determine which costs qualify as 'costs of the arbitration'. Such costs are, as a rule, payable by the 'losing party', as stated in Article 61(1) and (2).

The references to Articles 57, 58 and 60 make clear that three main heads of costs *shall* be included in the costs of the arbitration, i.e. administration costs (Article 57), fees and disbursements of the arbitrators (Article 58) and costs of legal assistance (Article 60). However, fees of party-appointed experts, interpreters, management time of company representatives and witnesses *may* also be part of the costs of the arbitration.[275]

Insofar as cost awards are concerned little case law and literature has been published from which guidance can be derived. In the comments on the articles of this Section 6, reference will be made to available sources.

2. Necessity of Incurrence of Costs

In this general provision, it is made clear that the arbitral tribunal must determine whether costs incurred in the arbitration (not being costs referred to in Articles 57, 58 and 60) have 'necessarily' been incurred. This entails the application of a test regarding both the reasonableness and proportionality of the costs claimed to

---

[275] In contrast, Art. 38 of the UNCITRAL Rules contains a limitative provision by stating which cost headings may be included under the 'costs of arbitration' and excludes other items.

be necessarily incurred. Article 60 contains a similar test concerning the necessity of costs of legal representation.

The application of this test may lead to the conclusion that, for example, costs of an expert instructed by either of the parties to inform the tribunal on a point that is clearly of little or no legal significance may be deemed to be not 'necessarily incurred'. Consequently, such costs will not form part of the costs of the arbitration and will thus not be included in an award on costs on the basis of Article 61(2).

Parties are well advised to both inform the arbitral tribunal of the costs incurred in their final written memorial or in a brief memorial on costs at the end of the arbitration and to support their statements by detailed accounts. In larger cases, an arbitral tribunal will, typically, give specific directions in relation to costs. Absent the provision of information by the parties, it is difficult to envisage the tribunal making a considered assessment on the necessity of costs incurred in larger cases.

3. In Exceptional Cases: Avoidance of Arbitration in View of Costs

It may be argued, *in highly exceptional cases*, that the costs of arbitration, including the deposits for administration and other costs as per the articles below, are prohibitive. Such may be the case to the degree that it would be unreasonable for a party to invoke an arbitration clause[276] if the party lacking funds brings the dispute in state courts (notwithstanding the valid conclusion of an arbitration agreement).[277] In such cases, a denial of jurisdiction (*onbevoegdverklaring*) by state courts, and thus direction of the parties to arbitration, could be argued to amount to a denial of access to justice. However, this may be averted if arrangements can be made for a party to claim financial assistance[278] in arbitral proceedings or if the NAI is prepared to make special provision to financially assist a party in need.[279]

---

[276] See Art. 1022(1) DCCP.

[277] Reference may be had to Meijer, 2008, 749-751 for a detailed discussion of this – little debated – issue. See also HR 21 Mar. 1997, NJ 1998, 219 (Meijer/OTM) and an annotation on this by H.J. Snijders, under (4).

[278] Parties may claim financial assistance to cover costs of representation in arbitral proceedings on the basis of *Besluit van 21 december 1999 tot vaststelling van het Besluit vergoedingen rechtsbijstand* (2000), Art. 1(b), and *Wet op de Rechtsbijstand*, Art. 12(1).

[279] G.J. Meijer (Meijer, 2008) notes a comment made by P. Sanders in 1988 (TvA 1988, 147) that the inability to pay deposits and costs tends to be addressed by making arrangements for reduction in administration costs as well as requesting arbitrators not to charge (full) fees and an arbitration institute providing for the compensation of costs incurred by the arbitrators.

ARTICLE 57 – ADMINISTRATION COSTS

---

1. Upon commencement of the arbitration, a fixed amount for administration costs shall be due from the claimant to the NAI, to be determined in accordance with the provisions of the next paragraph. The Administrator shall notify the claimant of this amount as soon as possible after receipt of the request for arbitration.

2. The administration costs shall be determined on the basis of a schedule fixed by the Governing Board, which schedule is contained in the Appendix to these Rules. This schedule may be revised from time to time by the Governing Board in accordance with the provisions of Article 67. If the administration costs cannot be determined on the basis of said schedule, the Administrator shall decide thereon.

3. In case of a counterclaim, administration costs shall also be due from the respondent, to be determined in accordance with the provisions of the previous paragraph.

4. In case a claim or counterclaim is increased, additional administration costs, to be determined in accordance with the provisions of paragraph (2), shall be due from the claimant or the respondent, respectively.

5. The Administrator shall be in charge of collecting the administration costs that are due. If a party fails, within 14 days[*] after a second reminder in writing by the Administrator, to pay the administration costs due, he shall be deemed to have withdrawn his claim or counterclaim, as the case may be.

6. If a claimant withdraws his request for arbitration before transmission of the arbitration file to the arbitrator(s), half of the administration costs as paid by him shall be reimbursed to him. The same shall apply if a respondent withdraws his counterclaim before transmission of the arbitration file to the arbitrator(s). In all other cases, no administration costs will be reimbursed.

7. If parties have agreed only to appointment of arbitrator(s) by the NAI as referred to in Article 14(7), half of the administration costs shall be due from the petitioner.

[*] This period of time is doubled in an international arbitration (Art. 5(2)).

---

1. Administration Costs

The NAI, like many other arbitration institutes, charges a fee to cover its costs of administering the case and its operations. The fee is to be paid by the claimant(s) in an arbitration.[280] The claimant(s) are notified by the Administrator of the amount due, after receipt of the request for arbitration by the NAI. Article 57(3) makes clear that the same fees are payable by the party or parties making a counterclaim.

The NAI does not charge additional administration costs for summary arbitral proceedings on the basis of Article 37 (i.e. pending an arbitration on the merits) as opposed to summary arbitral proceedings separate from proceedings on the merits (Article 42a and following). In respect of the latter, reference is made to the comments on Article 42n in conjunction with Section 6 (Articles 56-62).

2.   Level of the Administration Costs

The NAI's Governing Board has issued a schedule to the NAI Rules (Article 57(2)) entitled '*Appendix 2 to the Arbitration Rules of the Netherlands Arbitration Institute in Rotterdam, in force as of 13 November 2001*'. The most recent version of this schedule, which is periodically revised by the Governing Board pursuant to, and as further provided in, Article 67 is dated 1 March 2009. This schedule may be downloaded from the NAI's website and is usually included in the booklet containing the Rules.[281]

The schedule provides for the levels of administration costs. The level of administration costs ranges, under the current schedule, between EUR 340 for claims below EUR 50,000 if made by individuals to EUR 15,000 for claims made by corporate entities for claims of EUR 10,000,00 and above. The amounts listed do not include value-added tax (VAT). Nevertheless, VAT is applicable to the administration costs for parties domiciled in the EU.

Subsequent increases in the level of the claims and/or counterclaims may lead to the NAI charging additional administration costs. An increase in a claim or counterclaim will result in additional administration costs, the level of which is again to be determined by reference to the aforementioned schedule (see Article 57(4)).

Article 57(7) also separately provides for administration costs if the parties only require the NAI to act as appointing authority and not (also) to administer the arbitration. In such cases, only half of the administration costs listed on the aforementioned schedule will be due. The schedule also provides for an arrangement for specific administration costs if the NAI acts as appointing authority pursuant to the UNCITRAL Rules.

If a request for arbitration or a counterclaim included in a short answer is withdrawn before transmission of the arbitration file, only half of the administration costs relating to such claim are due and the other half will be reimbursed

---

[280]   The NAI Rules thus do not provide for joint and several liability of the parties to an arbitration (i.e. claimant(s) and respondent(s)) vis-à-vis the NAI and the arbitral tribunal for arbitration costs, as provided in Art. 28(1) of the LCIA Rules in relation to the LCIA.

[281]   See <www.nai-nl.org>.

(Article 57(6)). It is argued that this Article 57(6) should also apply if the NAI only appoints arbitrators. If that argument is followed 50% of the administration costs should be reimbursed if an arbitration is withdrawn before the transmission of the file to the arbitral tribunal (Article 57(6)).[282] Article 57(6) provides that this is the only situation in which administration costs are reimbursed.

3. Collection of Payment and Sanctions

Article 57(5) provides that the Administrator is in charge of collecting payment of the administration costs. Repeated failure to pay may lead to the claimant or counterclaimant being deemed to have withdrawn its claim. This is at issue if a party fails to make payment within 14 days, after a second reminder, in writing by the Administrator, proves to be unsuccessful (this period of time will be doubled in international arbitrations). The Administrator will, in principle, give a final warning before deeming the claim to be withdrawn. If a party refuses to pay administration costs that are due, the Administrator has the right to bring legal claims to retrieve these costs.

If a case is deemed to be withdrawn, the claimant will have to bring a new case. The consequences of this will vary according to the applicable substantive law. If a new case is brought under the NAI Rules, the claimant will be obliged to pay administration costs again.

ARTICLE 58 – FEES AND DISBURSEMENTS OF ARBITRATORS

---

1. The fees of the arbitrator(s) shall be determined by the Administrator after consultation with the arbitrator(s). In determining the fees, the time spent on the case by the arbitrator(s), the amount in dispute and the complexity of the case shall be taken into account.
2. The disbursement of an arbitrator include, among other things, reasonable costs for travel and lodging; secretarial assistance; conference rooms; mailing and telephone, telex and telefax.

Prior to the appointment of an arbitrator, the Administrator will consult with the prospective arbitrator(s) in order to agree on an applicable hourly rate, which rate is set by reference to guidelines drawn up by the NAI's Governing Board. The Dutch text of these guidelines has been published on the NAI website.[283]

The guidelines take into account the amount in dispute, the (expected) complexity of the case and the background of the arbitrator(s). The reason for taking the latter into account is that, inter alia, the costs that must be covered by such fees vary between prospective arbitrators. After all, partners at large commercial

---

[282] Vademecum Arbitrage, 2002 (H.J. Snijders), 97.
[283] See <www.nai-nl.org>.

law firms and retired members of the judiciary are not equal in this respect, for example in terms of overhead costs. The hourly fees run in principle from EUR 150 up to EUR 350, but in exceptional cases – including complex international arbitrations – the Administrator may allow higher hourly fees. In order to calculate the arbitrators' fees, the agreed hourly rates are multiplied by the hours spent by the relevant arbitrator on the case.

The fees of a secretary to the tribunal (if appointed) are also covered by this article and fall into either a low (for inexperienced secretaries) or higher (for more experienced secretaries) category (see also Article 59(2)). The secretary's fees in principle run from EUR 70 up to EUR 130 for every experienced secretaries.

The total fees, subsequent to the completion of the case but prior to the issuance of an award, will be determined in consultation by the arbitrator(s) and the Administrator. Generally, the fees are determined on the basis of the statements of hours spent by the arbitrators and (if appointed) the secretary to the tribunal.[284] Assuming Dutch law applies to the relationship between members of an arbitral tribunal and the parties (see Part I, Chapter 1, Section 6), it may be argued that the parties have (final) say in the level of the arbitrator's fees. However, the parties should be considered to have conferred this power on the Administrator (Article 58(1)).

Article 58(2) provides that arbitral tribunals, including the secretary to the tribunal, will be reimbursed for certain expenses. The cost of travel and lodging, assistance and other matters mentioned in this article may be included. Given that Article 58(2) does not provide an exhaustive list of disbursements, the tribunal may also claim other costs such as relating to the use of electronic aids (internet charges etc.).

Given the considerable level of costs that may be reached in arbitration, it is advisable to take a critical view at the number of arbitrators that will be appointed. As a general rule, the NAI indicates that the costs of an arbitral tribunal consisting of three arbitrators are roughly twice the amount of fees of an arbitral tribunal consisting of one arbitrator.[285] The calculation of fees on the basis of hours spent typically results in a total amount of fees that is substantially lower than the determination of fees within the range set by the ICC (Appendix III, Article 4, scale B to the ICC Rules). In contrast to, for example, arbitration on the basis of the ICC Rules, neither the aforementioned guidelines nor the NAI provide for minimum or maximum fees for arbitrators. For arbitrations that have commenced (see Article 6(2)) after 29 August 2006, VAT is applicable to the arbitrators' fees. This may be different for non-Dutch arbitrators. This follows from a decision of the

---

[284] A similar provision is contained in Art. 31(2) of the ICC Rules, which provides for an express power for the ICC Court to 'fix the fees of the arbitrators at a figure higher or lower than that which would result from the application of the relevant scale should this be deemed necessary due to exceptional circumstances of the case. The Administrator also has such power under the NAI Rules. This statement will not be provided to the parties.

[285] See the NAI website <www.nai-nl.org>.

Dutch Ministry of Finance to that effect.[286] A very limited exception applies to arbitrators that do not provide services in another professional commercial occupation and only act as arbitrator very occasionally. The NAI has consulted with the Dutch Ministry of Finance with respect to this decision and the resulting practical implications. Consequently, on 8 March 2007, the Ministry further refined the applicable arrangements and now permits VAT to be assessed by reference to the cost award in the arbitration.[287] As a result VAT can be added to the arbitrators' fees and may be included in the cost award at the end of the arbitration. VAT is not (yet) payable when a deposit for costs (Article 59) is made to the NAI. Each individual arbitrator is required to issue an invoice for his fees to each of the parties directly (and not through the NAI).[288]

Article 59 – Deposit for Costs

1. The Administrator shall be authorized to require that the claimant pay a deposit from which, to the extent possible, the fees and disbursements of the arbitrator(s) are to be paid. If the respondent has introduced a counterclaim, the Administrator may require him to pay a deposit as well.

2. The deposit referred to in the previous paragraph shall also serve to pay the costs of depositing the award at the Registry of the District Court. The costs of a secretary, an expert appointed by the arbitral tribunal, technical assistance and interpreter shall also be paid from the deposit, if and to the extent that such costs were incurred by the arbitral tribunal.

3. As soon as possible after the arbitration file is transmitted to it, the arbitral tribunal shall consult with the Administrator on the expected volume of work for the purpose of determining the amount of the deposit.

4. The Administrator may at all times require that the claimant and/or the respondent pay an additional deposit.

---

[286] The Ministry's decision is discussed, in detail, by M.J. Pelinck in 'BTW bij arbitrage', TvA 2007, 87-93 and by H.J. Snijders in an editorial comment, 'Arbitrale onafhankelijkheid en onpartijdigheid, complex en actueel', TvA 2008, 1-7.

[287] A letter to this effect may be downloaded from the website of the Ministry of Finance: <www.minfin.nl/nl/actueel/kamerstukken_en_besluiten,2007/03/CPP07-285.html>.

[288] The fact that individual arbitrators have to issue invoices is opposed in the literature on the basis of the argument that these invoices could disclose the extent to which an arbitrator has taken part in the decision-making process of an arbitral tribunal and/or drafted the arbitral award. This is argued to be irreconcilable with the independence of the arbitrators. However, the arbitrators' invoices will only reveal information that allows the parties to get an impression of the time spent by the relevant arbitrator. We consider it hard to imagine how such information can affect the arbitrators' independence. The debate is still ongoing, see H.J. Snijders, 'Arbitrale onafhankelijkheid en onpartijdigheid, complex en actueel', TvA 2008, 1-7.

5. The Administrator shall notify the arbitral tribunal of the deposit.

6. The arbitral tribunal shall be authorized to suspend the arbitration with regard to the claim or counterclaim, including a claim or counterclaim in summary arbitral proceedings as referred to in Article 37(2) until the party concerned has paid the deposit for costs required of him. If, within 14 days* after a second reminder in writing by the Administrator, a party does not pay the deposit required of him, he shall be deemed to have withdrawn his claim or counterclaim, as the case may be.

7. The NAI shall not be liable for payment of any costs which are not covered by a deposit. No interest shall be paid on the amount of a deposit.

* This period of time is doubled in an international arbitration (Art. 5(2)).

---

1. Payment of a Deposit (Article 59(1))

Article 59 provides for the Administrator with a discretionary power to request payment of a deposit from a party making either a claim or a counterclaim.[289] In practice, the Administrator will, as a rule, request payment of a deposit, the amount of which is determined by reference to Article 59(3). The request is made in writing to the parties with an instruction to make payment to the NAI's bank account.

Given the fact that the Administrator will have to consult with the arbitral tribunal (as per Article 59(3)), the request for the payment of a deposit will only be made subsequent to the appointment of an arbitral tribunal and the transmission of the file to the arbitral tribunal, in order to enable the tribunal to make an informed assessment of the expected volume of work and adequately consult with the Administrator in this respect.

2. Purpose of the Deposit

The deposit is used to provide a form of security for the discharge of various costs relating to the arbitration. Article 59(1) refers to costs of the arbitral tribunal. Article 59(2), in turn, covers various other cost headings connected to the administration and organization of the arbitration, to the extent incurred by the arbitral tribunal.

---

[289] A similar provision is contained in Art. 30 of the ICC Rules, which empowers the ICC's Secretary General to request the payment of a provisional advance. The NAI Rules, however, do not make a distinction between on the one hand a provisional advance set by the Secretary General (see Art. 30(1) ICC Rules) and on the other hand a (further) advance set by the ICC Court (see Art. 30(2) ICC Rules).

Article 59(2) also makes reference to costs connected to the filing of 'the arbitral award'. This is an obligation that arises from Article 1058 DCCP with respect to partial final and final awards. Upon receipt of such an award, and as provided in Article 50(1)(b), the Administrator will make the deposit on the arbitral tribunal's behalf. The costs for making such deposit are, at present, EUR 102 per award and are payable to the clerk of the District Court at which the deposit is made.

3.   Amount of the Deposit

The amount of the deposit is set by reference to the expected workload for the arbitral tribunal and complexity of the case, on the basis of information provided by the arbitrators as per Articles 58(1) and 59(3). In addition, the parties' views on the organization and conduct of the proceedings may appear in the request for arbitration and/or the short answer and will also have a bearing on the expected workload and complexity of the case. The parties, for example, may have indicated a wish to conduct cross-examinations and use court reporters.

Furthermore, Article 59(4) provides that the Administrator may request payment of a further deposit. This will occur if the expected fees and costs of the arbitrators (are likely to) exceed the initial deposit made by the (counter)claimant(s). In this respect, it is up to the arbitral tribunal and, if appointed, notably the secretary to the tribunal, to keep track of the amount of fees and costs that have been incurred and the level of the deposit held by the NAI.

In practice, arbitral tribunals are well advised to ask the Administrator for a timely increase of the deposit, and in any event prior to the issuance of a (final) arbitral award, in order to avoid having to collect payment from the party against whom an award to pay costs has been issued. The final increase should result in a deposit sufficient to pay the amounts due. In order to avoid surprising the parties with a request to increase the deposit, the arbitral tribunal should approach the Administrator during the course of the arbitration if the fees are likely to exceed the deposit and ask to arrange for an increase.

In order to keep the arbitral tribunal informed of the status of the deposit, the Administrator is obliged to notify the arbitral tribunal of the status of the amount of the deposit.

4.   Sanctions in Case of Late Payment

Article 59(6) confers an authority on the arbitral tribunal to suspend the proceedings with respect to either the claim(s) and/or the counterclaim(s), if payment of the deposit is not made upon request by the Administrator. In addition, failure to pay a deposit within 14 days after the date of a second reminder by the Administrator, the (counter)claim(s) shall be deemed to have been withdrawn. In international arbitrations, the period of 14 days is doubled as per Article 5(2).

This sanction for non-payment of a deposit (or an additional deposit) is indeed harsh and is not applied lightly.[290] In practice, the NAI Secretariat will attempt to contact the party requested to make a deposit for costs by telephone in order to provide an additional warning and ensure that its earlier communications have been received.

Article 42n provides a slightly different arrangement for summary arbitral proceedings (see the comments on that article).

5. Recourse and Interest on Deposits

In Article 59(7), the NAI Rules explicitly provide that the NAI shall not be liable for the payment of costs not covered by a deposit. This implies that the arbitral tribunal will, timely, have to ask for the issuance of a request for the payment of an additional deposit by the Administrator (Article 59(4)).

This provision is directed at both arbitral tribunals, secretaries, experts and other parties that are covered by Article 59(1) and (2) as well as the parties to an arbitration. The strength of this exclusion of recourse has not been tested in court, but will probably be sufficient to prevent recourse by either of the parties and the arbitral tribunal, assuming they have agreed to the applicability of the NAI Rules.

Consequently, arbitral tribunals will have to make a claim for costs themselves if they are left unpaid. Such can be complicated. Assuming Dutch law is applicable with respect to the relationship between an arbitral tribunal and the parties, this relationship will qualify as an instruction agreement (*overeenkomst van opdracht*) (see also Article 1029 DCCP).[291] This type of agreement is provided for in Articles 7:400-413 DCC. A claim for the payment of fees will in that case have to be brought in the competent state courts and is based on Article 7:405 DCC.

Article 59(7) provides that no interest is payable on deposits made.

ARTICLE 60 – COSTS OF LEGAL ASSISTANCE

The arbitral tribunal may award against the losing party the costs of legal assistance incurred by the party in whose favour the award is rendered if and to the extent that these costs are deemed necessary by the arbitral tribunal.

---

[290] For a published example of an arbitral award on costs in a case involving a party that had failed to timely pay its share of a deposit for costs and whose claim was deemed to be inadmissible, reference is made to the judgment of the Rotterdam District Court of 25 Jan. 2006 in subsequent proceedings to set aside an award, which was published in TvA 2007, 32-37. The award was not set aside.

[291] For a further exposé on the relationship between an arbitrator and the parties, see Part I, Ch. 1, Section 6.

1. Cost Award

Legal practice in the Netherlands is adverse to high cost awards in particular with respect to costs of (outside) legal assistance. In order to avoid excessive cost awards, Dutch state courts apply a table that sets out fixed tariffs for awards of costs for legal assistance applicable in the vast majority of cases. This table is generally applied by the courts.[292] Although this table may be deviated from, such is rarely done.[293] Until recently, arbitrations used to be the exception, with some arbitral tribunals being prepared to award full costs on the basis of the costs actually made. However, the NAI faced the problem that there was only little consistency in the approach taken by arbitral tribunals. Where some arbitral tribunals issued full cost awards, others stuck to cost awards on the basis of fixed tariffs similar to those contained in the table used by Dutch state courts. This resulted in a lack of predictability. Consequently, cost awards in almost identical cases could differ substantially, depending on the individual arbitrators' preferences. In order to break with this situation the NAI issued new (informal) guidelines (*handreikingen*), that steer away from full cost awards in national arbitrations (*Handreiking voor arbiters. Veroordeling tot betaling van kosten van juridische bijstand in NAI-arbitrages*). These guidelines are published on the NAI's website and may be accessed via a link on the NAI site's website page on costs.[294]

The NAI guidelines promote the use of a tariff system, which is similar to practice in the state courts. These guidelines are, however, non-binding and the arbitral tribunal remains entitled to exercise its full discretion in respect of an award on costs for legal assistance.

From published arbitral case law and experience, it appears that these NAI guidelines are gaining acceptance. Given that cost orders are generally not supported by extensive reasoning, it is not yet possible to conclude whether the NAI guidelines will develop into becoming as stringent in application as the state courts' system from which these guidelines are derived.

It is also unclear whether the costs of 'legal assistance' can be assumed to include costs of engaging a party's in-house counsel or in-house legal experts to deal with the case. Such costs are rarely, if ever, part of cost awards in the Netherlands, given that Dutch substantive law and practice does not support an award for these costs. There may be ground for awarding costs of inhouse

---

[292]   The point system is based on an arrangement that is known as the '*Liquidatietarief rechtbanken en hoven*' and the '*Liquidatietarief kantonzaken*'. Although the point system is non-binding, it is applied. The system originates from the Dutch Bar Association (*Orde van Advocaten*) and has been adopted by the National Body of Presidents of Civil Law Sections of the District Courts and also of the Courts of Appeal.

[293]   A judgment by the Utrecht District Court of 26 Dec. 2006 in proceedings to set aside an award and reported in TvA 2007, 85-86, makes the point clear that the tariffs are only rarely deviated from. Notwithstanding the baseless nature of the proceedings in this case to set aside an arbitral award and the fact that the parties had agreed to arbitration with a view to resolving the dispute in an expedient and final form, this parties did not also present a case in which the court felt inclined to deviate from the fixed tariffs notwithstanding a specific request by the defendant in these proceedings.

[294]   See <www.nai-nl.org>.

counsel, in particular, if a party has not engaged outside counsel to represent it in the arbitral proceedings. If awarded, these costs can be considered part of costs of an arbitration and brought under the scope of Article 56. One consequence of this is that the tribunal will have to be prepared to concluded that the incurrence was necessary in order to be able to make them part of an award on costs on the basis of Article 61(1) and (2). If parties choose to consider claiming these costs, they are well advised to document their claim in detail in order to optimize the chances of the tribunal making them part of an award on costs.[295]

2. Discretion: Relevant Considerations

Article 60 includes the wording '*may award*'. This wording serves to confer considerable discretion on an arbitral tribunal with respect to an award on costs for legal assistance.

The NAI guidelines provide that the arbitral tribunal may consider not to award full costs against the losing party. This is suggested if both parties' counsel have contributed significantly to providing the tribunal with information on complicated factual and/or legal matters, on which the tribunal has reached a balanced decision. In this case, the losing party's counsel's efforts have been instrumental in enabling the tribunal to resolve the dispute.

In addition, the arbitral tribunal is invited, by the NAI guidelines, to have regard to both the type of proceedings and nature of the parties. No further information or guidance is given on the latter two considerations. We take the view that a full cost award against a consumer or party not represented by legal counsel is not preferable.

In addition, Article 60 states that an award may be issued for costs against the 'losing party'. Whether or not a party has lost or won may be hard to determine if, for example, a claim is only granted in part. If a case is not decided clearly in favour of either of the parties, the arbitral tribunal should attempt to make a reasonable apportionment of costs. This may be done by equal application of the principle stated in the second sentence of Article 61(2) (see below): '*if both parties have lost in part, the tribunal may divide the costs between them wholly or in part*'.[296]

Furthermore, Article 60 provides that costs that are 'deemed necessary' may be awarded. The NAI's guidelines are tacit on the necessity of such costs. In practice, much will depend on the impression of the arbitral tribunal with respect to the procedural conduct of the parties and their respective counsel and the application of the standards of reasonableness and proportionality. In larger cases, parties are well advised to request permission to submit a costs submission prior to the issuance of a final award. This submission should contain sufficient information for the arbitral tribunal to assess the necessity of costs that have been incurred and not merely a print out, for example, of a law firm's time entry and billing system.

---

[295] Further guidance may be derived from Bühler and Webster, 2008, 445-447 who discuss, inter alia, fees for in-house lawyers, paralegals and management time in the context of an ICC award on costs.

[296] As suggested by Snijders, Vademecum Arbitrage, 2002 (H.J. Snijders), 101.

3.   Level of Costs

The NAI guidelines contain a table, attributing points to the submission of state-ments and other actions that typically occur in arbitral proceedings. The number of points indicates the relative weight of a specific procedural step and is set out in Table 1. The level of costs that could be awarded is calculated by multiplying the total number of points by the amount per point set in Table 2. These tables apply equally to claims and counterclaims.

The NAI guidelines indicate that the cost levels have been set by reference to the fees and charges applicable to proceedings in Dutch Courts of Appeal and are only intended to guide the arbitral tribunal in the exercise of its discretion. Given that the tables are derived from Dutch legal practice, they are intended to apply to arbitrations seated in the Netherlands and not to arbitrations outside the Netherlands.

In connection herewith, it is important that the NAI guidelines do not limit an arbitral tribunal's discretion with respect to the contents of an award on costs. Hence, an arbitral tribunal may decide to award full costs against the losing party notwithstanding the contents of the guidelines. In addition, the parties may agree to exclude the operation of the NAI guidelines altogether.

The amount at stake, referenced in Table 2 is the amount of the claim made plus interest at the time of issuance of the award. The amount per point will be determined by the tribunal exercising its discretionary power in respect of cost awards. If a case does not have a clearly identifiable monetary interest, the arbitral tribunal may decide which standard to apply.

The NAI table is reproduced below, with the addition of a more explanatory heading and an additional first row with a text in bold:

Table 1. Points Applicable to Proceedings on the Merits and
Summary Arbitral Proceedings

Procedural Step	Points
Request for arbitration/statement of claim, combined	2
Short answer and statement of answer, combined	2
Each further written submission as per Article 24	1
Oral hearing	2
Oral hearing in an incident	1
Witness examinations outside oral hearing	1
Procedural hearing/site visit	1

Table 2. Amount per Point on the Basis of the Monetary Interest at Stake in the Proceedings

	Amount at Stake (in euro)	Amount per Point (in euro) (see Table 1)
I	less than 50,000	500-1,200
II	50,000-100,000	1,200-2,000
III	100,000-200,000	2,000-3,000
IV	200,000-400,000	3,000-4,000
V	400,000-1 million	4,000-5,500
VI	1 million-5 million	5,500-10,000
VII	5 million and higher	10,000 and higher

The application of these tables appears from the following example. An arbitration relating to an amount at stake of EUR 1 million and involving a request for arbitration, a short answer and one round of written submissions and an oral hearing will thus result in an award of EUR 5,500 × 6 = EUR 33,000.

ARTICLE 61 – DETERMINATION AND AWARD OF COSTS

1. The arbitral tribunal shall determine the costs of the arbitration, having regard to the provisions of Article 58(1).
2. The losing party shall be condemned to bear the costs, except in special cases at the discretion of the arbitral tribunal. If both parties have lost in part, the arbitral tribunal may divide the costs between them, wholly or in part.
3. In awarding the costs, the arbitral tribunal shall take into account the deposit made in accordance with Article 59. To the extent that a deposit made by a party is used to pay costs that were awarded against the other party in accordance with the provisions of the previous paragraph, the latter party shall be condemned to reimburse the former party for these costs.
4. Costs may also be awarded if they were not expressly claimed by a party.

1.   Authority of Arbitral Tribunal to Make an Award on Costs

Article 61(1) affirms that the arbitral tribunal's mandate includes making an award on the costs of the arbitration (Article 56). In doing so, it will have to take Article 58(1) into account, i.e. the outcome of its consultations with the Administrator and the determination of the fees by the Administrator. Notwithstanding the explicit reference to Article 58(1), the provision in Article 61(1) refers to costs and thus the full scope of costs referred to in Article 56.

2.   Losing Party to Bear the Costs

The general principle that the party losing the arbitral proceedings will have to bear the costs of the proceedings is set out in Article 61(2). This applies to both claims and counterclaims.

This general principle is subject to a number of caveats, the first of which is expressed in the second sentence of Article 61(2). It will not always be clear which party 'loses' the case. In such cases a reasonable attribution of costs may be made. In addition, cost awards are not unlimited and may be mitigated by the arbitral tribunal using its discretionary power to do so.

The award on costs, typically, will be part of a final arbitral award and can thus be executed (see the comments on Article 1062 DCCP in Part III, Chapter 3). A party expecting a cost award in its favour may apply for a pre-judgment attachment (as per Article 1022(2) DCCP and Articles 700-770c DCCP). However, state courts requested to grant leave for a pre-judgment attachment may question the certainty of a cost award being issued by the arbitral tribunal. Such may lead to the application not being successful or the attachment being lifted, if challenged.

3.   Settlement of Costs with Deposit

If money deposited by the winning party has been used to pay costs that, pursuant to the arbitral award, are payable by the losing party, the losing party is obliged to reimburse the winning party as per Article 61(3). This provision makes clear that the deposit may be used to pay costs as provided for in Article 58, notwithstanding the fact that the party that has made the deposit is not liable for the payment of such costs. Consequently, the winning party will seek reimbursement through the (enforcement of the) cost award against the losing party.

4.   Tribunal's Mandate in Absence of Claim, Aimed at Award on Costs

Article 61(4) provides that the arbitral tribunal has the mandate to issue an award on costs, notwithstanding such claim not having been made part of the relief sought. This provision thus makes clear that the arbitral tribunal does not render an award that is *ultra petita* if costs are awarded without there being a corresponding claim. In any event, a party is well advised to include a detailed claim for costs in its (costs) submission(s).

ARTICLE 62 – COSTS IN CASE OF PREMATURE TERMINATION

1. If an arbitrator is released from his mandate before the last final award, he may claim reasonable compensation for the work performed by him, with the exception of special circumstances as determined by the Administrator. This compensation shall be determined by the Administrator and shall fall under the costs of the arbitration. It will be included by the arbitral tribunal in the determination and award of costs in accordance with the provisions of Article 61.

2. If the mandate of the arbitral tribunal is terminated before the last final award, the arbitrator or arbitrators may also claim reasonable compensation for the work performed by them, to be determined by the Administrator, unless termination takes place on the ground that the mandate was performed in an unacceptably slow manner.

3. In case of a decision that jurisdiction is lacking, the provisions of this article shall apply accordingly, provided that the costs as determined shall be awarded against the claimant.

1. General Comments

This Article 62 provides for three instances in which costs are payable, and in which instances costs cannot be ordered by the arbitral tribunal (or at least not in its original composition) in the last final award. Article 62 thus provides that either the arbitral tribunal (in a new composition but with a remaining mandate) may make such award (Article 62(1)) or the Administrator (Article 62(2)).

2. Release from Mandate Prior to Issuance of Final Award

Article 62(1) provides for the situation in which an arbitrator is released from his mandate, (see Article 17) prior to the issuance of the last final award, but in which a tribunal with a mandate remains in place.

In such case, an arbitrator may claim reasonable compensation for work performed. The Administrator has a discretionary power to determine the level of such compensation and will do so upon being provided, if possible, with a statement of fees and disbursements (Article 58(1) and (2)). Furthermore, in special circumstances, the Administrator may deny a claim for reasonable compensation. Such circumstances could, for example, be tortuous behaviour in the form of gross misconduct vis-à-vis either or both parties leading to release of his mandate.

The compensation, if any, determined by the Administrator will become part of the costs of the arbitration (Article 56) and will be awarded against either or both of the parties on the basis of Article 61(2).

3.   Termination of Mandate Prior to Final Award

If the arbitral tribunal's mandate is terminated prior to the issuance of the last final award, for example due to the fact that the parties reach a settlement, the tribunal will not be able to issue an award on costs.[297] In such cases, and absent the mandate of the tribunal ending on the ground that it was performed in an unacceptably slow manner (see in that respect also Article 23(3)), the Administrator determines the amount of compensation that is reasonable for the work performed by the tribunal, on the basis of an indication thereof to the Administrator. If the mandate is terminated in light of the parties having reached a settlement, it is recommended that the tribunal does not end its mandate prior to issuing an award on costs (either in a separate award or award on agreed terms (*schikkingsvonnis*), as provided in Article 1069 DCCP).[298] Concerning administration costs, reference may also be made to Article 57(6), discussed above.

4.   Mandate to Make an Award on Costs in the Event of Lack of Jurisdiction

If the arbitral tribunal comes to the conclusion that it lacks jurisdiction, Articles 56-61 should be taken to apply (see Article 9, note 3). However, given that the claimant has thus demonstrably brought a case in the wrong forum, an award on costs will be made against the claimant (Article 62(3)). See for the somewhat theoretical discussion on the question whether the arbitral tribunal has the power to render such award Article 9, note 3.

---

[297] The NAI Rules do not contain a provision for the premature termination of a tribunal's mandate. In this context, reference may be had to Art. 1031 DCCP (discussed above in Art. 17, note 3).

[298] See Vademecum Arbitrage, 2002 (H.J. Snijders), 100.

FINAL PROVISIONS (Articles 63-67)

ARTICLE 63 – VIOLATION OF RULES

In case of an action violating any provision of these Rules or a failure to act in accordance with any provision of these Rules, a party shall object thereto in writing as soon as possible after the violation became known to him, on pain of being barred from doing so thereafter, in the arbitral proceedings or in court proceedings.

---

1. General Comments

Article 63 provides for an implied waiver of the right to raise an objection – in the arbitral proceedings or in subsequent court proceedings – to any act or omission in violation of the NAI Rules, if an objection thereto has not been made as soon as possible after the violation became known to the party concerned. This article embodies the general principle (also known as estoppel) that a party should not be allowed to object to procedural irregularities long after their occurrence if that party did not do so when it originally could have.[299] Article 63 advances arbitral proceedings being carried out efficiently and in good faith.

2. Conditions for the Implication of a Waiver

Article 63 stipulates certain conditions for the implication of a waiver.

2.1. Act or Omission Contrary to NAI Rules

First, Article 63 requires an act or omission contrary to any provision of the NAI Rules. This may concern an act or omission of any of the persons that play a role

---

[299] Derains and Schwartz, 2005, 379; H.M. Holtzmann & J.E. Neuhaus, *A Guide to the UNCITRAL Model Law on International Commercial Arbitration* (Deventer, Kluwer Law and Taxation Publishers, 1989), 196. See also for example Art. 33 ICC Rules, Art. 32(1) LCIA Rules, Art. 4 UNCITRAL Model Law, Art. 30 UNCITRAL Rules, Art. 25 ICDR Rules and Art. 58 WIPO Arbitration Rules.

in NAI arbitrations, such as the other party, the individual arbitrators, the arbitral tribunal, the secretary, the NAI, the Administrator and the Executive Board. If a party to the arbitration does not comply, or complies insufficiently, with any provision contained in Section 4 of the NAI Rules, or with an order, decision or measure issued by the arbitral tribunal pursuant to that section, the arbitral tribunal may draw therefrom the conclusions it deems appropriate (Article 42).

The waiver provision of Article 63 is limited to acts or omissions contrary to provisions of the NAI Rules. It does not – as many other arbitration rules and arbitration laws[300] – provide for an implied waiver in the case of an act or omission contrary to other rules that apply to the arbitral proceedings, such as the applicable arbitration law, agreements made between the parties, or directions given by the arbitral tribunal. Furthermore, Article 63 does not make a distinction between provisions in the NAI Rules that relate to issues that may be freely determined by the parties and provisions that are based on mandatory law or public policy. The waiver rule of Article 63 should therefore be taken to operate in respect of non-compliance with, in principle, every applicable provision in the NAI Rules, whether mandatory or not. However, as will be discussed in note 3, fundamental procedural defects, i.e. violation of public policy including non-arbitrability, are excluded from its operation.

2.2. Knowledge of Non-Compliance

Second, for the implication of a waiver, Article 63 requires knowledge of the party concerned of the non-compliance. It follows from this requirement that Article 63 is intended only to prevent objections from being raised late in bad faith and not to preclude parties from raising objections to matters they could not have known earlier. The wording of Article 63 seems to indicate that actual knowledge is required. However, imputed knowledge will often suffice, as knowledge may often be proved by facts and circumstances from which actual knowledge may be concluded.

In principle, Article 63 also provides for a waiver if the party concerned does not object because it believes that it would be pointless to do so with the arbitrators or because it does not yet appreciate the relevance of the procedural irregularity concerned. After all, in such cases, knowledge of the non-compliance exists.

2.3. Objection as Soon as Possible

Third, for the implication of a waiver, Article 63 requires a failure to object as soon as possible after the party concerned became aware of the non-compliance.

---

[300] See for example Art. 33 ICC Rules, Art. 32(1) LCIA Rules, Art. 4 UNCITRAL Model Law and Art. 58 WIPO Arbitration Rules.

The exact time limit for raising an objection will depend on all relevant circumstances of the specific case, such as the violated rule, the seriousness of the violation, the respective party's adopted course of action during the proceedings, the respective party's legal expertise and the pace of the proceedings.

Some provisions in the NAI Rules stipulate explicit time limits for objecting to a violation. For example, Article 19(3)[301] provides that a challenge notification must be made within one week[302] after receipt of the notification referred to in Article 11 or, in the absence thereof, after the challenging party became aware of the grounds for the challenge.

The requirement that the party concerned objects as soon as possible implies that a party will not be deemed to have waived its right to raise an objection if the failure to object was caused by circumstances beyond its control. Many other arbitration rules and arbitration laws explicitly set out the requirement that the party concerned, without stating its objection, proceeds with the arbitration.[303] This, in order to prevent a party from being deemed to have waived its right to object in the case that it is not able to proceed with the arbitration – and, thus, to raise an objection – because of circumstances beyond its control. Although Article 63 does not explicitly set out this requirement, its result is essentially the same.

2.4. Failure to Object in Writing

Fourth, for the implication of a waiver, Article 63 requires a failure to object in writing. Article 4(1) generally provides that notices must be given or confirmed in writing. It could be argued that the wording of Article 63 – having regard to the wording of Article 4(1) – indicates that an objection as meant in this article may not be made orally and subsequently be confirmed in writing. We do not believe it to be likely, however, that an oral objection would not be deemed to be a valid objection, provided that a written confirmation is sent as soon as possible.

Particularities regarding the sending of an objection or the confirmation of an objection, both being a notice as meant by Article 4(4), are discussed in the comments on the Articles 4(2) and 20(2).

In practice, during arbitral proceedings, an arbitral tribunal may request each of the parties after a hearing whether they have any complaints regarding the conduct of the hearing, or, more in general, the arbitral proceedings. The respective answers of the parties will usually be included in the record of the hearing. The arbitral tribunal will generally try to ameliorate if not delete the complaints of the party or parties. We do not believe it to be necessary for a party that raises

---

[301] This article applies without exception in the case of summary arbitral proceedings (Art. 42f(3)).

[302] In an international arbitration, this will be two weeks (Art. 5(2)).

[303] See, for example, Art. 33 ICC Rules, Art. 32(1) LCIA Rules, Art. 4 UNCITRAL Model Law, Art. 30 UNCITRAL Rules, Art. 25 ICDR Rules and Art. 58 WIPO Arbitration Rules.

an objection in answer to the arbitral tribunal's request, to subsequently confirm its objection in writing, provided that the objection is actually included in the minutes of such conference or the record of the hearing. Parties are, therefore, advised to carefully verify such record.

3. Effect of Waiver

The wording 'in the arbitral proceedings or in court proceedings' in Article 63 makes clear that any waiver under Article 63 extends not only to subsequent phases of the arbitral proceedings, but also – and this is of even greater practical importance – to court proceedings. Thus, pursuant to Article 63, a party that is deemed to have waived its right to object under that article, may not invoke non-compliance as a ground for setting aside the award or as a reason for refusing recognition or enforcement thereof.

However, state courts reviewing an arbitral procedure, could come to a different conclusion than the arbitral tribunal as to whether each of the requirements discussed above for the implication of a waiver is met and, thus, as to whether a waiver may properly be implied. The court may nevertheless be expected to attach great importance to the judgment of the arbitral tribunal in this respect, as the arbitral tribunal is usually better acquainted with all relevant circumstances such as the facts and circumstances of the non-compliance with the NAI Rules and of the delay of the objection.

Furthermore, the waiver provision of Article 63 has effect in subsequent court proceedings only to the extent that the matters deemed to be waived thereunder are actually able to be waived. This will be no problem with respect to matters that the parties are free to decide on. But the same is not necessarily true in all jurisdictions with respect to matters that are governed by mandatory rules. With respect to public policy matters, the operation of the waiver of Article 63 will often be excluded. On the other hand, non-compliance with the NAI Rules to which a valid objection has been raised, has effect in subsequent court proceedings only to the extent that the applicable law recognizes the non-compliance concerned as a ground for setting aside or refusal of recognition and enforcement of an arbitral award.

> Dutch arbitration law – as found in the DCCP and in case law – provides for a waiver of the right to invoke a non-compliance regarding certain procedural matters as a ground for setting aside the award or as a reason for refusing recognition or enforcement thereof. The grounds for setting aside or for refusal of the recognition or enforcement of an arbitral award under Dutch law are discussed in Part III, Chapter 1 and 3 respectively.

4. Follow-Up after Objection

In order not to waive the right to invoke a non-compliance with the NAI Rules, Article 63 requires the party concerned to timely raise its objections. It does, however, not mandate the objecting party to immediately challenge an arbitral tribunal's negative decision that is the subject of the objection in court proceedings, prior to the arbitral tribunal's final award. Nor does Article 63 preclude the objecting party from continuing its participation in the arbitral proceedings, subject to that objection.[304] On the contrary, an objecting party should continue its participation in the arbitral proceedings, as Article 42 provides that, if a party to the arbitration does not comply, or complies insufficiently, with any provision contained in Section 4 of the NAI Rules, or with an order, decision or measure issued by the arbitral tribunal pursuant to that section, the arbitral tribunal may draw therefrom the conclusions it deems appropriate. After the arbitral tribunal has received the complaint of a party, it will either honour the complaint or reject the complaint. If the arbitral tribunal rejects the complaint, the arbitral proceedings will continue.

ARTICLE 64 – DISTRICT COURT PRESIDENT HAVING JURISDICTION

If the place of arbitration is within the Netherlands, the President of the District Court of Rotterdam shall have jurisdiction in the matters referred to in Article 1027(3) CCP with regard to the appointment of the arbitrator(s), Article 1028 CCP with regard to the privileged position of a party in the appointment of the arbitrator(s), Article 1035(2) CCP with regard to the challenge of an arbitrator, and Article 1041(2) CCP with regard to the examination of an unwilling witness.

---

1. General Comments

The Dutch arbitration act contains several mandatory provisions that apply next to or, if necessary, overrule the provisions in the NAI Rules, if the place of arbitration is in the Netherlands (Article 1073(1) DCCP).[305] Pursuant to a number of these mandatory provisions, a party may apply to the President (*voorzieningenrechter*) of the District Court in order to obtain a decision in the short term on certain matters regarding the arbitration. Among these provisions are Articles 1027(3), 1028 and 1035(2) DCCP regarding the appointment of the arbitrators and certain issues related thereto and Article 1041(2) DCCP regarding the examination of unwilling witnesses.[306] With respect to these matters, Article 64 designates the President of the Rotterdam District Court in the Netherlands as the judge having territorial jurisdiction. This designation is authorized by virtue

---

[304] See in this respect also Art. 9(1).

[305] See for a discussion Part I, Ch. 2, Sections 4 and 6.

[306] See for Art. 1027(3) DCCP, Art. 13, note 2 and Art. 14, note 2; for Art. 1028 DCCP, Art. 13, note 1; for Art. 1035(2) DCCP, Art. 19, note 4; for Art. 1041(2) DCCP, Art. 29, notes 3 and 4.

of Article 1072 DCCP. The designation of the President of the Rotterdam District Court is a result of the fact that the NAI has its registered office, as well as its actual place of business, in Rotterdam.[307]

2. Requirement of Place of Arbitration Seated in the Netherlands

Article 64 designates the President of the Rotterdam District Court in the Netherlands as the competent forum for the purpose of Articles 1027(3), 1028, 1035(2) and 1041(2) DCCP, provided that the place of arbitration is somewhere in the Netherlands.

If the parties have not determined the place of arbitration, the place of arbitration, in principle, will be determined by the arbitral tribunal (Article 22(1)). However, issues regarding the appointment or challenge of the arbitrators could arise before the arbitral tribunal has been able to determine the place of arbitration, for example because the arbitrators have not yet been appointed. In order to ensure that the arbitral proceedings occur, Article 1073(2) DCCP provides that, if the parties have not determined the place of arbitration, the appointment or challenge of the arbitrator or arbitrators or the secretary engaged by an arbitral tribunal may take place in accordance with the Articles 1020-1035 DCCP if at least one of the parties is domiciled or has its actual residence in the Netherlands.[308] Thus, Articles 1027(3), 1028 and 1035(2) DCCP confer jurisdiction upon the President (*voorzieningenrechter*) of the District Court, not only if the place of arbitration is in the Netherlands, but also if it has not, or not yet, been determined by the parties and at least one of the parties is domiciled or has its actual residence in the Netherlands. In that case, the wording of Article 64 does not seem to designate the President of the Rotterdam District Court as the judge having territorial competence. In our view, however, this is not the aim of Article 64. We believe it to be strongly arguable that also in that case the President of the Rotterdam District Court is the judge having territorial competence. See in this respect Article 65.

Article 1073(2) DCCP does not provide for the applicability of Article 1041(2) DCCP regarding the examination of unwilling witnesses if the place of arbitration has not been agreed upon by the parties. In practice, this will not be problematic because the place of arbitration must be determined by the arbitral tribunal as soon as possible after receipt of the arbitration file (Article 22(1)) and, thus, will usually be determined long before the issue of unwilling witnesses arises.

3. Exclusion of Appeal

Pursuant to Article 1070 DCCP, no appeal may be lodged against the decisions of the President (*voorzieningenrechter*) of the District Court on the basis of Articles 1027(3), 1028, 1035(2) and 1041(2) DCCP, since these provisions concern

---

[307] See Part I, Ch. 1, Section 1.

[308] Parliamentary History TK 1983-1984, 18.464, No. 3, 33.

situations in which a quick decision is required.[309] Thus, in principle, an appeal of such decision of the President of the Rotterdam District Court to the Court of Appeal as well as to the Supreme Court is excluded. This exclusion of appeal proceedings of Article 1070 DCCP in combination with the designation of the President of the Rotterdam District Court by Article 64 brings about that decisions of the President of the Rotterdam District Court as meant in Article 64 create significant precedents.[310] An appeal may nevertheless be assumed to be possible if the President of the District Court has wrongly applied or has wrongly failed to apply the statutory provision on the basis of which he acts, or if the President of the District Court has failed to observe essential procedural rules. In such appeal proceedings, the Court of Appeal of The Hague is the competent Court of Appeal.

ARTICLE 65 – UNFORESEEN MATTERS

> In all matters not provided for in these Rules, the spirit of these Rules shall be followed.

1. General Comments

The present NAI Rules are a detailed set of arbitration rules in order to (i) combine all relevant provisions, including those of the Dutch arbitration act, in the NAI Rules, so that it would not be necessary to consult the Dutch arbitration act in addition to the NAI Rules for an average arbitration and (ii) provide parties and arbitrators with clear information on the course and conduct of an NAI arbitration. The NAI Rules, nevertheless, are not intended to be a comprehensive code for the conduct of an NAI arbitration. Therefore, Article 65 provides for gaps in the NAI Rules to be filled in the spirit of these Rules. It thus serves the useful purpose of providing guidance and authority to act in respect of matters which the NAI Rules do not address.

Unlike similar provisions in certain other arbitration rules,[311] Article 65 does not specify on which person it imposes the obligation to follow the spirit of the NAI Rules in case of a gap. It may, therefore, be assumed that it applies to any person that plays a role in NAI arbitrations, such as the arbitral tribunal, the individual arbitrators, the parties, the secretary, the NAI, the Administrator and the Executive Board. Obviously, it will often be the arbitral tribunal that needs to determine how to proceed on matters not provided for in the NAI Rules.

---

[309] Ibid., 32.

[310] J.L.W. Sillevis Smitt, 'Naschrift bij het artikel van B.E.L.J.C. Verbunt. President Rotterdamse rechtbank zet wrakingsregeling NAI-reglement opzij', TvA 1999, 10-11.

[311] See for example Art. 35 ICC Rules and Art. 32(2) LCIA Rules.

2. Matters not Provided for

Although the wording 'all matters not provided for in these Rules' does not explicitly state so, the scope of Article 65 is limited to procedural matters. After all, the NAI Rules are of a procedural nature. Although the substantive decisions of the arbitral tribunal are indeed required to be made on the basis of the requirements of the NAI Rules as well as on the basis of the parties' relevant agreements and the applicable arbitration law, Article 65 does not impose any additional obligations in this regard.

Article 65, according to its wording and contrary to similar provisions in certain other arbitration rules,[312] only applies regarding matters that are not at all, i.e., neither explicitly nor implicitly, dealt with in the NAI Rules. It is a matter of interpretation whether a specific matter is not, either explicitly or implicitly, dealt with (see Part I, Chapter 1, Section 4.2). For example, the absence of an explicit provision on a certain right of the parties could mean that the NAI Rules implicitly provide for the parties not having that right, in which case Article 65 does not apply. It could, however, also mean that the NAI Rules do not deal with this matter, in which case Article 65 applies and the arbitral tribunal may determine whether or not to grant this right to the parties, thereby following the spirit of the NAI Rules. This, nevertheless, will often be a mere theoretical distinction, as the practical result will usually not substantially differ, particularly since in interpreting the implicit arrangements of the NAI Rules, the spirit of these rules will be an important factor.

Matters that the NAI Rules do not provide for include: (i) several issues with respect to multi-party arbitrations,[313] (ii) extension of the time limits for requesting the rectification or correction of an award and for the rendering of an additional award in exceptional cases, (iii) application for the interpretation of an arbitral award,[314] (iv) designation of the territorial competent judge regarding the matters mentioned in Articles 1027(3), 1028 and 1035(2) DCCP, if the place of arbitration has not been determined by the parties and at least one of the parties is domiciled or has its actual residence in the Netherlands,[315] and (v) applicable version of the NAI Rules in case of a remission and an amendment of these Rules during the period between the commencement of the original and the new arbitral proceedings.[316]

---

[312] Ibid.

[313] See, however, Art. 4(2) which addresses the number of copies of notices and other written submissions in multi-party arbitrations.

[314] However, see Art. 52, note 4: the interpretation of an arbitral award is not possible under the NAI Rules (nor under Dutch arbitration law).

[315] See the discussion thereon in Art. 64, note 2.

[316] See the discussion thereon in Art. 67, note 3.

3.   The Spirit of the NAI Rules

A question may arise as to the spirit of the NAI Rules. In this respect, the obligation of Article 65 is not – as in some other arbitration rules[317] – connected to an obligation of the arbitral tribunal to make every effort to ensure that the arbitral award is legally enforceable. Nevertheless, it may be assumed that the NAI Rules are also drawn up to ensure orderly and fair arbitral proceedings, leading to a legally enforceable arbitral award.

4.   Deviating and Supplementary Arrangements by Parties

Parties should exercise restraint in making arrangements in derogation from the NAI Rules, if the NAI Rules do not explicitly allow the parties to make such arrangements, without discussing these arrangements beforehand with the NAI. This is to prevent running the risk of the NAI refusing to administer the arbitration on the basis of such arrangements between the parties. However, with respect to matters not provided for in the NAI Rules, parties may, or would sometimes even be well advised to make additional arrangements, although it would still be advisable to discuss such arrangements beforehand with the NAI.[318] In our view, Article 65 is not intended to apply if the parties have made such additional arrangements, although this does not explicitly follow from the wording of Article 65.

Supplementary provisions of the applicable arbitration law apply only if the parties have not made any explicit arrangements – whether or not by reference to arbitration rules – with respect to the matter involved (see Part I, Chapter 2, Section 4).

ARTICLE 66 – EXCLUSION OF LIABILITY

> Neither the NAI, nor any member of its Governing Board personally, nor the Administrator, nor any arbitrator can be held liable for any act or omission with regard to an arbitration governed by these Rules.

1.   General Comments

Article 66 aims at providing arbitrators, the NAI, the members of the Governing Board and the Administrator with protection against lawsuits to the fullest extent possible.

---

[317] See for example Art. 35 ICC Rules and Art. 32(2) LCIA Rules.

[318] G.J. Meijer 2008 (T&C Rv), Art. 1020 DCCP, note 8(d).

2. Liability of Arbitrators in General

In many jurisdictions, arbitrators, in their quasi-judicial capacity, enjoy varying degrees of immunity from liability for the performance of their arbitral duties.[319] Often, the usually lenient standards that apply to the liability of regular judges apply accordingly to the liability of arbitrators. This means that, under most national laws, arbitrators can only be held liable in exceptional cases, also if liability has not been excluded by contract.

> Under Dutch law, indeed the same criteria apply to the liability of arbitrators as those regarding the liability of regular judges formulated by the Dutch Supreme Court. This means that liability can only be established if such fundamental rights have been violated during the formation of the arbitral decision, that (i) fair and impartial proceedings are out of the question and (ii) there are and were no legal remedies against the arbitral award. Such legal remedy is the setting aside of the arbitral award, as provided for in Article 1065 DCCP. Arbitrators, thus, cannot be held liable for an arbitral award that cannot be set aside. Otherwise, the arbitral award would remain valid, but the losing party could, in fact, undo this award.[320] However, the above does not imply that the setting aside of an award alone is a ground for liability of the arbitrators.

In this respect, the IBA Rules of Ethics[321] should be mentioned. These rules were drafted as an elaboration on the main rule that '[i]nternational arbitrators should be impartial, independent, competent, diligent and discreet' and are, thus, meant to provide guidance to arbitrators in performing their duties.[322] The rules are, however, explicitly not meant to constitute grounds for setting aside arbitral awards or arguments in national court proceedings against international arbitrators.[323]

3. Exclusion of Liability

Article 66 provides for the exclusion of liability of the arbitrators and – in conformity with the rules of other arbitration institutes[324] – of certain other persons

---

[319] A. Redfern, M. Hunter, N. Blackaby & C. Partasides, *Law and Practice of International Commercial Arbitration* (London, Sweet & Maxwell, 2004), 240-242; Derains and Schwartz, 2005, 381; Fouchard, Gaillard and Goldman, 1999, 619-621.

[320] Breda District Court 11 Sep. 1990 and Den Bosch Court of Appeal 28 Oct. 1992, both published in NJ 1993, 339. See for annotations P. Sanders, TvA 1991, 28-31; P. Sanders, TvA 1992, 231-232; P. Sanders, *De rechter en arbitrage* (2nd edn, The Hague, VUGA, 1996), 115-118 and 193. See also The Hague Court of Appeal 6 Sep. 2007, case number 05/1404 (unpublished). It should be noted that an appeal in cassation has been filed against this judgment. See for the criteria regarding the liability of regular judges as formulated by the Supreme Court: HR 3 Dec. 1971, NJ 1972, 137; HR 17 Mar. 1978, NJ 1979, 204; HR 8 Jan. 1993, NJ 1993, 558 and HR 29 Apr. 1994, NJ 1995, 227.

[321] See <www.ibanet.org/images/downloads/pubs/Ethics_arbitrators.pdf> or, for example A.J. van den Berg (ed) *Yearbook Commercial Arbitration*, Vol. 12 (Deventer, Kluwer Law and Taxation Publishers, 1987), 199 et seq.

[322] See the Introductory Note to the IBA Rules of Ethics.

[323] Ibid.

[324] See for example Art. 34 ICC, Art. 31(1) LCIA Rules, Art. 35 ICDR Rules and Art. 77 WIPO Arbitration Rules.

that play a role in NAI arbitration and that cannot be considered to fall within the quasi-judicial function and corresponding immunity of arbitrators, namely the NAI, the members of its Governing Board and the Administrator.

Article 66 is stated in terms of an absolute exclusion of liability. It excludes all liability of the persons mentioned, without exception. First, Article 66 – contrary to some corresponding provisions of other arbitration rules[325] – does not provide for an exception to the exclusion of liability in case of misconduct or gross negligence (but see note 4). Second, Article 66 provides for an exclusion of liability for 'any act or omission'. Arbitrators are, thus, not only exonerated for their own acts and omissions, but also for those of third parties for which they are responsible.[326] Third, Article 66 provides for an exclusion of liability for any act or omission 'with regard to' the arbitration.

4. Legal Effect of the Exclusion of Liability

The broad exclusion of Article 66 will probably not be effective in all jurisdictions where the conduct of the arbitrators, the NAI, the members of its Governing Board or the Administrator in NAI arbitrations may become the subject of a liability suit. Liability suits are normally brought at the place of arbitration or at the place of domicile of the person concerned. The rules of private international law of either of those jurisdictions then determine the applicable law. The mandatory provisions of this applicable law ultimately determine whether and to what extent Article 66 may be given effect. The provisions of such laws vary widely from jurisdiction to jurisdiction. In most jurisdictions, however, a contractual, absolute exclusion of liability, as provided for in Article 66, will be ineffective if the arbitrator is accused of misconduct or gross negligence.[327] The broad exclusion of Article 66 can, therefore, only ensure an exclusion of liability to the fullest extent possible under the applicable law. However, in certain countries an absolute exclusion of liability as provided for in Article 66 may be void and, thus, not have the effect of excluding any liability at all.[328] Furthermore, Article 66 may be useful in deterring disappointed parties from bringing liability claims as specified in this provision.[329]

In view of the possibly limited effect of the absolute exclusion of liability in Article 66, the NAI is insured for liability claims against arbitrators appointed by

---

[325] See for example Art. 31(1) LCIA Rules, Art. 35 ICDR Rules and Art. 77 WIPO Arbitration Rules. However, Art. 34 ICC Rules, like Art. 66 NAI Rules, provides for an exclusion of liability without exception in case of misconduct or gross negligence.

[326] Vademecum Arbitrage, 2002 (H.J. Snijders), 93.

[327] Derains and Schwartz, 2005, 382; Craig, Park and Paulsson, 2000, 412; W. Melis, 'Taak en verantwoordelijkheid van arbitrage-instituten', TvA 1988, 30.

[328] Derains and Schwartz, 2005, 383, No. 23.

[329] Annotation by P. Sanders in TvA 1991, 31 and P. Sanders, *De rechter en arbitrage* (2nd edn, The Hague, VUGA, 1996), 118. Regarding Art. 34 ICC Rules, see also Craig, Park and Paulsson 2000, 411.

the NAI.[330] As far as we know, neither NAI arbitrators, the NAI, the members of its Governing Board, nor the Administrator have been successfully sued for damages in recent years.[331]

For the exclusion of liability of Article 66 to be legally effective, it is also required that the persons involved are contractually bound by the NAI Rules and in particular by Article 66. For a discussion of the different contractual relationships between the persons involved, reference is made to Part I, Chapter 1, Section 6. Persons that, by virtue of Article 66, wish to actually exclude their potential liability to the fullest extent possible under the applicable law, should make sure that clear contractual relationships with the other persons involved exist on the basis of which these persons are contractually bound by Article 66.

> Under Dutch law, a contractually exclusion of liability in case of misconduct or gross negligence will be inoperative, since any state court or arbitrator is likely to ignore such exclusion on the basis of the principles of reasonableness and fairness, if requested to do so.

5. Liability of the Secretary and Other Persons Involved in the Arbitration

Article 66 does not mention the secretary to the arbitral tribunal (see Article 39). It has been argued that Article 66 could be read to provide for the exclusion of liability of the secretary by construing an implicit third-party clause.[332] Article 66 also does not mention other persons that may be involved in the arbitration, such as tribunal-appointed experts, interpreters and court reporters. Although we are not aware of cases in which the secretary to the arbitral tribunal or other persons involved in the arbitration have been successfully held liable, it is recommended that they request the parties to explicitly accept an exclusion or limitation of liability if they wish to ascertain the exclusion or limitation of their liability.

ARTICLE 67 – AMENDMENT OF RULES

1. The Governing Board may at all times amend these Rules. Such amendments shall have no effect with regard to arbitrations that have already been commenced.

---

[330] P. Sanders, *Het Nederlandse arbitragerecht. Nationaal en internationaal* (Deventer, Kluwer, 2001), 85.

[331] See for a recent unsuccessful attempt in the Netherlands to hold the NAI and the arbitrators appointed by the NAI liable a judgment of the Court of Appeal of The Hague of 6 Sep. 2007, case number 05/1404 (unpublished). An appeal in cassation has been filed against this judgment before the Dutch Supreme Court.

[332] Vademecum Arbitrage, 2002 (H.J. Snijders), 93-94.

2. These Rules shall apply in the form as they are in force at the time the arbitration is commenced.

1. Amendments of the NAI Rules (Article 67(1), First Sentence)

Pursuant to the NAI Articles of Association, the Governing Board draws up regulations that amongst other things provide rules with respect to the appointment of arbitrators and binding advisors (*bindend adviseurs*) and the way in which they shall hear disputes submitted to them, as well as rules with respect to costs (Article 6 of the NAI Articles of Association). This has resulted in the NAI Rules. Article 67 makes clear that the Governing Board may at all times amend the NAI Rules. The Governing Board has made use of its authority to amend the NAI Rules several times in the past.

2. Effect of Amendments (Article 67(1), Second Sentence)

Article 67(1) provides that amendments of the NAI Rules have no effect with respect to an arbitration that has already been commenced. The moment of commencement of an arbitration is deemed to be the day on which the request for arbitration is received by the NAI Secretariat (Article 6(2)). In our view, this provision has no added value next to the second paragraph of Article 67, from which also follows that amendments have no effect with respect to an arbitration that has already been commenced.

Parties may – after or even before they become aware of an impending amendment of the NAI Rules – agree on the applicability of amendments of the NAI Rules that become effective after the commencement of the arbitration. Changes in the applicable arbitration rules during the arbitral proceedings are, in principle, not desirable, as they may give rise to conflicts, depending on the changes involved. Nevertheless, the NAI leaves some scope for such agreement, as the Introduction to NAI Arbitration Rules state that the present version of the NAI Rules, *in principle*, applies only to arbitrations which are commenced after these Rules entered into force on 13 November 2001 (see Introduction to NAI Arbitration Rules, para. 2.6).[333]

3. Applicable Version of the NAI Rules (Article 67(2))

Article 67(2) stipulates that the NAI Rules apply as they are in force at the time of the commencement of the arbitration. As the present version of the NAI Rules entered into force on 13 November 2001, they, in principle, apply to arbitrations which are commenced after 13 November 2001.

---

[333] See also J.L.W. Sillevis Smitt, 'Het NAI introduceert het arbitraal kort geding; een toelichting', TvA 1997, 127 and Vademecum Arbitrage, 2002 (H.J. Snijders), 79.

The wording of Article 67(2) does not seem to allow parties to derogate from the NAI Rules and to agree on the applicability of an earlier or later version of these Rules. The NAI, however, usually honours the parties' choice of an earlier version of the NAI Rules, in particular choosing the NAI Rules in the form as they were in force at the time of the conclusion of the parties' arbitration agreement. Also, as noted above, the NAI leaves some latitude for the parties to choose a later version of the NAI Rules, as the Introduction to NAI Arbitration Rules state that the present version of the NAI Rules, *in principle*, applies only to arbitrations which are commenced after these Rules entered into force on 13 November 2001 (see Introduction to NAI Arbitration Rules, para. 2.6).[334] Parties are, nevertheless, well advised to discuss an agreement on another – earlier or later – version beforehand with the NAI.

Choosing the version of the NAI Rules in force at the time of the conclusion of the parties' arbitration agreement has the advantage that the parties are aware of the rules they agree on and that will apply to their potential future arbitration. Nevertheless, arbitrators may apply later amendments by virtue of Article 23(2) or Article 65, to the extent that these later amendments are not contrary to but are an addition to the provisions of the applicable version of the NAI Rules. Further, amendments to the NAI Rules will be made for good reasons. For example, because amendments to the Dutch arbitration act or to other relevant procedural rules necessitate amending the NAI Rules. By choosing the version of the NAI Rules in force at the time of the commencement of the arbitration, the parties profit from the most up-to-date rules that will be tailored to potential relevant amendments in Dutch procedural law. This is particularly important, as it may take many years before arbitral proceedings are instituted after the conclusion of an arbitration agreement. In addition, relevant amendments in Dutch mandatory procedural law will be applicable to such proceedings, provided that the place of arbitration is in the Netherlands (see Article 1073(1) DCCP). Finally, the application of the NAI Rules in force at the time of the commencement of the arbitration is the most convenient from an administrative point of view.

As will be discussed below (see the comments on Article 1067 DCCP in Part III, Chapter 1), neither the NAI Rules nor the Dutch arbitration act provide for the submission of the case to new arbitral proceedings following an arbitral award being set aside.[335] Article 67, thus, does not deal with the situation of remission. The parties may, however, agree on this, although in practice this is rarely done. In case of a remission, it is not entirely clear which version of the NAI Rules applies if the NAI Rules were amended during the period between the commencement of the original arbitral proceedings and the new arbitral proceedings. This issue would need to be resolved following the spirit of the NAI Rules, as provided for in Article 65.

---

[334] Ibid.

[335] However, the Draft Bill proposes to include the possibility of remission in the Dutch arbitration act.

4.   Applicable Version of the Appendix on Administration Costs

Article 57(2) provides that the schedule of administration costs that is contained in Appendix 2 to the NAI Rules may be revised from time to time by the Governing Board in accordance with the provisions of Article 67. The present schedule of administration costs applies to all arbitrations commenced on or after 1 March 2009 and irrespective of the version of the NAI Rules that is applicable to the arbitration. Obviously, the latitude left by the NAI for a choice by the parties for another – particularly an earlier – version of the NAI Rules, does not apply to the schedule of administration costs contained in Appendix 2.

PART III

POST-ARBITRATION COURT PROCEEDINGS

A good understanding of post-arbitration court proceedings is indispensable for conducting the arbitration itself. The rules for setting aside, revocation, recognition and enforcement of arbitral awards have a direct impact on the approach and conduct of the parties to NAI arbitration and on how the arbitral proceedings are conducted. For that reason, this Part III deals with those rules. It focuses on the rules of the DCCP because the vast majority of arbitrations conducted under the NAI Rules are seated in the Netherlands (this is true also for international NAI arbitrations), which means the DCCP applies (Article 1073(1) DCCP).[336] For ease of reference, this Part III contains the full translated text of the relevant provisions of the DCCP. Article headings are included for ease of reference as well: they do not appear in the text of the DCCP.

The DCCP also contains rules on the recognition of enforcement within the Netherlands of arbitral awards rendered outside the Netherlands. These will be discussed in Chapter 3 of this Part III. Part of that discussion includes the application of the New York Convention by Dutch state courts.

---

[336] If the arbitration is seated outside the Netherlands and a party seeks to set aside the award, or if recognition and enforcement is sought outside the Netherlands, the arbitration law of the respective foreign legal system applies. A discussion of the ramifications of such laws falls outside the ambit of this book.

CHAPTER 1

SETTING ASIDE

.

In arbitration practice in the Netherlands, proceedings to set aside an arbitral award remain the exception rather than the rule, and claims for setting aside an award are seldom successful. An application to set aside an award made in the Netherlands can be made to the District Court. A judgment of a District Court is subject to appeal to a Court of Appeal and, finally, to the Supreme Court. Proceedings to set aside an award may potentially take several years – in particular if all instances are used. Though this inevitably leads to uncertainty, proceedings to set aside an award generally do not impede the effectiveness of arbitration. First of all, proceedings to set aside an award do not suspend the enforcement of the arbitral award unless the court, upon application, so decides. Second, the Supreme Court has consistently stressed that in the interest of the effectiveness of arbitration, state courts should use the power to set aside awards with restraint. Practice shows that the courts observe this restraint.

The provisions of the DCCP on the setting aside of arbitral awards are largely based on the UNCITRAL Model Law. Notable differences, that practitioners from outside the Netherlands may not be readily aware of, are for example the time limit for application of setting aside an award and the possibility of setting aside an award on the ground that it does not contain reasons. Also, Article 1068 DCCP, which deals with revocation, contains three grounds on the basis of which the award can also be set aside (Article 1068(3) DCCP). These grounds are not part of the UNCITRAL Model Law either (see further Part III, Chapter 2).

Article 1064 DCCP – Setting Aside, in General

1. Recourse to a court against a final or partial final arbitral award which is not open to appeal to a second arbitral tribunal, or a final or partial final award rendered on arbitral appeal, may be made only by an application for setting aside or revocation in accordance with this Section.

2. An application for setting aside shall be made to the District Court with whose Registry the original of the award shall be deposited by virtue of Article 1058(1).

3. An application for setting aside may be made as soon as the award has acquired the force of res judicata. The right to make an application shall be extinguished three months after the date of deposit of the award with the Registry of the District Court. However, if the award together with leave for enforcement is officially served on the other party, that party may make an application for setting aside within three months after the said service, irrespective of whether the period of three months mentioned in the preceding sentence has lapsed.

4. An application to set aside an interim arbitral award may be made only in conjunction with an application for setting aside a final or partial final award.

5. All grounds for setting aside shall, on pain of being barred, be mentioned in the writ of summons.

1. Finality of the Award

An application for setting aside can only be made against a final or partial final arbitral award (Article 1064(1) DCCP). An award is (partially) final if it contains a final decision on the claim or a part of the claim (see the comments on Article 44 NAI Rules on what constitutes a final or partial final award). Article 1064(4) DCCP provides that the claim for setting aside of an interim award may be made only in conjunction with an application for setting aside a final or partial final award. If in doubt as to whether an interim award is partially final, it is generally prudent to apply to have the award set aside within the given time limit. If a court rules that the application to set aside is not admissible because the award does not contain a final decision, the application can be made at a later stage. However, when applying to have the last final award set aside and in conjunction with this a previous partial final award, a court most likely will not admit the application against that partial final award (as far as it concerns the final decisions contained therein), as that application could (and should) have been made when the partial final award was rendered (assuming that the time limit for setting aside the partial final award has already lapsed). Therefore, when in doubt as to whether an interim award is (in part) final, a party should file an application to set aside the partial award to avoid the risk of being precluded to do so at a later stage.

However, if a party files an application to set aside an arbitral award that does not contain a final decision, and subsequently a final award is rendered in the same arbitration, that party cannot ask to have the final award set aside by merely increasing its claim in the proceedings to set aside the award. The party will have to apply to have the final award set aside in a separate writ of summons.[337]

2.   Res Judicata Effect

An application to set aside an award can only be made against an award which has res judicata effect (i.e. not open to arbitral appeal) (Article 1064(1) DCCP). The application can be made as soon as the award has acquired the force of res judicata. An arbitral award has res judicata effect as of the date it is rendered,[338] unless the parties have agreed to arbitral appeal. In that case the award acquires the force of res judicata when the time limit for lodging an appeal has lapsed and none of the parties has lodged an appeal, or when an award is rendered in arbitral appeal and such award affirms the award in first instance (Article 1059(2) DCCP).[339] An application to set aside can also be made against a (partial) final award in summary arbitral proceedings (Article 1051(3) DCCP), unless the parties have agreed to arbitral appeal against an award in summary arbitral proceedings. Whether the parties have agreed to that is a matter of interpretation of the arbitration clause or the agreement to arbitrate. If the parties have agreed to arbitral appeal without mentioning whether this also applies to appeal against arbitral awards in summary proceedings, it may be assumed that arbitral appeal is not open to an award in summary proceedings.[340]

The NAI Rules do not provide for arbitral appeal, though they do not exclude the possibility that the parties agree on arbitral appeal under the NAI Rules.[341] Therefore, the parties have not agreed on arbitral appeal if the parties have agreed to arbitration pursuant to the NAI Rules (for instance by using the standard NAI arbitration clause), without making any reference to arbitral appeal. The fact that the NAI Rules do not contain any rules on arbitral appeal and that, in practice, arbitral appeal is not or seldom used in NAI arbitrations, does not mean that it is not possible. If the parties provide for arbitral appeal, they are well advised to conform to the 'regular' arbitration rules as much as possible and clearly provide how the specifics of arbitral appeal should be arranged (e.g. whether the partic-

---

[337] See HR 20 Jun. 2003, NJ 2004, 569 (Waterschappen/Milieutech Beheer) where this is determined for revocation. The same reasoning also applies to setting aside.

[338] Article 1059(1) DCCP and Art. 51 NAI Rules.

[339] When the award on arbitral appeal overturns the award in first instance, the award on appeal has res judicata effect as of the date it is rendered (Art. 1059(1) DCCP). If the award on appeal partially overturns and partially confirms the award in first instance, each has res judicata effect (albeit the award in first instance only to the extent it is confirmed) as of the date of the award on appeal.

[340] Parliamentary History TK 1983-1984, 18.464, No. 3, 20.

[341] See also Part I, Ch. 1, Section 5.

ularities of the grievance system (*grievenstelsel*), applicable in appeal proceedings in the state courts, apply).[342]

3. Competent Court

An application to set aside an award must be made to the District Court where the original of the award must be deposited, which is the District Court in whose district the arbitration is seated (Article 1064(2) DCCP).[343] This also applies if, in error, the arbitral award has actually been deposited with another court. Parties cannot litigate proceedings to set aside an award in person; they must be represented by a practicing lawyer (*advocaat*).

Parties can agree that an application to set aside can only be made to one factual instance, either the District Court (on the basis of Article 333 DCCP) or the Court of Appeal (on the basis of Article 329 DCCP).[344] Though the law is less clear on the question whether parties can also waive their right to appeal to the Supreme Court, we deem it likely that such waiver will be effective in court.[345] A waiver of one factual instance (District Court or Court of Appeal) and, possibly, of the right to appeal to the Supreme Court would limit setting aside proceedings to one instance, thereby reducing one of the main disadvantages of proceedings to set aside an award: a protracted battle before three instances of state courts. Parties who wish to avoid this, could add such a waiver to their arbitration clause. However, such waivers are only possible in regard to matters which may be freely determined by the parties. A waiver is void if it concerns matters which may not be freely determined by the parties (Articles 329 and 333 DCCP). Hence, if the application to set aside an award is based on the ground that the dispute was not capable of being settled in arbitration (see further the comments on Article 1065(1)(a) and (e) DCCP), the right to litigate the setting aside application before three instances of state courts cannot be waived.

4. Time Limitations

The application must be made (a) within three months after the date of the deposit of the arbitral award with the office of the clerk of the court, *or* (b) within three months after the arbitral award (together with leave for enforcement) is officially served on the other party, in which case only that party may make an application

---

[342] The *grievenstelsel* has been held to apply in arbitrations under the Arbitration Rules of the Arbitration Council for the Construction Industry, which provide in Art. 28(3) and (5) that an appeal must be lodged by submitting 'a statement of grounds for appeal' (see Amsterdam District Court 14 May 2008, LJN: BF0816 (Laco/Ruedisulj)).

[343] See Art. 50 NAI Rules, note 2 on the filing of the award with the District Court clerk's office, as prescribed by Art. 1058 DCCP.

[344] Art. 329 DCCP and Art. 62 Judiciary Organization Act (*Wet op de Rechterlijke Organisatie*).

[345] See also the Opinion of Advocate General Loeff to HR 3 Dec. 1954, NJ 1955, 56.

to set aside the award. The application to set aside can also be made before the award has been deposited.

(a) Article 1064(3) DCCP provides that the right to make an application extinguishes three months after the date of deposit of the arbitral award with the office of the clerk of the District Court. The arbitral tribunal is required to deposit the award with the District Court (Article 1058(1)(b) DCCP). Under the NAI Rules, the Administrator, on behalf of the arbitral tribunal, deposits the award with the court clerk's office (Article 50 NAI Rules). This office is not required to give notice to the parties that the award has been deposited. In practice, the NAI will deposit an award usually no later than a few days after it has been rendered. The Administrator will immediately inform the parties of the date of deposit (Article 50(2) NAI Rules).

(b) The party, against whom enforcement of an arbitral award is sought, may benefit from an additional time limit. A party seeking enforcement of an arbitral award in the Netherlands must ask for leave for enforcement (*exequatur*).[346] If the award together with leave for enforcement is officially served on the other party (which is a prerequisite to the actual execution), such other party may make an application to set aside within three months after the said service, irrespective of whether the period of three months as from the day of deposit of the award has already lapsed. Only the party against whom enforcement is sought can apply to have the award set aside within this time limit. In most cases this will be the party who lost in the arbitration. The losing party cannot always rely on this time limit. First of all, this time limit will not apply if the award only contains a declaratory or constitutive judgment, which cannot and need not be enforced. Such judgments may be the basis for further litigation or arbitration between the parties however, including enforcement measures, which enforcement would effectively amount to enforcement of the previous declaratory judgment, which has res judicata effect between the parties. Secondly, the time limit only applies when a leave for enforcement is necessary and the award together with leave for enforcement must be officially served on the other party. The time limit is written against the background of the enforcement requirements in the Netherlands, but this may not work for enforcement outside the Netherlands, if for such execution it is not necessary that the award together with leave for enforcement is officially served on the other party. It is unclear what applies in such cases. It could be argued that the time limit starts to run as from the date on which the respective foreign conditions for execution

---

[346] See Art. 1062 DCCP for enforcement of arbitral awards rendered in the Netherlands and Arts 1075 and 1076 DCCP for enforcement of arbitral awards rendered outside the Netherlands. See further Part III, Ch. 3.

have been fulfilled. However, it can also be argued that the additional time limit does not apply at all.

If an application to set aside is based on the ground that the tribunal has failed to decide on one or more matters submitted to it, a specific time limit applies. Such an application can only be made by a party who has first requested the tribunal to render an additional award (Article 1065(6) DCCP).[347] The time limit for applying to have an award set aside in that case starts to run as from the day the additional award is deposited or as from the day the denial of the request for rendering an additional award is deposited (Article 1065(7) DCCP). This time limit only applies to the ground that the tribunal has failed to decide on one or more matters submitted to it. At the same time, the party who seeks to set aside the award may also wish to use other grounds for setting aside, which the party must do within three months after the date the original award was deposited. Thus, several time limits may run in relation to different grounds. This may be very impractical, especially since the additional award may give rise to other, closely connected grounds for setting aside.

5. Grounds for Setting Aside in Writ of Summons

Article 1064(5) DCCP provides that all grounds for setting aside must be mentioned in the writ of summons, on pain of being barred from relying on them at a later stage. The arbitration act does not determine whether it is sufficient to merely mention one of the grounds stipulated in Article 1065 DCCP – e.g. to state that the award violates public policy or that the tribunal has not complied with its mandate without asserting why public policy is violated or why the tribunal has not complied with its mandate. The general view is that this is not sufficient, since it would enable a party to merely mention all grounds of Article 1065 DCCP and give the reasons for setting aside only at a (much) later stage. It would make the time limit merely a formality and considerably increase the time within which the reasons for the action to set aside are given. It also follows from the general requirements for a writ of summons under Dutch law that the claim must be substantiated in the writ.[348] To what extent certain factual allegations are within the ambit of the grounds presented in the writ of summons remains for the court to decide.

---

[347] On the request to render an additional award, see Art. 1061 DCCP and Art. 53 NAI Rules, see the comments on Art. 53 NAI Rules.

[348] A claimant has a duty to substantiate (*substantieringsplicht*) the claim in the writ of summons, which means that the writ must contain the facts and remedies on which the claim is based (Art. 111 DCCP).

ARTICLE 1065 DCCP – GROUNDS FOR SETTING ASIDE

1. Setting aside of the award can take place only on one or more of the following grounds:
   (a) absence of a valid arbitration agreement;
   (b) the arbitral tribunal was constituted in violation of the rules applicable thereto;
   (c) the arbitral tribunal has not complied with its mandate;
   (d) the award is not signed or does not contain reasons in accordance with the provisions of Article 1057;
   (e) the award, or the manner in which it was made, violates public policy or good morals.

2. The ground mentioned in paragraph (1)(a) above shall not constitute a ground for setting aside in the case mentioned in Article 1052(2).

3. The ground mentioned in paragraph (1)(b) above shall not constitute a ground for setting aside in the cases mentioned in Article 1052(3).

4. The ground mentioned in paragraph (1)(c) above shall not constitute a ground for setting aside if the party who invokes this ground has participated in the arbitral proceedings without invoking such ground, although it was known to him that the arbitral tribunal did not comply with its mandate.

5. If the arbitral tribunal has awarded in excess of, or differently from, what was claimed, the arbitral award shall be partially set aside to the extent that the part of the award which is in excess of or different from the claim can be separated from the remaining part of the award.

6. If and to the extent that the arbitral tribunal has failed to decide one or more matters submitted to it, the application for setting aside on the ground mentioned in paragraph (1)(c) above shall be admissible only if an additional award mentioned in Article 1061(1) is made, or the request for an additional award mentioned in Article 1061(1) has wholly or partially been rejected.

7. Notwithstanding the provisions of the second sentence of Article 1064(3), the time limit for making an application for setting aside mentioned in the preceding paragraph shall be three months from the date of deposit of the additional award or the copy of the notification mentioned in Article 1061(5) with the Registry of the District Court.

1. General Comments

In applying the grounds for setting aside, courts must act with restraint. The Supreme Court has consistently held that courts should act with restraint in setting aside arbitral awards. Proceedings to set aside an award may not be used as an appeal in disguise. The public interest in the effectiveness of arbitration requires that a court only sets aside in clear-cut cases.[349] The Supreme Court has made these statements in general, without distinguishing between the five grounds for setting aside.

Although Article 1065(1) DCCP, first sentence, states that setting aside an award 'can' take place on one of the grounds mentioned therein, this should not be interpreted as giving discretion to the court in deciding whether it sets aside, if it finds that one of the grounds for setting aside applies. It merely means that the grounds for setting aside are limited to those mentioned in Article 1065(1) DCCP, and that the court therefore 'can only' set aside an award based on one of those grounds.[350] That is not to say that in each instance where a ground for setting aside applies, the award should be completely annulled, since the court may also partially set aside the award, if the award contains decisions which are not inextricably entwined, so that a certain part of the award can be set aside, while the remainder of the award, not being inseparably connected, can be upheld.[351]

The provisions of Articles 1064 and 1065 DCCP contain mandatory law. For instance, the constitutional right to access to state courts and the fundamental right to be heard, which is also protected by Article 6 ECHR, cannot be waived. A party cannot be forced into arbitration where the party has not voluntarily agreed to arbitration, waiving its right to access to state courts. Accordingly, an award can always be set aside based on a violation of this right, either because there is no agreement at all (Article 1065(1)(a) DCCP), or where the tribunal has been constituted differently from what was agreed (Article 1065(1)(b) DCCP), or has exceeded its mandate (Article 1065(1)(c) DCCP). Though this means that parties cannot categorically waive their right to set aside, it should be possible to effectively limit the grounds for setting aside.[352] For instance, the parties could

---

[349] See for example HR 17 Jan. 2003, NJ 2004, 384 (IMS/Ministry of Defence), HR 9 Jan. 2004, NJ 2005, 190 (Nannini/SFT) and HR 22 Dec. 2006, NJ 2008, 4 (Kers/Rijpma).

[350] See however the Amsterdam Court of Appeal 7 Apr. 2005, NJF 2005, 274, TvA 2006, 115-118 which held that even though the award had not been signed in accordance with the provisions of Art. 1057 DCCP, this did not require the court to set aside the award; whether it should do so depends on the circumstances of the case. Snijders (Burg. Rv, 2006 (H.J. Snijders), Art. 1065 DCCP, note 1) and Roelvink (in his commentary to this judgment, TvA 2006, 117-118) provide compelling arguments why the Amsterdam Court of Appeal is wrong.

[351] See e.g. HR 20 Jan. 2006, NJ 2006, 77 (ASB/Sagro).

[352] Since it is not possible to categorically waive the right to set aside under Dutch law, it is uncertain what the effect is of a general clause, in which the parties waive their right to set aside insofar as such waiver can be validly made under Dutch law. Art. 28(6) ICC Rules contains such a clause. It provides that 'By submitting the dispute to arbitration under these Rules, the parties (...) shall be deemed to have waived their right to any form of recourse insofar as such waiver can validly be made.'

give the arbitrators a very broad mandate from the start of the arbitration, which would reduce the risk of arbitrators exceeding their mandate (setting aside ground (c)). Also, the parties could agree to firm cut-off date(s) for the submission of evidence and reduce the possibility to respond to one written statement and a hearing, which would prevent protracted proceedings based on the allegation that parties should time and again be given the right to be heard (setting aside ground (e)).

2.   Ad 1065(1)(a) Absence of a Valid Arbitration Agreement

The award can be set aside if the tribunal has declared it has jurisdiction, but there is no valid agreement to arbitrate. The ramifications of the arbitration agreement and its validity under Dutch law are discussed in the comments on Article 1, note 3 in Part II, Section 1. One of the reasons for invalidity of the arbitration agreement involves arbitrability. If an arbitral tribunal renders an award on a matter which is not capable of being settled by arbitration because it concerns legal consequences which may not be freely determined by the parties (Article 1020(3) DCCP), the award can be set aside on the ground that the agreement, which referred the dispute to arbitration, was invalid.[353] See Part I, Chapter 2, Section 2 on the issue of arbitrability.

Even though the Supreme Court has held that, in general, state courts should act with restraint when asked to set aside an arbitral award, this should not be held to apply to the assessment by state courts of whether a valid arbitration agreement existed. Article 17 of the Dutch Constitution (*Grondwet*) grants a right of access to state courts and Article 6 of the ECHR grants the right to a trial by an independent and impartial tribunal established by law. A choice of arbitration is a renunciation by the parties of a procedure before state courts satisfying all the guarantees of Article 6 ECHR (since arbitral proceedings need not satisfy all requirements of Article 6 ECHR[354]). In view of the fundamental nature of the right of access to state courts, state courts should fully assess whether an arbitral tribunal correctly established that a valid arbitration agreement existed, not just in clear-cut cases. This may still be aligned with Supreme Court case law however, since the Supreme Court has not specifically ruled that state courts should apply restraint also when assessing this particular ground for setting aside (i.e. whether a valid agreement to arbitrate existed).

A party is barred from an application to set aside the arbitral award due to the absence of an arbitration agreement if that party took part in the arbitration and did not raise this jurisdictional defence during the arbitration prior to all defences (Articles 1065(2) and 1052(2) DCCP).[355] 'Prior to all defences' means that the

---

[353]   Parliamentary History TK 1983-1984, 18.464, No. 3, 29.

[354]   See for example European Commission for Human Rights 27 Nov. 1996, NJ 1997, 505 (Nordström/Nederland).

[355]   See also Art. 9(2) NAI Rules.

plea that the arbitral tribunal lacks jurisdiction on the ground that there is no valid arbitration agreement must be made not later than in the statement of defence or, in the absence thereof, in the first written or oral defence. The short answer referred to in Article 7 NAI Rules is not deemed to constitute a defence (Article 9(2) NAI Rules).

Article 1027(4) DCCP provides that by cooperating with the appointment of the arbitrators, a party is not considered to have agreed to arbitration; this party may still allege that there is no valid arbitration agreement.

If the tribunal incorrectly declared it has jurisdiction with regard to one of the parties to the arbitration, but correctly established that there was a valid arbitration agreement between other parties to the arbitration, a court may partially set aside the award (i.e. only in respect of the party who was not party to the arbitration agreement).[356]

3. Ad 1065(1)(b) Constitution of Arbitral Tribunal in Violation of the Applicable Rules

The requirements for the constitution of the tribunal are determined by the Dutch arbitration act and the agreement between the parties.[357] If the arbitral tribunal is not constituted in accordance with those requirements, the arbitral award rendered by that tribunal can be set aside. However, if a party participated in the constitution of the arbitral tribunal without complaining that its constitution was not in accordance with the prevailing requirements, that party is barred from applying to have the award set aside on this ground (Articles 1065(3) and 1052(3) DCCP).

4. Ad 1065(1)(c) Arbitral Tribunal Has Not Complied with its Mandate

A tribunal violates its mandate if it awards in excess of, or differently from, what was claimed, if it fails to decide on a claim, if it fails to take into account an essential defence, if it violates the agreed procedural rules, or if it decides in accordance with the rules of law instead of as amiable compositeur or vice versa. These instances will be discussed below. The tribunal's failure to comply with its mandate is not a ground for setting aside if the party who invokes this ground has participated in the arbitral proceedings without invoking such ground, although this party could have done so and knew that the arbitral tribunal did not comply with its mandate (Article 1065(4) DCCP).

If the arbitral tribunal has *awarded in excess of, or differently from, what was claimed*, the arbitral award shall be partially set aside to the extent that the part of

---

[356] HR 20 Jan. 2006, NJ 2006, 77 (ASB/Sagro).

[357] See Part II, Section 3.

the award which is in excess of or different from the claim can be separated from the remaining part of the award (Article 1065(5) DCCP).

If the arbitral tribunal has *failed to decide one or more matters submitted to it*, the application to set aside based on the ground that the arbitral tribunal has not complied with its mandate is admissible only if the tribunal has been requested to render an additional award and such additional award was made or wholly or partially rejected (Article 1065(6) DCCP).[358] A party may, not later than 30 days after the date of deposit of the award, request the arbitral tribunal to render an additional award (Article 1061(1) DCCP and 50(1) NAI Rules). 'Matters submitted to it', as meant in Articles 1065(6) and 1061(1) DCCP, refers to one or more parts of the claim in arbitration.[359] There is no standard case law on the question of whether the tribunal should not only decide on all claims submitted to it, but also on each of the grounds presented for each claim. In the latter case, if a party for example files a single claim for an amount of 10 million euro, primarily as damages for breach of contract and alternatively on account of unjustified enrichment, the tribunal cannot merely deny the claim by giving reasons why the contract was not breached. It will have to rule on the alternative ground (unjustified enrichment) as well. In view of the uncertainty whether arbitrators indeed should address all grounds for the claim, parties are well advised to formulate these grounds as alternative claims, in which case it is certain the tribunal will have to address them as part of their mandate.

It has been established in case law that the defendant can ask for an award to be set aside for the reason that the tribunal has *failed to decide on a separate and essential defence*.[360] Not every defence must be addressed in the award: the defence must have some significance.[361] There is no clear yardstick for determining what constitutes a separate and essential defence. But in many instances it will be clear which defences must be addressed by the tribunal. For instance, if the defendant has made and maintained well-reasoned arguments that a claim for breach of contract should be denied, primarily because the claim is time-barred, alternatively because the defendant has not breached the contract and more alternatively that the damages must be imputed to the claimant, the tribunal will need to address all of these defences when it finds for the claimant. As mentioned above, if the arbitral tribunal has failed to decide one or more matters submitted to it, meaning that the tribunal has not decided on a part of the *claim*, the claimant can apply for an additional award. The defendant cannot do

---

[358] Even if an additional award is rendered, the party who requested the addition may still want to set aside the award, if the additional award insufficiently addresses the relevant matters or, again, fails to address them at all.

[359] HR 14 Feb. 1997, NJ 1998, 109 (Mannaerts qq/Van Rhienen); Parliamentary History TK 1983-1984, 18.464, No. 3, 26.

[360] HR 30 Mar. 1973, NJ 1973, 226 (De Kaaphoeve/Swinkels); HR 30 Dec. 1977, NJ 1978, 449 (De Ploeg/Kruse) and HR 14 Feb. 1997, NJ 1998, 109 (Mannaerts qq/Van Rhienen).

[361] Burg. Rv, 2006 (H.J. Snijders), Art. 1065 DCCP, note 4.

the same if one of its defences to the claim is not taken into account.[362] Therefore, if the tribunal has failed to take into account a separate and essential defence, the defendant can ask that the award be set aside, without having to resort to a request for an additional award first.

A tribunal violates its mandate if it *violates the procedural rules agreed by the parties* in the arbitration agreement. The state court must establish what these rules are, interpret these rules and decide whether they have been violated.[363] No breach of their mandate exists if the arbitrators violate their own internal procedural rules which they have set themselves.[364] A specific question arises with regard to procedural rules agreed to by the parties after the tribunal has been constituted. Though arbitrators are bound to the rules agreed to by the parties in the arbitration agreement, upon which their mandate is based,[365] this does not mean that they are also bound by the procedural rules agreed to by the parties thereafter. After the constitution of the tribunal, the tribunal determines the manner in which the procedure shall be conducted (Article 23(2) NAI Rules, see also the comments thereto). In doing so, they shall take account of – amongst others – the arrangements by the parties, but they are not required to apply them in any event. In our opinion, this means that, if the parties wish the arbitrators to apply certain procedural rules (e.g. the submission of statements of reply and rejoinder, the application of predetermined time limits, the rules of evidence, etc.) and wish the award to be set aside if those rules are violated, they will have to include the rules in their arbitration agreement.[366]

The award may be set aside if the arbitrators *applied the wrong decision making standard*, i.e. if they decided in accordance with the 'rules of law' though the parties have agreed that they should decide as amiable compositeur (or vice versa). A court must establish which measure the tribunal should have used and whether the tribunal has done so. However, state courts are not permitted to consider the way the tribunal (applying the right measure) has applied that measure and the result it has achieved (e.g. whether a decision in accordance with the rules of law applies the applicable law correctly).[367]

---

[362] HR 14 Feb. 1997, NJ 1998, 109 (Mannaerts qq/Van Rhienen).

[363] HR 28 Sep. 1990, NJ 1991, 230 (Huybregts/Van Tuyl).

[364] HR 25 Feb. 2000, NJ 2000, 508 (Benetton III).

[365] See the comments on Art. 23(2) NAI Rules.

[366] Also in those cases, however, the court being asked to set aside the award may decide not to set aside the award if it deems the violation of the agreed rules immaterial or if the violation does not in any way detrimentally affect the party who seeks to set aside the award. So, for instance, it can be doubted whether the failure by the arbitrators to comply with a time limit for rendering the award always leads to the award being set aside.

[367] HR 22 Dec. 1978, NJ 1979, 521 (Zaunbrecher/Muyzert).

5. Ad 1065(1)(d) Award Is Not Signed or Does Not Contain Reasons

The award must be signed in accordance with Article 1057 DCCP,[368] failing which it can be set aside. This rarely provides a ground for setting aside.[369] It is particularly unlikely in NAI arbitrations, since the Administrator usually checks whether the award is properly signed.

An award can be set aside if it does not contain reasons. An arbitral award can only be set aside based on this ground, if it contains no reasons at all, not if the reasons given are unsound. State courts are not permitted to review an arbitral award on the merits.[370] However, the Supreme Court complicated this ground for setting aside by ruling in the *Nannini* case that an award which does contain reasons, but in which no convincing explanation for the decision can be ascertained, must be equated with an award that does not contain reasons.[371] This criterion has lead to considerable debate in arbitration practice, since it is unclear what is meant by a 'convincing explanation' (*steekhoudende verklaring*).[372] As it could arguably mean that the standards for the reasoning of the award were raised (requiring the reasoning to be convincing), this ground for setting aside became more frequently used. In a later case, however, the Supreme Court added that the *Nannini* criterion must be applied with restraint and that the court must only apply it in clear-cut cases. State courts may set aside an award only if the award contains no reasons at all or if it is so deficiently reasoned that it must be equated with an award without reasons.[373] The Supreme Court also ruled that, if the reasoning of the tribunal is based on the wrong rules or an incorrect interpretation of the applicable rules, the award cannot be set aside for that reason, because this does not mean that the award can be put on par with an award that does not contain any reasoning at all.[374] In such case, it would be difficult to say that such reasoning is 'convincing'. It is safe to say that the wording 'convincing' (*steekhoudend*) as contained in the *Nannini* decision was ill-chosen and does not accurately reflect what is meant.

How explicit an arbitral tribunal must address the matters submitted to it depends on the nature of those matters, considering the dispute as a whole. A decision can also be given implicitly and without specific reasoning.[375]

---

[368] See Art. 48, note 1.

[369] See for such a rare example: HR 5 Dec. 2008, NJ 2009, 6 (Bursa/Güris).

[370] HR 25 Feb. 2000, NJ 2000, 508 (Benetton III).

[371] HR 9 Jan. 2004, NJ 2005, 190 (Nannini/SFT).

[372] 'Steekhoudend' also translates as 'sound' and 'well-founded'.

[373] HR 22 Dec. 2006, NJ 2008, 4 (Kers/Rijpma).

[374] See e.g. HR 22 Dec. 2006, NJ 2008, 4 (Kers/Rijpma), para. 3.5.

[375] HR 30 Dec. 1977, NJ 1978, 449 (De Ploeg/Kruse).

6. Ad 1065(1)(e) Award, or Manner in which It Was Made, Violates Public Policy or Good Morals

A violation of public policy[376] can be a matter of procedure and a matter of substance.

As to procedure, an award may be set aside if the manner in which it was made violates public policy. This typically involves violations of fundamental principles of due process and fair trial. In particular the right to be heard has generated quite some case law in proceedings to set aside an award. This fundamental right must, in principle, be applied just as strictly as it is applied to regular state court proceedings.[377] It means for instance that a party preserves its due process rights unless the party has unambiguously renounced its right to be heard.[378] Also, the tribunal may only decide on the basis of evidence which has been made available to the parties and which the parties have been given sufficient opportunity to respond to.[379] In a recent judgment[380] the Supreme Court has reiterated the stringent application of the principle of *audiatur et altera pars*. The Supreme Court again held that the restraint state courts must observe in proceedings to set aside applies also in cases where a violation of principles of due process is alleged, but does not apply to violations of the fundamental right to be heard. The judgment involved a case in which the tribunal had based its decision primarily on the statement of a witness. One of the parties had taken this person to a hearing, without having offered to hear him as a witness. The other party objected to his presence at the hearing; the tribunal granted that objection. However, the tribunal thereafter considered it relevant to hear this person as a witness, even though no witness testimony was offered or ordered. The other party was given the opportunity to ask questions to the witness and had not asked to hear witnesses of its own or to respond to his statement. Nevertheless, the Supreme Court ruled that the tribunal should have stated the purpose of the hearing and should have actively offered the other party the opportunity to contest the statement of the witness and to hear witnesses of its own.

The importance of this fundamental right to be heard sometimes leads to protracted arbitral proceedings, as parties keep on submitting new statements or evidence in response to the statements or evidence submitted by the other party, and arbitrators do not cut off this process, fearing that the right to be heard would be violated if they do so. However, it is very well possible under Dutch law to provide for a cut-off date for new evidence and still respect the right to be

---

[376] The term 'good morals' is a superfluous addition – it offers no addition to what is already covered by 'public policy'; see also P. Sanders, *Het Nederlandse arbitragerecht. Nationaal en internationaal* (Deventer, Kluwer, 2001), 197.

[377] HR 27 Mar. 1987, NJ 1988, 130 (Pensioenfonds/Geerlings).

[378] HR 18 Jun. 1993, NJ 1994, 449 (Van der Lely/VDH).

[379] HR 27 Mar. 1987, NJ 1988, 130 (Pensioenfonds/Geerlings).

[380] HR 25 May 2007, NJ 2007, 294 (Spaanderman/Anova).

heard, in particular where such cut-off date is followed by a hearing, in which the parties and their representatives, experts and witnesses can be heard and respond to each other.

Other examples of situations in which the manner in which the arbitral award was made violates public policy, involve violations of the impartiality and independence that arbitrators are required to observe. An award can only be set aside on this basis, when based on established facts an arbitrator was not impartial or independent when rendering the decision, or when – taking into account the circumstances of the case – there is such severe doubt as to his impartiality or independence, that it would be unacceptable to uphold the arbitral award.[381] If a party could have challenged the arbitrator during the arbitral proceedings, because the facts amounting to a violation of impartiality or independence were already known, that party is barred from using the same facts to set aside the award.[382] The grounds for challenging an arbitrator for lack of impartiality or independence are less strict: justifiable doubts (including outward appearance of partiality) are sufficient for a successful challenge (see Article 19 NAI Rules, notes 1 and 2).

As to substance, an award may be set aside if its contents violate public policy. It violates public policy if it is contrary to mandatory law of such fundamental nature that its application must not be impeded by procedural constraints.[383] A notable example is the incorrect application of or failure to apply European Community (EC) competition law. In regard to EC competition law, the European Court of Justice (ECJ) determined in the *Eco Swiss* case[384] that, where domestic rules of procedure require a national court to grant an application for setting aside of an arbitration award where such an application is founded on failure to observe national rules of public policy (as Article 1065(1)(e) DCCP does), it must also grant such an application where it is founded on failure to comply with the prohibition laid down in Article 81 EC. The same applies to EC consumer law.[385] In the *Mostaza Claro* case the ECJ ruled that the Directive concerning unfair terms in consumer contracts, must be interpreted as meaning that a national court seized of an action for setting aside of an arbitration award must determine whether the arbitration agreement is void and annul that award where that agreement contains an unfair term, even when the consumer has not pleaded that invalidity in the course of the arbitral

---

[381] HR 18 Feb. 1994, NJ 1994, 765 (Nordström/Nievelt); European Commission on Human Rights 27 Nov. 1996, NJ 1997, 505 (Nordström/Nederland).

[382] Ibid.

[383] HR 21 Mar. 1997, NJ 1998, 206 (Benetton/Eco Swiss).

[384] ECJ 1 Jun. 1999, C-126/97 (Eco Swiss China Time Ltd v. Benetton International NV), European Court reports 1999, I-03055; also in: NJ 2000, 339.

[385] ECJ 26 Oct. 2006, C-168/05 (Elisa María Mostaza Claro v. Centro Móvil Milenium SL), European Court reports 1999, I-10421.

proceedings, but only in that of the action for setting aside.[386] In these cases, the ECJ has not answered the question of whether arbitrators should go *ultra vires* and determine whether the relevant consumer law provisions were violated, even where this was not pleaded by the parties.[387] It could be argued that it would be a breach of the mandate if the arbitrators did so, and accordingly would make the award susceptible to being set aside on the basis of Article 1065(1)(c) DCCP. In our opinion, however, it should be regarded as an intrinsic part of the arbitrators' mandate to apply rules of public policy, even where parties have not pleaded these.[388]

If a dispute is not capable of being settled in arbitration, but was decided by arbitrators nonetheless, the award can be set aside not only because the arbitration agreement was invalid (ground (a), see above), but also because the award in that case is contrary to public policy (ground (e)).[389]

7. Partial Setting Aside

As mentioned, while Article 1065(5) DCCP specifically provides that, if the arbitral tribunal has awarded in excess of, or differently from, what was claimed, the arbitral award shall be partially set aside to the extent that the part of the award which is in excess of or different from the claim can be separated from the remaining part of the award, partial setting aside is possible also in the case of application of the other grounds for setting aside. From case law it follows that it is possible to apply to have an arbitral award partially set aside if the award contains decisions which are not inextricably entwined, so that a certain part of the award can be set aside, while the remainder of the award, not being insep-arably connected, can be upheld.[390] For instance, in an arbitration with two defendants, the court may set aside the award insofar as it concerns one of the defendants (e.g. for lack of a valid arbitration agreement), while upholding the award in regard to the other defendant.[391] Also, if the fundamental right to be heard is violated in regard to one of many claims, the award can be upheld for the decision on the other claims. In our view the courts should opt for partial settings

---

[386] ECJ 26 Oct. 2006, C-168/05 (Elisa María Mostaza Claro v. Centro Móvil Milenium SL), European Court reports 1999, I-10421.

[387] Dutch courts are required to do so, see e.g. HR 3 Dec. 2004, NJ 2005, 118 (Vreugdenhil/Floraholland); Amsterdam Court of Appeal, 12 Oct. 2000, NJ 2002, 111.

[388] It also prevents that arbitrators are faced with an impossible dilemma: either apply the EC rules *ultra vires* and face setting aside on the basis of Art. 1065(1)(c) DCCP, or render an award in violation of EC rules and face setting aside on the basis of Art. 1065(1)(e) DCCP. See also Burg. Rv, 2006 (H.J. Snijders), Art. 1054 DCCP, note 2. See for an application ex officio by an arbitral tribunal NAI 3 Sep. 2007, TvA 2008, 3.

[389] Parliamentary History TK 1983-1984, 18.464, No. 3, 29.

[390] HR 20 Jan. 2006, NJ 2006, 77 (ASB/Sagro).

[391] Ibid.

aside where possible, given the restraint that courts must apply in setting aside proceedings.

ARTICLE 1066 DCCP – SUSPENSION OF ENFORCEMENT

1. An application for setting aside shall not suspend the enforcement of the award.
2. However, the court which decides on an application for setting aside may, at the request of either party, if it considers the request to be justified, suspend enforcement until a final decision is made on the application for setting aside.
3. A copy of the request for suspension shall be communicated by the Court Clerk to the other party without delay.
4. The court shall decide on the request after the other party has been given an opportunity to be heard.
5. Upon granting the request, the court may order the petitioner to give security. Upon denying the request, the court may order the other party to give security.
6. If enforcement is suspended, either party may request the court to lift the suspension. The provisions of paragraphs (3) to (5) inclusive shall apply accordingly.

1. General Comments

Article 1066(1) DCCP provides that an application to set aside an award does not suspend the enforcement of the award. However, the court which decides on an application for setting aside may, at the request of either party, if it considers the request to be justified, suspend enforcement until a final decision is made on the application for setting aside (Article 1066(2) DCCP).[392] Whether a request is justified is at the discretion of the court, which makes its decision based on the interests of the parties and its prima facie analysis of the merits of the application to set aside.[393] It is assumed that suspension of enforcement not only stays the forced execution of the award, but also the *execution par suite d'instance*, which includes, for instance, the situation in which a party is requested to produce evidence based on the award.[394]

A request for suspension must be made by petition. The clerk of the court must send a copy of the petition requesting suspension to the other party

---

[392] The competent court may either be the District Court, the Court of Appeal or the Supreme Court, depending upon the stage of the proceedings to set aside an award.

[393] HR 21 Mar. 1997, NJ 1998, 206 (Benetton/Eco Swiss).

[394] G.J. Meijer 2008 (T&C Rv), Art. 1066 DCCP, note 1.

forthwith (Article 1066(3) DCCP). The court decides on the request for suspension after it has given the other party or parties the opportunity to be heard, which means that the other party will have the opportunity to file a statement of defence (Article 1066(4) DCCP). Thereafter, the parties have a right to an oral hearing. The decision by the court is subject to appeal to the Court of Appeal, which in turn is subject to appeal to the Supreme Court. The request for suspension does not suspend the award. As long as the court has not decided on the request, the award may be executed. However, a party against whom enforcement is sought could ask the summary proceedings judge for an injunction to stay the execution until the court has decided on a request for suspension, and it is likely that – if a prima facie bona fide request for suspension is made – the summary proceedings judge would grant such an injunction.

When granting the request for suspension, the court may order the petitioner to provide security, normally in the form of a bank guarantee. Upon denying the request, the court may order the other party to give security (Article 1066(5) DCCP). In both cases the security is meant to protect the party, who in the end wins the proceedings to set aside an award, against the risk that the opposing party by that time no longer has sufficient means to either pay the amount ordered by the tribunal or to pay compensation for wrongfully enforcing an arbitral award that in the end is set aside. Parties are well advised to ask the court to determine that, if a party fails to give the security in the form or timing as ordered, the other party may execute the award, or, as the case may be, that the enforcement is suspended.

If enforcement is suspended, either party may request the court to lift the suspension, in which case the same procedure applies as for a request for suspension (Article 1066(6) DCCP). Whether to lift the suspension is again up at the discretion of the court, which should base its decision on the interests of the parties and its prima facie analysis of the merits of the application to set aside the award. At the time the court rules on the request to lift the suspension, the interests of the parties and the court's prima facie analysis of the merits of the application to set aside may have changed in such a way that lifting the suspension is warranted. The interests of the parties may have changed as a result of new facts and circumstances. The (prima facie) analysis of the merits of the application to set aside may have changed in view of the possibility that during the original request for suspension the grounds for setting aside were not clearly argued, but have been elaborated on thereafter.

A party may have an urgent interest in suspending the execution of the arbitral award directly after it has been rendered, while on the other hand that party may wish to thoroughly prepare the application to set aside. In such case it is possible to ask the President (*voorzieningenrechter*) of the District Court to suspend the execution of the arbitral award, even though an application for setting aside has not (yet) been made.[395]

---

[395] HR 3 Jan. 1997, NJ 1998, 127 (Prudential/Diepgrond).

ARTICLE 1067 DCCP – CONSEQUENCES OF SETTING ASIDE

Unless the parties have agreed otherwise, as soon as a decision setting aside the award has become final, the jurisdiction of the court shall revive.

---

1. General Comments

The Dutch arbitration act does not contain a provision on remission. The courts cannot refer a case in which they have set aside an award back to arbitration.[396] When a judgment setting aside the award has become final, the courts regain jurisdiction in regard to the matters dealt with in the respective arbitration (Article 1067 DCCP). The judgment setting aside the arbitral award becomes final if no ordinary remedy is available against it – i.e. if appeal and Supreme Court appeal are exhausted or no longer available.

The parties may agree, however, that the jurisdiction of the court does not revive. They can agree – both beforehand and after the award has been set aside – that the arbitration agreement becomes operative again and submit the case to arbitration.[397] Remarkably, this is rarely done in practice.

There are good reasons for parties to provide that the jurisdiction of the courts does not revive. For instance, the revival of the jurisdiction of the courts may be particularly impractical where a partial final award is partially set aside. In that case, a part of the proceedings will be continued before the tribunal, whereas the part which has been set aside, will start from scratch in state courts (potentially in three instances), with the inevitable risks of conflicting decisions. In addition, the parties may also want to stick to arbitration in international cases involving multiple parties where it may be difficult to establish which state courts have jurisdiction. Moreover, the parties may simply want to start arbitration again, since it respects their original agreement to arbitrate their disputes. Article 1067 DCCP presumes that the parties no longer wish to use arbitration, if it has 'failed' once, but in practice that presumption is often incorrect. The parties, or at least one of them, may not wish to refer the case back to the same arbitrators if the award is set aside on the basis of one of the grounds mentioned in Article 1065(1) DCCP, since this means that the arbitrators have made a (grave) mistake.[398]

---

[396] The Draft Bill contains a new Art. 1065A which provides for remission. It enables the courts to refer a case back to the tribunal, allowing them to redress the ground for setting aside. See Art. 1065A of the Draft Bill.

[397] It should be noted that this is different from remission. Remission generally entails that a court does *not* set aside the award, but suspends the proceedings to set aside in order to give the arbitral tribunal the opportunity to resume the arbitral proceedings in order to eliminate the ground for setting aside.

[398] Though in cases of partial setting aside it may be practical to have one and the same tribunal decide on the entire dispute.

Nevertheless, the parties may still want to refer the case to arbitration again, starting new arbitral proceedings with new arbitrators being appointed. If the parties wish to do so, as the law currently stands,[399] the parties would have to provide in their arbitration agreement that in case of setting aside[400] the arbitration agreement remains in force. If the parties do so in an arbitration clause that refers to NAI arbitration, the NAI should administer the case just as it would administer any other case. This may be different where the parties provide that in case of setting aside, the case will be referred to the same arbitrators. There is much to be said for the position that in such case the original tribunal should again decide on (the part of) the case that has been set aside. After all, setting aside typically involves situations in which the arbitrators have not fully fulfilled their mandate, so that in the contractual relationship with the parties, they are obliged to again render an award, taking into account the court judgment in the proceedings to set aside.

---

[399] The Draft Bill provides that if the award is set aside, the arbitration agreement remains in force, except that the jurisdiction of the courts revives if the award is set aside on the basis of Art. 1065(1)(a) DCCP. See Art. 1067 DCCP of the Draft Bill.

[400] Save, of course, for the setting aside on the basis of the absence of a valid arbitration agreement (Art. 1065(1)(a) DCCP).

CHAPTER 2

REVOCATION

Although proceedings to set aside an award are addressed in Article 1065(1) DCCP, additional grounds for setting aside may be found in Article 1068 DCCP, which deals with revocation. Article 1068 DCCP makes it possible to set aside an award which is wholly or partially based on fraud or forgery of documents, or if relevant documents have been withheld. In this respect, Dutch law deviates from the UNCITRAL Model Law, which does not contain any similar provisions. When discussing proposals for the Model Law, the UNCITRAL Secretariat, however, did recommend including additional grounds for setting aside, amongst others for the situation that new facts or evidence have been discovered or that the award was improperly procured by the other party by fraud, bribery or forgery.[401] These grounds were all rejected by the Working Group. It was considered that grounds for setting aside should be limited to grounds for refusing recognition and enforcement under the New York Convention. Also, it was contemplated that the additions suggested were all covered by the 'public policy' ground for refusing recognition and enforcement (Article V(2)(b) New York Convention).[402] Whether indeed all cases of fraud or forgery of documents, or the withholding of relevant documents will be vindicated under the 'public policy' ground, is open to doubt. More importantly, the time limit for setting aside may have lapsed, before the fraud or forgery of documents, or withholding of relevant documents is discovered. For that reason, too, revocation serves its own purpose. Unless the parties have opted for prorogation of proceedings to set aside an award (see Article 1065 DCCP, note 3 above), parties cannot file claims for setting aside (based on of the grounds of Article 1065(1) DCCP) and for revocation in the same court proceedings, since an application for revocation must be brought before a Court of Appeal, whereas the application for setting aside must be made to a District Court.

---

[401] Comments on Art. 34 Model Law, in H.M. Holtzmann & J.E. Neuhaus, *A Guide to the UNCITRAL Model Law on International Commercial Arbitration* (Deventer, Kluwer Law and Taxation Publishers, 1989), 912 et seq.

[402] Ibid., 913-914.

A successful claim for revocation leads to the award being set aside. Under the New York Convention the recognition and enforcement of awards made in the Netherlands may therefore also be refused on the ground that the award has been suspended or set aside on a ground for revocation. One of the grounds for refusing recognition and enforcement is, in particular, suspension or setting aside of the award in the country of origin (Article V(1)(e) New York Convention).

Article 1068 DCCP has seldom been used. For case law, reference may be made to the provisions on revocation of court decisions (Articles 381-392 DCCP), which contain the same grounds for revocation. Article 1068 DCCP is based on these provisions.

ARTICLE 1068 DCCP – REVOCATION OF THE AWARD IN CASE OF FRAUD, FORGERY OR NEW DOCUMENTS

1. Revocation of the award can take place only on one or more of the following grounds:
   (a) the award is wholly or partially based on fraud which is discovered after the award is made and which is committed during the arbitral proceedings by or with the knowledge of the other party;
   (b) the award is wholly or partially based on documents which, after the award is made, are discovered to have been forged;
   (c) after the award is made, a party obtains documents which would have had an influence on the decision of the arbitral tribunal and which were withheld as a result of the acts of the other party.
2. An application for revocation shall be brought before the Court of Appeal which would have had jurisdiction to decide on an appeal relating to the application for setting aside mentioned in Article 1064, in corresponding application of Article 1064(3) or if this will result in a later date within three months after the fraud or forgery has become known or the party has obtained the new documents. If the party that has reason to apply for revocation dies within the term mentioned in the first sentence of this paragraph, Article 341 shall apply accordingly. The proceedings are commenced with the issuance of a writ of summons in conformity with the requirements of Article 111 and are conducted in the manner determined by Book One, Title Two. The provisions of Article 1066 shall apply accordingly.
3. If the judge considers the ground(s) for revocation to be correct, he wholly or partially sets aside the arbitral award. The provisions of Article 1067 shall apply accordingly.

1. General Comments

Article 1064(1) DCCP provides that an application for revocation of an award can only be made for an award which is final or partially final and which has res judicata effect (i.e. not open to arbitral appeal). An application for revocation can also be made against an award in summary arbitral proceedings.[403] These requirements are discussed above in the comments on Article 1064(1) DCCP. Article 1068 DCCP contains the grounds for revocation and the procedure that has to be followed.

2. Procedure

Revocation proceedings are commenced with the issuance of a writ of summons and are conducted in accordance with the rules applicable to litigation in first instance (Articles 78-260 DCCP), albeit that the competent court in first instance is the Court of Appeal.[404] This means that there is only one fact-finding instance, after which only appeal to the Supreme Court is possible, which is, in short, limited to review on errors in law, not in fact.

The time limit for issuing the writ of summons is three months. This time limit may start on three different dates. Equal to the time limit for the application to set aside, the writ of summons must be served (i) within three months after the date of deposit of the award with the court clerk's office, *or* (ii) within three months after the award (together with leave for enforcement) is officially served by the party seeking enforcement of the award (see Article 1064(3) DCCP above). Since the time limit for setting aside may have lapsed, before the fraud or forgery of documents, or withholding of relevant documents has been discovered, Article 1068 DCCP provides that the writ may be served (iii) within three months after the fraud or forgery has become known or the party has obtained the new documents. If a party is a natural person and dies within any of these time limits, his heirs may use an additional limitation period.[405]

Although the text of Article 1068 DCCP may suggest otherwise, Article 1068 DCCP does not lead to the revocation of the award, but to the award being set aside. In this respect, the provisions for revocation in arbitration cases are different from those for court decisions, which provide for the reopening of the case and the possibility that the court revokes the contested decision and gives a new decision on the merits of the case (Articles 382-391 DCCP).[406] This is different for arbitration. If the arbitral award is set aside based on a ground for

---

[403] Parliamentary History Revision DCCP, 2002, 474.

[404] Proceedings to set aside are also conducted in accordance with the rules applicable to litigation, but proceedings to set aside are conducted in three instances (District Court, Court of Appeal and Supreme Court).

[405] Article 1068 DCCP refers to Art. 341 DCCP, on the basis of which a three-month period starts to run as of the date on which the party died, which period may be extended by a maximum of four months.

[406] Art. 1068 formerly adopted the same procedure, but this was changed in a revision of the DCCP.

revocation, the party having initiated the arbitration will have to start from scratch by initiating proceedings before state courts (Article 1068(3) in conjunction with Article 1067 DCCP). The parties may agree, however, that the jurisdiction of the courts does not revive if they agree to submit the case to arbitration again (Article 1068(3) in conjunction with Article 1067 DCCP). The NAI Rules do not provide for this and in practice parties do not do so either, but there are good grounds for the parties to agree that – after the award has been set aside – the case will go back to arbitration (see the comments on Article 1067 DCCP above). This is even truer for revocation. As mentioned above, the parties, or at least one of them, may not wish that the case be referred back to the same arbitrators, if the award is set aside on the basis of one of the grounds mentioned in Article 1065(1) DCCP, since this means that the arbitrators have made a (grave) mistake. This is different for an award being setting aside based on a ground mentioned in Article 1068(1) DCCP, in which case the reason for setting aside lies with one of the parties. Another reason why referral to the same arbitrators is desirable is that these arbitrators do not have to redo the entire case, but merely decide whether the grounds for revocation presented lead to a different outcome of the case.[407]

As with proceedings to set aside, revocation proceedings do not suspend the enforcement of an award (Article 1068(2) in conjunction with Article 1066(1) DCCP). However, the court which decides on the revocation may, upon a justified request thereto, suspend enforcement until a final decision is made on the revocation (Article 1068(2) in conjunction with Article 1066(2) DCCP). The provisions on suspension of enforcement are the same as those for proceedings to set aside (see the comments on Article 1066 DCCP above), save that, of course, the request for suspension should be made to the Court of Appeal instead of the District Court.

Article 1068(3) DCCP provides that the court may wholly or partially set aside the arbitral award if it finds the grounds for revocation to be correct. The provision does not contain criteria in regard to the question of whether an award should be set aside completely or only partially. A court could apply the same criterion as has been established for proceedings to set aside, by partially setting aside the part(s) of the award containing decisions which are not inextricably entwined, so that a certain part of the award can be set aside, while the remainder of the award, not being inseparably connected, can be upheld (see the comments on Article 1065 DCCP above). In cases of wilful acts of fraud or forgery, the court may however feel tempted to penalize the party guilty of such conduct by wholly setting aside an award, even where the award is only partially based on such circumstances.

---

[407] The Arts 1065A and 1067 of the Draft Bill apply to revocation as well. See Art. 1068(3) of the Draft Bill in TvA 2005, 112.

3.   Ground for Revocation: Fraud

Revocation of the award can take place if the award is wholly or partially based on fraud. The Dutch text reads '*bedrog*', which could also be translated as 'deceit'.

The term fraud, as used in Article 1068 DCCP, has a broad meaning. Concealment and non-disclosure of relevant facts could also be considered as fraud.[408] Fraud includes the soliciting of false witness statements.[409] Fraud also includes situations in which a party's dishonest course of action during the proceedings precludes that facts are revealed, which could have been beneficial for the other party.[410]

Whether the award is based on fraud is a question of causality. Even if the alleged fraud has taken place, there is no basis for revocation if the award would not have been rendered differently, either in regard to its reasoning or in regard to the decisions in the operative part (dictum) of the award, if the fraudulent acts had not taken place.[411]

However, as the Supreme Court decided in one of its *Benetton* decisions, it is not required that it is *certain* that the alleged fraud would have led to a different decision; whether that is the case should be determined in subsequent proceedings on the merits.[412] This decision was made under the previous text of Article 1068 DCCP (which was amended in 2002), which provided for reopening of the case. After reopening, the parties would continue the already existing debate. The court could either deny the claim for revocation, or revoke the contested decision and give a new decision. Under the new text of Article 1068 DCCP, the grounds for revocation do not lead to a reopening of the case, but to setting aside the award, after which entirely new proceedings must be initiated. The consequences under the new text of Article 1068 DCCP are therefore more severe: the parties must start from scratch, even though it is not certain that the decision will be different.[413]

The fraud must be committed during the arbitral proceedings by or with the knowledge of the other party. It is not required that the fraud be contained in formal submissions to the tribunal. It could also be included in correspondence between the parties or with the tribunal.[414]

---

[408]   See for instance the Amsterdam Court of Appeal, 23 Nov. 2000, TvA 2001, 187-189, with an annotation by W.D.H. Asser.

[409]   Parliamentary History Revision DCCP, 2002, 475.

[410]   HR 4 Nov. 1996, NJ 1998, 45 (Goosen/Goosen); Parliamentary History Revision DCCP, 2002, 475.

[411]   HR 21 Mar. 1997, NJ 1998, 206 (Benetton/Eco Swiss).

[412]   Ibid.

[413]   This is clearly the intention of the legislature; see Parliamentary History Revision DCCP, 2002, 576-577.

[414]   Parliamentary History Revision DCCP, 2002, 475.

Only fraud which is discovered after the award is made can be a ground for revocation. If the fraud is discovered during the arbitral proceedings or could have been discovered by the deceived party after reasonable inquiry, the award will not be set aside for reasons of fraud.[415] In that case the party should bring the fraud to the attention of the tribunal in the arbitration. Reasonable inquiry does not mean that a party must adopt a thorough investigation, however.[416]

If a party suspects that the other party has committed fraud before the award is rendered, this party may report this to the tribunal, stating the reasons upon which the suspicion is based. It may do so even if the fraud relates to a part of the dispute, on which the tribunal has already given an interim award or partial final award. Arbitrators must give that party the opportunity to state its case in regard to the alleged fraud, and should give the other party the opportunity to respond. If the tribunal agrees that fraud has been committed and finds that this influenced their decision when rendering the interim award or partial final award, then the tribunal should render an award in which it reconsiders its decision.[417]

4. Ground for Revocation: Forged Documents

An award may be set aside if it is wholly or partially based on documents which, after the award is made, are discovered to have been forged. Documents are forged if they turn out to be false or untruthful. A typical example includes the pre-dating of written evidence. Untruthful witness statements could also be a basis for setting aside on this ground, though no case law has been reported yet. It is ultimately up to the court to decide whether the evidence brought before it warrants the conclusion that the documents are false.

5. Ground for Revocation: Documents Withheld

An award can also be set aside if, after the award is made, a party obtains documents which would have had an influence on the decision of the arbitral tribunal and which were withheld as a result of the acts of the other party. It is not required that the documents be withheld with fraudulent intent (in which the claim for revocation could also be based on fraud).[418] A court will have to assess whether the documents would have had an influence on the decision of the arbitral tribunal. It does not have to be certain that the documents would have been decisive – since a court cannot know for certain what the arbitrators would have done.[419]

---

[415] Parliamentary History Revision DCCP, 2002, 576.

[416] HR 20 Jun. 2003, NJ 2004, 569 (Waterschappen/Milieutech Beheer).

[417] Ibid.

[418] Parliamentary History Revision DCCP, 2002, 475.

[419] Parliamentary History Revision DCCP, 2002, 577.

CHAPTER 3

RECOGNITION AND ENFORCEMENT

The NAI rules do not include an express provision, stating that parties undertake to carry out the award without delay, as opposed to, for example, the ICC Rules and the UNCITRAL Rules.[420] Dutch arbitration law does not contain such a rule either. Nevertheless, arbitral awards are generally complied with voluntarily and practice shows that there is little use of enforcement proceedings in state courts. There is a firm understanding that arbitration is meant to arrive (within a reasonable time) at a binding award that is carried out without delay.[421]

However, if the losing party fails to abide by the award, the winning party needs to take measures to enforce the award. Typically, a losing party may refuse to abide by the award because it has started proceedings to set aside the award, but which, in principle, does not suspend the res judicata effect of the award (see the comments on Article 1066 DCCP above).

The arbitral tribunal has no role in the execution of its decision.[422] Article 1058(2) DCCP provides that, when the arbitral tribunal has rendered its final award and the award has been deposited, the arbitrators are *functus officio*. The NAI Rules provide that the mandate of the tribunal ends when it renders its final award (see the comments on Article 43(2) NAI Rules).[423] An arbitral award only becomes enforceable after a leave for enforcement (exequatur) is granted by the President (*voorzieningenrechter*) of the District Court. Once the exequatur has

---

[420] See Art. 28.6 ICC Rules ('By submitting the dispute to arbitration under these rules, the parties undertake to carry out any award immediately and without delay...') and Art. 32.2 UNCITRAL Rules ('...The parties undertake to carry out the award without delay').

[421] See also Art. 50 NAI Rules.

[422] An arbitral tribunal which is not yet released from its mandate may take measures which can effectively aid the winning party in enforcing its decision against the losing party, should the latter refuse to comply voluntarily. For instance, if a partial final award has been rendered, in which a party is ordered to perform in a certain way, but refuses to do so, the winning party may request the tribunal to impose a penalty on such non-performance. These are no formal execution measures however – a party would still have to obtain an exequatur from a court if it wishes to impose a penalty. See, in regard to the imposition of a penalty by an arbitral tribunal, Art. 421 NAI Rules, note 2.

[423] In practice, this is at most a few days earlier than the date following from Art. 1058(2) DCCP, since the Administrator will file the award without delay (Art. 50(1) NAI Rules).

been granted, the arbitral award may be enforced in the Netherlands in the same way as a judgment by a Dutch state court.

The Dutch arbitration act distinguishes between the enforcement of arbitral awards rendered in the Netherlands[424] (Articles 1062 and 1063 DCCP) and arbitral awards rendered outside the Netherlands (Articles 1075 and 1076 DCCP). We will first discuss the legal regime applicable to arbitral awards rendered within the Netherlands and subsequently the regime for awards rendered outside the Netherlands.

Article 1062 DCCP – Granting Leave for Enforcement

1. Enforcement in the Netherlands of a final or partial final arbitral award which is not open to appeal to a second arbitral tribunal, or which is declared provisionally enforceable, or a final or partial award rendered on arbitral appeal, can take place only after the President of the District Court with whose Registry the original of the award shall be deposited by virtue of Article 1058(1), has, in pursuance of a request of one of the parties, granted leave for enforcement.

2. Leave for enforcement shall be recorded on the original of the arbitral award or, if no deposit of the arbitral award has taken place, shall be laid down in a decision. The Court Clerk shall communicate without delay to the parties a certified copy of the arbitral award on which leave for enforcement is recorded or a certified copy of the decision in which leave for enforcement is granted.

3. If an appeal can be lodged from the award to a second arbitral tribunal, leave for enforcement of an award rendered at first instance which is not declared provisionally enforceable may be granted only after the time limit for lodging the appeal to a second arbitral tribunal has lapsed without the appeal having been lodged or earlier, if the right to appeal is renounced in writing.

4. If the President of the District Court grants leave for enforcement, the means of recourse mentioned in Article 1064(1) shall be the only means of recourse available to the respondent. The setting aside or the revocation of an arbitral award causes by operation of law the annulment of any leave for enforcement.

1. General Comments

The execution within the Netherlands of a final or partial final award made within the Netherlands can take place only after the President (*voorzieningenrechter*) of the District Court with whose clerk the original of the award has to be

---

[424] I.e. with its place of arbitration in the Netherlands, Art. 1073(1) DCCP.

deposited (on the basis of Article 1058(1) DCCP or Article 50 of the NAI Rules) has, at the request of one of the parties, granted leave for enforcement. A party is not required to retain local counsel to submit the request for leave for enforcement (Article 1071 DCCP). Once the leave for enforcement is granted, a party wishing to take enforcement measures must serve the arbitral award together with the leave for enforcement on the other party (Article 430 DCCP).

The President of the District Court may only grant leave for enforcement of a final or partial final award which is not (or no longer) open to appeal to a second arbitral tribunal, or which is declared provisionally enforceable, or a final or partial final award rendered on appeal. Article 1062(3) states in this respect that if the award is open to an appeal to a second arbitral tribunal, the leave for enforcement of an award rendered in first instance which is not declared provisionally enforceable may be granted only after the time for instituting the appeal to a second arbitral appeal has lapsed without the appeal having been instituted or earlier, if the right to appeal is renounced in writing.

The President of the District Court with whose office of the court clerk the original of the award has to be deposited is competent to grant the leave for enforcement. It is not decisive where the award *has actually been* deposited, but where the award has to be or should have been deposited on the basis of Article 1058 DCCP or Article 50 of the NAI Rules.

The enforcement procedure commences with a request for enforcement. In principle, the parties will not be summoned to appear before the President of the District Court. However, this may be different if the losing party, upon receipt of the award, has asked the District Court to be heard in the event a request for enforcement is filed.

The President of the District Court may not refuse the request for enforcement without giving the party requesting the enforcement the opportunity to elaborate on its request in an oral hearing. It is likely that in that event, the respondent will also be given the opportunity to be heard.

The President of the District Court will only perform a summary assessment of the award. The grounds on which the enforcement of an award may be refused are set out in Article 1063 DCCP and are discussed below.

On the basis of Article 1062(2) DCCP, the leave for enforcement shall be recorded on the original of the arbitral award or, if no deposit of the arbitral award has taken place, shall be laid down in a decision. A certified copy of the arbitral award on which the leave for enforcement is recorded, or a certified copy of the decision in which leave for enforcement is granted shall be communicated to the parties without delay by the clerk of the court. The same is true for the refusal to grant leave for enforcement (Article 1063(2) DCCP).

If the President of the District Court grants leave for enforcement, an application for revocation and for the setting aside of the award are the only means of recourse available to the respondent against such decision (Article 1062(4) DCCP). There is no appeal against the decision in which the leave for enforcement is granted. The setting aside or the revocation of an arbitral award automatically causes any leave for enforcement being set aside. If the request is denied, the party requesting leave for enforcement may appeal the decision within two months. If it is denied again, this party may lodge an appeal before the Supreme Court within two months after the decision of the Court of Appeal.

ARTICLE 1063 DCCP – REFUSAL OF LEAVE FOR ENFORCEMENT

1. Enforcement of an arbitral award may be refused by the President of the District Court only if the award or the manner in which it was made is manifestly contrary to public policy or good morals, or if enforcement is ordered notwithstanding the lodging of an appeal in violation of Article 1055, or if a penalty for non-compliance is imposed in violation of Article 1056. In the latter case, the refusal shall be limited to the enforcement of the penal sum.
2. The Court Clerk shall without delay send to the parties a certified copy of the President's decision to refuse leave for enforcement.
3. The petitioner may lodge an appeal to the Court of Appeal against refusal to grant leave for enforcement within two months after the date on which the decision is signed.
4. If refusal to grant leave for enforcement is affirmed on appeal, the time limit for recourse to the Supreme Court shall be two months after the date on which the decision on appeal is signed.
5. If leave for enforcement is granted on appeal or after recourse to the Supreme Court, the provisions of the first sentence of Article 1062(4) shall apply accordingly.

1. General Comments

The grounds for refusal of leave for enforcement are provided in Article 1063(1) DCCP. Enforcement may be refused if the award or the manner in which it was made is manifestly against public policy or good morals. The court has to make a prima facie assessment whether this is the case; the actual analysis whether the award must be set aside because it is contrary to public policy (either in substance or in the manner in which it was rendered) must be made in proceedings on the merits to set aside an award. The term 'public policy or good morals' is the same as the identically worded ground for setting aside in Article 1065(1)(e) DCCP.

Leave for enforcement can also be refused if the arbitral tribunal declares its award provisionally enforceable in violation of Article 1055 DCCP. This ground for refusal will seldom apply in NAI cases, since it is only relevant if the parties have provided for arbitral appeal proceedings, which they generally have not when they agree to NAI arbitration.

Finally, leave for enforcement can be refused if a penalty for non-compliance is imposed in violation of Article 1056 DCCP. This may be the case, for instance, where the parties have not asked for a penalty, or where a penalty is imposed for the payment of a monetary sum. In that case, the refusal shall be limited to the enforcement of the penalty. The claim as awarded can otherwise be enforced in full.

The clerk of the court will send a certified copy of the decision of the President of the District Court to refuse leave for enforcement to the parties without delay (Article 1063(2) DCCP).

The decision refusing enforcement may be appealed before the Court of Appeal within two months after the date on which the decision is signed (Article 1063(3) DCCP). If the refusal to grant leave for enforcement is affirmed on appeal, the time limit for an appeal to the Supreme Court will be two months after the date on which the decision on appeal is signed (Article 1063(4) DCCP). If leave for enforcement is granted on appeal or after recourse to the Supreme Court, an application for revocation and for the setting aside of the award are again the only means of recourse available to the respondent against such arbitral award (Article 1063(5) DCCP). Of course, a party can always address the court to ask for a suspension of the enforcement (see the comments on Article 1066 DCCP above).

ARTICLE 1075 DCCP – RECOGNITION AND ENFORCEMENT OF FOREIGN AWARD UNDER TREATIES

An arbitral award made in a foreign State to which a treaty concerning recognition and enforcement is applicable may be recognized and enforced in the Netherlands. The provisions of Articles 985 to 991 inclusive shall apply accordingly to the extent that the treaty does not contain provisions deviating therefrom and provided that the President of the District Court shall be substituted for the District Court and the time limit for appeal from his decision and for recourse to the Supreme Court shall be two months.

ARTICLE 1076 DCCP – RECOGNITION AND ENFORCEMENT OF FOREIGN AWARD WITHOUT TREATIES

1. If no treaty concerning recognition and enforcement is applicable, or if an applicable treaty allows a party to rely upon the law of the country in which recognition or enforcement is sought, an arbitral award made in a foreign State may be recognized in the Netherlands and its enforcement may be sought in the Netherlands,

upon submission of the original or a certified copy of the arbitration agreement and arbitral award, unless:

(A) the party against whom recognition or enforcement is sought, asserts and proves that:

    (a) a valid arbitration agreement under the law applicable thereto is lacking;

    (b) the arbitral tribunal is constituted in violation of the rules applicable thereto;

    (c) the arbitral tribunal has not complied with its mandate;

    (d) the arbitral award is still open to an appeal to a second arbitral tribunal, or to a court in the country in which the award is made;

    (e) the arbitral award has been set aside by a competent authority of the country in which that award is made;

(B) the court finds that the recognition or enforcement would be contrary to public policy.

2. The ground mentioned in paragraph (1)(A)(a) above shall not constitute a ground for refusal of recognition or enforcement if the party who invokes this ground has made an appearance in the arbitral proceedings and, before submitting a defence, has not raised the plea that the arbitral tribunal lacks jurisdiction on the ground that a valid arbitration agreement is lacking.

3. The ground mentioned in paragraph (1)(A)(b) above shall not constitute a ground for refusal of recognition or enforcement if the party who invokes this ground has participated in the constitution of the arbitral tribunal, or if he has not participated in the constitution of the arbitral tribunal, has made an appearance in the arbitral proceedings and, before submitting a defence, has not raised the plea that the arbitral tribunal lacks jurisdiction on the ground that the arbitral tribunal is constituted in violation of the applicable rules.

4. The ground mentioned in paragraph (1)(A)(c) above shall not constitute a ground for refusal of recognition or enforcement if the party who invokes this ground has participated in the arbitral proceedings without raising it, although it was known to him that the arbitral tribunal did not comply with its mandate.

5. If the award is in excess of, or different from, what was claimed, the arbitral award shall be capable of partial recognition or enforcement to the extent that the part of the award which is in excess of or different from the claim can be separated from the remaining part of the award.

6. The provisions of Articles 985 to 991 inclusive shall apply accordingly, provided that the President of the District Court shall be substituted for the District Court, the time limit for appeal from his decision and for recourse to the Supreme Court shall be two months, and no documents need be submitted evidencing the enforceability of the arbitral award in the country in which it is made.

7. If an application for the setting aside of an award made in a foreign State is made to a competent authority of the country in which the award is made, the provisions of Article 1066(2) to (6) inclusive shall apply accordingly when recognition or enforcement is sought in the Netherlands.

1.   Two Regimes for Recognition and Enforcement

Articles 1075 and 1076 DCCP contain the provisions concerning the recognition and enforcement of arbitral awards that have been rendered in a country outside the Netherlands (also 'foreign arbitral awards'). Although the number of NAI arbitrations with place of arbitration outside the Netherlands is relatively small, in such cases there is usually a connection with the Netherlands, for instance a holding company or other major assets are situated in the Netherlands. The provisions concerning the recognition and enforcement of arbitral awards are important for those cases.

Article 1075 DCCP provides that an arbitral award made in a foreign country to which a treaty concerning recognition and enforcement is applicable may be recognized and enforced in the Netherlands. The most important treaty for the recognition and enforcement of foreign arbitral awards, to which the Netherlands is a signatory, is the New York Convention.[425] The New York Convention applies to the recognition and enforcement of arbitral awards made in the territory of a state other than the state where the recognition and enforcement is sought. The Netherlands has made a declaration of reciprocity in which it confines the application of the Convention to arbitral awards made only in the territory of another contracting state.[426]

If no treaty can be applied, Article 1076 DCCP applies. Article 1076 may, however, also be relied on if the applicable treaty allows a party to rely on the law of the country in which recognition and enforcement is sought. This provision

---

[425] The Netherlands has also concluded several bilateral treaties that contain provisions concerning the enforcement of arbitral awards, such as the Belgian-Dutch Convention of 1925.

[426] Approval and Publication of New York Convention (Kingdom) Act, 14 Oct. 1963, Parliamentary History TK 1962-1963, 7055 (R 326).

reflects the possibility provided for in Article VII of the New York Convention (see below): the 'more-favourable law provision' which provides that a party may also seek to enforce an award on the basis of another treaty or the law of a country where the recognition and enforcement of the award is sought, if such law is more favourable in terms of allowing the recognition or enforcement. In practice, there is little use for this possibility, as the grounds for refusal of enforcement set out in Article 1076 DCCP are modelled on the New York Convention. As a consequence, there is hardly any difference between application of Article 1075 DCCP (i.e. the New York Convention) and 1076 DCCP. It has been noted in the literature that the requirements for the validity of the arbitration agreement are more stringent under the New York Convention (see Article 1 NAI Rules, note 3, in regard to the requirements for the validity of the arbitration agreement).[427] In a case where this could be at issue, a party could request the enforcement primarily on the basis of Article 1075 DCCP and the New York Convention and alternatively on the basis of Article 1076 DCCP (should the New York Convention requirements for the validity of the arbitration agreement, upon which the award is based, prove to be too restrictive). The likelihood of this scenario has further reduced as a result of the Recommendation regarding the interpretation of Article II, paragraph 2, and Article VII, paragraph 1, of the New York Convention adopted by UNCITRAL on 7 July 2006 at its 39th session and supported by the General Assembly of the United Nations.[428]

According to Article 1076(5) DCCP, partial leave for enforcement is possible if it is found that the award was in excess of, or different from, what was claimed. In that case, only the part which was not in excess of, or different from, what was claimed can be given leave for enforcement, if such part can be separated from that part which is. Under the New York Convention, partial enforcement should be considered possible as well.

Article 1076(7) DCCP provides (similar to Article VI of the New York Convention) that a court may suspend its decision on enforcement pending proceedings to set aside an award in the country where the award was made. In this event, the provisions on the suspension of enforcement contained in Article 1066(2)-(6) DCCP apply, which article is discussed in Part III, Chapter 1.

---

[427] For example G.J. Meijer 2008 (T&C Rv), Art. 1075 DCCP, note 2(b).

[428] Resolution 61/33, adopted at the 64th plenary meeting, 4 Dec. 2006. The Recommendation was drafted in recognition of the widening use of electronic commerce and enactments of domestic legislation as well as case law, which are more favourable than the New York Convention in respect of the form requirement governing arbitration agreements. It encourages states to apply Art. II(2) of the New York Convention, 'recognizing that the circumstances described therein are not exhaustive'. Art. II(2) provides that the requirement that the arbitration agreement is 'in writing' shall include an arbitral clause in a contract or an arbitration agreement, signed by the parties or contained in an exchange of letters or telegrams.

2.   Procedure to Obtain Leave for Enforcement

The procedure for obtaining a leave for enforcement of a foreign arbitral award is by and large the same as the procedure for obtaining leave for enforcement of a foreign court judgment. The Articles 985 to 991 DCCP contain the formalities of the enforcement of foreign enforceable titles. These provisions apply, save that the President (*voorzieningenrechter*) of the District Court is the competent judge (instead of the District Court itself), the time limit for appeal against his decision and for recourse to the Supreme Court is two months (instead of one) and that the requirement that documents need to be submitted which show that the decision is enforceable in the country of origin, does not apply to foreign arbitral awards (Article 1075, second sentence, and Article 1076(6) DCCP).

Article 985 DCCP determines that the decision must be enforceable on the basis of a treaty or on the basis of an Act. Accordingly, leave for enforcement can only be granted if the requirements of Article 1075 DCCP and the New York Convention, or the requirements of Article 1076 DCCP are met. Apart from the review that is necessary to verify that those requirements are satisfied, there will be no review of the merits of the award (no *revision au fond*). A court will only review whether one of the grounds for refusal of enforcement apply (those contained in the New York Convention, if enforcement is sought on the basis of Article 1075 DCCP, or those mentioned in Article 1076 DCCP). The party applying for the enforcement must submit the original arbitral agreement and the original arbitral award, or duly certified copies of these documents (Article IV(1) New York Convention; Article 1076(1) DCCP).

Article 986(1) DCCP (which is declared applicable by Articles 1075 and 1076 DCCP) determines that the request for leave for enforcement must be submitted by counsel. However, as explained above, counsel does not have to be retained for leave for enforcement of a domestic award (Article 1071 DCCP). Since Article IV of the New York Convention determines that 'There shall not be imposed substantially more onerous conditions or higher fees or charges on the recognition or enforcement of arbitral awards to which this Convention applies than are imposed on the recognition or enforcement of domestic arbitral awards', it can be argued that the use of counsel is not required for leave for enforcement under Article 1075, but is required for leave for enforcement under Article 1076 DCCP.

Article 1075 DCCP provides that the above procedure applies, to the extent that a treaty does not contain different provisions. The New York Convention contains such minor differences. One example is Article IV of the New York Convention, which provides that in addition to a duly authenticated original award or certified copy, also an original arbitral agreement or duly certified copy should be submitted.[429] Article 1076(1) DCCP also contains the additional

---

[429] Article 986 DCCP only provides that the request for leave for enforcement must be accompanied by a duly authenticated copy of the decision.

requirement to submit the original or duly authenticated copy of the arbitration agreement.

Article V New York Convention states that recognition and enforcement 'may' be refused. Article 1075 DCCP states that the award 'may' be recognized and enforced. The same is true for Article 1076 DCCP: the award 'can' be recognized and enforced. This prompts the question of whether courts have discretion when deciding whether to recognize or enforce a foreign arbitral award. Under Dutch law, if a ground for refusal exists, the courts must refuse recognition or enforcement when so requested. However, an exception may arise where a court is requested to enforce an award that has been set aside in the country of origin, but in regard to which the petitioner alleges that the proceedings to set aside were marked by fundamental flaws in procedural justice. In a well-reasoned case, the Amsterdam District Court held that the court at the place of arbitration (i.e. the competent authority), which is chosen by the parties, exclusively deals with the validity and setting aside of the arbitral award. If the award is set aside in the country of origin, the court should in principle respect this. However, the fact that an award is set aside in the country of origin does not automatically lead to the conclusion that enforcement abroad should be refused in all instances. In certain exceptional cases (such as violations of the right to a fair trial in the proceedings to set aside) a court may decide to ignore the setting aside of the award and grant leave for enforcement.[430]

3. Recognition and Enforcement on the Basis of the New York Convention[431]

The key provisions of the New York Convention in respect of the enforcement of arbitral awards are Articles IV and V.

Article IV contains the conditions that must be satisfied by a party applying for enforcement: such party shall supply a duly authenticated original award and an original arbitral agreement, or duly certified copies of these documents.

Article V contains the grounds for refusal of recognition and enforcement. As it is generally accepted, the court before which the enforcement of a foreign award is sought may not review an award on the merits but may only examine whether one of the grounds for refusal apply. These grounds include: the parties to the arbitration agreement were, under the law applicable to them, under some incapacity or the arbitration agreement is not valid under the law applicable thereto (Article V(1)(a)); the party against whom the award is invoked was not given proper notice

---

[430] Amsterdam District Court 28 Feb. 2008, No. 365094/KG RK 07-750 (Yukos/Rosneft).

[431] For a detailed discussion of the New York Convention, we refer to A.J. van den Berg, *The New York Arbitration Convention of 1958* (Deventer, Kluwer Law and Taxation Publishers, 1981), and, in regard to recent case law on refusals of enforcement under the New York Convention: A.J. van den Berg, 'New York Convention of 1958: Refusals of Enforcement', *ICC International Court of Arbitration Bulletin* 18, No. 2 (2007), 15-49.

of the appointment of the arbitrator or of the arbitral proceedings or was otherwise unable to present its case (Article V(2)(b)); the arbitral tribunal has not complied with its mandate (Article V(1)(c)); the composition of the arbitral tribunal was not in accordance with the agreement of the parties or, failing such agreement, was not in accordance with the law of the country where the arbitration took place (Article V(1)(d)); or the award has not yet become binding on the parties, or has been set aside or suspended by a competent authority of the country in which, or under the law of which, that award was made (Article V(1)(e)).

The court may also refuse recognition and enforcement if it finds that (a) the subject matter of the difference was not capable of settlement by arbitration or (b) the recognition or enforcement of the award would be contrary to the public policy of the country of enforcement (Article V(2)). The court must assess this on its own motion.

4. Recognition and Enforcement without Treaty

As mentioned before, Article 1076 DCCP applies if no treaty can be applied or if an applicable treaty allows a party to rely on the law of the country in which recognition and enforcement is sought.

Article 1076 DCCP contains the five grounds for refusal of enforcement, which are similar to those set out in Article V of the New York Convention (see above). These grounds are also similar, but not identical, to the grounds for setting aside of the award, as set out in Article 1065 DCCP. The grounds contained in Article 1076 DCCP are the following:

- A valid arbitration agreement under the law applicable thereto is lacking (Article 1076(1)(A)(a)).
- The arbitral tribunal has been constituted in violation of the rules applicable thereto (Article 1076(1)(A)(b)).
- The arbitral tribunal has not complied with its mandate (Article 1076(1)(A)(c)).
- The arbitral award is still open to an appeal to a second arbitral tribunal, or to a court in the country in which the award is made (Article 1076(1)(A)(d)).
- The arbitral award has been set aside by a competent authority of the country in which that award is made (Article 1076(1)(A)(e)).
- The court may also refuse the enforcement and recognition if it finds that the recognition or enforcement would be contrary to public policy (Article 1076(1)(B)). The enforcement of an award could be considered contrary to public policy if it was found, for example, that the subject matter of the dispute was not capable of settlement by arbitration. So also in this respect Article 1076 is on a par with the New York Convention, even though Article 1076 – contrary to Article V(2) New York Convention – does not explicitly provide the incapability of settlement by arbitration as ground for refusal of enforcement.

As with the New York Convention, the grounds for refusal to granting leave for enforcement will not be considered ex officio, except for the ground that enforcement would violate public policy.

The grounds mentioned in Article 1076(1)(A)(a)-(c) are virtually identical to those set out in Article V of the New York Convention. However, as to the ground that a valid arbitration agreement is lacking, this ground cannot lead to refusal of enforcement if the party seeking to rely on it has made an appearance in the arbitral proceedings and has not raised the plea that the tribunal lacks jurisdiction on the ground that a valid arbitration agreement is lacking before submitting a defence on the merits (Article 1076(3) DCCP). Similarly, the second ground for refusal, namely that an arbitral tribunal has been constituted in violation of the rules applicable thereto, cannot be invoked if the party invoking the ground has participated in the constitution of the arbitral tribunal or if a party who has not participated in the constitution has made an appearance but failed to raise the plea that the tribunal lacks jurisdiction in the arbitral proceedings before submitting a defence on the merits (Article 1076(4) DCCP). The third ground, failure to comply with its mandate, is also barred if a party was aware of this failure and failed to raise this argument in the arbitral proceedings (Article 1076(5) DCCP).

THE NETHERLANDS ARBITRATION ACT

The Netherlands Arbitration Act,* in force 1 December 1986 and current to 30 June 2004**

CODE OF CIVIL PROCEDURE
BOOK FOUR: ARBITRATION

Title One. Arbitration in the Netherlands

Section One. Arbitration Agreement and Appointment of Arbitrators

ARTICLE 1020
ARBITRATION AGREEMENTS IN GENERAL***

1. Parties may agree to submit to arbitration disputes which have arisen or may arise between them out of a defined legal relationship, whether contractual or not.

---

* Unofficial translation.

** On 1 January 2002, an important amendment to the first chapter of the Dutch Code of Civil Procedure entered into force. This amendment deals with the proceedings before the District Courts, Court of Appeals and Supreme Court. In order to reflect this amendment, some minor adaptations to the Dutch Arbitration Act were required. These changes are indicated in italics.

On 30 June 2004, the Emendation Act in implementation of the Directive on Electronic Commerce (*Aanpassingswet richtlijn inzake elektronische handel*) entered into force. This Act states in the New Sect. 6:227a of the Dutch Civil Code that for any agreement or contract which existing legislation requires to be made in written form in order to be valid, this condition is deemed to have been met also if the agreement was made by electronic means and

  – it may be consulted by parties;
  – the authenticity of the agreement is guaranteed to a sufficient degree;
  – the time the agreement was made may be established with sufficient certainty; and
  – the identifies of the parties to the agreement may be established with sufficient certainty.

In order to reflect this Act, a new sentence has been added to Art. 1021 of the Dutch Code of Civil Procedure stating that the existence of an arbitration agreement can also be proved by electronic means, in accordance with Sect. 6: 227a of the Dutch Civil Code. This change is indicated in italics.

*** Article headings do not appear in the original text of the Act; they are provided in the translation for reference purposes only.

2. The arbitration agreement mentioned in paragraph (1) includes both a submission by which the parties bind themselves to submit to arbitration an existing dispute between them and an arbitration clause under which parties bind themselves to submit to arbitration disputes which may arise in the future between them.
3. The arbitration agreement shall not serve to determine legal consequences of which the parties cannot freely dispose.
4. Parties may also agree to submit the following matters to arbitration:
   (a) the determination only of the quality or condition of goods;
   (b) the determination only of the quantum of damages or a monetary debt;
   (c) the filling of gaps in, or modification of, the legal relationship between the parties referred to in paragraph (1).
5. The term "arbitration agreement" includes an arbitration clause which is contained in articles of association or rules which bind the parties.
6. Arbitration rules referred to in an arbitration agreement shall be deemed to form part of that agreement.

ARTICLE 1021
FORM OF ARBITRATION AGREEMENT

The arbitration agreement must be proven by an instrument in writing. For this purpose an instrument in writing which provides for arbitration or which refers to standard conditions providing for arbitration is sufficient, provided that this instrument is expressly or impliedly accepted by or on behalf of the other party. *The arbitration agreement can also be proven by electronic means. Article 227a, paragraph 1 of the Civil Code shall apply accordingly.*

ARTICLE 1022
ARBITRATION AGREEMENT AND SUBSTANTIVE CLAIM BEFORE COURT; ARBITRATION AGREEMENT AND INTERIM MEASURES BY COURT

1. A court seized of a dispute in respect of which an arbitration agreement has been concluded shall declare that it has no jurisdiction if a party invokes the existence of the said agreement before submitting a defence, unless the agreement is invalid.
2. An arbitration agreement shall not preclude a party from requesting a court to grant interim measures of protection, or from applying to the President of the District Court[432] for a decision in summary proceedings in accordance

---

[432] In the Dutch text, the President of the District Court is now called the '*voorzieningenrechter*', which could be translated as 'interim measures judge' or 'provisional measures judge'. Since it is still customary in the context of international arbitration in the Netherlands to use the term 'President of the District Court', we retain this terminology.

with the provisions of article *254*. In the latter case the President shall decide the case in accordance with the provisions of article 1051.

3. *An arbitration agreement shall not preclude a party from requesting a court to order a preliminary witness examination, a preliminary expert report or a preliminary site visit, unless at the time of this request arbitrators have been appointed. Article 187(1) is applicable as if no arbitration agreement has been concluded.*

ARTICLE 1023
WHO MAY BE APPOINTED AS AN ARBITRATOR

Any natural person of legal capacity may be appointed as arbitrator. Unless the parties have agreed otherwise, no person shall be precluded from appointment by reason of his nationality.

ARTICLE 1024
SUBMISSION AGREEMENT: COMMENCEMENT OF ARBITRAL PROCEEDINGS

1. The submission agreement shall describe the matters which the parties wish to submit to arbitration.
2. The arbitration shall be deemed to have been commenced by the conclusion of the submission agreement, unless the parties have agreed to another method of commencement.
3. If the parties have agreed that a third person shall appoint the arbitrator or arbitrators, or any of them, either party shall send to the third person a copy of the submission agreement.

ARTICLE 1025
ARBITRATION CLAUSE: COMMENCEMENT OF ARBITRAL PROCEEDINGS

1. In the case of an arbitration clause, the arbitration shall be deemed to have been commenced on the day of receipt of a notice in writing in which a party informs the other that he is commencing arbitration. The said notice shall contain a description of the matters which the party commencing the arbitration wishes to submit to arbitration.
2. If the parties have agreed that a third person shall appoint the arbitrator or arbitrators, or any of them, the party who commences arbitration shall send to the third person a copy of the notice mentioned in paragraph (1).
3. The parties may agree that the arbitration shall be commenced in a different method from that provided for in this article.

ARTICLE 1026
NUMBER OF ARBITRATORS

1. The arbitral tribunal shall be composed of an uneven number of arbitrators. The arbitral tribunal may also consist of a sole arbitrator.
2. If the parties have not agreed on the number of arbitrators, or if the agreed method of determining that number is not carried out and the parties cannot reach agreement on the number, the number shall, at the request of either party, be determined by the President of the District Court.
3. If the parties have agreed on an even number of arbitrators, the arbitrators shall appoint an additional arbitrator who shall act as the chairman of the arbitral tribunal.
4. Failing agreement between the arbitrators in appointing the additional arbitrator, such arbitrator shall, unless the parties have agreed otherwise, be appointed, at the request of either party, by the President of the District Court.

ARTICLE 1027
APPOINTMENT OF ARBITRATORS

1. The arbitrator or arbitrators shall be appointed by any method agreed by the parties. The parties may entrust to a third person the appointment of the arbitrator or arbitrators or any of them. If no method of appointment is agreed upon, the arbitrator or arbitrators shall be appointed by consensus between the parties.
2. The appointment shall be made within two months after the commencement of the arbitration, unless the arbitrator or arbitrators have already been appointed. In the event, however, that any of the cases mentioned in article 1026(2) occurs, the period of two months shall start to run on the day on which the number of arbitrators is determined. The period for appointment shall be extended to three months if at least one of the parties is domiciled or has his actual residence outside the Netherlands. These periods may be shortened or extended by agreement between the parties.
3. If the appointment of the arbitrator or arbitrators is not made within the period prescribed in the preceding paragraph, the arbitrator shall, at the request of either party, be appointed by the President of the District Court. The other party shall be given an opportunity to be heard.
4. The President or the third person shall appoint the arbitrator or arbitrators without regard to the question whether or not there is a valid arbitration agreement. By participating in the appointment of the arbitrator or arbitrators, the parties do not forfeit the right to challenge the jurisdiction of the arbitral tribunal on the ground of absence of a valid arbitration agreement.

ARTICLE 1028
PRIVILEGED POSITION OF A PARTY IN APPOINTING ARBITRATORS

If the arbitration agreement gives one of the parties a privileged position with regard to the appointment of the arbitrator or arbitrators, the other party may, despite the method of appointment laid down in that agreement, request the President of the District Court within one month after the commencement of the arbitration to appoint the arbitrator or arbitrators. The other party shall be given an opportunity to be heard. The provisions of article 1027(4) shall apply accordingly.

ARTICLE 1029
ARBITRATOR'S ACCEPTANCE AND RELEASE OF MANDATE

1. An arbitrator shall accept his mandate in writing.
2. An arbitrator who has accepted his mandate may, at his own request, be released from his mandate either with the consent of the parties or a third person designated by the parties, or in the absence thereof, by the President of the District Court.
3. An arbitrator who has accepted his mandate may be released from his mandate by agreement between the parties.
4. An arbitrator who has accepted his mandate and who has become de jure or de facto unable to perform his mandate, may, at the request of either party, be released from his mandate by a third person designated by the parties, or in the absence of such third person, by the President of the District Court.

ARTICLE 1030
APPOINTMENT OF A SUBSTITUTE ARBITRATOR

1. Unless the parties have agreed otherwise, an arbitrator who has been released from his mandate in accordance with the provisions of article 1029(2), (3) or (4) shall be replaced pursuant to the rules applicable to the initial appointment. The same shall apply to an arbitrator who has died.
2. If the parties have named the arbitrator or arbitrators in the arbitration agreement, their replacement shall also take place in the cases prescribed in paragraph (1) above, unless the parties have agreed that the arbitration agreement shall terminate in such a case.
3. Unless the parties have agreed otherwise, the arbitral proceedings shall be suspended by operation of law in case of replacement. Unless the parties have agreed otherwise, the arbitral proceedings shall, after the suspension ceases, continue from the stage they had reached.

ANNEX

Article 1031
Termination of the Arbitral Tribunal's Mandate; Tribunal's Failure to Proceed

1. The parties may agree to terminate the mandate of the arbitral tribunal.
2. At the request of either party and after having heard the other party and the arbitrator or arbitrators, the third person designated by the parties, or in the absence thereof, the President of the District Court, may, having regard to all circumstances, terminate the mandate of the arbitral tribunal if, despite repeated reminders, the arbitral tribunal carries out its mandate in an unacceptably slow manner. In these circumstances, the jurisdiction of the court shall revive, unless the parties have agreed otherwise.

Article 1032
Death of a Party

1. Unless the parties have agreed otherwise, neither the arbitration agreement nor the mandate of the arbitral tribunal shall terminate by reason of the death of one of the parties.
2. The arbitral tribunal shall suspend the arbitral proceedings for such period as may be determined by it. The arbitral tribunal may, at the request of the legal successors of the deceased party, extend such period. The arbitral tribunal shall give the other party an opportunity to be heard in respect of such request.
3. Unless the parties have agreed otherwise, the arbitral proceedings shall, after any suspension, continue from the stage they had reached.

Article 1033
Challenge of an Arbitrator: Grounds

1. An arbitrator may be challenged if circumstances exist that give rise to justifiable doubts as to his impartiality or independence. A secretary engaged by an arbitral tribunal may be challenged on the same grounds; the provisions of article 1035 shall apply accordingly to such a challenge.
2. A party may only challenge an arbitrator appointed by him on grounds of which he has become aware after the appointment has been made.
3. A party may not challenge an arbitrator appointed by a third person or the President of the District Court if he has acquiesced in this appointment, unless he has become aware of the ground for challenge after the appointment has been made.

ARTICLE 1034
DUTY TO DISCLOSE

1. A prospective arbitrator or secretary who presumes that he could be challenged shall disclose in writing to the person who has approached him the existence of such grounds.
2. A person who has been appointed as arbitrator or secretary shall, if the parties have not previously been notified, immediately notify the parties as prescribed in the preceding paragraph.

ARTICLE 1035
CHALLENGE OF AN ARBITRATOR: PROCEDURE

1. The challenge and the grounds therefor shall be notified in writing by the challenging party to the challenged arbitrator, the other members of the arbitral tribunal, the other party and, if a third person has appointed the challenged arbitrator, this third person. The arbitral tribunal may suspend the arbitral proceedings as of the day of receipt of the notification.
2. If the challenged arbitrator does not withdraw within two weeks after the day of receipt of the notification, the President of the District Court shall, at the request of either party, decide on the merits of the challenge. If such request is not made within four weeks after the day of receipt of the notification, the right to challenge shall be barred and the arbitral proceedings, if suspended, shall continue from the stage they had reached.
3. If the challenged arbitrator withdraws, or if the challenge is upheld by the President of the District Court, the arbitrator shall, unless the parties have agreed otherwise, be replaced in accordance with the rules governing his initial appointment. The provisions of article 1030(2) and (3) shall apply accordingly.
4. If the challenged arbitrator or one or both of the parties is domiciled or has his actual residence outside the Netherlands, the periods mentioned in paragraph (2) above shall be six and eight weeks respectively.

Section Two. **The Arbitral Proceedings**

ARTICLE 1036
DETERMINATION OF RULES OF PROCEDURE

Subject to the provisions of this Title, the arbitral proceedings shall be conducted in such manner as agreed between the parties or, to the extent that the parties have not agreed, as determined by the arbitral tribunal.

ARTICLE 1037
PLACE OF ARBITRATION

1. The place of arbitration shall be determined by agreement of the parties, or failing such agreement, as determined by the arbitral tribunal. The determination of the place of arbitration establishes also the place where the award shall be made.
2. If the place of arbitration has not been determined either by the parties or the arbitral tribunal, the place of making the award as stated by the arbitral tribunal in the award shall be deemed to be the place of arbitration.
3. The arbitral tribunal may hold hearings, deliberate, and examine witnesses and experts at any other place, within or outside the Netherlands, which it deems appropriate.

ARTICLE 1038
REPRESENTATION AND ASSISTANCE

1. The parties may appear before the arbitral tribunal in person, be represented by a practising lawyer, or be represented by any other person expressly authorised in writing for this purpose.
2. The parties may be assisted in the arbitral proceedings by any persons they may choose.

ARTICLE 1039
EQUAL TREATMENT OF PARTIES; HEARING; RIGHT TO PRODUCE WITNESSES AND EXPERTS; PRODUCTION OF DOCUMENTS; RULES OF EVIDENCE

1. The parties shall be treated with equality. The arbitral tribunal shall give each party an opportunity to substantiate his claims and to present his case.
2. The arbitral tribunal shall, at the request of either party or on its own initiative, give the parties an opportunity of making an oral presentation.
3. The arbitral tribunal may, at the request of either party, allow a party to produce witnesses or experts. The arbitral tribunal shall have the power to designate one of its members to examine witnesses or experts.
4. The arbitral tribunal shall have the power to order the production of documents.
5. Unless the parties have agreed otherwise, the arbitral tribunal shall have discretion in the rules of evidence to be applied.

ARTICLE 1040
DEFAULT OF A PARTY

1. If the claimant, without showing good cause, fails to communicate his statement of claim or duly to explain the claim, in spite of having had a reasonable opportunity to do so, the arbitral tribunal may terminate the arbitral proceedings by means of an arbitral award.
2. If the respondent, without showing good cause, fails to submit his defence, in spite of having been given a reasonable opportunity to do so, the arbitral tribunal may render an award forthwith.
3. In the circumstances mentioned in paragraph (2) above, the arbitral tribunal shall render an award in favour of the claimant, unless it considers the claim to be unlawful or unfounded. Before rendering an award, the arbitral tribunal may require the claimant to produce evidence in support of one or more of his allegations.

ARTICLE 1041
EXAMINATION OF WITNESSES

1. If an examination of witnesses takes place, the arbitral tribunal shall determine the time and place of the examination and the manner in which the examination shall proceed. If the arbitral tribunal deems it necessary, it shall examine the witnesses *after they have sworn the oath to tell the whole truth and nothing but the truth, in the manner determined by the law.*
2. If a witness does not appear voluntarily or, having appeared, refuses to give evidence, the arbitral tribunal may allow a party who so requests, within a period of time determined by the arbitral tribunal, to petition the President of the District Court to appoint a judge-commissary before whom the examination of the witness shall take place. The examination shall take place in the same manner as in ordinary court proceedings. The Clerk of the District Court shall give the arbitrator or arbitrators an opportunity of attending the examination of the witness.
3. The Clerk of the District Court shall communicate without delay to the arbitral tribunal and the parties a copy of the record of the examination.
4. The arbitral tribunal may suspend the proceedings until the day on which it has received the record of the examination.

ARTICLE 1042
EXPERTS APPOINTED BY ARBITRAL TRIBUNAL

1. The arbitral tribunal may appoint one or more experts to give advice. The arbitral tribunal shall communicate as soon as possible to the parties a copy of the appointment and the terms of reference of the experts.

2. The arbitral tribunal may require a party to provide the experts with the information required by them and to give them the necessary cooperation.
3. Upon receipt of the expert's report, the arbitral tribunal shall provide a copy of the report to the parties without delay.
4. At the request of either party, the experts shall be examined at a hearing. A party wishing to make such request shall inform the arbitral tribunal and the opposing party thereof without delay.
5. The arbitral tribunal shall give the parties an opportunity to examine the experts and to produce their own experts.
6. The provisions of article 1041 (1) shall apply accordingly.

ARTICLE 1043
ORDER FOR PERSONAL APPEARANCE OF THE PARTIES

At any stage of the proceedings the arbitral tribunal may order the parties to appear in person for the purpose of providing information or attempting to arrive at a settlement.

ARTICLE 1044
REQUEST FOR INFORMATION ON FOREIGN LAW

1. The arbitral tribunal may, through the intervention of the President of the District Court at The Hague, ask for information as mentioned in article 3 of the European Convention on Information on Foreign Law, concluded at London, 7 June 1968 (Dutch Treaty Series 1968, 142). The President shall, unless he considers the request to be without merit, send the request without delay to the agency mentioned in article 2 of said Convention and notify the arbitral tribunal thereof.
2. The arbitral tribunal may suspend the proceedings until the day on which it has received the answer to its request for information.

ARTICLE 1045
THIRD PARTIES

1. At the written request of a third party who has an interest in the outcome of the arbitral proceedings, the arbitral tribunal may permit such party to join the proceedings, or to intervene therein. The arbitral tribunal shall send without delay a copy of the request to the parties.
2. A party who claims to be indemnified by a third party may serve a notice of joinder on such a party. A copy of the notice shall be sent without delay to the arbitral tribunal and the other party.

3. The joinder, intervention or joinder for the claim of indemnity may only be permitted by the arbitral tribunal, having heard the parties, if the third party accedes by agreement in writing between him and the parties to the arbitration agreement.

4. On the grant of a request for joinder, intervention, or joinder for the claim of indemnity, the third party becomes a party to the arbitral proceedings. Unless the parties have agreed thereon the arbitral tribunal shall determine the further conduct of the proceedings.

ARTICLE 1046
CONSOLIDATION OF ARBITRAL PROCEEDINGS

1. If arbitral proceedings have been commenced before an arbitral tribunal in the Netherlands concerning a subject matter which is connected with the subject matter of arbitral proceedings commenced before another arbitral tribunal in the Netherlands, any of the parties may, unless the parties have agreed otherwise, request the President of the District Court in Amsterdam to order a consolidation of the proceedings.

2. The President may wholly or partially grant or refuse the request, after he has given all parties and the arbitrators an opportunity to be heard. His decision shall be communicated in writing to all parties and the arbitral tribunals involved.

3. If the President orders consolidation in full, the parties shall in consultation with each other appoint one arbitrator or an uneven number of arbitrators and determine the procedural rules which shall apply to the consolidated proceedings. If, within the period of time prescribed by the President, the parties have not reached agreement on the above, the President shall, at the request of any of the parties, appoint the arbitrator or arbitrators and, if necessary, determine the procedural rules which shall apply to the consolidated proceedings. The President shall determine the remuneration for the work already carried out by the arbitrators whose mandate is terminated by reason of the full consolidation.

4. If the President orders partial consolidation, he shall decide which disputes shall be consolidated. The President shall, if the parties fail to agree within the period of time prescribed by him, at the request of any of the parties, appoint the arbitrator or arbitrators and determine which rules shall apply to the consolidated proceedings. In this event the arbitral tribunals before which arbitrations have already been commenced shall suspend those arbitrations. The award of the arbitral tribunal appointed for the consolidated arbitration shall be communicated in writing to the other arbitral tribunals involved. Upon receipt of this award, these arbitral tribunals shall continue the

arbitrations commenced before them and decide in accordance with the award rendered in the consolidated proceedings.

5. The provisions of article 1027(4) shall apply accordingly in the cases mentioned in paragraphs (3) and (4) above.

6. An award rendered under paragraphs (3) and (4) above shall be subject to appeal to a second arbitral tribunal if and to the extent that all parties involved in the consolidated proceedings have agreed upon such an appeal.

ARTICLE 1047
SECTION TWO NOT APPLICABLE TO QUALITY ARBITRATION

With the exception of the provisions of article 1037, the provisions of this Section shall not apply to arbitrations concerning the matters mentioned in article 1020(4)(*a*). In that case the proceedings shall be conducted in the manner agreed upon by the parties or, to the extent that the parties have not agreed thereon, as determined by the arbitral tribunal.

ARTICLE 1048
TIME LIMIT FOR MAKING THE AWARD

The arbitral tribunal is free to determine the time when the award shall be made.

Section Three. **The Arbitral Award**

ARTICLE 1049
TYPES OF AWARD

The arbitral tribunal may render a final award, a partial final award, or an interim award.

ARTICLE 1050
APPEAL TO SECOND ARBITRAL TRIBUNAL

1. An appeal from the arbitral award to a second arbitral tribunal is possible only if the parties have agreed thereto.

2. Unless the parties have agreed otherwise, an appeal to a second arbitral tribunal from a partial final award can be lodged only in conjunction with an appeal from the last final award.

3. Unless the parties have agreed otherwise, an appeal to a second arbitral tribunal from an interim award can be lodged only in conjunction with an appeal from a final or partial final award.

4. Unless the parties have agreed otherwise, an appeal to a second arbitral tribunal shall be lodged within three months after the date of deposit of the award with the Registry of the District Court.

ARTICLE 1051
SUMMARY ARBITRAL PROCEEDINGS

1. The parties may agree to empower the arbitral tribunal or its chairman to render an award in summary proceedings, within the limits imposed by article *254(1)*.
2. In the event that, notwithstanding such agreement, the case is brought before the President of the District Court in summary proceedings, he may, if a party invokes the existence of the said agreement, taking into account all circumstances, declare to have no jurisdiction by referring the case to the agreed summary arbitral proceedings, unless the said agreement is invalid.
3. A decision rendered in summary arbitral proceedings shall be regarded as an arbitral award to which the provisions of Sections Three to Five inclusive of this Title shall be applicable.
4. In the case of a referral to the summary arbitral proceedings mentioned in paragraph (2) above, no appeal may be lodged against the decision of the President of the District Court.

ARTICLE 1052
PLEAS AS TO THE JURISDICTION OF THE ARBITRAL TRIBUNAL

1. The arbitral tribunal shall have the power to decide on its own jurisdiction.
2. A party who appeared in the arbitral proceedings shall raise a plea that the arbitral tribunal lacks jurisdiction on the ground that there is no valid arbitration agreement, unless the plea is made on the ground that the dispute is not capable of settlement by arbitration by virtue of article 1020(3), before submitting a defence; thereafter that party will be barred from raising this plea in the arbitral proceedings or in proceedings before the court.
3. A party who has participated in the constitution of the arbitral tribunal may not, in the arbitral proceedings or in proceedings before the court, raise the plea that the arbitral tribunal lacks jurisdiction on the ground that the arbitral tribunal is constituted in violation of the applicable rules. A party who has made an appearance in the arbitral proceedings and who has not participated in the constitution of the arbitral tribunal, shall raise the plea that the arbitral tribunal lacks jurisdiction on the ground that the arbitral tribunal is constituted in violation of the applicable rules before submitting a defence; thereafter that party will be barred from raising this plea in the arbitral proceedings or in proceedings before the court.

4. Any decision in which the arbitral tribunal declares that it has jurisdiction can be challenged only by the means of recourse mentioned in article 1064(1) in conjunction with the challenge of a subsequent final or partial final award.
5. Unless the parties have agreed otherwise, the court shall have jurisdiction to try the case if the arbitral tribunal declares that it lacks jurisdiction.
6. Appeal to a second arbitral tribunal shall, if agreed, be allowed against both a decision of the arbitral tribunal that it has jurisdiction and a decision that it lacks jurisdiction. In such event the court shall have jurisdiction under paragraph (4) or (5) above only after a decision is made on appeal to the second arbitral tribunal or after the time limit for appeal has lapsed without the appeal having been lodged or earlier, if the right to appeal is renounced in writing.

ARTICLE 1053
SEPARABILITY OF THE ARBITRATION CLAUSE

An arbitration agreement shall be considered and decided upon as a separate agreement. The arbitral tribunal shall have the power to decide on the validity of the contract of which the arbitration agreement forms part or to which the arbitration agreement is related.

ARTICLE 1054
RULES APPLICABLE TO THE SUBSTANCE OF THE DISPUTE

1. The arbitral tribunal shall make its award in accordance with the rules of law.
2. If a choice of law is made by the parties, the arbitral tribunal shall make its award in accordance with the rules of law chosen by the parties. Failing such choice of law, the arbitral tribunal shall make its award in accordance with the rules of law which it considers appropriate.
3. The arbitral tribunal shall decide as *amiable compositeur* if the parties by agreement have authorised it to do so.
4. In all cases the arbitral tribunal shall take into account any applicable trade usages.

ARTICLE 1055
ENFORCEABILITY OF AWARD NOTWITHSTANDING
ARBITRAL APPEAL

Where an appeal from the award to a second arbitral tribunal is provided for, the arbitral tribunal may declare its award provisionally enforceable in cases where the court has the power to do so. The arbitral tribunal may determine that such enforceability of the award is subject to the giving of security.

ARTICLE 1056
PENALTY FOR NON-COMPLIANCE

The arbitral tribunal has the power to impose a penalty for non-compliance in cases where the court has such power. The provisions of articles 611*a* to 611*i* inclusive shall apply accordingly, although in the cases mentioned in article 611*d*, an application for the revocation, suspension or reduction of the penalty shall be made to the President of the District Court with whose Registry the original of the award shall be deposited in accordance with article 1058(1).

ARTICLE 1057
MAJORITY DECISION; REFUSAL OF MINORITY TO SIGN; FORM AND CONTENTS OF AWARD

1. Unless the parties have agreed otherwise, if the arbitral tribunal is composed of more than one arbitrator, it shall decide by a majority of votes.
2. The award shall be in writing and signed by the arbitrator or arbitrators.
3. If a minority of the arbitrators refuses to sign, the other arbitrators shall make mention thereof beneath the award signed by them. This statement shall be signed by them. A similar statement shall be made if a minority is incapable of signing and it is unlikely that this impediment will cease to exist within a reasonable time.
4. In addition to the decision, the award shall contain in any case:
   (a) the names and addresses of the arbitrator or arbitrators;
   (b) the names and addresses of the parties;
   (c) the date on which the award is made;
   (d) the place where the award is made;
   (e) the reasons for the decision, unless the award concerns merely the determination only of the quality or condition of goods as provided in article 1020(4)(*a*) or the recording of a settlement as provided in article 1069.

ARTICLE 1058
NOTIFICATION AND DEPOSIT OF AWARD; TERMINATION OF MANDATE OF ARBITRAL TRIBUNAL

1. The arbitral tribunal shall ensure that without delay:
   (a) a copy of any award, signed by an arbitrator or the secretary of the arbitral tribunal, is communicated to the parties;
   (b) the original of the final or partial final award is deposited with the Registry of the District Court within whose district the place of arbitration is located.

2. Without prejudice to the provisions of articles 1060 and 1061, the mandate of the arbitral tribunal shall terminate upon the deposit of the last final award with the Registry.

ARTICLE 1059
RES JUDICATA OF THE AWARD

1. Only a final or partial final arbitral award is capable of acquiring the force of *res judicata*. The award shall have such force from the day on which it is made.
2. If, however, an appeal to a second arbitral tribunal is provided for, the final or partial final award shall have the force of *res judicata* from the day on which the time limit for lodging appeal has lapsed or, if the appeal has been lodged, the day on which a decision is rendered on appeal, if and to the extent that the award rendered at first instance is affirmed on appeal.

ARTICLE 1060
RECTIFICATION AND CORRECTION OF THE AWARD

1. Not later than thirty days after the date of deposit of the award with the Registry of the District Court, a party may request in writing that the arbitral tribunal rectify in the award a manifest computing or clerical error.
2. If the details referred to in article 1057(4)(*a*) to (*d*) inclusive are stated incorrectly or are partially or wholly absent from the award, a party may, not later than thirty days after the date of deposit of the award with the Registry of the District Court, request in writing that the arbitral tribunal correct the mistake or omission.
3. A copy of the request mentioned in paragraph (1) or (2) above shall be communicated by the arbitral tribunal to the other party.
4. An arbitral tribunal may, not later than thirty days after the date of deposit of the award with the Registry of the District Court, also make on its own initiative the rectification or the correction mentioned in paragraph (1) or (2) above.
5. In the event that the arbitral tribunal makes the rectification or correction, it shall record and sign it on the original and copies of the award, or set it out in a separately signed document, which shall be treated as forming part of the award. The provisions of articles 1057(1) to (3) inclusive and 1058(1) shall apply accordingly.
6. If the arbitral tribunal rejects the request for rectification or correction, it shall inform the parties thereof in writing.
7. A request under this article does not suspend the enforcement or setting aside of the award unless the President or the District Court deems that there are serious reasons for so doing while a decision on the request is pending.

ARTICLE 1061

ADDITIONAL AWARD

1. If the arbitral tribunal has failed to decide on one or more matters which have been submitted to it, either party may, not later than thirty days after the date of deposit of the award with the Registry of the District Court, request the arbitral tribunal to render an additional award.
2. A copy of the request shall be communicated by the arbitral tribunal to the other party.
3. The arbitral tribunal shall give the parties an opportunity to be heard before deciding on the request.
4. An additional award shall be regarded as an arbitral award to which the provisions of Section Three to Five inclusive of this Title shall be applicable.
5. If the arbitral tribunal rejects a request for an additional award, it shall inform the parties accordingly in writing. A copy of this notification, signed by an arbitrator or the secretary of the arbitral tribunal, shall be deposited with the Registry of the District Court, in accordance with the provisions of article 1058(1).
6. If an appeal to a second arbitral tribunal has been agreed, the arbitral award rendered at first instance may only be supplemented on appeal. Any request for supplementation shall be made within the period of time applicable to the lodging of the appeal.

Section Four. Enforcement of the Arbitral Award

ARTICLE 1062

GRANTING LEAVE FOR ENFORCEMENT

1. Enforcement in the Netherlands of a final or partial final arbitral award which is not open to appeal to a second arbitral tribunal, or which is declared provisionally enforceable, or a final or partial award rendered on arbitral appeal, can take place only after the President of the District Court with whose Registry the original of the award shall be deposited by virtue of article 1058(1), has, in pursuance of a request of one of the parties, granted leave for enforcement.
2. Leave for enforcement shall be recorded on the original of the arbitral award or, if no deposit of the arbitral award has taken place, shall be laid down in a decision. The Court Clerk shall communicate without delay to the parties a certified copy of the arbitral award on which leave for enforcement is recorded or a certified copy of the decision in which leave for enforcement is granted.
3. If an appeal can be lodged from the award to a second arbitral tribunal, leave for enforcement of an award rendered at first instance which is not declared

provisionally enforceable may be granted only after the time limit for lodging the appeal to a second arbitral tribunal has lapsed without the appeal having been lodged or earlier, if the right to appeal is renounced in writing.

4. If the President of the District Court grants leave for enforcement, the means of recourse mentioned in article 1064(1) shall be the only means of recourse available to the respondent. The setting aside or the revocation of an arbitral award causes by operation of law the annulment of any leave for enforcement.

ARTICLE 1063

REFUSAL OF LEAVE FOR ENFORCEMENT

1. Enforcement of an arbitral award may be refused by the President of the District Court only if the award or the manner in which it was made is manifestly contrary to public policy or good morals, or if enforcement is ordered notwithstanding the lodging of an appeal in violation of article 1055, or if a penalty for non-compliance is imposed in violation of article 1056. In the latter case, the refusal shall be limited to the enforcement of the penal sum.
2. The Court Clerk shall without delay send to the parties a certified copy of the President's decision to refuse leave for enforcement.
3. The petitioner may lodge an appeal to the Court of Appeal against refusal to grant leave for enforcement within two months after the date on which the decision is signed.
4. If refusal to grant leave for enforcement is affirmed on appeal, the time limit for recourse to the Supreme Court shall be two months after the date on which the decision on appeal is signed.
5. If leave for enforcement is granted on appeal or after recourse to the Supreme Court, the provisions of the first sentence of article 1062(4) shall apply accordingly.

Section Five. **Setting Aside and Revocation of the Arbitral Award**

ARTICLE 1064

SETTING ASIDE IN GENERAL

1. Recourse to a court against a final or partial final arbitral award which is not open to appeal to a second arbitral tribunal, or a final or partial final award rendered on arbitral appeal, may be made only by an application for setting aside or revocation in accordance with this Section.
2. An application for setting aside shall be made to the District Court with whose Registry the original of the award shall be deposited by virtue of article 1058(1).
3. An application for setting aside may be made as soon as the award has acquired the force of *res judicata*. The right to make an application shall

be extinguished three months after the date of deposit of the award with the Registry of the District Court. However, if the award together with leave for enforcement is officially served on the other party, that party may make an application for setting aside within three months after the said service, irrespective of whether the period of three months mentioned in the preceding sentence has lapsed.

4. An application to set aside an interim arbitral award may be made only in conjunction with an application for setting aside a final or partial final award.

5. All grounds for setting aside shall, on pain of being barred, be mentioned in the writ of summons.

ARTICLE 1065
GROUNDS FOR SETTING ASIDE

1. Setting aside of the award can take place only on one or more of the following grounds:
   (a) absence of a valid arbitration agreement;
   (b) the arbitral tribunal was constituted in violation of the rules applicable thereto;
   (c) the arbitral tribunal has not complied with its mandate;
   (d) the award is not signed or does not contain reasons in accordance with the provisions of article 1057;
   (e) the award, or the manner in which it was made, violates public policy or good morals.

2. The ground mentioned in paragraph (1)(*a*) above shall not constitute a ground for setting aside in the case mentioned in article 1052(2).

3. The ground mentioned in paragraph (1)(*b*) above shall not constitute a ground for setting aside in the cases mentioned in article 1052(3).

4. The ground mentioned in paragraph (1)(*c*) above shall not constitute a ground for setting aside if the party who invokes this ground has participated in the arbitral proceedings without invoking such ground, although it was known to him that the arbitral tribunal did not comply with its mandate.

5. If the arbitral tribunal has awarded in excess of, or differently from, what was claimed, the arbitral award shall be partially set aside to the extent that the part of the award which is in excess of or different from the claim can be separated from the remaining part of the award.

6. If and to the extent that the arbitral tribunal has failed to decide one or more matters submitted to it, the application for setting aside on the ground mentioned in paragraph (1)(*c*) above shall be admissible only if an additional award mentioned in article 1061(1) is made, or the request for an additional award mentioned in article 1061(1) has wholly or partially been rejected.

7. Notwithstanding the provisions of the second sentence of article 1064(3), the time limit for making an application for setting aside mentioned in the

preceding paragraph shall be three months from the date of deposit of the additional award or the copy of the notification mentioned in article 1061(5) with the Registry of the District Court.

ARTICLE 1066
SUSPENSION OF ENFORCEMENT

1. An application for setting aside shall not suspend the enforcement of the award.
2. However, the court which decides on an application for setting aside may, at the request of either party, if it considers the request to be justified, suspend enforcement until a final decision is made on the application for setting aside.
3. A copy of the request for suspension shall be communicated by the Court Clerk to the other party without delay.
4. The court shall decide on the request after the other party has been given an opportunity to be heard.
5. Upon granting the request, the court may order the petitioner to give security. Upon denying the request, the court may order the other party to give security.
6. If enforcement is suspended, either party may request the court to lift the suspension. The provisions of paragraphs (3) to (5) inclusive shall apply accordingly.

ARTICLE 1067
CONSEQUENCES OF SETTING ASIDE

Unless the parties have agreed otherwise, as soon as a decision setting aside the award has become final, the jurisdiction of the court shall revive.

ARTICLE 1068
REVOCATION OF THE AWARD IN CASE OF FRAUD, FORGERY OR NEW DOCUMENTS[433]

1. Revocation of the award can take place only on one or more of the following grounds:
   (a) the award is wholly or partially based on fraud which is discovered after the award is made and which is committed during the arbitral proceedings by or with the knowledge of the other party;
   (b) the award is wholly or partially based on documents which, after the award is made, are discovered to have been forged;

---

[433] *Translator's note.* The Dutch text for the term 'revocation of the award' reads literally: 'revocation by reason of *request civiel*', which expression originates from the French '*requête civile*'.

    (c) after the award is made, a party obtains documents which would have had an influence on the decision of the arbitral tribunal and which were withheld as a result of the acts of the other party.

2. An application for revocation shall be brought before the Court of Appeal which would have had jurisdiction to decide on an appeal relating to the application for setting aside mentioned in article 1064, *in corresponding application of article 1064(3) or if this will result in a later date* within three months after the fraud or forgery has become known or the party has obtained the new documents. *If the party that has reason to apply for revocation dies within the term mentioned in the first sentence of this paragraph, article 341 shall apply accordingly. The proceedings are commenced with the issuance of a writ of summons in conformity with the requirements of article 111 and are conducted in the manner determined by Book One, Title Two. The provisions of article 1066 shall apply accordingly.*

3. *If the judge considers the ground(s) for revocation to be correct, he wholly or partially sets aside the arbitral award. The provisions of article 1067 shall apply accordingly.*

Section Six. **Arbitral Award on Agreed Terms**

ARTICLE 1069

1. If during the arbitral proceedings the parties reach a settlement, the arbitral tribunal may, at the joint request of the parties, record the contents of the settlement in the form of an arbitral award. The arbitral tribunal may refuse the request without giving reasons.

2. An arbitral award on agreed terms shall be regarded as an arbitral award to which the provisions of Sections Three to Five inclusive of this Title shall be applicable, provided that:
    (a) the award may be set aside only on the ground that it is contrary to public policy or good morals,
    (b) notwithstanding the provisions of article 1057, the award does not need to contain reasons, and
    (c) the award is also signed by the parties.

Section Seven. **Final Provisions**

ARTICLE 1070
NO APPEAL AGAINST CERTAIN DECISIONS OF PRESIDENT OF DISTRICT COURT

No appeal may be lodged against the decisions of the President of the District Court mentioned in Sections One to Three inclusive of this Title.

ANNEX

ARTICLE 1071
NO ATTORNEY REQUIRED FOR CERTAIN REQUESTS

In the cases mentioned in articles 1026(2) and (4), 1027(3), 1028, 1044(1), and 1062(1), the application and if applicable the answer need not be filed by an attorney.

ARTICLE 1072
AGREEMENT ON COMPETENT PRESIDENT OF DISTRICT COURT IN CERTAIN CASES

The parties may designate by agreement the President of a specific District Court as the President competent for the matters mentioned in articles 1026(2) and (4), 1027(3), 1028, 1029(2) and (4), 1031(2), 1035(2) and 1041(2).

ARTICLE 1073
APPLICABILITY OF TITLE ONE TO ARBITRATION WITHIN THE NETHERLANDS; APPOINTMENT OF ARBITRATORS IN CASE PLACE OF ARBITRATION IS UNKNOWN

1. The provisions of this Title shall apply if the place of arbitration is situated within the Netherlands.
2. If the parties have not determined the place of arbitration, the appointment or challenge of the arbitrator or arbitrators or the secretary engaged by an arbitral tribunal may take place in accordance with the provisions contained in Section One of this Title if at least one of the parties is domiciled or has his actual residence in the Netherlands.

Title Two. **Arbitration Outside the Netherlands**

ARTICLE 1074
FOREIGN ARBITRATION AGREEMENT AND SUBSTANTIVE CLAIM BEFORE DUTCH COURT; FOREIGN ARBITRATION AGREEMENT AND INTERIM MEASURES BY DUTCH COURT

1. A court in the Netherlands seized of a dispute in respect of which an arbitration agreement has been concluded under which arbitration shall take place outside the Netherlands shall declare that it has no jurisdiction if a party invokes the existence of the said agreement before submitting a defence, unless the agreement is invalid under the law applicable thereto.
2. The agreement mentioned in paragraph (1) shall not preclude a party from requesting a court in the Netherlands to grant interim measures of protection, or from applying to the President of the District Court for a decision in summary proceedings in accordance with the provisions of article 289.

ARTICLE 1075
RECOGNITION AND ENFORCEMENT OF FOREIGN AWARD UNDER TREATIES

An arbitral award made in a foreign State to which a treaty concerning recognition and enforcement is applicable may be recognised and enforced in the Netherlands. The provisions of articles 985 to 991 inclusive shall apply accordingly to the extent that the treaty does not contain provisions deviating therefrom and provided that the President of the District Court shall be substituted for the District Court and the time limit for appeal from his decision and for recourse to the Supreme Court shall be two months.

ARTICLE 1076
RECOGNITION AND ENFORCEMENT OF FOREIGN AWARD WITHOUT TREATIES

1. If no treaty concerning recognition and enforcement is applicable, or if an applicable treaty allows a party to rely upon the law of the country in which recognition or enforcement is sought, an arbitral award made in a foreign State may be recognised in the Netherlands and its enforcement may be sought in the Netherlands, upon submission of the original or a certified copy of the arbitration agreement and arbitral award, unless:
   (A) the party against whom recognition or enforcement is sought, asserts and proves that:
      (a) a valid arbitration agreement under the law applicable thereto is lacking;
      (b) the arbitral tribunal is constituted in violation of the rules applicable thereto;
      (c) the arbitral tribunal has not complied with its mandate;
      (d) the arbitral award is still open to an appeal to a second arbitral tribunal, or to a court in the country in which the award is made;
      (e) the arbitral award has been set aside by a competent authority of the country in which that award is made;
   (B) the court finds that the recognition or enforcement would be contrary to public policy.
2. The ground mentioned in paragraph (1)(A)(*a*) above shall not constitute a ground for refusal of recognition or enforcement if the party who invokes this ground has made an appearance in the arbitral proceedings and, before submitting a defence, has not raised the plea that the arbitral tribunal lacks jurisdiction on the ground that a valid arbitration agreement is lacking.
3. The ground mentioned in paragraph (1)(A)(*b*) above shall not constitute a ground for refusal of recognition or enforcement if the party who invokes this ground has participated in the constitution of the arbitral tribunal, or if he has not participated in the constitution of the arbitral tribunal, has made an appearance in the arbitral proceedings and, before submitting a defence, has not

raised the plea that the arbitral tribunal lacks jurisdiction on the ground that the arbitral tribunal is constituted in violation of the applicable rules.

4. The ground mentioned in paragraph (1)(A)(c) above shall not constitute a ground for refusal of recognition or enforcement if the party who invokes this ground has participated in the arbitral proceedings without raising it, although it was known to him that the arbitral tribunal did not comply with its mandate.

5. If the award is in excess of, or different from, what was claimed, the arbitral award shall be capable of partial recognition or enforcement to the extent that the part of the award which is in excess of or different from the claim can be separated from the remaining part of the award.

6. The provisions of articles 985 to 991 inclusive shall apply accordingly, provided that the President of the District Court shall be substituted for the District Court, the time limit for appeal from his decision and for recourse to the Supreme Court shall be two months, and no documents need be submitted evidencing the enforceability of the arbitral award in the country in which it is made.

7. If an application for the setting aside of an award made in a foreign State is made to a competent authority of the country in which the award is made, the provisions of article 1066(2) to (6) inclusive shall apply accordingly when recognition or enforcement is sought in the Netherlands.

Miscellaneous Provisions, Including Transitional Law*

ARTICLE II

1. Title One of Book Three of the Code of Civil Procedure is repealed, subject to the provisions of article III of this Act.

2. This Act shall apply to arbitrations which have been commenced before the day on which this Act enters into force, subject to the provisions of article III of this Act.

ARTICLE III

1. This Act shall not apply to cases which, before the date on which this Act enters into force, were commenced before the court by means of a summons or a request. These cases shall continue to be governed by the provisions of Title One of Book Three of the Code of Civil Procedure in force before the entry into force of this Act.

2. Cases in which, before the date on which this Act enters into force, an appeal to a court was reserved, shall continue to be governed by articles 646 and 647

---

* Article I of the Act contains Arts 1020-1076.

of the Code of Civil Procedure as in force before that date, provided that upon the expiry of a period of five years after that date the reservation of appeal shall be extinct.

ARTICLE IV

When this Act comes into force, articles 429*a* to 429*r* inclusive of the Code of Civil Procedure shall become applicable to matters which must be initiated by means of a request, and article 345 of this Code shall become inoperative.

ARTICLE V

1. Article 29(3) of the Code of Civil Procedure is repealed.
2. The words 'arbitral award or' mentioned in article 993(1) of the Code of Civil Procedure are deleted.

ARTICLE VI

This Act comes into force on the first day of the fifth calendar month following the month in which the Act is published in the Official Gazette.

INDEX